BIBLICAL & THEOLOGICAL FOUNDATIONS
of the
FAMILY

Joseph C. Atkinson

BIBLICAL & THEOLOGICAL FOUNDATIONS

of the FAMILY

The Domestic Church

THE CATHOLIC UNIVERSITY
OF AMERICA PRESS
WASHINGTON, D.C.

Copyright © 2014

The Catholic University of America Press

All rights reserved

The paper used in this publication meets the minimum
requirements of American National Standards for
Information Science—Permanence of Paper for Printed
Library Materials, ANSI z39.48-1984.

∞

Library of Congress Cataloging-in-Publication Data

Atkinson, Joseph C.

Biblical and theological foundations of the family : the
domestic church / Joseph C. Atkinson.

pages cm

Includes bibliographical references and index.

ISBN 978-0-8132-2170-0 (pbk. : alk. paper)

1. Families—Religious aspects—Catholic Church.

2. Catholic Church—Doctrines.

I. Title

BX 2351.A85 2014

261.8′3585—dc23   2013048932

For Nancy, in whom my heart trusts

אֵשֶׁת־חַיִל מִי יִמְצָא וְרָחֹק מִפְּנִינִים מִכְרָהּ
בָּטַח בָּהּ לֵב בַּעְלָהּ וְשָׁלָל לֹא יֶחְסָר
צוֹפִיָּה הֲלִיכוֹת בֵּיתָהּ וְלֶחֶם עַצְלוּת לֹא תֹאכֵל
קָמוּ בָנֶיהָ וַיְאַשְּׁרוּהָ בַּעְלָהּ וַיְהַלְלָהּ:
רַבּוֹת בָּנוֹת עָשׂוּ חָיִל וְאַתְּ עָלִית עַל־כֻּלָּנָה

An excellent wife, who can find? For her worth is far above jewels.

The heart of her husband trusts in her, and he will have no lack of gain.

She looks well to the ways of her household, and does not eat the bread
   of idleness.

Her children rise up and bless her; her husband also, and he praises her,
   saying:

"Many daughters have done nobly, but you excel them all."

Proverbs 31:10–11, 27–29 NASB

And our beloved "domestic church"
Jennifer, Joe, and Saiorse
William, Luke, Edward and Maile, Charles and Peter

CONTENTS

Preface by José Granados   ix
Foreword by Francis Martin   xv
Author's Preface   xix
Notes on Hebrew Language and Sources   xxiii

Introduction: The Need for a Theology of the Family   1

PART 1. FOUNDATIONS OF THE FAMILY IN THE OLD TESTAMENT   13

1. The Family in Mythological Thought   19
2. The Principles of Creation and Covenantal Reality   33
3. Abraham and the Family of Faith   78
4. Family as the Carrier of the Covenant   91
5. Family as Image of the Covenant   128
6. Hebraic Anthropological Principles: Corporate Personality   161

PART 2. FOUNDATIONS OF THE FAMILY IN THE NEW TESTAMENT, EARLY CHURCH, AND VATICAN II   193

7. The Family of Abraham in the New Testament   197
8. The Corporate Dimension of Baptism in the New Testament   220
9. Appropriation by the Church Fathers   269
10. Vatican II and the Problems of Appropriation   301

Bibliography   327
Scriptural Indexes   337
Index of Names   343
General Index   346

PREFACE

In the documents of the Second Vatican Council, of which we now celebrate the 50th anniversary, we find the expression that "the family is, so to speak, the domestic Church" (*Lumen Gentium* 11). The rich magisterium of John Paul II on the family has made it clear that this sentence is not an isolated fragment without implications for the whole reception of the Council. If Vatican II was centered in the dialogue between the Church and modernity, *Gaudium et Spes* 47–52 sees the family as the first place of this encounter of the Christian vision with the modern world. It is in this context that the idea of the family as domestic church reveals its central place.

First, the term expresses clearly the importance of the family for the dialogue between Christianity and the world. The family is both a natural institution, essential for the development of humanity and culture, and a place where God makes himself present, revealing his love through the love of the spouses, parents, and children. In addition, the family is transformed by the Gospel so that it shows at its core the love of the Father, from which all fatherhood comes (Eph 3:14–15).

Secondly, the idea of the domestic Church conveys a vision of the Church as a family, the family of God, which preserves the pathway towards the fullness of communion. The structure of the family, in which we learn our being in relationship as children, spouses, and parents, is the basic analogy for understanding the Church. The image of the family is a point of connection of different descriptions of the Church: the Church as communion, as the Body of Christ, as the sacrament of unity.

It appears then a fruitful relationship between Church and the family. The family cannot stand by itself: it needs to enter into the Church, a family of families, in which the new measure Christ brought to human love is preserved. The Church, on her part, needs the family to connect his message with the foundational experience of all human beings and their call to love.

It is in this context that we welcome Dr. Joseph Atkinson's work on the domestic Church. Taking as its departure point this connection between family and Church, the author explores its foundations, both in Scripture and in the Fathers of the Church. The question is whether the family could serve as a way to read the covenant between God and Israel in the Old Testament and the essence of the new people of God founded by Jesus.

Atkinson starts with a description of other cultures surrounding Israel, a study that enables him to highlight the novelty of the Bible's view. His analysis presents a pre-Abrahamic religious environment in which sexuality is connected to the divine, and in which sexual intercourse/fecundity becomes a way of entering directly into contact with God. In this context, Israel's novelty is described as the secularization of sexuality, but not, as the author carefully notes, in the modern sense of the loss of its connection with the divine. In fact, sexuality preserves in Israel a link with God, not as direct knowledge of Yaweh, but as a way to find him and to receive his blessing. Sexuality is no longer sacred, but it is still symbolic of the divine presence and action in the world.

A key point in Atkinson's approach is his analysis of God as Creator, which he binds with the concept, developed later in the Christian tradition, of *creatio ex nihilo.* The initial distance between God and creation, God's total freedom to create and thus to become the ultimate origin of everything, guarantees that sexuality is lived out not as a confusion with the divine but as a path that allows for growth and personal relationship with the Creator. In this way sexuality is seen as a path, with a concrete origin and *telos,* and offers the foundation for the historical consciousness of Israel. Israel's sense of history is thus rooted in the People's conception of the family. God's creative act, which is not sexual, institutes a distance between God and human sexuality, thus inaugurating a pathway that can be dynamically covered. By leaving his father and mother and uniting to his wife, thus becoming in his turn father, the man of the Bible appears as the carrier of a promise that is fulfilled only in its historical development.

Having presented the importance of creation for Israel's sense of history and having described how the generations (*tôledôt*) are the way in which God's blessing concretely reaches the People of God, Atkinson considers in the third chapter the singular case of Abraham's family. Abraham is elected with a calling that requires him to leave his own family in order to become a blessing for a multitude of people. This election takes place, not only by the generation in the flesh, but also through a sacred sign, circumcision. Circumcision, which marks the presence of God's covenant upon the flesh, reveals that the family is the center of the covenant. In this way Atkinson sets the foundation for considering, in a later chapter, the link between the family and Baptism.

Chapters four and five form a diptych. The first deals with the connection between the family and the covenant: the family is the *carrier* of the covenant; the second accomplishes the same task, but looking at the family as an *image* of the covenant. (McLuhan's sentence, "the medium is the message," offers a description of the unity of both approaches.)

Chapter four, by showing the importance of hallowing time, of education into the covenant as a way of remembering the past, and of the priesthood of the father in the family, establishes a clear connection between family life and the religion of Israel. Three concrete examples are given: redemption of the first-born, circumcision (the father acts as a representative of Abraham), and the Passover.

In chapter five a relationship is drawn between the family and God's behavior regarding the People. The two main images of God as a Father and a Spouse of Israel are developed, singularly in the prophets. The laws of holiness are also examined, and their importance for understanding the meaning of sexuality for Israel is properly highlighted. An interesting excursus explains the parallel between the creation of man and woman in Genesis 2 and the building of the sanctuary in Exodus 40.

A crucial chapter is devoted to examining the "family-anthropology" of the Old Testament. I consider this analysis one of the most important contributions of the book, for it shows the consequences of the proposal for theological anthropology and for the broader question of the relationship between the human being and God. Atkinson describes well how the concept of corporate personality is not a primitive and underdeveloped vision of the human being, and how it is maintained throughout the Old Testament and into the New. In the eyes of Scripture, the human person, while retaining a concrete personality irreducible to the community, is not an isolated being. The human being "is" inasmuch as he belongs (in a unique way) to others. It is in this openness of the person to the People, that God reveals himself and acts with his blessing.

The New Testament section examines the continuity between the Old Testament idea of the Abrahamic family and corporate personality with Jesus' revelation. The book shows how Christ belongs to the _tôldôt_ of Israel and offers salvation through a new generation that, while it goes beyond Old Testament expectations, is still radically based on the Hebrew vision of the human person: Jesus' family is grounded in Abraham's figure. The author argues that there is no developed theology of the family in the New Testament precisely because the covenantal family of the Old was still valid and operative. Atkinson then focuses on Baptism to show the connection with Old Testament anthropology. Both the concepts of corporate personality and of anamnesis / salvation history, rooted in the experience of the family, are essential to explain Christian salvation.

The last part of the book deals with the expression "domestic church." After examining some New Testament texts, Atkinson concludes that the philological New Testament evidence does not ground the concept of the domestic church. What is important, however, are not the words, but the anthropological background, which allows us to see the connection between family and Israel, between family and Christian Church. The following chapter deals with the same philological analysis in some Fathers of the Church (mainly Augustine and John Chrysostom), accounting for the development of the expression, which now explicitly describes the link between Church and family. In a last chapter the author deals with the recovery of the term at Vatican II and in John Paul II's magisterium, thus showing the potential of his study for contemporary theology.

This book offers an important and needed contribution to the topic

of the family in Scripture, especially in the biblical foundational analysis of the first seven chapters. Dr. Atkinson gathers many results of biblical scholarship around a unifying vision rooted in the family. He is
careful and balanced in his judgments, offering solid scholarly analyses
of the texts, rooted in a serious study of the biblical sources and rich
with secondary literature. His study goes deep into the central questions of biblical anthropology, thus providing an example of what Paul
Ricoeur called "to think the Bible."

Publications on family in Scripture abound. Most of these proposals, however, are interested in the Bible in order to "solve" modern
moral and cultural issues. Dr. Atkinson's work offers a novelty in that
it lets the Bible not only propose the solutions but also frame the debate
and the structure of the answers. He goes deep into the questions, not
only analyzing some of the texts, but examining the anthropological
and theological foundations. His proposal becomes thus more credible
and durable, able to offer a lasting answer to the difficult questions society and Church face regarding the family.

This work has been prepared and written in the context of Dr. Atkinson's teaching and researching at the John Paul II Institute for Studies
on Marriage and Family, an international academic institution founded by the late pope to deepen the truth of God's plan for human love.
I had the privilege of teaching with Dr. Atkinson for several years in
Washington, D.C., and I have continued in contact with him through
the central session of the John Paul II Institute in Rome. To the institute he founded, Blessed John Paul II conveyed not only an object of
study (marriage and the family) but also a method, which puts together in a fruitful way human experience and divine revelation, both centered on God's call to love. It is in the spirit of this method, within a
communion of persons and in a prolonged conversation between fac-
ulty and students, that this book has been written. I am grateful to Dr.
Atkinson for his careful study on this important topic, which fosters
the work of the John Paul II Institute and offers a fruitful proposal for
the understanding of the domestic church.

José Granados, Vice President, Pontifical John Paul II Institute for Studies
on Marriage and Family, Rome

FOREWORD

It is said that Gilbert K. Chesterton declared, as early as 1927, that the next great crisis which the Catholic Church would have to face would be in the area of sexuality. The obvious confirmation of that prediction in our own day must evoke a response on the part of Catholic theologians. Atkinson's return to the patristic understanding of the family as a domestic church is a good example of a response which is also a valuable modern teaching on the ecclesial dimension of the family.

One of the key advantages of this study is that it begins by taking seriously the teaching on family life and its actual practice among our predecessors, the Jewish people. This reflects, the ancient view, well summed up by Thomas Aquinas, who sees continuity along with transposition in the relation between the Old and New Covenants. He invokes Aristotle's principle (in *On Memory and Recall*) that movement toward an image, in so far as it is an image, is the same as the movement toward the reality.

> And therefore the ancient Fathers, by observing the sacraments (liturgical practices) of the Law, were brought toward Christ through the same faith and love by which we are still brought toward him. For this reason the ancient Fathers belonged to the same Body of Christ to which we belong.[1]

---

1. *Summa Theologiae* 3,8,3 ad3. For further discussion and distinction in the application of this principle see "The Spiritual Sense (*Sensus Spiritualis*) of Sacred Scripture: Its Essential Insight," in F. Martin, *Sacred Scripture: The Disclosure of the Word* (Ave Maria, Fl.: Sapientia Press, 2006), 249–76.

Extending this principle, we can get a certain idea of the revealed understanding of marriage in the OT, to some of which teaching Jesus himself appealed (Mk 10:1–12). After briefly recreating for us the mental and religious world of the surrounding nations, Professor Atkinson takes us through the foundational teaching on human sexuality in the first three chapters of Genesis. He then proceeds to show how the family is the carrier of the covenant and what this implies regarding the corporate nature of the relationship between God and his people. To this day, the basic way in which someone is made a part of the covenant between God and the Jews, a covenant completed but never revoked, is to be born of a Jewish mother. In order to establish this covenantal reality in the context of the New Covenant we are led into an appreciation of the context of *corporate personality*, a concept long awaiting the clarification given to it in this study. The Church, the Body of Christ, as its designation implies, is a physical reality nurtured by the Body and Blood of its Savior. In this sense we are part of the Abrahamic covenant: "If you belong to Christ, then you are the seed of Abraham, and heirs according to the promise" (Gal 3:29).

Very helpful is the ensuing section recalling for us the nuclear reality of the family as a domestic church, the account of the loss of this concept in the post-patristic era and its recovery in the post–Vatican II era. Such an understanding gives the family its theological place as a human reality caught up into the life and structure of the Church. It also restores the proper understanding of corporality and sexuality in human life, liberating them from a return to the mythological thrall of cosmic religion and the banality of modern attitudes. Atkinson's study accomplishes this by a careful and balanced understanding of what the Bible does with the attitudes and theories about sexuality which, in one form or another, are perennially present and which re-assert themselves whenever an understanding of creation is obfuscated and associated with violence and sexuality.

Doctor Atkinson's careful biblical study is an important contribution to the Christian understanding and defense of God's plan for marriage. Particularly helpful is the extended consideration of the _tôledôt_ or "generations" lists. History, including salvation history, moves by

and through generations. This fact establishes the importance, holiness, and true nature of generation: it is the basic material of God's
plan, not merely the "side effect" of sexual pleasure and certainly not
the chance result of scientific manipulation. It is also the prime analo-
gate of that process by which believers are reborn in baptism. It is in
that light that we may understand this prayer to be found in the concluding ceremony of the marriage rite itself.

> May you always bear witness to the love of God in this world
> so that the afflicted and the needy
> will find in you generous friends,
> and welcome you into the joys of heaven.

Francis Martin, S.T.L., S.S.D.

AUTHOR'S PREFACE

The value of the family is, in many ways, self-evident. We owe our origins to our father and mother and to the long family line from which we come. Our culture, the language we speak, the values we hold, the traditions we observe, and above all the life of which we are given the stewardship, all of this is a gift. We are, because they were. Family is the primary cell, the heart so to speak, of society. But today this truth about family is no longer self-evident. In our modern rush to affirm the autonomous self-determination of the individual, we have forgotten the truth of family. The modern emphasis on freedom is correct, but detaching it from objective truth outside of the individual and from the corporate reality of the family leads to a destructive subjectivism. It is a misconstrual of the truth when the freedom of the individual is pitted against all other mediating forms (be they family, Church, culture, or whatever). True freedom is found only when we take account of our human nature for what it is. We are created, but never in isolation, always oriented towards another. We come from another and are meant for the other. Both the subjective and the corporate dimension of the human person must always be accounted for in a genuine anthropology of the human person.

Very little has been written about the theology of the family per se. In fact, we are not yet ready to develop such a systematic theology until some preliminary ground work has been done. We need first to develop and clarify the foundations on which such a theology can be built. Key to that theology is identifying the principles and concepts that are operative in the biblical worldview. This requires a profound recovery of an authentic theology of creation. What are the dynamic principles that inform creation and affect both the nature of created reality and how created things relate to each other? How are created realities free, and how is that freedom exercised? What constitutes the human person's nature? Is that nature primarily individualistic or is it primarily corporate? How does that nature affect the salvific plan of God?

This present study attempts to identify the Biblical and theological foundations of both man and creation and to show how the family is of critical importance to the covenant God has with His people. This is done both with regard to the original Abrahamic covenant and with regard to the teleological fulfillment of the covenant in Christ. My hope is that this study will help in some small way in the recovery of the genuine Biblical and theological foundations of the family.

This work has been many years in the making. I wish to thank the John Paul II Institute in Washington, D.C., for enabling me to work on this project through many years of teachings and lecturing. The institute has both provided me with a place to carry out this critical research and given me colleagues who have helped create an atmosphere where the search for the truth and a love of the faith is paramount. Special thanks go to Fr. Francis Martin, who served as the director for both my licentiate thesis and my doctoral dissertation. His scholarship and faith-filled approach to study has served as a profound example. This project on the theology of the family began as a paper in one of his courses, and he continues to graciously help in this study. He has kindly read and offered critiques, as well as patiently helped with the translations of ancient language texts. I wish also to express my gratitude to my students, who have urged me to publish this book, seeing the need for the development of this theology.

I wish to thank CUA Press for publishing this book and its staff who have helped me in the many details necessary to a book's publication. Special thanks go to my editor, Jim Kruggel, who has patiently shepherded me through this process. Thanks to those who have given of their time, reading and re-reading this manuscript, offering criticism and insights. Special thanks go to Susan Needham, who carefully went over the text, giving invaluable comments. I also wish to thank Fr. Granados, who has been a supportive colleague and whose insights into the ecclesial dimension of the family are profound; thanks to Dr. Mary Shivanandan, who has reviewed the text and given support over the long duration of this project; to my wife, Nancy, who has tirelessly proofread the text and helped it become clearer and more understandable, and to all others who carefully read and critiqued the manuscript and have given encouragement. I would like to thank especially Fr. James McDermott of Sacred Heart Seminary in Detroit, who forced me to think afresh through many areas of the text. It is to be hoped that the text has become much stronger through my responses to his excellent critiques. All shortcomings, of course, remain my own responsibility.

Some material in Chapter 6 first appeared in "Root of the Christian Family in the Old Testament: Corporate Personality," *Liberty, Life and Family: An Interdisciplinary Journal of Common Concerns* 4, no. 1 (1999): 57–87, and is used here with permission.

Family is a great mystery. It is the place of great joy and sorrow; it is the place where we work out a large part of our salvation. Family proclaims that while we are individuals, we are never alone but always a part of a greater whole. It is the place where we taste heavenly joys: the love of husband and wife, the gift of new life. But, because we are fallen, it is also the place where we experience great pain and wounds. The great mystery is that God desires to transform even our pain and sorrow so that they become the means of healing for our families and for the world.

This book on family was written within the context of a family, my own. This is where I have learned the truth about family. My wife and I have been blessed with six children. As my wife says, I did the theoretical work, she did the practical! I wish to give thanks for each of their lives, for the inestimable gift they are, and for the grace God has given and continues to give us along this pilgrimage of life.

May we all become instruments of His love and grace to each other, especially in our families.

NOTES ON
HEBREW LANGUAGE
AND SOURCES

Transliteration shown in the following table is modified to aid pronunciation.

	dagesh (⊙)			vowels
א	'			
ב	b̲ = v sound	בּ = b	בַ	ba
ג	g		בָ	bā
ד	d		בֱ	bă
ה	h		בֶ	be
ו	v		בֵ	bê
ז	z		בְ	bě
ח	ḥ = (Bach)		בֵי	bê
ט	t		בֶי	bê
י	y		בְ	b'
ך / כ	ḥ (Bach)	ך / כ = k	בִ	bi
ל	l		בִי	bî
מ	m		בֹ	bō
ן / נ	n		בוֹ	bô
ס	s		בָ	bō
ע	'		בֻ	bu
ף / פ	ph / f	ף / פ = p	בוּ	bû
צ	ts			
ק	q			
ר	r			
שׁ	sh			
שׂ	s			
ת	t̲			

RABBINIC AND OTHER JEWISH WRITINGS
REFERENCED IN TEXT

11Q13	Melchizedek (Qumran text 11 QMelch)
BaMidbar Rabbah	Midrashic explanations of Numbers
b. Bek.	*Bekorot* (Babylonian Talmud) on the first born
b. Shab	*Shabbat* (Babylonian Talmud) on the Shabbath
b. Yeb	*Yebamot* (Babylonian Talmud) on Levirate marriage
Genesis Rabbah	Rabbinical Commentary on Genesis
Ger.	Post-Talmudic tractate *Gerim* dealing with proselytes
J. Bik	*Bikkurim* (Jerusalem Talmud) dealing with offering of first fruits
Kiddushin	Talmudic tractate dealing with marriage
K'ritot	Talmudic tractate on divorce
Midrash on Psalms	Midrashic explanation of Psalms
Midrash Rabbah	Large collection of Midrashic material
Midr. Sam	Midrashic explanations of Samuel
Mishnah Pesahim	Midrashic explanations on Passover
Pesikta Rabosai (Pesikta Rabbati)	Midrashic explanations of the Jewish feast days and Sabbaths
Pirke DeRabbi Eliezer	Midrashic explanations on Genesis and Exodus by Rabbi Eliezer
Qoh. R.	Midrashic commentary on *Qohelet Rabba* (Ecclesiastes)
Shir HaShirim Rabbah	Midrashic explanations of the Song of Songs
Test. Levi	Testament of Levi
Tg. Neof.	*Targum Neofiti* commentary on the Pentateuch

BIBLICAL & THEOLOGICAL FOUNDATIONS *of the* FAMILY

THE NEED FOR
A THEOLOGY OF
THE FAMILY

The future of humanity passes by way of the family.
Familiaris Consortio 22:8

The *Catechism of the Catholic Church* states: "The Christian family constitutes a specific revelation and realization of ecclesial communion, and for this reason it can and should be called a domestic church" (section 2204).[1] Its inclusion in the Catechism reveals that the term "domestic church" has become a fundamental concept in regard to the family. Its essential meaning is that the family (the father, mother, and children converted to Christ and baptized into Him) has been endowed with an ecclesial nature. This organic unit is considered to be the smallest articulation of the Church and the sphere in which, in a concrete way, primary ecclesial activities such as catechesis, conversion, and prayer are carried out.[2] In other words, the baptized family has become a church.[3]

---

1. *Catechism of the Catholic Church* (New York: Catholic Book Publishing, 1994), 532 (hereafter *CCC*).

2. Cf. *Lumen Gentium* 11: "In what might be regarded as the domestic church, the parents...are the first heralds of the faith with regard to their children." Austin Flannery, ed., *Vatican Council II: The Conciliar and Post Conciliar Documents* (Northport, N.Y.: Costello Publishing Company, 1975), 362.

3. This is always to be understood as a church within the Church, in the same way as Christians are understood to be sons in the Son.

What is surprising is that this ancient doctrine was virtually un-heard of in modern times until it was introduced by Bishop Pietro Fior-delli during the debates of Vatican II. Prior to that, the term had lain virtually dormant for almost fifteen hundred years. Before this latent period, it is clear the term possessed vitality as evidenced in the writings of key Church Fathers and was an accepted part of the Christian vocabulary by the era of St. Augustine. In fact, both he and St. John Chrysostom used the concept explicitly to denote the family trans-formed by the grace of Christ. This was not a theological innovation on their part. Rather, the family had followed a long trajectory with-in salvation history, starting from being the "carrier of the covenant" in the Abrahamic covenant to becoming the "sphere of eschatological activity" when it reached its teleological conclusion in Christ. Howev-er, due to the phenomenal growth of the early Church, Christianity's acceptance as the state religion, and the rise of monasticism as the ide-al of Christian life, the importance of the family began to recede after the early Church period, and the term "domestic church" virtually dis-appeared from the theological landscape. Some Protestant reformers of the sixteenth century, in their desire to "return to the Scriptures," attempted to revitalize the place of the family in Christian life, but they did not add much to its theological understanding. Even though Church Fathers used this term (grounding it in the Scriptural text and the reality of baptism), the reformers did not take up the terminology. Then, amazingly, after a fifteen-hundred-year hiatus, the concept of the family as an ecclesial reality suddenly emerged in the debates at Vati-can II. In the years following the Council, there have been important theological developments of the concept in the magisterium, and these developments were evident in the universal catechism, which was is-sued in 1994.[4] At this point, the idea of the baptized family, having both

4. There has been little (if any) development of the ecclesiological nature of the family in Protestant circles in the modern period, perhaps because of Protestantism's emphasis on individualism and the increasing loss of the corporate nature of the faith. This emphasis is ultimately tied to Protestants' specific understandings of ecclesiology. It can be hoped that a recovery of the corporate understanding of the family as domestic church will contrib-ute positively to both Catholics and Protestants in their understanding of the nature of the Church.

an *ecclesial* identity and an *ecclesial* mission, was finally accepted as the *primary* hermeneutic by which the family was to be understood.

Initially, at the time of its inclusion during Vatican II, the concept of the family as "domestic church" caused little notice. Since that time, however, it has grown exponentially in importance and has become entrenched in Catholic teaching, particularly through the writings of John Paul II. A major problem, however, remains: while this term is officially sanctioned and has become the principal theological construct for the family, it still remains relatively rootless. Its novel status can be seen by an examination of John Paul II's *Love and Responsibility* (published in Polish in 1960, just prior to Vatican II). In this work, the family is defined simply as "an educational institution within the framework of which the personality of a new human being is formed";[5] nowhere is there ever a consideration that the family has an ecclesial identity, and nowhere is it referred to as the domestic church![6] The truth is simply that the term "domestic church" is a relatively new appropriation of the earlier patristic term whose theological foundations have yet to be sufficiently secured.[7] While the term is used extensively in a pastoral sense, little formal research has been carried out to deter-

5. K. Wojtyla, *Love and Responsibility*, trans. H. T. Willetts (London: William Collins and Sons, 1982), 242.

6. Wojtyla says of the family, "[It is] a small society, and the existence of all large societies—nation, state, Church—depends on it," and further, it is "an institution based on marriage" (ibid., 217). This is a somewhat minimalist definition of the family, especially compared to the rich and complex theological description which he gives in *Familiaris Consortio* (hereafter *FC*). This wide difference underlies the profound development that took place in both Wojtyla's and the Church's understanding of the nature of the family in those few short years.

7. See A. Scola, *The Nuptial Mystery* (Grand Rapids, Mich.: Eerdmans's, 2005) and M. Ouellet, *Divine Likeness: Toward a Trinitarian Anthropology of the Family* (Grand Rapids, Mich.: Eerdman's, 2006). Both books include profound theological reflections on the family, but neither deals with the Biblical foundations of the family per se. The essential work that still remains is to establish the Biblical foundations of the domestic church. Without this preliminary work, inevitable and unresolvable conflicts will arise regarding, amongst other things: the degree to which "ecclesial" language can be applied to the family; the "realism" of this language; whether or not ecclesial structures also exist in the family; and what the ground of this concept actually is. Only through a rigorous examination of the family and its relationship to the Old and New covenants can these questions be resolved.

mine its biblical and theological grounding. The grave danger here is that this ambiguity will inevitably result in distortions. Consequently, the fundamental principles which inform and ground this concept need to be (re)discovered if it is to become a fruitful construct and not distorted or misused in modern cultural wars. This first step must be taken if a construction of an adequate theology of the family and especially of its identity as the "domestic church" is to be achieved. This is the purpose of our present study.[8]

HEBRAIC FOUNDATIONS

The New Testament understanding of the family is fundamentally predicated on the theological role of the family within the Hebraic covenant. Not to take this into account would prove fatal for any analysis of the Christian understanding of the family. Historically, while this lack of appreciation of the Jewish roots of the domestic church may be understandable, it nevertheless remains a salient fact that all Christian reality is grounded in the prior revelation of God to Israel. To ignore this foundation would result in a severely diminished understanding of the structure and meaning of the Christian family. In fact, without reference to its Old Testament roots, the nature of the New Testament

8. Rarely, if ever, is the question of the theological and Biblical grounding of the domestic church concept adequately raised, and consequently little research has been done in this area. Indeed, one can go to virtually any database or topical index in a book and, in all probability, there will be no reference to "domestic church." Neither the original *Catechism of the Catholic Church* nor Wojtyla's *Love and Responsibility* carried such indexed references. Some have attempted to make a contribution towards a theology of the domestic church but without paying sufficient attention to its theological foundations in salvation history and its relationship to creation, the Hebraic covenant, and baptism. John Paul II's great contribution in this area was his development of the theme in *Familiaris Consortio,* where he speaks of the ecclesial identity of the family. That document has greatly helped this understanding of the family and embedded it within the magisterium of the Church. This is a good beginning point, but a proper grounding for the concept will require the examination of the theological meaning of the family in the Hebraic covenant and its fulfillment in Christ, along with the concomitant theological structures and functions of the family that ensue. There is also confusion whether baptism or the sacrament of marriage is the ultimate ground for the family as the domestic church. This question cannot be resolved until the Scriptural and theological work has been done.

family cannot be fully grasped. Therefore, the indispensable first step in constructing an adequate theology of the family and especially its identity *as the domestic church* is the examination of the theological nature of family in the Old Testament.

The difficulty here is that very little Jewish or Christian scholarship has been carried out in this area. This is evidenced by the remarks of Shaye Cohen in his introduction to *The Jewish Family in Antiquity,* part of the Brown Judaic Studies series: "The family in classical antiquity has been the subject of intense study in recent years.... But this scholarship has not yet had an impact on the study of Jewish antiquity. I know of no monograph-length study of the subject. Even the number of relevant articles is small."[9]

This paucity of scholarly pursuit and lack of attention in so foundational an area is both remarkable and strange. As one rabbi observed, however, this lack itself can be seen as a theological statement. In Judaism, family is everything; everything in life is experienced with the family as a backdrop. Family is such a part of the fabric of all other experiences that it has never been separated out. It is always background, never foreground. In essence, the family mediates all other experiences of life.[10] In both Judaism and Christianity, the value of the family is never questioned but is always assumed. It is perhaps this which accounts for the fact that little scholarly progress has been made in the *theological* understanding of the family.

AIM OF THIS STUDY

It is premature to think of constructing a comprehensive theology given the present state of research. Rather, a new approach or paradigm

9. Shaye Cohen, ed., *The Jewish Family in Antiquity,* Brown Judaic Studies 289 (Atlanta: Scholars Press, 1993), 1. While these studies deal with Judaism primarily in Roman times, the thesis that will be later developed is that, because of the unique revelation to Israel, her whole self-understanding and life were always radically differentiated at the deepest levels from those of her pagan neighbors, starting from the inception of the covenant.

10. I am indebted to Rabbi Irving Breitowitz (professor at the University of Maryland Law School and rabbi of Woodside Synagogue, Silver Spring, Maryland) for this insight, which he shared with me during a private discussion.

needs to be developed to study the family which allows its foundations, its constitutive properties, and the purposes for which it was created to be discovered. We will identify the theological meaning that the family acquired in salvation history. This requires a critical examination of the theological functioning of the family at each major juncture in the Judeo-Christian revelation. Thus, this work is divided into two distinct parts. It will begin by discovering the foundations and functioning of the family in the narrative of creation and the Hebraic covenants and cult, that is, the Old Testament section. This is followed by the New Testament section, which examines both how the salvific family is affected by its insertion into the new covenant in Christ and how the idea of the family as the domestic church was appropriated in subsequent ages, particularly by the early Church Fathers and later at Vatican II. The thesis of our work is that within revelation there is a developing theological trajectory moving towards fulfillment. That is, the truth and meaning of the family are gradually disclosed within revelation. Our approach, which attempts to examine this trajectory sequentially, will allow us to uncover the Scriptural identity of the family and the pivotal role it plays in salvation history. It will provide the fundamental theological and Scriptural foundations necessary to construct an adequate theology of the domestic church.

STRUCTURE OF THE STUDY—PART I

Part I of this book will explore the *theological functioning* of the family in the Old Testament. The essential question is whether the family is only a sociological construct (albeit a fundamental one) or whether it actually possesses a *theological* dimension and has, at some stage, been assumed into the creative and salvific will of God. It is to the latter understanding that the Hebrew Scriptures give witness.[11] In the Old Testament, the essential structure of the family is discovered in terms of its irreplaceable role within the Hebraic covenant. In fact, it becomes

11. This is a twofold reality. Already, as we shall see, marriage and family were created having a covenantal dimension (see Gn 2). Later, the family of Abraham becomes the soteriological center of God's covenant with mankind.

the essential "carrier of the covenant." The following three subsections outline the three key themes that Part I explores.

Principles of Creation Inform the Family

The Hebraic revelation provides us with key principles that are not only operative *within* the process of creation but also become the constitutive principles of the created realities themselves. That is, they continue to inform specific created realities, providing us with critical information about the nature of the human person and the specified forms of human relationality we call marriage and family.[12] Specifically, we will use contemporary pagan myths and their radical differences from Hebrew thought to show that, in the latter, a process of *demythologization* took place which radically transformed Israel's understanding of both the human person and sexuality.[13] In Chapters 1 and 2, we will examine the effects of a monotheistic understanding of God; the constituent structures of creation (especially the human person and relationality); and the emergence of historical (linear) consciousness and its consequences. It is *only* within this context that the family is seen as having a teleological and salvific purpose. Only *after* having been demythologized can human sexuality and the family be assumed into the divine plan and become an intrinsic part of the Hebraic covenant.

---

12. Genesis 1 and 2 are the key texts here. In much modern scholarship, these texts are seen as being at odds with each other and presenting differing accounts of creation. This work sees them as a fundamental unity, each needing the other for completion. For example, the tension in Gn 1:26 between the singular (him) and plural (them) is only resolved by the account of woman's creation from the man in Gn 2. As we shall see, the tensions in one text are resolved in the other, and *together* they provide a more complete and unified understanding of the human person than either account offers alone. E.g., Gn 1 knows nothing of communion between the genders, whereas Gn 2 does not speak of procreation. Together they form what we will call the *narrative of creation*.

13. The term "to demythologize" refers to the process by which phenomena (such as sexuality, gender, family, etc.) that have been understood by a culture in terms of mythological constructs (often for religious reasons), are freed from those constructs. In this way, their objective nature and the ends towards which they are moving are able to be grasped more clearly. Essentially, it means that phenomena are stripped of their mythological guise and their true nature is allowed to be seen.

Functioning of the Family within
the Hebraic Covenant

The second key theme deals with the salvific role of the family in the Abrahamic covenant. The organic family unit is at the core of covenantal theology and plays an indispensable role, such that *without the family there is no covenant*. In Chapters 3 through 5 we will see how the intersection between the family and the covenant is most profoundly achieved in the person and the very body of Abraham. In fact, he and his family become paradigmatic for all the faithful—including Christians (Rom 4:16 and Gal 3:29).[14]

Within the Hebraic covenant, the family becomes the *medium* of faith and is the indispensable *carrier of the covenant*. It becomes the miniature representation of the sanctuary and is an essential component in the hallowing of time (Chapter 5). It is not at the Temple but within his own home that the father carries out the three father-led rituals that are at the heart of the covenant (Chapter 4). The family is the primary place of education and a primary locus of the cult, providing the necessary links between the generations. These family functions and rituals all flow from the identification of the family with God's salvific will. The family is, in its essence, the carrier of the covenant and essential if Israel is to realize her vocation to holiness. Without the family and its holiness, there is no covenant.

Hebraic Anthropology

The third theme in the Old Testament section deals with the underlying principles that inform Hebraic anthropology. The Semitic understanding in this area is radically different from our own modern under-

14. "To the ones of the faith of Abraham, who is the father of all of us" (+Rom 4:16). "And if you are of Christ, then you are of the seed of Abraham" (+Gal 3:29).

The Hebrew texts are from Bibloi/SilverMount Software. Almost all original texts are provided. In general, translations have been chosen to reproduce the original text as closely as possible. Consequently, various sources of translations have been used, including the author's own (marked with +), the New American Bible (marked with •) and the Revised Standard Version (marked with ^). Any other translations are identified. I have developed a slightly modified transliteration and have referred extensively to the transliteration found in BibleWorks 6.

standing, particularly in the West. We have lost the profound sense of corporateness which is the mainspring of Semitic thought. Consequently, if we limit ourselves to modern categories, it will be impossible to understand the Hebraic concept of the human person or of the covenantal design of history. It is necessary to go beyond modern conceptualization, which sees the person in atomistic terms, and begin wrestling with the Hebraic principle of *corporate personality* and understanding of the soul (*nephesh*).[15] Surprisingly, this Semitic understanding of the person pervades *both* the Old and the New Testaments and maintains a *positive* tension between, on the one hand, the value of the personal/ subjective element, and, on the other, the recognition that each person is formed by, and is determined by, a prior corporate reality (the family, tribe, and / or nation). These two realities are *inextricably* linked and cannot be divided. This Semitic understanding, which always maintains both the personal and the corporate, is foundational for the New Testament's worldview. Consequently, in the new covenant in Christ, both the corporate and personal dimensions co-exist and never collapse into one another. In the New Testament's understanding of the Church, one finds personal salvation, but it is always found in terms of belonging to the corporate body of the Church. In household baptisms, there is personal response on the part of the head of the family, but this response also profoundly affects all who are a part of that family so that baptism becomes a familial reality (cf. Acts 16). The myth of the autonomous, self-determining individual does not function within the anthropology of either the Old or the New Testament. Rather, both the constitutive personal and corporate dimensions of the person are safeguarded.

STRUCTURE OF THE STUDY—PART II

Part II focuses on the family as it has been reconfigured in Christ and brings us into the New Testament era. Because the very first Christians were all Jews, the fundamental principles concerning the nature

---

15. Certainly one can form a noetic idea of this corporate dimension, but it takes sustained exposure to this concept before one begins to see how pervasive and informing this concept is in Semitic thought.

and functioning of the family *had already been received* and were being lived out in the community. Hence, there was no need for a developed theology of the family per se in the New Testament. But the NT presents us with a dynamic shift in this paradigm nonetheless. The New Testament does not repudiate the Old but rather fulfills it.[16] In the NT, the family of Abraham finds its teleological fulfillment in the body of Jesus Christ, which manifests itself as the (organic) Church. The individual family now takes on a Christological form and participates in the ecclesial design of salvation. That is to say, the family becomes what it was always intended to be—the "domestic church," the icon of Christ's unending love within the created order. Hence, the family, the carrier of the covenant, now takes on its final and Christological form, realizing its vocation by becoming the sphere of *eschatological* or *pneumatological* activity. Within the family we are to become conformed to Christ and enter into His mission.

In order to uncover the theological principles operative in this reconstituted family, we will examine the three critical stages in the development and appropriation of the theology of the domestic church, which will help us to see more clearly the transformative changes in the family effected by baptism into Christ.

Transformation in Christ:
New Testament Foundations

The first Christians, having initially inherited the Jewish tradition, carried with them the understanding of the family they received from the Torah and the covenant. A fundamental question for our study is, how was the structure of the Old Testament covenantal family affected by its insertion into Christ and to what degree? The key issue is, did the New Testament Church, because of its emphasis on the personal relationship with Christ, diminish or even replace the OT idea of corporate salvation with an exclusively individualistic one?[17] Our task here is to

---

16. •Mt 5:17, which sets out this hermeneutical principle. Jesus, during the Sermon on the Mount, states, "Do not think that I have come to abolish the law or the prophets. I have come not to abolish but to fulfill (πληρῶσαι)."

17. This is a key issue and is evident in the different understandings of salvation within

see whether or not the principle of corporate personality is overcome by some form of NT personalism or does this corporate principle *continue* to inform the family structure in the new covenant, now modified within a Christological framework (Chapters 7 and 8). A second critical need is to carry out a philological study of the usage and provenance of the phrase "domestic church" in the New Testament canon. Here we will see that conceptually this phrase is linguistically tied to the house-church experience of the early church. Our need will be to discover how the NT theologically grounds its understanding of the family (chapter 8). There are serious problems and limitations with the phrase "domestic church" within the NT canon; thus a technical discussion is essential and will help prevent confusion over its meaning and ensure that the concept is properly grounded in the NT reality of baptism.

Appropriation by the Fathers

In the patristic period the practice of referring to the Christian family as a "domestic church" was well established. The question here is how the early Church Fathers appropriated and understood the term "domestic church" and how they worked out its ecclesial identity (Chapter 9). Augustine and Chrysostom located actual *ecclesial* structures *and* order *within* the Christian home; they taught that those structures and the attendant order flow from the participation of the family in the nature of the Church. For both Fathers, the baptized family was indeed a micro-church (*micra ekklesia*) which participated in the formal Body of Christ and was the locus where the mission and life of the Church were being lived out in a concrete manner in daily life.

---

the Christian community. The debates usually focus covenantal theology, infant baptism, the nature of original sin, etc. Evangelicals tend to diminish the corporate nature of salvation per se and emphasize the individual act of faith. Those with a catholic sense understand that the salvific process is always corporate. The consequences of these understandings are not negligible. Each proceeds from and/or produces an anthropology that is distinct from and at variance with the other. This, in turn, has profound ramifications in other major areas of theology. See A. Das's work on the debates in Pauline thought, especially his treatment of *covenantal nomism*, in *Paul, the Law and the Covenant* (Peabody, Mass.: Hendrickson Publishing, 2001), 70–144.

Reappropriation at Vatican II

Finally, we will examine how the term "domestic church," after a hiatus of 1500 years, emerged within the Vatican II debates. Some of the Council fathers had theological problems with this concept, and it was accepted only tentatively during this period, was mentioned only briefly in two of the conciliar documents, and then only in metaphorical language. It is necessary to study the Vatican II debates as they reveal (1) the contemporary theological mind set (which at that point gave little theological value to the family); (2) the tensions that existed within the Council concerning the holiness of the family; and ultimately, (3) the Council's theological justifications for seeing the family as being a constitutive part of the Church and having (analogously) an ecclesial identity.

This study provides the essential foundations upon which a comprehensive theology of the domestic church can be constructed. By uncovering the informing principles of the family and, at the same time, identifying the family's theological meaning and purpose within the divine covenant, this study will aid in the recovery of a biblical vision of the family, which culminates in the family's Christological identity.[18] Any theology not informed by the foundational Biblical principles uncovered in this study will inevitably falter. It is hoped that, as the principles discussed in this work are understood, the genuine ecclesial vocation of the family (both its mission and its structure) will be more deeply grasped and lived out.

---

18. The research in this book lays the foundations so that a more fully developed theology of the domestic church can emerge. This work provides indications of what areas will need further investigation. In the Old Testament area, studies need (1) to explore the Hebraic concept of holiness and the specific water rituals of Israel and their relationship to the family and their link to baptism, and (2) to develop an adequate hermeneutic which deals with the symbolic structure of Scripture and which allows the family to acquire a depth dimension beyond its sociological construction. In the area of New Testament studies, further research is required to develop a renewed understanding of the multifaceted dimensions of baptism, along with its connection to Old Testament purity rituals, and its relationship to the family.

PART ONE

FOUNDATIONS OF THE FAMILY IN THE OLD TESTAMENT

The New is hidden in the Old and the Old is revealed in the New.

St. Augustine, *Quest. in Hept.* 2, 73

APOLOGIA FOR THE "ELDER BROTHER"

The whole trajectory of salvation history is a single revelation of God's encounter with His fallen creation. As the Catechism puts it, "Through all the words of Sacred Scripture, God speaks only one single Word, his one Utterance in whom he expresses himself completely."[1] From the very first, Christians refused to view the Old Testament antagonistically[2] and knew it to be not only the revelation of God but also the foundation for the Chris-

---

1. *CCC*, section 102. Similarly, section 112 states: "different as the books which comprise it may be, Scripture is a unity by reason of the unity of God's plan, of which Christ Jesus is the center and heart."

2. One of the earliest heresies of the Church concerned the relationship of the New and Old Testaments. Marcion and his followers were condemned for the proposal that there was a fundamental opposition between the Old and New Testaments that required the Old Testament to be rejected.

tian revelation.[3] Because there is only the one divine will being worked
out in time and history, there is of necessity an organic connection among
all parts of that revelation. This means that there is an *intrinsic* relationship between Israel and the Church, which, unfortunately, is not evident to
everyone. Therefore, before proceeding, we will need to briefly examine the organic unity that exists between Israel and the Church, which,
in turn, will explain the Church's need *always* to situate herself within
the revelation to Israel and never apart from it. As the *elder brother in the
faith*,[4] Israel possesses a revelation that is foundational for Christianity.
Because of their underlying organic unity, the Jewish and Christian rev-
elations cannot be seen as opposing entities.[5] In the OT, as the Fathers of
Vatican II noted, "the mystery of our salvation is present in a hidden way,"
and thus Hebrew revelation is intimately linked with the New Covenant.[6]
The Council affirmed this by stating that "the books of the Old Testament,
all of them caught up into the Gospel message, attain and show forth their
full meaning in the New Testament...and, in their turn, shed light on it

3. See Paul's explanation of the continuing role of Israel and its place in the mystery of
God's divine economy in Romans 11, especially verses 25–29.

4. John Paul II, in his historic visit to the Synagogue of Rome on April 13, 1986, said that
the Jews could be said to be the elder brothers of Christians. David G. Dalin, in his article
"John Paul II and the Jews," noted that "the Wadowice of Karol Wojtyla's childhood was also,
as Weigel has noted, 'a place where the Polish poet Adam Mickiewicz's description of Jews as
the 'elder brothers' of Christians was taken seriously by many local Catholics'" (http://www.
firstthings.com/web-exclusives/2007/12/john-paul-ii-and-the-jews [accessed May 29, 2009]).

5. This is certainly how the Church views the relationship between the Old and New Testaments. However, from the Jewish perspective, the fulfillment which Christianity claims to
have experienced in Christ is still being awaited. But the dialogue between Christians and
Jews since Vatican II has generated much goodwill and greater reciprocal respect and gen-
erosity on both sides, without the fundamental differences that exist being denied. See the
Vatican II declaration *Nostrae Aetate* and the Jewish publication of *Dabru Emet: A Jewish
Statement on Christians and Christianity* (2002) from the National Jewish Scholars Project.
There has been criticism of *Dabru Emet*, notably from within the Orthodox community,
notably in the response by Dr. David Berger issued by the Institute for Public Affairs of the
Orthodox Union on September 14, 2000.

6. *Dei Verbum* 4:14 in *Vatican Council II*, 759.

and explain it."[7] Saint Paul, in his epistle to the Romans, explained the relationship between the two covenants: "For if you were cut from what is by
nature a wild olive tree, and grafted, contrary to nature, into a cultivated
one, how much more will they who belong to it by nature be grafted back
into their own olive tree" (•Rom 11:24).

Christians are grafted into the prior experience of God's revelation to
Israel. This must never be forgotten, especially if one hopes to understand
with ever-increasing clarity the depths of the Christian faith. This explains
why it is essential to locate the roots of "domestic church" in the OT. By so
doing, the theological foundations and the richness of this concept will begin to emerge for us.

A propos this discussion is Paul's teaching on the effect of salvation: "if
you belong to Christ, then you are Abraham's descendant, heirs according
to the promise" (•Gal 3:29). Paul is showing the Galatian Christians that
being incorporated into Christ causes one to become *organically* a part of
the family of Abraham, the father of Judaism. To reject the Judaic basis of
Christianity, as did Marcion, is to reject the foundation of one's own salvific identity. To disregard its relevance is to be profoundly mistaken as to
the proper relationship between Judaism and Christianity.[8]

FAMILY IN THE OLD TESTAMENT

In his study *Marriage: Human Reality and Saving Mystery,* Schillebeeckx realized the need to root his theology in the experience of Israel
and articulated why this was necessary:

---

7. Ibid., 4:16, pp. 759–60. The Scriptural references given are Mt. 5:17; Lk 24:27; Rom.
16:25–26; 2 Cor 3:14–16.

8. Jesus' teaching in the Sermon on the Mount shows the foundational importance of the
Hebrew revelation: "Do not think that I have come to abolish the Law or the Prophets; I have
not come to abolish them but to fulfill them" (Mt 5:17).

> [T]he fact remains that it pleased God to reveal himself within a Se-
> mitic society and in the course of a Semitic history.... We can ignore
> this history and civilization only at our peril, for it is impossible to
> grasp the word of God as a pure, divine reality somehow divorced
> from its human expression. It is precisely in Israelite man that the
> Old Testament revelation comes to us.... Many aspects of Israel's so-
> cial and historical setting bear the imprint of divine revelation or of
> her association with the living God.[9]

The divine imprint is precisely what we are seeking to discover, especially in terms of family. The term "domestic church," of course, appears
nowhere in the Hebrew canon; therefore, one cannot do a philological
analysis of the term "domestic church" or an examination of its philological development. Instead, the proper question to pose is: "How was the
family understood *theologically* in the Israelite context?" It is here that one
can discover the Jewish roots of the domestic church. Schillebeeckx's comments clarify our question even further:

> Our search is for the word of God concerning marriage, the word
> which has been heard with a gradually increasing clarity throughout
> salvation history.... In the first place this means that we must seek
> to answer the question: How did Israel, as the people of God, expe-
> rience the reality of marriage? I stress, *Israel as the people of God*....
> Expressions such as "biblical anthropology"...may just denote...the
> ancient oriental, and more particularly Semitic, view of man or of
> marriage.... The dogmatic question as to what is "biblical" in the Old
> Testament in the theological sense of the word—that is, as the ex-
> pression of God's word which is binding on Christians—remains un-
> answered.[10]

This present study is neither a sociological nor an historical analysis of
the family and its structures. Rather it is an attempt to discover how the

9. Edward Schillebeeckx, *Marriage: Human Reality and Saving Mystery*, trans. N. D.
Smith (New York: Sheed and Ward, 1965), 9.
10. Ibid., 8.

family operates *theologically* in God's revelation to Israel. In order to discover the critical principles that are constitutive of the OT family, we will examine: (1) how the concept of family was worked upon and shaped by the demythologizing processes active in the Old Testament; (2) how this newly "dimensioned" family functioned within the Israelite covenant; and (3) what concept of the person and his relationships made this possible. Together, these elements will provide the key anthropological principles operating in the text.

Central to our investigation are the related processes of demythologization and historicization, both of which are predicated on the revelation of monotheism. These forces shaped and altered every facet of Israel's self-perception and experience, including her understanding of sexuality and family life. Through them, Israel became fundamentally differentiated from her pagan environment, and it was this separation that allowed sexuality and family to be conceived in wholly different terms. Once freed from false constructions, human sexuality and the family were assumed into the divine salvific process.

CHAPTER 1

THE FAMILY IN MYTHOLOGICAL THOUGHT

The family, in order to assume its proper functioning with the Judeo-Christian covenants, had first to undergo a process of demythologization. In the ancient Near East, sexuality, marriage and fecundity were understood within a mythological context that united them to the divine sphere and made them instruments by which the natural world order could continue. In this context, sexuality and fecundity were means by which the divine sphere could be manipulated magically. Thus, these basic human realities were not understood on their own terms but as parts of a complex mythological worldview. This understanding had first to be purified before marriage and family could be assumed into the covenant with God.

THE NEAR EASTERN CONTEXT

A key question to examine at the beginning of our study is whether there was something unique about the revelation to Israel or did Israel simply borrow heavily from the mythologies of her pagan neighbors. Hellmut Brunner, in his introduction to *Near Eastern Religious Texts Relating to the Old Testament,* articulates clearly for us what the central problem is:[1]

> It is obvious how many issues must necessarily remain unresolved in a comparison between ancient Near Eastern texts and the religious witness of the Old Testament. Indeed, the situation is so open that we even have limited possibilities in using parallels to elucidate such important questions as whether and how far the religion...to be found in the Old Testament traditions is a stranger to the world of the religions of the ancient Near East, or whether it is a part of that world, rooted in it, shaped by it, and incomprehensible without it.[2]

To examine fully the important question of Israel's dependence on her pagan neighbors is beyond the scope of our present study. But the question of Israel's distinctiveness is critical to our discussion. Until the rise of the higher critical movement in the latter part of the nineteenth century, the revelation to Israel was generally considered to be divine, unique, and in opposition to the pagan world around it. However, this understanding was seriously challenged by the rise of higher critical scholarship. As it developed, modern critical studies saw the faith of Israel as having been greatly influenced by the surrounding pagan cultures and as incorporating large amounts of the prevailing pagan myths into its own religious experience. Indeed, Israel was but a part of the cultural matrix of the ancient Near East.[3]

While today there are serious debates over the presuppositions of

---

1. It was formerly assumed that monotheism gradually arose from polytheism. But E. O. James rejects this. "Monotheism in this sense is the prerogative of the higher living religions...but it has not evolved from polytheism and animism in a lineal development in the manner formerly surmised.... Each of these several theistic traditions has emerged within its own proper context and conditions" (E. O. James, *The Worship of the Sky-God* [New York: Oxford University Press, 1963], 21).

2. Walter Beyerlin, ed., *Near Eastern Religious Texts Relating to the Old Testament,* trans. J. Bowden (London: SCM Press, 1978), xxiv–xxv.

3. There is a fundamental problem with this conclusion: the revelation to Israel of the oneness of God inevitably caused her to be *separated* from all her polytheistic neighbors. In fact, the very identity of Israel was predicated on these differences and became one of the great admonitions to Israel: be separate from the surrounding cultures. (See Ezr 10:11.) This distinctiveness is further confirmed in Israel's vocational call to holiness—which has as its primary meaning the idea of separation. All that is holy is separated unto God.

the higher critical methodology and over many of its conclusions, it remains a major (but not exclusive) framework for most modern scholars.[4] But this approach *has* focused the question of Israel's uniqueness very sharply for us: is there anything fundamentally distinctive about Israel, her faith and her self-understanding, or is Israel, in reality, indistinguishable from her pagan neighbors? Shaye Cohen, in *The Jewish Family in Antiquity*, concluded: "The Jewish family in antiquity seems not to have been distinctive by the power of its Jewishness; rather its structure, ideals, and dynamics seem to have been virtually identical with those of its ambient culture(s)."[5]

In opposition to this view, the thesis to be developed in this work is that there is something fundamentally unique in Israel's experience that shaped and controlled not only the destiny of Israel but also all of her beliefs, thus differentiating her from the culture in which she found

4. G. Wenham, in his commentary on Genesis, states that "some of the most deeply rooted convictions of the critical consensus have been challenged in recent years.... The striking thing about the current debate is that it emanates from within the heart of critical orthodoxy…[and] there is now widespread recognition of the hypothetical character of the results of modern criticism" (*Genesis 1–15*, Word Biblical Commentary, vol. 1 [Waco, Tx.: Word Books, 1987], xxxiv–xxxv). He offers a summary of current Pentateuchal research on pages xxv–xlv. Claus Westermann also provides an extensive summary with many of its variations (both pro and con) in *Genesis 1–11: A Commentary*, trans. John J. Scullion (Minneapolis: Augsburg Publishing House, 1984), 567–606. While modern criticism is the framework for most current scholars, Westermann reviews its opponents as well. Yehezkel Kaufmann, who sees some validity to critical methodologies, rejects the late dating of the Torah, and he labels some of this scholarship "paganistic"—see *The Religion of Israel: From Its Beginnings to the Babylonian Exile*, trans. Moshe Greenberg (Chicago: University of Chicago Press, 1960), 156n1. U. Cassuto rejects the Documentary Hypothesis and maintains that "it is inconceivable that the Torah would allude to a pagan epic of gentile origin" (*A Commentary on the Book of Genesis: From Adam to Noah*, trans. I. Abrahams [Jerusalem: Magnes Press, 1961], 73). He favors some preexisting Israelite literature which contained some of the ancient stories of beginnings (ibid., 8). Cardinal Ratzinger presented an insightful analysis of the current problems in this area of hermeneutics in his *Biblical Interpretation in Crisis*, ed. R. Neuhaus (Grand Rapids, Mich.: Eerdmans, 1989); see also the newly revised version edited by J. Granados (Eerdmans, 2008), in which it is shown that academic conjecture has turned into rigid dogma in this area and needs to be challenged and purified.

5. Cohen, *The Jewish Family in Antiquity*, 2. There are many who would reject this syncretic position. For an articulate presentation of the opposing view holding to the uniqueness of the revelation to Israel and providing the theological underpinnings for this position, see Cassuto's *From Adam to Noah*.

herself.[6] Our task is to discover what this "differentiating" factor is and how it affected Israel's understanding and experience of family.

THE ESSENCE OF POLYTHEISM:
A COMMON MYTHOLOGY

The Biblical witness portrays Israel as being surrounded by a multitude of polytheistic religions which had to be utterly rejected and avoided if Israel was to remain holy.[7] The pagan gods were sexually active and licentious and their rituals were orgiastic and tied to fertility rites. To grasp what is truly significant about the Israelite experience, it is best to see it against the background of the ancient Near East where it emerged. Therefore, our first need is to establish what were the primary understandings that informed and motivated paganism.

Samuel Kramer in *The Sumerians* established that while the religious cultures of the ancient Near East were not uniform, they were heavily dependent on each other.[8] His extensive work lay in establish-

---

6. This viewpoint is strengthened by the conclusions of the sociologist Irving Zeitlin, who contends that "one way to assess the validity of the syncretism theory is to look at these elements of Canaanite culture and to ask whether they were borrowed or absorbed by the Israelites." He then shows how Israel differed radically from Canaanite culture and concluded: "In this light, we have to say that no evidence exists of a Canaanite-Israelite syncretism in technology and social organization. Accordingly, we should treat with extreme skepticism the prevailing theory of a Canaanite-Israelite syncretism in religion" (Irving M. Zeitlin, *Ancient Judaism* [Glasgow: Polity Press, 1984], 23–25).

7. The following verses condemn relating to foreign gods and set a clear line of demarcation between Israel and all other nations: "Do not be led astray into adoring them [the sun, moon and stars] and serving them. These, the LORD, your God, has let fall to the lot of all other nations under the heavens." (•Dt 4:19); "You shall not worship any other god, for the LORD is 'the Jealous One'; a jealous God is he." (•Ex 34:14) This is reinforced during the covenant process in Ex 19:5 in which God calls Israel His special possession (סְגֻלָּה / s⁰gullāʰ) which He has separated out "from all people" (מִכָּל־הָעַמִּים / mikkol-hāʿammîm).

8. Samuel Noah Kramer, *The Sumerians: Their History, Culture, and Character* (Chicago: University of Chicago Press, 1963). See also David Tasker's *Ancient Near Eastern Literature and the Hebrew Scriptures about the Fatherhood of God*, Studies in Biblical Literature 69 (Washington, D.C.: Peter Lang, 2004). He states: "The budding empire of Babylon germinated in the same geographic region as Sumer, and although they spoke a different language, the Babylonians borrowed copiously from Sumerian theology and culture, adapting them to suit their own purposes" (29).

ing the priority in time of the Sumerian culture and how influential it was for later civilizations.[9] His conclusion was that "for a proper appraisal of the cultural and spiritual development of the entire ancient Near East the significance of the Sumerian literary documents can hardly be overestimated. The Akkadians, that is, the Assyrians and Babylonians, took these works over almost *in toto.* The Hittites, Hurrians, and Canaanites translated some of them into their own languages and no doubt imitated them widely."[10] As Tasker notes in his 2004 study, the myths developed in Sumer became "the basic creed and dogma of much of the ancient Near East."[11]

Thus the ancient Near East cultures can be understood as sharing, to some extent, a common religious heritage or ambience which was polytheistic and pagan in its orientation. While significant differences existed, many themes, stories, and even gods and goddess were shared or adapted to the different emerging civilizations. Syncretism was the operative dynamic in the developing religious systems in the ancient Near East and led to an essential religious commonality amongst those nations. It is in the midst of this common mythological worldview that ancient Israel found itself.

It is evident that these religions were directly connected with the processes of nature and were in fact nature religions. Their mythologies and rituals were often attempts at explaining, as well as manipulating, natural phenomena, especially fertility. Walter Eichrodt, in *Theology of the Old Testament,* points out their primary impulse:

> Especially evident is the naturalistic character of these deities; they have their being in the natural phenomena of their district, in the vegetable and animal life and in the natural resources on which these depend for their growth, springs and rivers, the storm and the heat of the sun. Hence fertility rites, with their physical mimicry of natural processes, play a great part in the cult. Similarly, the Baals are constantly coupled

9. "In the course of the third millennium B.C. the Sumerians developed religious ideas and spiritual concepts which have left an indelible impress on the modern world, especially by way of Judaism, Christianity, and Mohammedanism" (Kramer, *The Sumerians,* 112). See also "The Legacy of Sumer," chapter 8 in ibid., 269–99.

10. Kramer, *The Sumerians,* 166.

11. Tasker, *ANE Fatherhood,* 16.

with a female consort, who as goddess of Love and Motherhood is found
sometimes as Baalah, at others [times] as Astarte or Asherah.[12]

The rituals of the cult were exercised expressly for the purposes of
inducing fertility for both nature and man. Max Weber, in his study of
this Near Eastern context, states: "Like most ancient agricultural cults,
those of Baal were and remained orgiastic, specifically, of a sexual and
alcoholic character."[13] The sociologist Irving M. Zeitlin, who recently
revised and updated Weber's classic, concurs with this interpretation.
In his own *Ancient Judaism,* he succinctly defines the nature of these
religions as "the deification of natural processes."[14]

How this deification played out in these ancient societies can be concretely illustrated in the following two examples. It will be clear from
these examples that in the ancient pagan world, there was a penetra-
tion of the divine and natural worlds such that there was constant and
necessary interplay between them and that this relationship was highly
sexualized. This admixture then would greatly determine the functioning and value of sexuality within those societies. While Sumer was the
first to record its beliefs,[15] it nevertheless did not do so in a systematic
manner. Rather, one has to piece together what were actual beliefs by
examining their myths, poems, etc.[16] The first example is an extract
from the second-millennium Sumerian story "Enki and the World Order," which mythically explains how the fertility of the world is accomplished and maintained. Enki, the god responsible for the universe and

12. Walter Eichrodt, *Theology of the Old Testament,* vol. 1, trans. J. A. Baker (Philadelphia: Westminster Press, 1960), 200 (hereafter, *TOT*). Eichrodt's point is that the b^e'alim
appear in other mythologies under different titles. There was thus a common underlying
structure amongst the pagan religions that can be referred to as *ba'alism.*

13. Max Weber, *Ancient Judaism,* trans. and ed. H. H. Gerth and D. Martindale (Glencoe, Ill.: Free Press, 1952), 189.

14. Zeitlin, *Ancient Judaism,* 33.

15. "Because the Sumerians were the first in recorded history to develop ethical, religious, social, political and philosophical ideas, this study of the fatherhood of the gods must
commence with them" (Tasker, *ANE Fatherhood,* 15).

16. "No texts uncovered to date deal specifically with the creation of the universe...so
Sumerian cosmogony must be 'ferreted out' from myths, epic talks, and hymns" (Tasker,
ANE Fatherhood, 16).

its fertility, is portrayed as a bull who "mates with the river imagined as a wild cow":[17]

> Enki, the king of the Abzu, overpowering (?) in his majesty, speaks up with authority:
>
> My father, the king of the universe,
> Brought me into existence in the universe,
> My ancestor, the king of all the lands,
> Gathered together all the *me's*, placed the *me's* in my hand...
> I am the fecund seed, engendered by the great wild ox, I am the first born
>   son of An...
> I am the "big brother" of the gods, I am he who brings full prosperity...
> After father Enki had lifted it over the Euphrates,
> He stood up proudly like a rampant bull,
> He lifts the penis, ejaculates,
> Filled the Tigris with sparkling water...
> [The Tigr]is surr[endered] to him, as (to) a rampant bull...
> The water he brought is sparkling water...
> The grain he brought, is checkered grain, the people eat it...[18]

The natural process of seasonal rains upon which the crops depended was conceived in mythological terms and greatly sexualized. Rain became the semen of the gods that made the earth fecund. Four things are of particular note here:

1. The gods themselves are merely a part of nature; they do not have absolute control.
2. All things are controlled by fate (in Sumerian, the *me's*).[19]
3. The ordinary processes of nature are mythologized.[20]
4. The divinities, which are gendered beings, relate to nature in a sexualized manner.

17. Kramer, *The Sumerians,* 172–73.
18. "Enki and the World Order" (Kramer, *The Sumerians,* 181).
19. See Kramer, *The Sumerians,* 123–25, for explanation of these fated decrees. The word *me's* refers to the idea of fate and fated decrees.
20. This means that created realities were agents in the mythological explanations for the processes and events found in nature. Sexuality, for example, becomes a means by which the gods can be induced to grant fecundity to the fields. Thus, the proper nature of a created reality is overlaid with a mythological meaning.

The second example is Kramer's description of the Sumerian New Year rite which included the *hieros gamos*—that is, the sacred marriage of the king with the divinity.

> The most significant rite of the New Year was the *hieros-gamos,* or holy marriage, between the king, who represented the god Dumuzi, and one of the priestesses, who represented the goddess Inanna, *to ensure effectively the fecundity and prosperity of Sumer and its people....* The tutelary deity of Erech was Inanna, a goddess who throughout Sumerian history was deemed to be the deity primarily responsible for sexual love, fertility, and procreation.... [An] idea arose that the king of Sumer, no matter who he was or from what city he originated, must become the husband of the life-giving goddess of love, that is, İnanna of Erech, *if he was to ensure effectively the fecundity and prosperity of the land and its people....* It was carried out in ritual practice by the consummation of a marriage ceremony, which was probably repeated every New Year, between the king and a specially selected hierodule from Inanna's temple in Erech.[21]

In each example, sexuality, rather than being seen on its own terms, is assumed into the mythological realm and becomes part of the way in which the gods interact with human beings. It becomes an instrument in the divine cosmic drama that is being played out in the different processes of nature and in the preservation of society. In essence, sexuality was divinized.[22]

CULTS AND FERTILITY

Divine sexuality and the fecundity of nature and man were thoroughly intermingled in the cultus of the ancient Near East,[23] which has

21. Kramer, *The Sumerians,* 140–41 (emphasis added).

22. In the ancient world, human sexuality was assumed into the mythological/divine world and its creaturely status was not sufficiently guarded. In the Judeo-Christian view, sexuality is a created good which is intended to have a sacramental dimension. While there is an interpenetration between the creaturely and the divine in the Christian view of human sexuality, they are not confused as they were in pagan thought.

23. "The cycles of nature are commonly conceived of as the perennial mating and procreating of the gods" (Kaufmann, *Religion of Israel,* 23). See also Jeffrey H. Tigay, *The Evolution of the Gilgamesh Epic* (Philadelphia: University of Pennsylvania Press, 1982), 175, where the sacred-marriage ritual for agricultural fertility is mentioned.

been described as the "sexualization of the world."[24] This had profound consequences for how sexuality was understood and what practices followed from these mythological beliefs. Gerhard von Rad, in *Old Testament Theology*, explored the beliefs and practice in the Canaanite territories:

> The cults there practiced were pure fertility cults, as was appropriate to a farming population: Baal was the owner (the term was originally taken as appellative) of a mountain, or an oasis, or some other place. His relationship to the earth was that of a *hieros gamos*; he is the mythical generative power that fructifies the earth by means of the sperm of the rain. Human beings share in this fertilizing power by entering this mystery and imitating it. Cultic prostitution was therefore an essential characteristic of this worship; sacred prostitutes lived at the sanctuaries (*qdsh* I Kings XV.12; II Kings XXIII.7; Deut. XXIII. 18).[25]

In the pagan cultic practices, human sexuality became an essential instrument in worship and in securing the favor of the gods. Sexual intercourse was seen as an imitation of how the pagan god related to nature and in fact, when included in the cult, was seen as participating in this divine relationship and somehow released power to control the natural processes.

There is also the question of the sexual nature of the gods, themselves. Even a cursory examination of the ancient mythologies reveals a highly sexualized divine realm.[26] To begin with, the gods were always sexually differentiated as either male or female deities. The mythologies often contained theogonies which purported to give the genealogies of the gods who themselves were often sexually generated. For example, the Sumerian Enki impregnates several of his own family line, including his daughter Ninmu. He is quoted as saying:

> Shall I not kiss the young one, the fair,
> (Kiss) Ninmu, the fair...
> He embraced her, he kissed her,

24. Nahum Sarna, *Understanding Genesis* (New York: McGraw-Hill, 1966), 34n21.

25. Gerhard von Rad, *Old Testament Theology*, vol. 1: *The Theology of Israel's Historical Traditions*, trans. D. M. G. Stalker (New York: Harper and Row, 1962), 22 (hereafter, *OTT*).

26. See Michael Coogan, ed., *Stories from Ancient Canaan* (Philadelphia: The Westminster Press, 1978), 100.

> Enki poured the semen into the womb
> She took the semen into the womb, the semen of Enki.[27]

From this, Ninmu gives birth to Enki's granddaughter, Ninkurra, who in turn is impregnated by Enki who gives birth to Uttu.[28]

In an Egyptian myth of creation, sexuality is again the *modus operandi* by which the created order comes into existence.[29] The Egyptian god Re explains:

> I planned in my own heart, and there came into being a multitude of forms of beings.... I was the one who copulated with my fist, I masturbated (xxvii I) with my hand. Then I spewed with my own mouth: I spat out what was Shu and I sputtered out what was Tefnut.[30]

The divine sphere was completely sexualized, and their relationships were highly capricious and licentious.[31] In the Ugaritic myths, the god Baal copulates with a heifer seventy-seven times and this results in the birth of Math.[32] In the Hittite myth *Kingship in Heaven* the god Kumarbis bites the male generative organs of Anus who consequently is impregnated with three gods: the Storm-god, Aranzahas, and Tasmisus.[33] This same sexual promiscuity abounds in the Ugaritic myths.[34] This conception of the gods prevented any sense of absolute power being given to them. They too were contingent beings, powerful, yet not fully self-determining but caught in the matrix of natural forces and desires.

27. James B. Pritchard, *Ancient Near Eastern Texts,* 2d ed. (Princeton, N.J.: Princeton University Press, 1955), 39 (hereafter, *ANET*).

28. Pritchard, *ANET,* 39.

29. Cf. James, *Worship of the Sky-God,* 19.

30. Pritchard, *ANET,* 6.

31. See Kramer, *The Sumerians,* 146, for Enlil's raping of Ninlil.

32. Pritchard, *ANET,* 139.

33. The Sumerian text graphically describes the sexual activity of these gods: "He [Kumbaris] bit his 'knees' [meaning male parts] and his manhood went down into his inside. [Anus said]: 'Firstly I have impregnated thee with the noble Storm-god. Secondly I have impregnated thee with the river Aranzahas, not to be endured. Thirdly I have impregnated thee with the noble Tasmisus. Three dreadful gods have I planted in thy belly as seed'" (Pritchard, *ANET,* 120b).

34. In Poem IV AB, which deals with Ba'al and Anath, their sexual behavior is graphically portrayed: "He seizes and holds [her] womb; / [She] seizes and holds [his] stones / Baal ... *to an ox* / [...the Mai]den Anath / ...to conceive and bear" (Pritchard, *ANET,* 142).

As noted above, the sexual motif was often central to the agricultural nature motif:

> Enki (before) the wise Nintu, (the mother of the land),
> Causes his phallus to water the dikes,
> Causes his phallus to submerge the reeds...
> Poured the semen in the womb of Ninhursag.[35]

Using his own sexuality as a paradigm, ancient man understood the cycles and forces in nature as expressions of divine sexuality. Thus, the sexuality of the gods, as well as his own, became an essential ingredient in his understanding of the nature of the world and his purpose and place in it. Cultic sexual intercourse became a necessary way by which to obtain divine favor and to secure crops and water, the essentials of a secure life.

It is precisely on this point that Israel is radically differentiated from her neighbors. In the Hebraic revelation, the nature of the divinity and the role of the cult are premised on a radically different basis. First and foremost, there is only one God; there simply does not exist a host of competing divine powers or complementary genders. There is only Yahweh. There is no female counterpart. Divine sexual congress could not be essential to the creation of the world. The impact of this revelation of monotheism cannot be overestimated; it fundamentally changed the whole worldview of its adherents. The fundamental basis of the pagan system is undermined with this one revelation.

FATE AND THE PAGAN "GODS"

A basic tension and uncertainty about the control and destiny of the world underlies polytheistic thought.[36] The very plurality of the gods— who, by necessity, are in competition with one another—causes tension and uncertainty; there is no single, overarching divine will governing all things. The myths are replete with the stories of the gods battling each other for control, frequently with the sub-theme of the younger

---

35. Pritchard, *ANET*, 39, 142.
36. See James, *Worship of the Sky-God*, 41.

gods attempting to usurp the place of the older deities (the father-gods), often with the help of the mother goddesses.[37] Indeed, as E. O. James noted, this father-son battle for control is a fundamental motif of the Near Eastern mythology.[38] Moreover, as the Jewish historian Yehezkel Kaufmann pointed out, the pagan gods are never self-existent; rather, they emerge out of something else. "All these embodiments involve one idea which is the distinguishing mark of pagan thought: the idea that there exists a realm of being prior to the gods and above them, upon which the gods depend, and whose decrees they must obey."[39]

On this point, Israel's conception of God and the creation is fundamentally different from the ideas of its surrounding neighbors. The pagan deities are dependent on a prior realm.[40] It is here that the impersonal forces of the "fates" reside which control even the gods.[41] In the Sumerian mythology, this was represented by the *me's* noted in the Enki story above.[42] Kaufmann mentions that even the gods "are depicted as calling upon metadivine forces to surmount their own predestined limitations."[43] This effects a highly conflictual relationship between the gods and creation. The gods do not have supreme power,

37. See Coogan's development of this theory in *Stories from Ancient Canaan*, 81. Also see 29–31.

38. "In the background lay the struggle for power between the different generations of gods in the heavens, so fundamental in Near Eastern mythology" (James, *The Worship of the Sky-God*, 40). This point is central to Miller's thesis in his book *Biblical Faith and Fathering: Why We Call God "Father"* (New York: Paulist Press, 1989), 43–54. Miller demonstrates that at the heart of the pagan myths was a very weak understanding of fatherhood: the younger sons, often abetted by their mothers, rose in rebellion against the weak fathers. In contrast, at the heart of the Biblical revelation is a strong Father who cares for, and protects, His children.

39. Kaufmann, *Religion of Israel*, 21–22.

40. This is sometimes portrayed as the primal sea, *Hammu*, as in the Sumerian mythological texts. Cf. Kramer, *The Sumerians*, 150.

41. The Akkadian Creation Myth in Pritchard's *ANET* (p. 61, lines 6ff.) is a good example of the pagan understanding of theogony: "When no gods whatever had been brought into being,/Uncalled by name, their destinies undetermined—/Then it was that the gods were formed within them." This view has been confirmed and further developed by Zeitlin who traces the existence of this "belief in a supradivine force" in the different ancient mythologies including the Akkadian (Babylonian and Assyrian), the Geek (*Moira*), Sumerian (*me's*) and Egyptian (*Maat*) versions. See Zeitlin, *Ancient Judaism*, 1–9.

42. See Kramer, *The Sumerians*, 115–16, 125.

43. Kaufmann, *Religion of Israel*, 23.

nor do they ultimately determine the nature of created reality, for they themselves, at some level, are a part of that same order. In the pagan worldview, both the gods and human beings have to accept the power of the fates.[44]

These two realities (competing gods and impersonal fates) determined man's relationship both to the divine realm and to nature itself. Religion was a means by which he hoped to manipulate these competing forces for his own ends and this allowed for the emergence of magic.[45] As Sarna observed:

> Since, according to pagan concepts, man's destiny is controlled by two separate forces, the gods and the powers beyond the gods, it was inevitable that magic became an integral part of pagan religion. Man had to be able to devise the means of activating those forces superior even to the gods.[46]

This illustrates a point essential to our discussion. In the pagan worldview, the gods were formed and were merely a part of the created order; further, because there existed a supradivine impersonal realm (the controlling fates), the will of the gods was not absolute or sovereign.[47] *Hence, man in the ancient world experienced a fundamental uncertainty which could never be alleviated.* Underlying the experience of the world within the pagan framework was a fundamental angst that proceeded from the pagan conception of the gods and the pagan understanding of fate or time:

44. "They [the gods] are, rather, part of a realm precedent to and independent of them. They are rooted in this realm, are bound by its nature, are subservient to its laws.... This is the radical dichotomy of paganism; from it spring both mythology and magic.... In myth the gods appear not only as actors, but as acted upon" (Kaufman, *Religion of Israel*, 21–22).

45. Von Rad quotes E. Sprangler on this point:" Magic is originally a technique, a way of actively influencing the world rather than an attitude in which it is contemplated.... Primitive man wants to maintain himself over against the world; he believes that he possesses means through which he can render the powers which in a sinister way surround his existence tractable. To this extent magic is the primitive threshold of technology" (E. Spranger, *Die Magie der Seele* [Tubingen 1947], 66, quoted in von Rad, *OTT*, vol. 1, 34n52).

46. Sarna, *Understanding Genesis*, 11.

47. See Kaufmann, *Religion of Israel*, 43–45: "In it [divination] the gods manifest their knowledge of matters not necessarily dependent upon them."

It is not to be wondered at that Mesopotamian society suffered from a malaise which scholars have characterized as "overtones of anxiety." The nature of the gods could give no feeling of certainty and security in the cosmos.... To aggravate the situation still further, there was always that inscrutable primordial power beyond the realm of the gods to which man and gods were both subject. Evil, then, was a permanent necessity and there was nothing essentially good in the pagan universe.... History and time were but a repeating cycle of events in which man played a passive role, carried along relentlessly by the stream of existence to his ineluctable fate.[48]

This is the inevitable consequence of a mythological worldview that not only sexualizes the divine realm but also conversely provides a mythological understanding of the natural processes of generation in both nature and man. It was into this world of uncertainty and angst that the revelation to the Hebrews entered and fundamentally overturned these pagan conceptions.

48. Sarna, *Understanding Genesis,* 17–18. Cf. Kramer's assessment of Sumerian civilization: "Man's life was beset with uncertainty and haunted by insecurity, since he did not know beforehand the destiny decreed him by the unpredictable gods. When he died, his emasculated spirit descended to the dark, dreary nether world where life was but a dismal and wretched reflection of its earthly counterpart" (Kramer, *The Sumerians,* 123).

CHAPTER 2

THE PRINCIPLES
OF CREATION AND
COVENANTAL
REALITY

בְּרֵאשִׁית בָּרָא אֱלֹהִים אֵת הַשָּׁמַיִם וְאֵת הָאָרֶץ

In the beginning God created the heavens and the earth.

(+Gn 1:1)

THE SOVEREIGNTY
OF YAHWEH

With the first line of the Hebrew revelation, the fundamental principles of the mythological worldview were challenged and a radical vision of reality was set in opposition to the omnipresent pagan understanding.[1] The uniqueness of this view was captured by von Rad in his commentary on Genesis:

---

1. See Westermann, *Genesis 1–11,* 93–100, for an excellent summary of the literature on the exegesis of the creation narrative. Cf. Wenham, *Genesis 1–15,* 11–15; Walther Eichrodt, *Theology of the Old Testament,* trans. J. A. Baker, vol. 2, 5th ed., OTL (Philadelphia: Westminster Press, 1967), 93–106 [hereafter, *TOT,* vol. 2]; A. Dillmann, *Genesis: Critically and Exegetically Expounded,* trans. William B. Stevenson, vol. 1 (Edinburgh: T & T Clark, 1897), 53–60; E. A. Speiser, *Genesis,* Anchor Bible, vol. 1 (Garden City, N.Y.: Doubleday, 1964), 12–13; Alexander Heidel, *The Babylonian Genesis* (Chicago: University of Chicago Press, 1963),

The idea of creation by the word preserves first of all the most radical essential distinction between Creator and creature. Creation cannot be even remotely considered an emanation from God…but is rather a product of his personal will. The only continuity between God and his work is the Word.[2]

In the Hebrew world, there are no other gods but Yahweh, no mythic struggles from which creation emerges.[3] There is no fatalistic supradivine realm; hence magic and ritual manipulation are *de facto* eliminated from the cultus.[4] Rather, there is only the one God, whose will alone is absolute and sovereign, and He is the Creator of all.[5] This became the underlying foundation for the whole of Israel's understanding of created realities; all reality outside of God is contingent reality and possesses its nature and ultimate meaning (*telos*) only as it is found in Him.[6]

But it is important to note that Yahweh's sovereignty is not the sheer exercise of raw power. Rather, as Walter Brueggemann points out in his study of sovereignty in the Old Testament, it becomes sovereignty in relationship. This means that the God who is Creator is not disinterested in His creation and in particular His chosen people, but cares for them and also is deeply *affected* by them.

89–96; Gerhard von Rad, *OTT,* vol. 1, 142; Brevard Childs, *Myth and Reality in the Old Testament,* 2nd ed. (London: SCM Press, 1962), 41.

2. Von Rad, *OTT,* vol. 1, 51–52.

3. "The basic idea of Israelite religion is that God is supreme over all. There is no realm above or beside him to limit his absolute sovereignty" (Kaufmann, *Religion of Israel,* 60). See also p. 62.

4. See Zeitlin, *Ancient Judaism,* 21.

5. "Nowhere in the Bible, either in the primeval legends of Genesis or in the prophetic and poetic literature, is there the faintest suggestion of a force, condition or principle that is prior or superior to Yahweh. Neither is there the slightest indication that other autonomous principles exist in the universe. What we find instead in the biblical literature is that ideas which had originally emerged in a polytheistic culture have been radically transformed." Zeitlin, *Ancient Judaism,* 21; see also 26–27. It is this fundamental belief in the oneness of God and the concomitant beliefs which ensue from it that separated Israel from her surrounding cultures. There was no commonality such as existed amongst the pagans.

6. In the discussion that follows, we will establish the general principle that the Hebraic revelation of the nature of God fundamentally altered Israel's understanding of the relationship between the divine realm and creation. The specificity of this relationship then determines constitutively those realities which make up the domestic church, i.e., the human person, sexuality and institutions such as marriage and family.

But of course such a capacity to govern decisively is not the whole story of this sovereign, for Yahweh's sovereignty is sovereignty in relationship, an inexplicable mystery that is at the heart of biblical testimony.
As Israel attests, relationships of fidelity and loyalty to which YHWH is
committed...do decisively change the character of sovereignty so that
YHWH is not disinterested or unaffected by the reality of the partners
in the relationship.[7]

In essence, Yahweh is in control of all because He is Creator of all, but
His exercise of power is not in terms of domination or violence.[8] Rather, He has entered into relationship with his creation and especially His
people, who are now seen in filial terms.

CREATIO EX NIHILO

Until recently, the relationship of the divine to the created has always been understood within the Judeo-Christian worldview in terms
of *creatio ex nihilo*. However, certain modern scholarship has raised the
question whether, in fact, Israel held to a cosmology which was out of
nothing, or did she, like the pagan cultures around her, posit first a pre-
existent material out of which creation emerged? The answer has enormous consequences.[9] The latter would posit a primordial reality hav-

7. Walter Brueggemann, *Old Testament Theology: An Introduction* (Nashville, Tenn.:
Abingdon Press, 2008), 85–86. Brueggemann develops this relational aspect through a thematic exploration of Ex 2:24–25 and 3:7–8; Ex 34:6–7; and Ex 33:12–21—showing how they
"nicely summarize the claim of *sovereignty in relationship*" (86).

8. J. Alberto Soggin partially gets this right in *Israel in the Biblical Period: Institutions,
Festivals, Ceremonies, Rituals* (trans. J. Bowden [New York: T & T Clark, 2001]). He states
that "the almost spontaneous corollary of monotheism is belief in the divine creation of the
universe" (52). However, Soggin sees chaos as a force against which the creation must be
protected. This is antithetical to the interpretation that in Gn 1 and 2 there is an absence of
chaos precisely because God is the Creator and all powerful, against which there can be no
opposition.

9. See J. McKeown's commentary on Genesis, which proposes an historical trajectory
of this doctrine and deals with the philological intricacies. He acknowledges that "some
would argue that it has significant implications for our view of God: is he the God who simply works with the material to hand and subdues or orders it, as other deities were understood to do, or was he master of everything, creating even the materials that he would use?"
(*Genesis* [Grand Rapids, Mich.: Eerdmans, 2008], 265). He states that the doctrine of *creatio
ex nihilo* "exludes any possible hint of dualism" (ibid.). Oddly, in his survey he does not

ing an independent existence from God and forming a second basis of creation.[10] The answer to this question has enormous consequences for the relationship of God to all created realities, including sexuality, the human person, and family. The question, however, is controverted within modern scholarship and has generated a vast literature that is both complex and contradictory. To resolve this problem, we will examine two critical concepts presented in the Genesis narrative itself: the unique verb בָּרָא (bārā') and בְּרֵאשִׁית (bᵉrē'shît), which contains the idea of a "beginning point" to creation. While technical, this discussion is essential to establish the precise relationship of God to created realities.

בָּרָא (bārā'): to create

The Hebrew verb בָּרָא (bārā'—to create) is a technical term used to refer to the creative acts of God alone; it is used seven times in the opening account of creation.[11] It carries the sense of "initiating something new"[12] and "bring[ing] into existence."[13] In Hebrew, only God is ever the agent of this type of creative activity; only God is the subject of בָּרָא.[14] This points to a qualitative differentiation between the creative act of God and the activities of man. Wellhausen captures the distinction made by this word: "The most important point is that a special word is employed, which stands for nothing else than the creative agen-

---

include any reference to John's prologue, which clearly points to this doctrine. He goes over the usual philological ground. He does note that *creatio ex nihilo* "came as a response to Gnosticism. The Gnostics explained the existence of evil in the world as the result of preexistent deficient material" (269). But creation-out-of-nothing "means that the world is not, as the Gnostics claimed, an emanation from God but is a determined act of his free will" (269).

10. This would inevitably lead to a dualistic understanding of creation such as we see in the pagan mythologies and, later, in Gnosticism.

11. Gn 1:1, 21, 27 (3 times); 2:3, 4. This accounts for nearly one-fifth of its usage in the OT.

12. T. E. McComiskey, "ברא " in *Theological Wordbook of the Old Testament*, ed. R. L. Harris, G. Archer, and B. Waltke (Chicago: Moody Press, 1980), 127 (hereafter *TWOT*), which references Ps 51:10 (new heart); Is 48:6–7 (new creation); Is 65:7 (new heavens, new earth); Jer 31:22 (fundamental change in the natural order). Also note Gn 1:1–30 and Ps 148:5.

13. McComiskey, "ברא, w127, which references Is 43:1; Ezek 21:30 [H 21:35]; 28:13, 15.

14. Ibid.: "The word is used in the Qal of God's activity and is thus a purely theological term...appropriate to the concept of creation by divine fiat."

cy of God, and so dissociates it from all analogy with human making and shaping."[15] The question arises, what makes this form of "making" so unique and why can this not be said of mankind? The answer is perhaps contained in the fact that when this verb is used, the matter from which something is created is never mentioned. The Hebrew בָּרָא is free from any sense of pre-existent material.[16]

Contextually, in Genesis, the activity of בָּרָא is in distinct opposition to the pagan myths, where battles and conflict abound. In the Genesis narrative of creation, God merely speaks and created realities emerge in silence and in peace.[17] As Routledge states, "Rather than depicting rival gods fighting for power, the OT emphasizes that there is only one God who is Lord of heaven and earth."[18] This contrast to the surrounding pagan myths indicates that בָּרָא carries with it the sense of ease with which God creates. His creative acts are without effort. As W. H. Schmidt observed: "ברא ... preserves the same idea [of *creatio ex nihilo*], namely, 'God's effortless, totally free and unbound creating, his sovereignty.' "[19] Linguistically, as Heidel and others have noted, howev-

---

15. Julius Wellhausen, *Prolegomena to the History of Israel,* ed. Harry W. Gilmer, Scholars Press Reprints and Translation series (Atlanta: Scholars Press, 1994), 303. See also Eichrodt, *TOT,* vol. 2, 104 in which he describes ברא as "the technical term for that marvelous divine creativity which brings forth something new and astonishing." This unique agency of God will appear in the discussion of the image of God that is taken up later in this work.

16. Wenham, *Genesis 1–15,* 14. See also Heidel, *The Baylonian Genesis,* 89, citing Julian Morgenstern, "The Sources of the Creation Story—Genesis 1:1—2:4," *American Journal of Semitic Languages and Literatures* 36 (1920): 20: ברא "never takes the accusative of the material from which a thing is made, as do other verbs of making, but uses the accusative to designate only the thing made."

17. The pagan myths abounded with violence as the source of creation. This is referred to as *Chaoskampf* and "refers to the common depiction of creation as a battle between the creator god and the powers of chaos, usually represented by the primeval waters and the monster that rise from them" (Robin Routledge, *Old Testament Theology: A Thematic Approach* [Downers Grove, Ill.: InterVarsity Press Academic, 2008], 128). As Tsumura says, Gunkel tried to link phonologically the Hebrew word for the primordial waters (תְהוֹם / tᵉhôm) with the Babylonian name for the goddess Ti'âmat (David Tsumura, *Creation and Destruction: A Reappraisal of the Chaoskampf Theory in the Old Testament* [Winona Lake, Ind.: Eisenbrauns, 2005], 36). This would presumably establish a Babylonian dependency for the Hebrew creation story. However, as Tsumura concludes after careful linguistic analysis, this is "phonologically impossible" (38). See also Heidel, *The Babylonian Genesis,* 36ff.

18. Routledge, *OT Theology,* 129.   19. Wenham, *Genesis 1–15,* 14.

er, the verb בָּרָא does not explicitly require *creatio ex nihilo*.[20] However, given the context and its usage, it appears to lean in that direction. As T. E. McComiskey concluded: "Since the word never occurs with the object of the material, and since the primary emphasis of the word is on the newness of the created object, the word lends itself well to the concept of creation *ex nihilo,* although that concept is not necessarily inherent within the meaning of the word."[21]

בְּרֵאשִׁית (*bᵊrē'shit̠*—In the beginning)

An analysis of the second concept, בְּרֵאשִׁית (*bᵊrē'shit̠*—in the beginning), is more complex. This is the phrase with which the Hebrew Scriptures begin, and it is traditionally understood as a simple phrase and translated as "in *the* beginning." (I will refer to this construction as the absolute mode.)[22] However, the preposition בְּ (*bᵊ*), which means "in," is not pointed with the "a"-vowel, which is a dash under the letter (בַּ) called *patach* and which normally indicates the definite article.[23] Instead, it is pointed with the *shewa* (בְּ two dots below the letter). In this case, the phrase is not taken as being in the absolute mode ("in the beginning") but is construed as being "in construct," which in Hebrew links the phrase to another part of the sentence. In this case,

20. Alexander Heidel, *The Gilgamesh and Old Testament Parallels* (Chicago: University of Chicago Press, 1963), 89–92; S. R. Driver, *The Book of Genesis,* ed. Walter Lock, 3rd ed., Westminster Commentaries (London: Methuen, 1904), 3; Wenham, *Genesis 1–15,* 14.

21. McComiskey, "בָּרָא," H127. However, creation by divine *fiat* would seem to point clearly in that direction: "'Let there be light'; and there was light." (N.B.: Ps 51 speaks of the creation of a new heart, but heart here is the direct object of the action and not the material out of which something is made.)

22. Hebrew is a consonantal language and is not usually written with vowel sounds. The vowel pointing of the text was added much later to the original Hebrew text. However, the pointing that was adopted was not a creative exercise but rather preserved the way the text had traditionally been understood.

23. The theory of when vowel pointing was established and what historical stage it represents are debatable. Whereas the Masoretes of the seventh to tenth centuries AD have given the final form of the Biblical text known as the Masoretic text, it represents the vocalization that would have been used centuries earlier and seems to differ little in comparison with earlier texts that we have (e.g., from Qumran). However, there is wider divergence with the Septuagint, which is the Greek translation of the Hebrew text made in the second century BC.

the phrase is translated simply "in beginning" and connected to the verb "to create."[24] When this is done, the sentence is sometimes translated "when God was creating," which provides an opening to the idea that there was a material reality pre-existing God's act of creation and which co-existed eternally along with Him. Clearly, the correct reading is vital here, as it determines the extent of God's sovereignty over all reality. Should the phrase be taken in the absolute or the construct mode? Are both possible, or is one to be preferred over the other?

To resolve this dilemma, both Hebrew grammar and usage have to be invoked. Grammatically, בְּרֵאשִׁית (bᵉrēʾshît) can be read in Hebrew as being in construct. The construct case in Hebrew subordinates one noun to another, forming a unit, and this governs how the vowels are written.[25] Read this way, the phrase could be translated as a relative temporal clause, subordinated either to v. 2 or to v. 3.[26] The meaning then becomes "at the time when God was creating," thus giving the impression that the formless earth[27] existed before the divine creative act. While grammatically possible, this translation, as Wellhausen stated, "is desperate, and certainly not that followed by the punctuators, for the Jewish tradition (Septuagint, Aquila, Onkelos) is unanimous in translating, 'In the beginning, God created.'"[28] The witness of the Septuagint is particularly important, because it provides a written witness of how the Hebrew Scriptures were interpreted within the religious

24. However, it should be noted that this is transliterated in the ancient Greek versions of this passage as βαρησήθ, βρησέθ, βαρησίθ, βρισήθ, and βρησίδ (see Heidel, *The Babylonian Genesis,* 93). Note that the *patach,* which represents the definite article, is present in some of these transliterations. Heidel concludes that this shows that the inclusion or omission of the article is semantically irrelevant, as both expressions are essentially equivalent, thus strengthening the *ex nihilo* argument (ibid., 93).

25. See Wenham, *Genesis 1–15,* 11–12. Wenham notes that the famous Jewish exegetes Rashi (d. 1105) and Ibn Ezra (d. 1167) suggest that this phrase be taken as a temporal clause subordinated to other parts of text. The Septuagint (LXX) parallels this structure with *en arche.* The Vulgate renders it as *in principio* (see ibid., 11–12).

26. See Wenham, *Genesis 1–15,* 11–14. Cf. the New Jewish Version which, as H. Orlinsky comments, "has excluded altogether…the traditional 'In the beginning'" (H. Orlinksy, *Genesis: The NJV Translation* [New York: Harper and Row, 1966], xiv).

27. וְהָאָרֶץ הָיְתָה תֹהוּ וָבֹהוּ (vᵉhāʾāretz hāyᵉtāʰ tōhû vābōhû) (Gn 1:2).

28. Wellhausen, *Prolegomena,* 387, n. 1

Jewish community, and it is clear that בְּרֵאשִׁית was taken in the absolute mode, providing a beginning point to creation.

Furthermore, a study of the Hebrew canon shows that it is quite possible to construct such a phrase in Hebrew without the *patach* (_) and the phrase still retains its independence, not being subordinated to any other part of the text (that is, it is read in an absolute sense).[29] Numerous examples of this exact phrase *without the patach* are evident in Jeremiah (26:1, 27:1, 28:1, 49:34), which lists the kings, stating the beginning point of their reigns, clearly referring to a specific moment in time, before which this individual did not reign.

Both the absolute and construct interpretations are possible grammatically;[30] it is, though, possible to determine the more likely meaning from the following factors: (i) The Hebrews had no single inclusive word for the results of the divine creative act, such as the Greek *kosmos*. Instead, they referred to all created reality as "the heavens and the earth."[31] Therefore, v. 1 ("God created the heavens and the earth") can be understood as referring to the whole of reality, outside of which is

---

29. See Westermann, *Genesis 1–11*, 96, where he makes a thorough investigation of the differing interpretations. Reporting on the conclusions of O. Procksch, N. H. Ridderbos, and Walther Eichrodt ("In the Beginning"), Westermann states: "There is no convincing proof that the בְּרֵאשִׁית cannot be used in the absolute state at the beginning of a sentence to indicate time" (Westermann, *Genesis 1–11*, 96).

30. U. Cassuto rejects those attempts to put the phrase into construct. Syntactically, he compares Gn 1:1–2 with Jer 26:1, 27:1, 28:1, and Hos 1:2, which also contain בְּרֵאשִׁית. (*bᵉrēʾshît*). In each case, this phrase is subordinated to the following sentence, which is typified by the predicate preceding the subject. In Genesis 1:2 the subject, הָאָרֶץ (*hāʾāretz*), comes first, thus showing each phrase to be an independent clause. Therefore, the opening statement in Genesis is an encapsulation of all that will follow. See U. Cassuto, *From Adam to Noah*, 19–20. Westermann, along with Wellhausen, believed that "it would be completely out of harmony with P's style in Gn 1 to arrange the first three verses into one complete sentence" (Westermann, *Genesis 1–11*, 97, with reference to Wellhausen, *Prolegomena*, 387, n. 1). Eichrodt comments: "The idea of the absolute beginning of the created world thus proves to be a logical expression of the total outlook of the priestly narrator, an indispensable link in the working out of salvation on behalf of Israel in God's world order" (Walther Eichrodt, "In the Beginning," in *Israel's Prophetic Heritage: Essays in Honor of James Muilenburg*, ed. B. W. Anderson and W. Harrelson [New York: Harper and Brothers, 1962], 9).

31. See Wenham, *Genesis 1–15*, 13, 15; Heidel, *The Babylonian Genesis*, 90–91; Driver, *The Book of Genesis*, 3; Dillmann, *Genesis*, vol. 1, 53; Eichrodt, *TOT*, vol. 2, 104. Cf. Cassuto, *From Adam to Noah*, 20, for a slightly different understanding.

only God. That is, there is no pre-existing primal matter out of which the creation is fashioned. (ii) It is stated that God *created* the הָאָרֶץ (*hā'āretz*), which means the earth (Gn 1:1). It is this same created הָאָרֶץ which is subsequently described in verse 2 as תֹהוּ וָבֹהוּ (*tōhû vā vōhû*), meaning it was void and formless. This is often interpreted as referring to some kind of preexistent primordial matter. But, as noted, God had already created this formless earth. (iii) As well, there is other evidence outside the Hebrew canon, which is tied to the Jewish community's exegesis of this verse. The conception of *creatio ex nihilo* occurs formally in 2 Macc 7:28,[32] and this would certainly be an expression of the prevailing Jewish understanding of that period. In John's Gospel, which emerges from a Jewish context as well, the parallel between the prologue and Gn 1:1 is obvious: "In the beginning was the Word...apart from Him nothing came into being" (+Jn 1:1).[33] The prologue is careful to prove that all created realities were created by and through God and states this concept both positively and negatively within the same verse: "All things came to be through him, and without him nothing came to be" (+Jn 1:3). When understood in its fullness, this Johannine exegesis presents us with an unambiguous doctrine of *creatio ex nihilo*.[34] (iv) Finally, the standard Jewish view from the Septuagint (third century BC) until the Masoretic text (tenth century AD) favored *creatio ex nihilo*. As the Jewish historian Y. Kaufmann noted: "Nowhere do we find that the cosmic elements...were fashioned out of pre-existent stuff."[35]

Although textual ambiguities remain, it is most probable that the

---

32. This is noted by von Rad, *OTT*, vol. 1, 142: "The heavens and the earth...God did not make them out of things that existed." He notes that the question often raised here is whether or not this concept arose due to Hellenizing influences. See also Heidel, *The Babylonian Genesis*, 91.

33. See Heidel, *The Babylonian Genesis*, 91.

34. See G. May, *Creatio ex Nihilo: The Doctrine of "Creation out of Nothing" in Early Christian Thought*, trans. A. S. Worrall (Edinburgh: T & T Clarke, 2004).

35. Kaufmann, *Religion of Israel*, 68. He also uses Is 45:7 (God creates darkness); Prov 3:20; 8:24 (the creation of the watery abyss); and Job 26:7 (creation "upon the void") to support his conclusion. See also, Childs, *Myth and Reality*, 41: "Nevertheless, the omission of the accusative of material along with the simultaneous emphasis on the uniqueness of God's action could hardly be brought into a smooth harmony with the fact of a pre-existent chaos."

phrase בְּרֵאשִׁית (bᵉrēʾshît), which is translated "in the beginning," should be understood as linked to the concept of *creatio ex nihilo*. This understanding of creation, which establishes the absolute sovereignty of God over every aspect of creation, has profound implications. A creation on any other basis would be radically different.[36]

Within the Judeo-Christian understanding, the importance of *creatio ex nihilo* is twofold. First, it establishes that there is no principle of opposition within creation, as there is no other reality or force that is co-eternal with God. Thus, there can be no dualism. Second, this doctrine within the creation narrative establishes God as separate and *other than* His creation. There are only two options: to be created or to be non-created; not to be God is to be created. This specifically precludes the idea of "material emanation."[37] Thus, the divine agent of creation is never reduced to being a contingent part of the created reality. The divine is not a part of created reality as it was within pagan mythologies.[38]

This doctrine also establishes the relationship of created realities to God. All matter comes into being only through the will and power of God, who maintains sovereign control over it.[39] No created reality is a self-sustaining element, nor is it divine, but it receives its initial being and nature from God, who *remains* sovereign over it. Thus, the power for any created reality to sustain its existence and to flourish is derived from its own relationship to, and ontological dependence upon,

36. See comments below: in note 47 (Kaufmann) and in note 115 (Westermann).

37. Kaufmann, *Religion of Israel*, 68. As Kaufmann said: "The idea of a material emanation from the creator is foreign to the Bible" (ibid., 68).

38. Nahum Sarna describes the impact of the Hebrew cosmogony: "The clear line of demarcation between God and His creation was never violated.... Here we find no physical link between the world of humanity and the world of the divine.... The God of Creation is eternally existent, removed from all corporeality, and independent of time and space. Creation comes about through the simple divine *fiat*: Let there be!" (*Understanding Genesis*, 11–12). See Westermann, *Genesis 1–11*, 110–12.

39. As Brueggemann states, "YHWH is the sovereign creator who presides over the earth and over all creatures.... This affirmation is explicitly stated in Exodus 20:11 but is everywhere implied... what the narrative asserts of Yahweh's sovereignty over the Nile [in the Exodus] is everywhere extended in prophetic faith to all of creation. The God who creates is the God who may uncreate (Jeremiah 4:23–26)" (Brueggemann, *OT Theology*, 76–77).

the Creator, who alone gives it its specific nature and propensities and ordains the purposes for which it exists. Hence, every created reality possesses an interior logic which is given by God. Nature is not in competition with the divine realm but rather *is the expression* of His will.[40] To the degree that a thing conforms to this inner logic or nature, to that degree it is able to become fully what it was intended to be.[41] This is above all true of the human person and human relationships, especially marriage and family.

MYTHS AND THE SEXUALIZING OF CREATION

Another important difference between the Hebrew creation narrative and the pagan myths concerns the actual process by which creation emerges. The pagan myths present a cosmos that is the fruit of divine sexual activity or of cosmic battles, the latter providing mutilated corpses as the source for creation. In these myths, creation becomes a projection of the divine life that always had a sexual aspect to it. Consequently, in pagan thought, the created and divine realms interpenetrate and are intermingled, and the foundation is laid for the magical use of sexual practices within the cult. The Babylonian *Enûma Eliš* is a primary text that utilizes the cosmic battle motif as the basis for creation. The god Marduk vanquishes the goddess Ti'âmat and makes the world out of her mutilated corpse.

101. He [Marduk] shot off an arrow, and it tore her interior;
102. It cut through her inward parts, it split (her) heart.

40. This is echoed in Eichrodt's analysis of the creation by Word: "The same thought is represented in the Priestly account of creation in conceptually stronger terms, *by shifting the act of creation to the Word the origin of the creature is attributed entirely to the miracle of the transcendent creative will*" (*TOT*, vol. 2, 100; emphasis added).

41. With the revelation of Jesus as the Logos, all creation is understood to be Christocentric. "All things came into being by Him, and apart from Him nothing came into being that has come into being" (John 1:3). Rahner's explication of creation as being the expression of the divine nature and yet distinct from it is helpful here. See Karl Rahner, *Theological Investigations*, trans. Kevin Smith, vol. 4 (New York: Crossroad, 1982), 237–38.

135. The lord rested, examining her dead body,
136. To divide the abortion (and) to create ingenious things (therewith)
137. He split her open...into two (parts);
138. Half of her he set in place and formed the sky (therewith) as a roof...
144. And a great structure, its counterpart, he established (namely,) Esharra [i.e., the earth].[42]

Sarna correctly observes how in this epic sexuality is linked to the foundation of creation. "It will be remembered that in *Enûma Elish*, Apsû and Ti'âmat represent respectively the male and female powers which, through the 'commingling of their water' gave birth to the first generation of the gods. The sexual element existed before the cosmos came into being and all the gods were themselves creatures of sex."[43] We noted earlier that in one Egyptian cosmogenesis, the sun god, Re, created through self-pollution. In yet other mythologies, numerous gods resulted from the sexual escapades of other divinities.

Sarna sees a fundamental principle in operation here. "In polytheistic mythologies creation is always expressed in terms of procreation. Apparently, paganism was unable to conceive of any primal creative force other than in terms of sex."[44] This is evidenced in the myths of Sumer-Akkad. As Tasker notes, "the union of Enlil and his mother earth sets the stage for the organization of the universe—the creation of plants, animals, and man, and the establishment of civilization."[45] Since the origins of the cosmos are sexualizing, it is inevitable that within such a worldview the cult itself is also sexualized. Sexual relationships, instead

---

42. "Enûma Elish," trans. A. Heidel, in *The Babylonian Genesis,* 42–43. This book is of critical importance in evaluating the degree of influence that the pagan myths had on Israel (in this case, he is dealing with the *Enûma Eliš*). Heidel, against the pan-Babylonian position, shows that the type of borrowing that at one time was advocated was linguistically not possible.

43. Sarna, *Understanding Genesis,* 12.

44. Ibid. See Westermann, *Genesis,* 161: "The world in which Israel lived divinized the vital and explosive power of fertility and so gave birth to a whole range of myths and cultic practices, and of highly colored poetic, literary and ritual images."

45. Tasker, *ANE Fatherhood,* 28.

of being understood in terms of their effect within the created order, were seen as representations of what occurred in the divine realm, and in some cases they were the vehicle by which one participated in the divine sphere.[46] This instrumentalizing of the person and human sexuality is evident in the phenomena of cultic prostitution and ritual orgiastic feasts. A point needs to be made clear here, however: these were not merely hedonistic practices but actually possessed their own inner logic. Once creation was understood in sexual terms, then the relationship of the divine realm to the created world was inevitably eroticized with sexual practices becoming the focus of the cult. This could not help but profoundly affect the pagan understanding of the person, marriage, and family.

The Hebrew account of creation (Genesis 1–3) stands in stark contrast to the pagan cosmologies. The Genesis narrative contains not one word or hint of sexual activity from or in God. There is no preexistent material, no cosmic struggle, no other forces, gods or impersonal forces, and no abortive or mutilated matter from which either the gods or creation emerges. There is serenely only the one God, the ground of all being, who, in the exercise of His sovereign will, and in the speaking of His Word, brings forth all creation from an absolute beginning, while remaining distinct from it.[47]

The Hebraic creation narrative speaks not only of the relationship of the divine to the created order but also of the relationship of created realities to one another. This will become important when we want to understand the structure of human relationships. Genesis shows that the creation emerges through a series of graduated "separations," which reach their climax in the introduction of God's image into the created

46. This is particularly true of the *hieros gamos* phenomena, the sacred marriages between the earthly ruler and the reigning deity. On the idea of the "sexualization of the world," Sarna refers to M. Eliade, *The Forge and the Crucible*, 34–42; Jacobsen, *Before Philosophy*, 158f., 170ff.; and N. O. Brown, *Hesiod's Theogony*, 8, 19. See Sarna, *Understanding Genesis*, 34n21. Eliade's work as a cross-cultural anthropologist who specialized in symbolism is particularly relevant in this area.

47. Kaufmann shows the difference between these conceptions of the cosmos: "Biblical cosmology lacks also the basic pagan idea of a natural bond between the deity and the universe. Creation is not depicted as a sexual process" (Kaufmann, *Religion of Israel*, 69).

order through the creation of man.[48] Creation is not instantaneous; all things do not appear at the same instant. Nor are individual things created separately and then brought together into some form of ad hoc relationship. Rather, realities usually emerge within ones that have been created before, and so an organic interconnectedness to all of creation is thereby established.[49]

In Gn 1:9 the land emerges from the waters; in 1:11 the earth sprouts forth (תַּדְשֵׁא / tadshē') the trees; in 1:21, the waters teem with the fish; in 1:24, the earth brings forth (תּוֹצֵא / tōtzē') the animals, and in 2:7, man comes from the earth. Creation emerges organically and sequentially. In fact, Gn 2:4 uses the word תּוֹלְדוֹת (tôldôt—generations) to describe this process underlying creation's own organic nature. This generative process always remains outside of God. All is contingent upon the Creator-God, but creation itself remains outside (ad extra) the divine realm and is a separate reality from it.[50] Though there is a strong organic interconnectedness within creation, the all-sovereign will of God alone is the controlling factor, informing and grounding all realities in an absolute fashion.[51]

The Hebraic revelation is a total rejection of the mythic conceptualization of reality which believed in multiple sources of power (the gods

48. While this Semitic principle of separation was also known in others parts of the ancient world, no pagan myths understood the gradual emergence of the universe as being predicated on a single divine will which informed all things and which was outside of the process itself. In Hebrew, there was no *mutually* constitutive relationship between the divine realm and the created one.

49. This process of gradual separation from an original unity is called in Hebrew הִבְדִּיל (hibdîl) (derived from the root verb meaning "to separate").

50. The creation is not an emanation of God but is "outside of him" as it were. Theologically, this is described as *creatio ad extra*. See Jurgens Moltman's explanation of this in *God in Creation*, trans. M. Kohl (Minneapolis: Fortress Press, 1993), 86ff.

51. This concept is at the heart of our analysis. It is precisely because there is only one God and He is the all-powerful Creator that all of creation receives its constitutive nature and teleological design from Him. To understand the nature of any given reality, we must discover what the divine will is concerning it. This latter is expressed in terms of the Christocentric design of creation. Von Rad understood the importance and effect of monotheistic thought. The whole Hebraic worldview is ultimately based on this primary principle, and, without it, Israel could not exist. As he said, "Jahwism without the first commandment is positively inconceivable" (von Rad, *OTT*, vol. 1, 26).

and fates) and divinized sexuality, assuming both gods and sexuality into their myths about the beginning which rendered creation chaotic and violent.[52] Israel's worldview was wholly different, predicated on a unique relationship between God and His creation, which enabled human sexuality to be set free from its mythological encumbrances. What is most important for our study is the fact that "for Israel the polarity of the sexes was something belonging to Creation, and not to the deity himself."[53] This truth fundamentally altered man's understanding of his own sexuality and his place in the created order.

THE NATURE OF GOD AND
HUMAN SEXUALITY

וַיִּבְרָא אֱלֹהִים אֶת־הָאָדָם בְּצַלְמוֹ בְּצֶלֶם אֱלֹהִים בָּרָא אֹתוֹ זָכָר וּנְקֵבָה בָּרָא אֹתָם

And God created the man in His image, in the image of God He created him, male and female He created them.

(+Gn 1:27)

Given that Hebraic revelation diametrically opposed mythological thought, sexuality assumes its rightful place within the created order in a demythologized form in this new context.[54] The obscuring effects of mythologizing were now overcome by this new understanding of God and nature:

---

52. Max Weber concluded that, because of Yahweh's separate identity from nature, "this, above all, blocked the formation of true myths" (Weber, *Ancient Judaism*, 137, quoted in Zeitlin, *Ancient Judaism*, 35).

53. Von Rad, *OTT*, vol. 1, 146.

54. By its very first phrase, the creation narrative in Genesis undoes the whole mythological world in one single stroke. Emile Brunner, commenting on this opening phrase of Scripture, observed that it is "the immense double statement, of a lapidary simplicity, so simple indeed that we hardly realize that with it a vast world of myth and Gnostic speculation, of cynicism and asceticism, of the deification of sexuality and fear of sex completely disappears" (Brunner, *Man in Revolt*, 346, quoted by von Rad, *Genesis* [Philadelphia: Westminster Press, 1972], 60).

But, for the historian of religion, what is most astonishing is Jahwism's self-preservation vis-à-vis the mythicising of sex. In the Canaanite cult, copulation and procreation were mythically regarded as a divine event; consequently, the religious atmosphere was as good as saturated with mythic sexual conceptions. *But Israel did not share in the "diviniza-tion" of sex.* Jahweh stood absolutely beyond the polarity of sex, and this meant that Israel also could not regard sex as a sacral mystery.[55]

Sexuality was excluded from the Godhead and thus, as Eichrodt noted, "any disintegration of the Godhead into male and female principles was...firmly excluded."[56] Instead sexuality became "a phenomenon of the creature."[57]

But it is just Israel's polemical attitude towards any deification of sex, her exclusion of this whole sphere of life from the cult and the sacral events, which shows that, in actual fact, a very positive doctrine of Creation was in existence, at least *in nuce,* in Israel, even at an early period. This doctrine was already posited along with the desacralization of sex, *indeed, it has to be regarded as the real motivating power behind it.*[58]

Once the true nature of God is revealed, human sexuality is inevitably demythologized, and those institutions predicated on sexuality, namely marriage and the family, are transformed. They are removed from mythological trappings and are freed to function properly within the *created* order.[59] Schillebeeckx, in a perceptive analysis, shows how in Israel, marriage is rendered a created, human reality:

55. Von Rad, *OTT,* vol. 1, 27 (emphasis added). This statement is certainly true vis-à-vis the cult, but Israel did not turn sexuality into a mere secular phenomenon. The Jewish people came to understand that the covenant was to be understood in both familial and marital terms, but it was not sexualized per se.

56. "Yahweh never had a female consort; and thus any idea that he needed to be complemented—a fate which befell all the other major Semitic deities—was rejected. It is significant that in Hebrew there should be no word for "goddess"; El or Elohim has to serve to denote the heathen goddesses" (Eichrodt, *TOT,* 223).

57. Von Rad, OTT, vol. 1, 28.

58. Von Rad, OTT, vol. 1, 28 (emphasis added). John Grabowski of the Catholic University of America has made a perceptive comment on this in a written communication: "Here I disagree with von Rad who sees 'demythologize' and 'desacralize' as interchangeable. Sex remains holy or else it could not serve as an image of the covenant between Yahweh and Israel" (personal communication). Grabowski is correct here.

59. The effect of this can hardly be overestimated. By contrast, this can be particularly

It was through her association with the God Yahweh that Israel's conception of the creation was purified, becoming a faith in a Creator who was in no way restricted and who was generous and free, elective and loving in the sharing of his abundant riches. That is precisely why *marriage was first and foremost a secular reality* which could not be allowed to evaporate, to become an insubstantial representation of something that might previously have been enacted in the divine sphere. In Israel there existed *no divine prototype of marriage* which could then be directly associated with marriage at the human level by means of religious rites.... *It was, for Israel, a secular reality.*[60]

There could be no *hieros gamos* (sacred marriages) or temple prostitution which, in the pagan world, opened the way "for man to share in the divine world."[61] But a clarifying point needs to be made at this juncture, for many (wrongly) assume that the pagan understanding was simply a degenerate form of eroticism. We must realize that paganism *rightly* intuited that there was a profound relationship between sacredness and human sexuality, and this is later confirmed within the Judeo-Christian economy. But the pagan intuition was irremediably confused by the mythological framework in which it functioned. Once "demythologized," the relationship between the divine and sexuality could be properly worked out. Schillebeeckx's analysis here is helpful:

> Secular demythologized marriage...was a good gift of the creation, coming from Yahweh, the God of the covenant. *What was called into existence by God's creation was sanctified by the fact of creation itself* and subject to God's holy laws. It was not the sacred rites which surrounded marriage that made it a holy thing. *The great rite which sanctified marriage was God's act of creation itself.*[62]

---

seen in the modern era, where the attempt has been made to re-sexualize the world and deify sexuality itself. By that act, the proper function of sex, marriage and the family is lost.

60. Schillebeeckx, *Marriage,* 15 (emphasis added). Against Schillebeeckx's viewpoint, the following question can be raised: "Was anything in Israel's experience ever considered as strictly secular once the covenant was entered into?" His use of language here is imprecise, since everything in Israel, because it was within the covenantal context, was oriented towards holiness. However, Schillebeeckx's concept is essentially correct.

61. Von Rad, *Genesis,* 60.

62. Schillebeeckx, *Marriage,* 15 (emphasis added).

Inasmuch as marriage is part of God's creative order, it cannot be arbitrarily or subjectively defined, but rather it receives, *in the very act of its creation,* a constitutive nature which needs to be respected if man and society are to flourish. Gn 1:28 is crucial here: "God blessed them, and God said to them, 'Be fruitful and multiply.'" This shows that at the heart of this primary form of human relationality is fecundity and this is inextricably tied to the blessing that God continually desires to give to His creation. As our analysis will show, *fecundity is not opposed to marital communion but, in fact, presupposes it and establishes this communion in a specific modality.* As we will show, the creation narrative establishes that personal, communitarian life, to be true to its nature, must unfold integrally until it reaches its logical and somatic expression in the family. Modern anthropological and philosophical constructs emphasize the isolated subjectivity of the individual as being key to the person, and they also view the body instrumentally, as something which the person merely uses for his own purposes. Thus, the Scriptural understanding of the person is a great challenge to modern understanding, which resists the Biblical idea of a constitutive human nature that can only be received and that cannot be humanly constructed. Schillebeeckx addresses this when he speaks of the divine laws (*hoq/hoqqoth*) that were written into marriage at the beginning. "The things of the earth and man received their *hoq* or *huqqah* with their creation: each received, on creation, its intrinsic conditions or existence, its defined limits."[63]

Within the Hebraic understanding, everything has a purpose and function, including human sexuality, marriage, and family.[64] Westermann noted that "everything that God makes or creates is given a destiny."[65] As we shall see, this is closely tied to the new concept of history

63. Ibid., 24. In note 14 he explains that *hoq/huqqah* mean "firm law(s), the expression of God's will."

64. Westermann, *Genesis,* 88.

65. Ibid. Routledge see the *telos* of creation as a function of the *Urzeit wird Endzeit* paradigm. "This way of looking at the future in terms of the past is sometimes known as Urzeit wird Endzeit (primal history becomes the end time); the end of time is, therefore, a reflection of what happened at the beginning" (Routledge, *OT Theology,* 129–30). In essence, there is a form of recapitulation that occurs where the end is in the beginning. This theory does

that begins to emerge here. It is not accidental that as modernity becomes more and more ahistorical in its consciousness, the idea that our sexuality has a destined end (*telos*) given by a Creator becomes difficult to comprehend. In fact, there is almost a reversion to a "paganized" understanding of sexuality, inasmuch as it takes on a semidivinized status in popular culture. In the modern context, sexuality is seemingly the one thing worth living and dying for.[66] It is increasingly divorced from its teleological end which, in the Judeo-Christian view, is manifested in both a covenantal union and the blessing of fecundity. As these purposes are rejected, inevitably the nature of sexuality and the concomitant realities of marriage and family are de-constructed to fit a pleasure-centered ethos that ultimately is destructive of the family, the individual, and society. The only antidote to this is the retrieval of the biblical vision of marriage and family, which requires the recovery of an authentic theology of creation.

---

seem to cohere with the biblical witness and is a valuable way of understanding the *telos* of creation. However, Routledge proposes that "the primordial battle that resulted in creation and the defeat of rebellious and chaotic elements will be repeated in the eschatological overthrow of evil and the promise of the arrival of a new creation" (ibid., 129). This is based on what Routledge interprets as mythological references, found mostly in the Psalms but occasionally elsewhere (Job, Isaiah, Ezekiel). But, as shown above, the narrative of creation in Genesis is devoid of these references, and Routledge acknowledges that the Babylonian mythic basis for Genesis cannot be established as Gunkel had hoped. The beginning in Genesis is characterized by *shalom,* which is the operative principle of the creation. This will likewise be true of the new creation, which is manifested in the peace that Christ gives to the disciples on the eve of His death.

66. There is a difference, however, from the perspective of *Heilsgeschichte.* Within the framework of salvation history, pagan mythologies had intuitions about the divine life that were correct, but misconstrued and commingled with fundamental error. However, revelation invited Israel to emerge from this confusion into the clarity of truth, which gradually became clearer and develops in profundity until the advent of Christ. Today, there is a process of "paganization" going on which is all in the other direction. C.S. Lewis speaks to this when he said that what helped him in his conversion was realizing that in Christ all the myths had become true. We are in danger of doing the opposite and turning truth into myth—but with an ever-decreasing sense of the divine.

THE DIVINE IMAGE IN MAN

וַיֹּאמֶר אֱלֹהִים נַעֲשֶׂה אָדָם בְּצַלְמֵנוּ כִּדְמוּתֵנוּ

God said, "Let us make man in our image, after our likeness."

(+Gn 1:26)

The construal of the human person that is found in the Hebraic revelation differs radically from that found in the cultural matrix surrounding ancient Israel. First, Hebrew revelation clearly puts sexuality within the created realm, separating it, in its essence, from the divine sphere, thus undercutting the whole of the mythological worldview. The Hebraic understanding removed the reason for sexuality being instrumentalized as it was within the pagan cult.[67] Second, in Hebraic revelation there is a fundamental dignity to the human person that was lacking in the pagan myths. In the Hebrew account of creation, man is not the slave of the gods but is made in the image of God to act as His vice-regent.[68] While the concept of "divine image" can perhaps be found in some of the pagan myths, the purpose of his existence is fundamentally different. In the Babylonian *Enûma Elish*, man is portrayed as the slave of the deposed gods:

> Then will I set up *lulla*, "Man" shall be his name!
> Yes, I will create *lulla*: Man!
> (Upon him) shall the services of the gods be imposed that they [the gods] may be at rest."[69]

In this Babylonian legend, human subjects are created for the express purpose of freeing the lesser gods from their slave *labor* to the greater gods. The onerous tasks now will fall to the lots of the human creatures. This was how the meaning of human life was conceived. In

---

67. Thus there was an absolute hostility between the pagan and Israelite views. Whereas the common mythologies of the ancient world allowed for syncreticism because they had the same basis, Israel's revelation abhorred such a process. In fact, it was impossible to mix the two systems, as the prophets clearly showed. See Cassuto, *From Adam to Noah*, 8, n. 18.

68. Cf. •Jer 2:14: "Is Israel a slave, a bondman by birth? Why then has he become booty?"

69. Heidel, *The Babylonian Genesis*, 46.

contrast, in the Hebraic revelation, the person is freed from this mythological shackling and human life is given an absolute dignity because it is created in God's image and is free to enter into the acts of history and "fill the earth and subdue it" (+Gn 1:28). Being made in the divine likeness and image, man alone has the interior structure to image forth God's likeness on the earth.[70]

Third, it is critical to note that this "image" is revealed (at least implicitly) to be communitarian. There is a mysterious tension in Gn 1:26–27 that is never satisfactorily resolved in that text. The *imago* that is reflected in the human person is revealed to have a plural dimension to it. +Gn 1:26 does not have, "in my image"; rather the Hebrew has God saying, "Let *us* make man in *our* image (בְּצַלְמֵנוּ / *b*etzalmēnû)." Given the absolute requirement of monotheism, this statement, in which a reference to a plurality within God is indicated, appears contradictory to the foundations of Hebrew faith.[71] This text has occasioned a long history of interpretation, but several things are clear which help to establish reasonable parameters for interpretation. It is clear that within the act of creating mankind, God initiates a form of dialogue unique to the whole of the creative process.[72] What is crucial to interpreting this verse is the nature of the participants in this dialogue.

At issue is the Hebraic revelation's insistence that God is one (אֶחָד /

---

70. For a full explanation of the term "image forth," see note 2 in chapter 5.

71. It should be clear that the reference to "our" in this text is not *explicitly* a reference to the trinitarian nature of God. However, if one takes into consideration the unity of Scriptures and the divine pedagogical intention (as we see, for example, in the Suffering Servant songs), space can be made for some form of implicit reference here, particularly in light of John 1. In modern scholarship, it is proposed that "our" in this text simply refers to some form of a heavenly court and that the phrase "Let us make" is a form of *pluralis majestaticus*. However, the use of the plural of majesty seems to be a much later invention (cf. Richard N. Davies, *Doctrine of the Trinity* [Cincinnati: Granston and Stowe, 1981], 227ff.). The renowned Hebraist Genesius testifies to this, stating, "It is best explained as a plural of self-deliberation. The use of the plural as a form of respectful address is quite foreign to Hebrew." Theologically, there is a problem of associating "our" with something outside the Godhead, as man is made in God's image and not in the image of the angels or other parts of the heavenly host.

72. The whole creative process is halted in order for this divine dialogue to take place. This at once shows the uniqueness of this act and the drama it contains.

'eḥād).[73] Yet here, the biblical text has God referring to Himself in terms of plurality (us, our image). In fact, in this narrative the word for God, אֱלֹהִים ('elōhim), is itself the plural form of the singular אֵל ('ēl). The exegetical solution for this apparent contradiction has been to posit that God was speaking to an angelic court and was using a form of royal address. But this exegesis contradicts the tenor of the whole narrative and cannot be supported. The main problem is that in 1:26, God is presented as having a dialogue with someone who is addressed as being a *partner* in the creation of the human creature ("let us make"). Thematically, the essential point of the Genesis narrative is that it is *only* God who creates. To introduce an angelic court is possible, and even to address such a court is plausible, but to make them agents of creation is neither. Secondly, there is a problem with associating the image in which man is made with anything other than God. In addressing the dialogue partner(s), God speaks of making the human creature "in our image." If the dialogue partners were angels, then the image would be a confused hybrid of a divine-angelic nature. But the Scriptures strongly affirm that it is only in the image of God that man is made.[74] The next verse (1:27) further clarifies the intent of the passage: "God created man in his image (בְּצַלְמוֹ / b'tsalmô), in the image of God (בְּצֶלֶם אֱלֹהִים / b'tselem 'ĕlōhîm) He created him." The "our" image of 1:26 is qualified by the singular "his" image in 1:27. The double emphasis on

---

73. "Hear, O Israel, the Lord, our God, the Lord is one"—שְׁמַע יִשְׂרָאֵל יְהוָה אֱלֹהֵינוּ יְהוָה אֶחָד / s'ma' yisrā'ēl YHWH 'ĕlōhênû YHWH 'eḥād (Dt 6:4). The meaning of "one" (אֶחָד / 'eḥād) can be determined by its usage within the Hebrew canon. Its first instance is in Gn 1:5, which states that "there was evening and there was morning, day one." Clearly this single day is made up of two differentiated parts, the day and night. The next example is Gn 2:24, which states Adam and the woman had become "one flesh." This oneness-of-flesh is composed of the two differentiated realities, the man and the woman. Then we come to Dt 6:4, which states that the nature of God is "one." Based on the previous usage, one (אֶחָד / 'eḥād) here would seem to indicate a real oneness (unity), yet possessing within itself some form of real distinction.

74. The Letter to the Hebrews is addressed to a Jewish audience and deals with the Hebraic grounding of Christianity. Heb 1:1–14 draws a sharp contrast between the uncreated Son, in whom all things are made, and the angels, who are "ministering spirits sent to serve for the sake of those who are to inherit salvation." This text, which is reflective of first-century AD Jewish views, would not see man being made in an angelic image.

the divine origin of this image in 1:27 is striking.[75] From the above analysis, we move forward in securing the meaning of the text.[76] Since the
dialogue partner of 1:26 is also an agent in the creation process and is
the source, with God, for the divine image for the human person, then
it would seem that the partner addressed must also be divine. But the
text does not discuss this; it merely records the dialogue, which acts as
a preamble to the creation of man. At a minimum, the text is affirming
that this image, which is key to human nature, clearly has some dimension of plurality within it (our image) and is divine, since it is the image
of God. Given the aspect of plurality, it would seem plausible that this
image implicitly possesses some sense of communion or community
within itself, and this is underscored by the fact that the narrative takes
on a dialogic form.

Clearly, the text and context are sufficiently ambiguous to allow only
qualified affirmations at this point. Again, it is not that the trinitarian
nature of God is explicitly revealed here. But, since it is the trinitarian
God who is creating, it should not be totally unexpected to find traces (vestigia) of this plurality-within-singularity present.[77] It is accurate

75. A tension remains in Gn 1:27, for it leaves unresolved how man is created at once
singularly ("He created him") and yet maintains a plural aspect ("He created them"). This
dynamic tension is resolved in Gn 2, where Adam is created first and then the woman is created from Adam. Much later, the Johannine Gospel goes back to this early narrative of creation and provides a deeper glimpse at the workings of Creation, showing how God is one
and yet there is differentiation within God. John states that the Father creates through the
agency of the Son and both are divine, as both are of the Godhead (see Jn 1:1ff.).

76. Miguel de la Torre, in his Genesis (Louisville, Ky: Westminster John Knox Press,
2011), does not deal carefully with the Hebrew text (which clearly posits this tension between the singular (he) and the plural (them)). He states that a "proper translation of these
two texts [Gn 2:26–27] would be: 'So God created humans in the image of God, in the image
of God God created them'" (22). But this translation does not accurately portray what is
stated in the Hebrew text, which unambiguously contains the singular personal pronoun. It
states that "in the image of God, He created 'ōtô" (third person, singular, masculine).

77. This, of course, presupposes that revelation, though distinguishable into various
texts and time periods, is yet a single Word of God which is wholly integrated. See CCC 102,
quoting St. Augustine: "You recall that one and the same Word of God extends throughout
Scripture, that it is one and the same Utterance that resounds in the mouths of all the sacred writers, since he who was in the beginning God with God has no need of separate sylla-
bles; for he is not subject to time" (St. Augustine, Ennarationes in Psalmos 103,4,1: Patrologia

to say that within the text on image there is a tension between a plural sense and a unitive sense being predicated of God.[78] Given the monotheistic revelation of Judaism, it is clear that any plurality has to be accounted for in relationship to an interior unity, because God is one and cannot be divided. Certainly, viewed within the fuller tradition and especially given the Johannine revelation of the Christological nature of creation, it is plausible that the phrase "our image" points to some sense of communion existing within the one God.[79] Therefore, if man is to be like God (since we are created in His image), then at the heart of man there must be some form of communion as well. This is reflected specifically by the differentiation of the sexes that are ordered to each other for communion.[80] It is by understanding *imago* that the teleology of gender begins to emerge. It is not a societally or artificially constructed reality; rather, gender has a given nature, received in the act of its being created, that is deeply linked to the purposes of communion. This will be more deeply developed in Genesis 2.[81]

Latina [hereafter PL] 37:1378); *CCC* then references Ps 104 and Jn 1:1. Certainly, the Father of the Church believed this and concluded that there were trinitarian dimensions in the text. Today in academic analysis, there is often hesitation to make such claims.

78. E.g., *'ĕlōhîm* (pl.) + singlular verb *bārā'* followed by "our" image. The rabbis were aware of this and saw that this text could help the enemies of the Judaic faith because it seems to posit something more than one God (see Rabbi Samuel ben Nachman in *Genesis Rabbah*, VIII. 8, p. 59).

79. The early Church Fathers in examining Gn 1:26 saw there a reference to the trinitarian nature of God. See St. Justin Martyr, *Dialogue with Trypho* (trans. Thomas B. Falls, rev. Thomas P. Halton, Selections from the Fathers of the Church, vol. 3 [Washington, D.C.: The Catholic University of America Press, 2003], chap. 62), in which he uses Gn 3:22 to show that "us" must refer to a person numerically distinct from the Father. Irenaeus, in the preface to Book 4 of *Against Heresies*, notes that in Gn 1:26, the Father is speaking to the Son and the Spirit, hence the use of "us" (*Against Heresies*, ed. and trans. by Alexander Roberts et al., Ante-Nicene Fathers, vol. 1 [Buffalo, N.Y.: Christian Literature Publishing Co., 1885]). In the *Epistle of Barnabas* 5:5, this verse is understood as the Father speaking to the Son (in Apostolic Fathers, vol. 1, Loeb Classical Library, reprint [Cambridge, Mass.: Harvard University Press, 2003]). There is a clear sense in the Fathers that the communitarian nature of God was being revealed in the dialogue of Gn 1:26.

80. See John Paul II, *Theology of the Body*, trans. Michael Waldstein (Pauline Books and Media, 1997). Audience, November 14, 1979: "Man Becomes the Image of God by Communion of Persons."

81. Genesis 2 carefully articulates the meaning and purpose for the differentiation of the

MEANING OF GENDER

וּלְאָדָם לֹא־מָצָא עֵזֶר כְּנֶגְדּוֹ׃

*For Adam no suitable helper was found.... [Then the LORD
God built the rib that He had taken out of the man into a woman.... The man said, "This is now bone of my bones and flesh of
my flesh."]*

(+Gn 2:20–23)

The nature of the human person was reconceived in Hebrew revelation, and this had a profound effect upon the understanding of gender
and the purposes of sexuality. Within this newly demythologized context, the gender differentiation no longer participated in a mythologi-
cal-divine drama but rather pointed to man's own created status. The
attraction of the sexes was a gift from God and was, therefore, good,
but it was not to be misconceived as a representation on earth of divine
realities concerning gender. Nor was it to be conceived of as an instrument to manipulate the forces of nature and the gods.[82] The mythological linkage between the earthly and divine realms through sexuality was now completely severed. The sexual drive was now seen as a
witness to the truth that man is not meant to be alone; he is meant for
community.[83] As Westermann comments,

A consequence of this is that there can be no question of an 'essence of
man' apart from existence as two sexes. Humanity exists in community.... What is being said here is that a human being must be seen as one

---

sexes (loneliness, the need for the other, etc.) and develops this within a covenantal context.
It is revealing that in the early chapters of the Hebraic revelation, a seemingly dispropor-
tionate amount of time is spent on the theme of human sexuality. Indeed, after the general
presentation on creation in the first chapter, the next chapter is then devoted to explaining
the emergence of human gendered existence. This indicates the importance of the gender
distinction in the created order and that it mysteriously lies at the heart of the revelation.

82. Von Rad states, "The Jahwist's story of creation practically issues in this aetiological
explanation of the power of eros as one of the urges implanted in man by the Creator himself (vs. 24f.), and so gives the relationship between man and woman the dignity of being the
greatest miracle and mystery of Creation" (*OTT*, vol. 1, 150).

83. "By God's will, man was created alone but designated for the 'thou' of the other sex"
(von Rad, *Genesis*, 60).

whose destiny it is to live in community; people have been created to
live with each other.[84]

Man is not called to live in isolation or merely to have some form of
sexual congress with another. Rather man is called to live a deeper interpersonal relationship such that the very angst of existence is resolved
by the communal existence of the two.

ABSOLUTE DIGNITY OF
THE HUMAN PERSON

Any anthropology that posits that any human subject is inferior to
another is simply false to the biblical witness. As we shall see, all are
"subjects" and, therefore, there can be no domination of one over the
other. Consequently, there can be no sense of inferiority-superiority
within familial relationships. All have absolute dignity, and this paradigm for proper relationality emerges from the order of creation. Genesis 2 is a critical text in this regard, because with great precision it unfolds for us the basic principles operative within biblical anthropology.
In this portion of the creation narrative, it is clear that the human person exists in two modalities and that the man and woman are related to
each other in a highly determined manner. In order to understand the
import of Gn 2 we have to realize that it is answering a specific question: How do men and women relate to each other? The key to answering this lies in being able to see the Temple/covenantal subtext that acts
as a leitmotiv for Gn 2. The clues to securing the existence of this subtext are numerous.[85] First, the covenant name for God is used in the
text as contrasted with the generic name for God found in Genesis 1.[86]

Second, the text abounds with Temple imagery. The Temple and its
cult were an essential manifestation of the covenant God had with Israel. Like the Temple in Jerusalem, the Garden of Eden was oriented

84. Westermann, *Genesis,* 160.

85. See the section in this work titled "Sanctuary Symbolism in Gn 1–3" which will deal
with these specific elements in Gn 2 at greater length in Chapter 5.

86. Gn 1 is answering the generic question: How did everything get here? Consequently,
the generic name of God (*'ĕlōhîm*) is used.

toward the east (Gn 2:8), there is the mention of gold (2:11), which reminds one of the gold that overlaid virtually everything in the Temple (Ex 25:11ff.). The Tree of Life in the Garden is associated with the Temple menorah which is a stylized Tree.[87] There is also the mention of bdellium (2:12) whose color is related to the manna which was kept in the Temple (Nm 11:7 and Ex 16:33) and onyx stone (2:12), which was the stone used in the High Priest's breastplate on which were inscribed the names of the twelve tribes of Israel (Ex 28:9). These and numerous other correspondences show that the substructure of Gn 2 has to do with the Temple.[88] If this analysis is correct, then the text of Gn 2 is constructed to show that the relationship between man and woman is covenantal and is somehow related to the divine relationship of God with His people.

Third, this text provides the underlying dynamics that resolve the relationship between man and woman. The creation narrative is constructed with great precision at this point. Man has been created, but it is discovered that being alone is not good (Gn 2:18). Therefore, the Lord God creates the animals, but there is still no helper (עֵזֶר / 'ēzer) suitable for him. It is at this point that Yahweh puts the man into a deep sleep,[89] and He takes of the substance of the man and "builds it up" (וַיִּבֶן / vayyīben) into a woman. This text is the ground for the Semitic understanding of the relationship between the genders. The Lord could have separately created a number of men and then women and brought them together for sexual congress to propagate the species. But this would have resulted in a created reality different from the one we experience. In this hypothetical scenario, two autonomous principles (the male and female) would exist, morally related to each other for the purpose of propagation, but being mutually independent and only extrin-

87. See C. Selkin, Exegesis and Identity: The Hermeneutics of Miqwa'ôt in the Greco-Roman Period (Ph.D. diss., Department of Religion, Duke University, 1993).

88. See Gordon J. Wenham, "Sanctuary Symbolism in the Garden of Eden Story," in "I Studied Inscriptions from before the Flood," Ancient Near Eastern, Literary, and Linguistic Approaches to Genesis 1-11, ed. R. S. Hess and S. T. Tsumura (Winona Lake, Ind.: Eisenbauns, 1994), 399–403, and U. Cassuto, From Adam to Noah.

89. The word here is תַּרְדֵּמָה (tardēmāh), which means sleep; it is also used of Abraham when the covenant is revealed to him in Gn 15:12, underlining once again the covenantal nature of the relationship between man and woman.

sically related to each other. They would remain as autonomous principles, with the great potential to be antagonistically related towards each
other, not having the necessary mechanism of resolution between the
two principles. It would be a context not ordered to peace.

The whole creation narrative in both Gn 1 and Gn 2, unlike the violent pagan myths, is predicated on the establishment of peace. Whereas in pagan myths (such as the *Enûma Eliš*) creation emerges from violence and bloody conflict, in the Genesis account no such themes are
present. The first two chapters of Genesis are order to peace: Gn 1 reveals
that creation is by the word of God and it proceeds in peace, culminating with the Sabbath rest; Gn 2 reveals how the two distinct genders that
make up humanity are specifically ordered to each other and their ordering results in a fulfilled relationship without conflictual division.

Yahweh first creates the man and then, out of man's substance, He
creates the woman.

וַיִּבֶן יְהוָה אֱלֹהִים אֶת־הַצֵּלָע אֲשֶׁר־לָקַח מִן־הָאָדָם לְאִשָּׁה וַיְבִאֶהָ
אֶל־הָאָדָם:

The LORD God then built up the rib that he had taken from the man
into a woman and he brought her to the man. (+Gn 2:22)

It is important to note that the woman was not created in an independent fashion. In the creation narrative, it is from the substance of the
man that the woman is created, and her existence is thereby ontologically tied to that of the man. Being the first created and being source,
the man embodies an ordering principle for their relationship. That is,
the order of creation itself provides the ordering principle for the relationship between the genders. This "logic of creation" is explicitly used
by Paul in the New Testament when he teaches on the relationship of
man and woman (see 1 Tim 2:1ff.). The gender difference does not produce conflict but is interiorly ordered to peace precisely because they
are not autonomous, nor are they self-determining. It is by the encounter with the difference that the loneliness of the man is overcome and
he is brought to peace.[90] The male and female creation are not antag-

---

90. This idea of *shalom* is important to the concept of the corporate personality. As Schillebeeckx noted: "Because it [the relationship between man and woman] was always authen-

onistic toward one another, nor are they in conflict. Instead, the one comes from the other and *together* they form a unity, בָּשָׂר אֶחָד (*bāsār 'eḥād*), which is translated as "one flesh." The unity is not superimposed on the two distinct genders but is portrayed as something which *already* existed ontologically within the original "one" that was later differentiated. The unity is constitutive of both the male and the female. *They become one because they are one.*

Unfortunately, the modern world finds it difficult to accept that difference does not always betoken anything other than a superiority-inferiority nexus. However, the biblical text includes several precisions that are contrary to this falsified anthropology and serve as an antidote to it.[91] First, there is an emphasis on the distinctiveness of maleness and femaleness, showing that they are not reductive. Each gender is unique and each contributes to the fullness of creation; they are not interchangeable but each has its own unique dignity. In trying to resolve the existential angst of the man, Yahweh creates the animals as companions. However, they do not suffice, because the animals could not function as a suitable helper (*'ezer*). What was required was not just another being, but another who was like the man. The dignity of this role as עֵזֶר (*'ēzer*) is seen in that this word is also used of God, who is said to be the *helper* of Israel (Ps 54:6). It is clear that Yahweh is not inferior to His own creation but in fact helps it to fulfill its mission. Second, the verb וַיִּבֶן (*v°yyiven*), meaning 'to build' (fr. בָּנָה / *bānah*), is vitally important to this discussion. While the first *'ādām* is the source of the material from which the woman comes, he does not create her. Her being comes directly from the hand of God, who builds her up into being. The fact that he is resting in a deep sleep (תַּרְדֵּמָה / *tardēmah*) un-

---

tically human in the full sense of the word it was expressed as a *physical blood-relationship*. In this expression—as in the expression *básár ehádh* (one flesh)—three elements are fused together. The first is the idea of blood-relationship, seen as an extension of the idea of peace (*shálôm*) in the life of the clan and the solidarity of the family" (Schillebeeckx, *Marriage*, 19).

91. There are precisions in the narrative of creation in Genesis which, if accepted, would prevent these false ideas of superiority-inferiority/the person as subject–object, etc. from arising. In the Fall, these truths were rejected and a distorted view of the human person was accepted. Redemption of sexuality means returning to these truths and accepting the revelation of the true nature of the human person.

derlines that the man is not an active agent in her creation. The word
תַּרְדֵּמָה (*tardēmah*) can be connected to the deep sleep into which
Abraham is put in Genesis 15 and in which the covenant is revealed to
him. The assonance between these two texts indicates that the marital
relationship is somehow ordered to the divine covenant. The relationship between man and woman is not between two autonomous, self-
determining entities, only functionally connected. Nor can the relationship between the genders be described in terms of subject and object. Rather, the creation narrative reveals that both man and woman
are uniquely differentiated, non-reducible to each other, and ordered to
each other's existence. They receive their being directly from the hand
of God and thus each possesses absolute dignity. They are not autonomous; their radical difference as male and female is not intrinsically
antagonistic but is predicated on an already existing ontological unity
in the first *'ādǎm,* which only later is differentiated. In this way, they
are never objects, but both are always subjects.[92]

COMMUNION AND FRUITFULNESS

This dual-unity, this being-for-others, possesses an even greater depth
and richness because this communitarian life is never self-focused or
enfolded in upon itself. Rather, the logic of this community of the two-
in-one is oriented by its inner nature toward another third that becomes
the embodiment of the interpersonal union of the two. The union of the
male and female is not an end unto itself but reaches its full expression
in the child and the family. Here, again, we see the same principle of dif-
ferentiation-in-unity that has been operative in the creation narrative
of Genesis 1. This text reveals that life and divine blessing are always
seen in terms of communion, which possesses the possibility of fecundity, which then begets further communion. This alone is life; any other order is death. The text affirms that even in the non-personal world

92. This profound understanding of anthropology is at the heart of marriage, which
John Paul II called the sacrament of creation. Marriage in Eden ultimately finds its teleolog-
ical conclusion in Christ, who is the Bridegroom, and the people of God, who become the
Bride. This is a relationship where there is absolute dignity and where all are subjects.

of plants and animals each thing has life within itself and is willed by God to bear forth fruit and reproduce.[93] In the human sphere, precisely because we are made in the image of God, this fecundity is tied to interpersonal communion. The human family is always organically connected to, and grounded in, the original unity of the couple. Children are the embodiment and manifestation of personal communion of the couple.

REPLICATION OF THE IMAGE

וַיְבָרֶךְ אֹתָם אֱלֹהִים וַיֹּאמֶר לָהֶם אֱלֹהִים פְּרוּ וּרְבוּ

God blessed them and God said to them, "Be fruitful and multiply, [fill the earth and subdue it]."

(+Gn 1:28)

It is with the introduction of the generations that creation and history intersect. History can only become a reality once man has the ability to reproduce and generation can succeed generation. At the heart of the biblical understanding of history is the concept of blessing, which in the Hebraic setting means "to bestow with a dynamism to increase."[94] Gn 1:28 shows that the blessing God gave the primordial couple is linked to the command to be fecund. We should note that the dignity of this fruitfulness is elevated beyond that of the animals precisely because man is made in the image of God. Thus, as God has given His image into the world, now, as part of their vocational challenge, the man and his wife are to replicate that image by bringing forth children through their sexual communion, who likewise will bear the divine imprint. In other words, the work of God continues to be reproduced in creation though the family. Hence, we need to see procreation as a gift bestowed upon mankind in the form of a blessing that makes history possible.[95]

93. E.g., see Gn 1:11—"fruit trees which produce fruit according to its kind which has its seed in it."

94. Köhler, *Lexikon,* as cited by Westermann, *Genesis,* 88.

95. Von Rad draws out the essential distinction between Israel and her pagan neighbors: "It is noteworthy that procreative ability is removed from God's image and shifted to a special word of blessing" (von Rad, *Genesis,* 61).

The Hebrew text, with an insightful level of precision, gives two actual blessings and/or commands.[96] The first is פְּרוּ (pʰrû) which expresses the idea "be fruitful." The second imperative is רְבוּ (rʰbû) which means "become many." The latter phrase points to something far greater than mere physical reproduction, which is the essential meaning of the first term. Rabbi Samson Raphael Hirsch notes that the Hebrew word rʰbû initiates a process by which the original type (ʾādăm) with all his spiritual and moral developments is to be replicated in his offspring. This does not happen instantaneously but *requires* the creation of the family:

> Already the mere physical increase of the human race presupposes something more than just begetting children.... A human child would have no chance of survival at all were it not cared for by parents...the aftercare is the real factor of increase of the human race. But *rbh* is something more and higher. The parents are to multiply themselves by their children.... The children are to be replicas not only of the physical bodily traits of their parents, but also of their spiritual, intellectual and moral selves. In short, they have to form, educate and cultivate them. Only so have they reproduced themselves in their children and discharged the duty of *rbh*.[97]

Man is not merely to physically populate the earth (animals can do as much), but he is to take care to form and train his offspring to be like himself and thereby replicate (*rbh*) who he is in all his fullness. In this way, the *one* becomes the *many* who are a continuation of the original. At the heart of each generation is the mystery of the image of God, which is to be realized ever more deeply and lived out in all its fullness. To achieve this, the family now becomes the primary place where the truth about the person's nature and vocation is appropriated by children to enable them to become fully the image of God that they were intended to be. In this way, the family is taken up directly into the will of God. We will see that when man experiences alienation because of the Fall, God uses the family to accomplish His salvific purposes.

96. Samuel Raphael Hirsch, *Genesis*, vol. 1 of *The Pentateuch: Translated and Explained*, 2nd ed., trans. I. Levy. (Gateshead, England: Judaica Press, 1976), 34–35.
97. Ibid.

PROCREATION AND HISTORY

It is in the blessing and gift of procreation that we see the wedding of creation and history. Only a creation based on the sovereignty and absoluteness of God's will, a creation that is *ad extra* and separate from God, can properly accord sexuality its appropriate place. For Israel, this fundamental human reality is removed from the mythological realm and remains a part of the created order. Human sexuality is not a means of union with the divine or a technique by which the gods can be manipulated. Sexuality resides in man, but like everything else in creation, it receives its constitutive nature from Yahweh, who has determined its purpose and meaning. Through this divinely ordered instrument, generation will succeed generation, thereby initiating the process of history, which has its own divinely established end (*telos*). In history, through procreation, man will continually perpetuate the initial blessing of God and experience His salvific acts. "It is this [procreative blessing] that makes it possible for living beings to exist; in the case of humanity the blessing itself works itself out in the series of the genealogies which form the framework of the primeval story. *The blessing of animate creation binds creation with history.*"[98]

History is tied to the emergence of successive generations,[99] which provides the fundamental structure for salvation history. At the critical junctures of revelation where the relationship with God is furthered, the generational lines are recorded, to ensure that the fundamental blessing of God is preserved and passed on faithfully from one generation to the next. Interestingly, in Genesis 2:4, even the organic creation itself is described in terms of the *tôldôt* (generations).[100] In the creation narrative of Gn 1:1–2:3 there is an intentional progression in creation. It is accomplished in deliberate stages, "set into the categories of time and space,"[101] moving increasingly from inanimate to animate, culminat-

98. Westermann, *Genesis*, 88 (emphasis added).

99. For the human person, freedom is a critical factor which establishes history as human choices propel the trajectory of history along its path.

100. Westermann, *Genesis*, 26.

101. See ibid., 88.

ing in the creation of man. As Westermann notes, everything preceding the creation of man is only prologue: "There is a gradual progression in this arrangement: everything that God has created has a destiny; this destiny reaches its goal in humanity which God created as his counterpart; with human beings creation points the way into history."[102] The procreative blessing bestowed on man not only disclosed the purpose of man's sexuality but also inserted man into an historical context. This would cause the acts of history to be seen no longer as meaningless cyclical acts (which was the tenor of the pagan worldview).[103] Acts of history now assume a specific value and meaning in relation to an implied "end." The actions of history are the places where man will meet God and his destiny will be worked out.[104]

This procreative power situating man in history must be taken seriously. It is within human generation that the divine blessing is perpetuated, but it is only Yahweh who bestows the blessing of procreation. It is His and His alone to give.

> It is of the greatest importance for its understanding of God that Israel completely subsumed and subordinated this power under the activity of Yahweh, the God of Israel. Yahweh alone is the master of this power, *he alone as creator confers it on every living being,* he alone remains lord of creation, he alone disposes of the power.... The phraseology of the genealogies...shows that, in primeval time and in the period of the patriarchs, the blessing which effected *the succession of generations was understood as the basic power of history.*[105]

Without procreation and the creation of new families, there can be no history. The point here is that it is precisely within history that Yahweh acts and reveals Himself. The profound spiritual dimension of the covenant is worked out in the context of time and physical relationships. The activity of God and his blessing are to continue throughout

---

102. Ibid.

103. See Chapter 1, "Cults and Fertility." The pagan rituals were tied to the cyclical season of an agricultural society. Life was understood in terms of these cyclical seasons which were ever re-occurring and which had no *telos* or concluding point.

104. Cf. the quotation from Westermann in note 115.

105. Westermann, *Genesis,* 160–61 (emphasis added).

the generations of mankind.[106] This conception of history is radically different from that of the surrounding environment.[107] The Israelite concept of history is predicated on the belief in a demythologized creation.[108] The pagan conception of time was essentially cyclical, derived from the cycles of nature. Their cult practices were tied to the regular progression of the seasons. Orgiastic rituals developed as attempts to use ritualized sexuality as a means to influence the fecundity of the crops and their lives. By contrast, in Israel the idea of "linear history" broke into the religious consciousness of man and sharply differentiated this nation from the surrounding culture. Time was linear; the divine realm could not be manipulated, and human sexuality was properly situated as a created reality. This understanding powerfully reformulated the Israelites' frame of reference.[109] For Israel, "his-

106. "...God will remain effectively at work in them because of this action at creation" (ibid., 161).

107. "In contrast with the Israelites the ancient polytheistic peoples had no primary interest in history. Their attention was concentrated on nature, not on society" (Zeitlin, *Ancient Judaism*, 28).

108. See Schillebeeckx's *Marriage*, where he develops this theme extensively. There is much discussion concerning the exact nature of the first chapters in Genesis. Whatever exact genre they are, they can be distinguished from pagan mythology inasmuch as there is a real connection with history. Some have attempted to capture this distinction by contrasting myth (which as a literary genre is essentially ahistorical or imaginary) with mythos, which is the attempt to express primordial matters in a manner that gives an explanation of real events that are difficult to fully articulate. Eugene H. Maly states in his article "Genesis" (in *Jerome Biblical Commentary,* ed. Raymond E. Brown, Joseph A. Fitzmeyer, and Roland E. Murphy [Englewood Cliffs, N.J.: Prentice-Hall, 1968], 8, §6): "The first 11 chapters of Gn present truths based on historical facts.... Whereas these are religious explanations that in most cases transcend the competence of modern science, they are at the same time historical in that they explain historical events." In particular, the human experience of history, rather than being the experience of continuous cyclical events with no particular concluding point, is now a dramatic structure that is the paradigm for human life itself. There is a beginning which is now moving towards an implicit end which is yet to be revealed. Linear historical conscious now becomes a reality.

109. Von Rad brings out this distinction clearly: "This idea of history made a radical division between Israel and her environment...with her idea of saving history she completely parted company with these [neighboring religions]. Not one of them understood the dimension of history in the way that Israel did! The most that can be said of their concept of time is that there is a "primeval time."...The various conditions of creation were given their divine orders at that time, and the task assigned to the cult and ritual was that of giving continuing

tory" now had its own legitimacy and was free of the constraints of magic, the arbitrariness of the gods' conflicting decisions, and of the controlling influence of fate. "For the Israelites, existence in its entirety resulted from God's will and God's word."[110] Yahweh is the God of history, whose will alone is absolute and determinative of man's ways. "Accordingly, history, for the Israelites had a unity and meaning from the beginning of time to the 'end of days.'"[111] In Israel, history is now seen as "a meaningful process *en route* to a goal."[112] In other words, man was not to meet God in some divinized sexual drama that symbolized the sexual life of the gods, but in history. One of the great principles enunciated in the creation narrative is that human history has its own integral value and not as a mimic of the divine realm. Consequently, human sexuality and procreation are clearly seen as a part of the created and human sphere and not an instrumental means of entering into, mimicking, or influencing the divine realm. In this sense, sexuality is demythologized. Yahweh alone is the creator of all and it is He who controls history.[113] This stands in stark contrast to the pagan mythical experience. Kramer, in his classic presentation of Sumerian culture, succinctly portrays the angst of the pagan world:

---

effect to these primordial orders.... The ancient east's view of the world bears to a greater or lesser degree the clear impress of cyclical thinking in terms of myth, that is to say, of a way of thinking which understood the cultic event on the basis of the rhythm of the fixed orders of nature.... It was always this basically cyclical order of nature on which the ancient peoples of the east conferred the dignity of divinity and which they regarded as a divine event.... *This sacral understanding of the world is essentially non-historical*; at least, it leaves absolutely no place for the very thing which Israel regarded as the constitutive element in her faith, the once-for-all quality of divine saving acts within her history" (Gerhard von Rad, *Old Testament Theology*, vol. 2, *The Theology of Israel's Prophetic Traditions*, trans. D. M. G. Stalker (New York: Harper and Row, 1965), 110–11 (emphasis added).

110. Zeitlin, *Ancient Judaism*, 28.

111. Ibid.

112. Ibid.

113. G. E. Wright articulates this point of view clearly: "The Israelite eye was thus trained to take human events seriously, because in them was to be learned more clearly than anywhere else what God willed and what he was about" ("Theology as Recited," in *Old Testament Issues*, ed. Samuel Sandmel [New York: Harper and Row, 1968], 21, quoted in Zeitlin, *Ancient Judaism*, 29).

They were firmly convinced that man was fashioned of clay and created for one purpose only: to serve the gods by supplying them with food, drink, and shelter so that they might have full leisure for their divine activities. Man's life was beset with uncertainty and haunted by insecurity, since he did not know beforehand the destiny decreed him by the unpredictable gods. When he died, his emasculated spirit descended to the dark, dreary nether world where life was but a dismal and wretched reflection of its earthly counterpart.[114]

But the revelation to Israel broke through this despair and uncertainty. Historical acts and realities now had a purpose in realizing the divine will, including human sexuality and the family.

Israel and the pagan world each had a cultus that connected it to its understanding of the divine realm. But Westermann saw how radically different the cultus in Israel was in this regard compared to paganism. The stories of Israel were not recited to manipulate the gods. Rather the historical acts of man are now the *vehicle* for the divine.[115] That is, God is not working through an isolated and independent cosmic-drama enacted in the cultus, but now works through history, which provides the ground for the Israelite cult. This had profound implications for the understanding of the relationship between creation and history: "Creation is regarded as a work of Jahweh in history, a work within time. *This means that there is a real and true opening up of historical prospect.... Creation is itself a sequence in time, exactly marked out into days. But if the account of Creation stands within time, it has once for all ceased to be myth, a timeless revelation taking place in the natural cycle."[116]

Beyond that, there is the understanding that the divine will penetrates human experience and leads directly to the idea of *sacred* history. History is no longer the consciousness of man's cyclical experiences

---

114. Kramer, *The Sumerians*, 123.

115. "When the primeval story is seen as a prologue to the history of God acting with Israel, then each narrative and each genealogy is affected, and each individual text takes a new direction. *The texts no longer speak to Israel in the context of the action of the primeval period on the present—there is no cultic actualization—but through the medium of history*" (Westermann, *Genesis*, 65 [emphasis added]).

116. Von Rad, *OTT*, vol. 1, 139 (emphasis added).

of the power of nature. Rather, from the Israelite perspective, history takes on a primarily linear dimension, in that human generation is the means by which God passes down the primordial blessing from generation to generation. History (the human consciousness and understanding of time) is no longer cyclic or purposeless; it is directed toward an end (*telos*) that is predetermined by God.[117] *Precisely because it is the means by which each generation is conceived and formed, the family now becomes one of the chief instruments by which that goal is realized.* The story of man is the story of God's representative in creation (*imago dei*), acting within and responding to His will (*historical acts*), moving toward his destined fulfillment (*telos*). What Genesis 1 and 2 presents is that through the act of creation, man is inserted into history and dramatically given the opportunity to enter into the will of God.

> Genesis is but a prologue to the historical drama that unfolds itself in the ensuing pages of the Bible. It proclaims, loudly and unambiguously, the absolute subordination of all creation to the supreme Creator who thus can make use of the forces of nature to fulfill His mighty deeds in history. It asserts unequivocally that the basic truth of all history is that the world is under the undivided and inescapable sovereignty of God.... [T]here is a divine purpose behind creation that works itself out on the human scene.[118]

TÔLDÔT: THE CRITICAL LINK

The Hebrew word for human genealogies is *tôldôt*. While on the surface they may not appear crucial, in fact they provide the substructure on which divine revelation is based, up to and including the New Tes-

---

117. History, or the human consciousness and understanding of time, has two aspects, freedom and determination. This is the genius of the Hebraic revelation. Man has freedom to enter or refuse God's plan (see Gn 3). Hence, there is fundamental human freedom by which, through self-determined acts, man creates his own history. But these individual acts are encased within a greater reality, which is God's will. Man possesses a given nature, which he does not create, and an end, which is determined by God (revealed finally in Jesus Christ). The drama now consists in whether or not the human person will conform his own personal history to the design of God or not.

118. Sarna, *Understanding Genesis*, 9.

tament. The *tôldôt* are the critical link between the purposes of Yahweh and creation. Westermann, in explaining their function, comments:

> The genealogies are part of the human condition.... P states explicitly that they are the working out of the blessing given at creation and that it is the same blessing which is at work in the succession of generations leading up to Abraham as well as in the line which takes its beginning from him.... Israel was always conscious of its origin from one father. This, side-by-side with Israel's beginnings as a people based on a covenant with God, remained an essential element of its historical consciousness and persevered through all vicissitudes and failures. *This is the source of the importance of the family throughout the history of Israel.*[119]

Although the genealogies of the Torah are perhaps the least animated material in the Scriptures, they provide us with some of the most important theological statements in the Old Testament. Their very existence and the care with which they are preserved clearly show that they were of central importance in Israel's faith. The whole of mankind's development is chronicled up to the appearance of Abraham. From thence onwards, his family line alone is fully preserved, as it is linked to the divine blessing. It is clear from Gn 12:1–3 that the salvific purposes of God are destined to be accomplished through the instrumentality of this family. It is not mere random copulation but the actual reproducing, nourishing, and transmitting of the divine image in man and the faithful passing on of the covenantal blessing that becomes the means by which God's will is carried out in the world.

For man to become fully human and for him to rightfully discharge his role as image of God on earth, he *needs* a family. Thus, history can be understood as sacred familial history—the intersection between the human and the divine. The individual cannot exist without the familial

---

119. Westermann, *Genesis*, 66 (emphasis added). Westermann bases his comments on the modern academic consensus that the Genesis text is composed of several different sources representing different theologies. The "P" source is hypothesized to represent the priestly interests in Jerusalem and their validation of the cult as central to Israel's identity. Cassuto and others would argue contrariwise with these hermeneutical presuppositions. It should be noted that Westermann's thesis of the *tôldôt* is of critical help in OT studies and is particularly helpful in understanding the theological functioning of the family in the Old Testament.

context. Thus, the family emerges as the instrument God has created by which His primary blessing in creation is realized. It is the instrument through which creation will reach its final goal.[120] *For Israel, the family is assumed into the divine will.*

CREATION AS SALVIFIC

One further question needs to be investigated to help us properly situate the family theologically within Israel. That question is: What is the goal of creation? Creation, properly understood, is the sovereign act of Yahweh that opens up into the realm of historical reality. In 1935, von Rad first began exploring the relationship between creation and salvation. He asked what was "the *theological position* of belief in creation within the whole of Old Testament faith concerning salvation."[121] His conclusion was that one had to place creation in the context of Israel's history and allow the force of that history to provide the hermeneutic to properly interpret the meaning of creation. As Sarna points out, the history of Israel is centered on the experience of the Exodus.[122] "The theme of creation, important as it is in the Bible, is nevertheless only introductory to what is its central motif, namely, the exodus from Egypt. God's acts in history, rather than His role as Creator, are predominant in biblical thought."[123]

Von Rad contends that there was no understanding of creation in the oldest creeds or statement of faith of Israel. This understanding

120. This becomes particularly clear in the New Testament where those baptized into Christ become His family and indeed, it is discovered, that in salvation, Abraham becomes "the father of us all" (Rom 4:16).

121. The reference to this is found in the work of N. Lohfink, who, writing in about 1975, stated: "Here I am referring, for example, to the regularly reappearing question of the theological position of belief in creation within the whole of Old Testament faith concerning salvation.... [I]n the year 1935...Gerhard von Rad proposed this theme for the first time at a meeting in Gottingen.... Another question is that of the *antiquity* of Israel's belief in creation" (N. Lohfink, *Theology of the Pentateuch: Themes of the Priestly Narrative and Deuteronomy*, trans. L. M. Maloney [Minneapolis: Fortress Press, 1994], 118).

122. Von Rad, however, does not make this claim. He contends that whereas in the earlier strata this is true, later theological developments relativize this. Cf. von Rad, *OTT*, vol. 1, 115.

123. Sarna, *Understanding Genesis*, 8.

only came later as the older beliefs became completely transformed by her experience of the saving acts of Yahweh.[124] In von Rad's estimation, this took a considerable amount of time. What was fundamental to Israel's conceptual outlook was God's saving acts in Israel's history.[125] In particular, the call of Abraham and the covenant at Sinai form the ground of Israel's self-understanding. Israel alone had been chosen by God from all the nations to receive the revelation of His nature and His call. Israel was to be separated unto Him. But even within that experience of election, the need for the salvific activity of God was also revealed. As Abram was being initiated into the covenant, he was shown that his family would eventually become slaves in Egypt and would have to be rescued by Yahweh and brought to Canaan:[126]

In essence, election and salvation are two mutually related experiences of the one same eternal reality, namely, God's love. Israel experienced the reality of Yahweh as election and salvation. These were the preeminently saving actions of Yahweh on behalf of Israel and became her primary terms of reference.[127] Israel then read this salvific experience back into creation. This requires creation itself to be so structured that it can receive this interpretation. Precisely because creation itself is a salvific act, it can be brought into Israel's experience of the mighty acts of Yahweh in history. Von Rad puts it this way:

> [The creation account in Genesis] has only an ancillary function. It points the course that God took with the world until he called Abraham and formed the community; and it does this in such a way that Israel looked back in faith from her own election to the creation of the world,

124. "And Israel only discovered the correct theological relationship of the two when she learned to see Creation too as connected theologically with the saving history" (von Rad, *OTT*, vol. 1, 136).

125. There exists a multiplicity of theories regarding the time frame of the different ideas and documents of the Old Testament, exposition of which goes far beyond the scope of the present discussion. However, although these ideas are often antagonistic to each other, in the present context of trying to understand creation, history and genealogies, the contributions of different schools seem to complement one another.

126. See Gn 15:12–16, in which God reveals to Abram that his descendants will be slaves in Egypt.

127. The belief in the unity of God was a third point of reference.

and from there drew the line to herself from the outermost limit of the protological to the center of the soteriological.[128]

Thus, creation is understood through the lens of the Exodus and the Sinaitic covenant that God had established with Israel.

TÔLDÔT AND SALVATION HISTORY

Similarly, Westermann identifies the tôldôt as the link between creation and salvation history.[129] This conclusion is valuable whether or not one accepts the hypothetical framework he proposes for the formation of the canonical text. He contends that the account in Genesis is the reworking of pre-Israelite (i.e., pagan) stories, reshaped "to join them to Israel's own traditions which are the result of her confession of Yahweh as savior."[130] The primeval stories were later added after Israel had experienced the salvific power of God at Sinai. Israel, having been freed from a mythic existence, now was experiencing history as a meeting place with God. The defining moment for Westermann was when "J and P prefix the primeval story to a history which begins with the call of Abraham."[131]

> The genealogies are part of the human condition.... P states explicitly that they are the working out of the blessing given at creation and that it is the same blessing which is at work in the succession of generations leading up to Abraham as well as in the line which takes its beginning from him.[132]

Cassuto, on the other hand, was a Jewish exegete who pointed out serious problems with this approach.[133] While believing in the existence of an earlier Israelite literature, Cassuto totally rejected the idea that Israel would ever borrow from her *pagan* neighbors. "Generally speaking, it

---

128. Von Rad, *Genesis*, 46.

129. Like von Rad, Westermann saw no recognition of creation in the older creeds of Israel. See his *Genesis*, 66.

130. Ibid., 64.   131. Ibid., 65.

132. Ibid., 66.

133. Westermann bases his analysis on the documentary hypothesis. Cassuto, on the other hand, argues against this methodology in *The Documentary Hypothesis and the Composition of the Pentateuch* (translated by Israel Abrahams [Jerusalem: Shalem Press, 2006] [Hebrew, *Torat HaTeudot*, 1941]).

is inconceivable that the prophets and poets of Israel intended to seek support for their views in the pagan mythological works, which they undoubtedly detested and abominated."[134] This view seems probable. In fact, the perceptive insight of Westermann concerning the role of the family and its connection to the initial blessing is actually strengthened when associated with Cassuto's understanding. The *tôldôt* (generations) and the cultural reality they represented would serve no purpose if they were being constantly adulterated by outside pagan influences.

The truth that does emerge is that the family within Israel is seen as a witness to, and a bearer of, the original blessing from the hands of God. The family is also the means by which the salvific purpose of God is to be transmitted to future generations. The recitation of the *tôldôt* (genealogies) shows the interrelatedness of all things and how the generations (which in each era are instantiated as specific families) act as the conduit for the blessing and purpose of God.[135] Without families, there can be no transference of that blessing from one generation to another. Without families, the promise and purpose of God cannot be fulfilled in history. Without families, there can be no salvation history.

Rabbi S. R. Hirsch, in his exegesis of Genesis 2:27, focused on the blessing of *rbw* ("to multiply"). He concluded that "*rbw* demands the founding of the home, the family, the only nursery for human education...the parental home in which, and by which alone, the child blossoms to a Man, to an Adam."[136] More than mere random copulation or bare physical reproduction, the accomplishing of the divine will throughout each succeeding generation requires a framework within which the human person can grow and mature. In a word, this requires a family. Thus, the creation of the family is intrinsically linked to and emerges from the original blessing bestowed on man. Only by establishing a home which inwardly participates in the salvific purposes of God can one be said to have "discharged the duty of *rbw*."[137] Here we

---

134. Cassuto, *From Adam to Noah*, 8n18.

135. The genealogies in Genesis are recited at 5:1–32; 10:1–32; 11:10–32; 35:23–26; 36:1–43; 46:8–26.

136. Hirsch, *Genesis*, 35.

137. Ibid. He shows that education and formation are innate in the concept of *rbw*. The

see the *vocational* dimension of the family emerging. The *tôldôt* (generations) are the bridge between the fiat of creation and the salvific experience of election-and-covenant. More than mere linear descent, the generations become the carrier of the blessing and the instrument for God's purpose in history. Thus, the accomplishing of the divine will and the recitation of the family generations are directly tied to each other.[138] John Paul II, in examining this trajectory, draws the conclusion that marriage in the original state of man had hidden within it the deeper reality to which man is ultimately called. The primordial relationship of man to woman was always pointing toward the even greater relationship with God, which was to be fulfilled in His Son, Jesus Christ. He thus calls marriage a primordial sacrament.

> Thus, in this dimension, there is constituted a primordial sacrament, understood as a sign which effectively transmits in the visible world the invisible mystery hidden from eternity in God. This is the mystery of truth and love, the mystery of the divine life in which man really shares.... It is the original innocence which initiates this participation.... In the dimensions of the mystery of creation the election to the dignity of adopted sonship was proper only to the first Adam, that is, to the man created in the image and likeness of God, male and female.[139]

CONCLUSION

To understand aright the theological function of the family in the Old Covenant, it is essential to begin with the monotheistic nature of God and the creation which proceeds from this. The distinctiveness of the revelation to the Hebrews emerges when compared to the contemporaneous pagan myths. When creation, and human sexuality in particular, is freed from mythological constraints, the true nature of the family emerges. Only in a demythologized context can it be assumed into the process of salvation. Only then can the family be experienced

---

Catholic Church teaches that one of the primary purposes of marriage is for the *procreation* and education of children (see *CCC* 1652).

138. See above the quote from Westermann, *Genesis*, 66.

139. John Paul II, *Theology of the Body* (Audience: Oct. 11, 1982).

as a carrier of salvific power. Having an absolute beginning point, creation now enters into history. It will now be in and through the events of history that God will reveal Himself to man and bring all things to their destined completion. This includes the family, which in a special way, becomes the instrument by which God's will for man's salvation is accomplished in history: "The biblical story does not destine humans to minister to the gods; people are oriented to the fields and to the world which has been given them. It is here that everything will take place concerning God's dealing with people. One can understand then how this history leads ultimately to God becoming human."[140] Human sexuality, marriage and the family, once demythologized, were assumed into salvation history. For the Hebraic revelation, a long trajectory begins at this stage which culminates in the Incarnation. In the fullness of time, God, having providentially put His image within the creation at the beginning, will assume that same human nature and become man. He will be "born of a woman" (Gal 4:4) and enter into human history in the context of a family, becoming the *telos* of all the Old Testament genealogies (see Mt 1:1ff.).

140. Westermann, *Genesis*, 68. As we shall see, it is baptism that allows the family to be incorporated into Christ and in this way forms what can be considered an extension of the Incarnation. This insertion of Christ into the family and drawing the baptized family into the salvific sphere ultimately is the meaning of the domestic church.

CHAPTER 3

ABRAHAM
AND THE FAMILY
OF FAITH

From the previous chapter, it is evident that the role the family plays is vital not only for the individual but also for the covenant itself. Once the family had been freed from mythological deformations, it then could assume its proper function. Now the human person was inserted not only into chronological history but also into the salvific order (*Heilsgeschichte*). We now turn to investigate how this newly "dimensioned" covenantal family functioned within the Israelite covenant. Here, we will discover that the family had a threefold function: (1) it became the carrier of the covenant, (2) it imaged forth the covenant, and (3) it became the sphere of holiness. It is in these capacities that the *theological* nature of family begins to be manifested.

This theological nature of the family is intrinsically linked to the person and mission of Abraham, "father of all of us" (+Rom 4:16). In a fundamental sense, his family alone is *the* covenantal family. All who wish to enter into the salvific sphere (in both the Old Testament and the New) must in some manner be joined to Abraham and participate in him. The center of the dramatic action in Genesis is the person of Abraham and the establishment of the covenant with him and his family. It is true that the *tôldôt* sections establish the genealogies of all the nations. "From these the other nations of the earth branched out after the flood" (•Gn 10:32). But the initial genealogical lines always lead to one person alone, Abraham, who then becomes the starting point for all the ensuing genealogies that are recorded. Thus, within history there is one salvific family.[1]

This exclusivity can initially be puzzling. The purpose of the first chapter of Genesis is to reveal the origin of every living thing and to show their underlying interconnectedness. God the Creator is Lord of all. But if Westermann is right, all this is only prologue. From the appearance of Abram (who will later take on the name of Abraham) onwards, the *tôldôt* are concerned only with his family. This reveals a rather startling fact: the salvific concern of God is *seemingly* concentrated on this one chosen person alone and God's salvific activity in history is alone in relation to this chosen family.

THE ELECTION OF ABRAHAM

The call and election of Abraham are presented in a tripartite fashion in which each of the three successive stages is clearly defined and each is constitutive of the covenantal process. The process by which Abraham is established as the salvific point parallels the process of creation in the first chapter of Genesis. In Gn 1:2, a single organic foundation is revealed, from which other created realities emerge organically through a process of differentiation.[2] The establishment of the Abrahamic covenant in Gn 12–17 follows a similar pattern and the same fundamental principles are at work. As in Gn 1, a sequential pattern is followed, that gradually allows the fullness of God's purpose to emerge. These three successive stages are:

1. See •Jn 4:22, where Jesus says that "we worship what we understand, because salvation is from the Jews." It is this salvific line that is traced in Scripture up to the birth of the Messiah.

2. ^Gn 1:2: "the earth was without form and void (תֹהוּ וָבֹהוּ / *tōhû vābōhû*—an inchoate mass)."

1. The call *away* from family—(a form of differentiation) (Gn 12:1–5)
2. The promise of descendants—(the original blessing of creation) (Gn 15:1–21)
3. The sign of the covenant in circumcision—(comparable to the Sabbath) (Gn 17:1–27)

Stage One: The Call away from Family

The election of Abraham can be seen as a continuation of the original creation. As in the creation narrative, the principle of differentiation is key. Here, Abraham is "differentiated" from the rest of mankind and *alone* is chosen to be the instrument of God's will. As in Gn 1:1, this establishes a single beginning point (cf. בְּרֵאשִׁית). This differentiation is effected by separating Abram from his pagan context (his natural family and country) and calling him to move to a new space where the covenant can be lived out in its fullness.

וַיֹּאמֶר יְהֹוָה אֶל־אַבְרָם לֶךְ־לְךָ מֵאַרְצְךָ וּמִמּוֹלַדְתְּךָ וּמִבֵּית אָבִיךָ

The Lord had said to Abram, "Go from your land, from your kindred and your father's household. (+Gn 12:1–5)

Ironically, the first stage in establishing a new type of family, the *salvific family,* is the calling *away from* family. Of all the families that existed, only Abram's is separated out and consecrated for the purposes of God. God's desire was to establish a new *form* of family, a family that would be severed from its moorings in paganism and be created anew—a family where the will of God would be the determining factor. While there is an exclusive aspect to this choice, there is simultaneously present a universal horizon.

וְנִבְרְכוּ בְךָ כֹּל מִשְׁפְּחֹת הָאֲדָמָה

And in you all the families of the earth shall be blessed / find blessing / bless themselves. (•Gn 12:3)[3]

In fact, a certain ambiguousness or tension remains in the text. On one hand, Abraham was called to completely leave behind his family and

3. There is an extensive discussion of the translation of וְנִבְרְכוּ (*v'nibr'ḫu*) in W. J. Dumbrell's *Creation and Covenant* (Nashville, Tenn.: Thomas Nelson, 1984), 70ff.

kindred in order to establish a new covenantal family; he had to reject all that he had known in order to allow something new to come into existence. Only in this way could a new organic beginning be established which later will be opened up to include all families. While Abraham's family is the only salvific point within the created order, this new family is destined to become a blessing for all families of the earth.[4] In the text, there is a movement toward exclusivity which ultimately opens up to universality.[5] Here again we have the key principles of creation: the process of differentiation, the one source yielding the many, and the organic interconnection of all things.[6]

The salvific blessing is tied to the Abrahamic family, which ultimately will bless all other families. Only through this one family can the salvific will of God be accomplished.[7] There is an obvious tension set up within the call of Abram between exclusivity, the "scandal of particularity,"[8] and the simultaneous openness to a universal blessing which

---

4. It should be noted that the individualism of the call of Abraham is tempered (a) by its extension to all other families and (b) by the taking along of his wife and nephew. Thus, even the personal covenantal call of Abraham always exists within a corporate dimension.

5. McKeown provides an excursus on the technical difficulties surrounding the translation of Gn 12:3 and especially of the verb וְנִבְרְכוּ (v'nibr'ḫu), which McKeown states can translated as a passive reflexive, or (here he uses Dumbrell), in a middle sense meaning "win for themselves a blessing" (McKeown, *Genesis*, 77).

6. As McKeown notes, there appears to be an interplay between the five curses found in Gn 1–11 and the five blessings that are announced in this revelation to Abraham and the starting point of the salvific covenant. "It is probably not coincidental that cursing occurs five times in chs. 1–11 and the Hebrew root conveying the idea of blessing appears five times in the 'call of Abram'... The underlying message in this passage is that God now counters the power of cursing with blessing. Cursing began because of the disobedience of human beings (Adam)... blessing and the success it brings are possible through obedience and faith" (McKeown, *Genesis*, 74).

7. Pointed out by J. H. Hertz in *The Pentateuch and Haftorahs*, 2nd ed. (London: Soncino Press, 1977), 64. The uniqueness of Israel's election is strongly established by God's description of Israel on Mt. Sinai just before the giving of the Ten Commandments (Ex 19:5). He uses the term סְגֻלָּה (s'gullaʰ), which connotes a special or personal possession that a person can use for his own purposes. The phrase becomes "you shall be my special possession from all the peoples." The prophets also give witness to this uniqueness: "Only you have I known of all the families of the earth" (+Amos 3:2).

8. The "scandal of particularity" refers to the decision by God to work out His salvific plan beginning with one family/nation and not in a generalized manner.

is prophesied in Gn 12:3: "all families shall be blessed." This tension will finally be resolved only when the covenant family of the OT reaches its fulfillment in the emergence of the Church in the NT.[9] At that point, the family of Abraham becomes the Body of Christ and, through the one (i.e., Abraham), the many (i.e., all nations) will be blessed.

Stage Two: The Promise of Descendants

וַיֹּאמֶר לוֹ כֹּה יִהְיֶה זַרְעֶךָ

[Look now at the heavens and count the stars...] and He said to him, *"Thus shall your seed (offspring) be."* (+Gn 15: 5)

In the second stage, God establishes the covenant of promise with Abram once he has been separated from his pagan context. A key provision of the covenant was a space (which is revealed in the promise of land) where the covenant could be lived out freely. The acquisition of the land, Canaan, was to be realized specifically through his children. But as Abram advanced in years, no heirs were produced and the continuance of the covenant was in jeopardy. Consequently, in Gn 15 Abram came before God and expressed his complaint that without an heir, all was futile. Abram correctly realized that it was *through his body* and his natural offspring that the covenant was meant to pass. If there were no offspring, the covenant would die and all would be lost. The family was indeed the fundamental carrier of the covenant.

What is striking about their exchange is the frankness with which Abram addresses God and his request for assurances: "'O Lord GOD, what good will your gifts be, if I keep on being childless?'" (•Gn 15:2). The Lord promises Abram not only will he have a descendant "'which

---

9. The early Church understood this as being specifically fulfilled with the giving of the Holy Spirit on Pentecost (Acts 2:38–41), at which point the family of Abraham reaches its teleological conclusion in its emergence as the Body of Christ, the Church. In his address, Peter explains the outpouring of the Holy Spirit as the fulfillment of the original covenant: "For the promise [i.e., the promise made to Abraham] is made to you and to your children and to all those far off, whomever the Lord our God will call" (•Acts 2:39). The exclusivity of the Abrahamic call now yields to the universal dimension, which was always present within it. In later sections of this study, we will examine the organic relationship between this family of Abraham and the Church.

shall come from your body'" (15:4), but that they will be as numerous as
the stars. Abram asks for confirmation of this promise and God commands Abram to offer a sacrifice. ("'Lord, how shall I know?'...'Fetch
me a heifer'" [+15:8–9]). This human-divine dialogue demonstrates that
this is a genuine relationship where each party is transparent and free
to reveal who he is. There is no hiding behind a pious persona. There is
only a presenting of human need and fragility, which is then answered
by the merciful response that addresses human fear. "'Look up at the
sky and count the stars, if you are able to count them. Thus shall your
seed be'" (+Gn 15:5).

It is significant that in the midst of the requested sacrifice, God reveals (in a highly mysterious manner) the future enslavement and eventual deliverance of Abraham's family.[10]

> As the sun was about to set, a trance fell upon Abram, and a deep, terri-
> fying darkness enveloped him. "Know for certain that your descendants
> will be strangers in a country not their own, and they will be enslaved
> and mistreated four hundred years. But I will punish that nation they
> serve as slaves and afterward they will come out with great possessions."
> (•Gn 15:12–14)

Herein we touch the mystery of suffering which is intrinsically a part
of the divine vocation in a fallen world. Even as Abraham's election is
announced, it is inextricably linked with suffering. The promise of the
covenant cannot be realized without suffering. As part of its covenantal task, the covenantal family of Abraham is going to be enslaved, but
later it will be redeemed through the events of the Exodus, which will
become the epicenter of Israelite faith.[11] In Gn 15 we see that *within the
initial call of Abram, the future generations are already comprehended.*
Salvation is worked out in a familial and communal fashion such that
the generations are already and always bound together in the salvific
design of God. This is an example of corporate personality, which will
be discussed later.

10. The word used here for the trance or deep sleep is תַּרְדֵּמָה (*tardēmāʰ*) which is also
used in Gn 2:21, where Yahweh takes the rib from the man after first causing him to "fall
into a deep sleep." This word, thus, has covenantal overtones.

11. As noted above, Westermann's point was that Israel was fundamentally formed in the

Stage Three: The Sign of Circumcision

הִמּוֹל לָכֶם כָּל־זָכָר׃

Every male belonging to you shall be circumcised. (+Gn 17:10)

In creation, the Sabbath is established as the final point in the creative process and serves as a sign of God's lordship over creation.[12] In the third and final stage of the Abrahamic covenant, God establishes circumcision as the sign of the covenant that will provide the physical link between the generations and serve as a memorial of Abraham's experience. This covenant is cut into his very flesh. "This is my covenant which you shall keep, between Me and you and your seed (descendants) after you. Every male belonging to you shall be circumcised...and it will be a sign of the covenant between Me and you" (+17:10–11).

Given the structure of this essential sign of the covenant and the fact that it takes place within the family sphere, it is clear that the family was designed to be the *carrier of the covenant*.[13] The very fact that the covenant is cut into the generative organ of the male is a profound reminder of how sexuality has been demythologized and become an instrument for God's salvific purposes. This shows the critical importance of both human generation and the family for the covenantal process. Only one man received the covenantal promise, and this covenant continues to exist in history only through his family line. The

---

salvific experience of the Exodus and consequently began to see all her history in salvific terms. Yahweh was truly the God of deliverances and a Savior. In this context, the family becomes reconstituted so that the truth of the saving nature of God will be passed on from generation to generation through the rituals and education taking place within the family.

12. Gn 2:2–3 provides the account of the establishing of the Sabbath, while Ex 31:13–17 explains that the Sabbath is a covenant, linked to the creation, and becomes a memorial of the creation. "So shall the Israelites observe the sabbath, keeping it throughout their generations as a perpetual covenant" (•Ex 31:16).

13. This phrase which I have constructed is a crystallization of the theological function of the family within the OT. Its function as carrier must be understood as having an intrinsic relationship to the covenant itself precisely because the *tôldôt* are essential, not only for the continued existence of the covenant within the historical order, but also because the family becomes the primary means by which the truth and reality of the covenant are experienced. *No family equals no covenant.*

Abrahamic blessing was to be passed on from generation to generation through circumcision, which was a sign of the covenant. Any male not circumcised was cut off from the people of God; "he has broken my covenant" (+Gn 17:14). The passage at Gn 17:10–11 reveals the intrinsic link between the actual covenant and its memorial sign (circumcision).[14]

All this points to the fact that one could not share in the covenant unless he were a member of Abraham's family and (for the male) circumcised. Thus the instrumentality of family vis-à-vis the covenant is disclosed, but (astonishingly enough) at the same time it is relativized. Blood is not enough; the covenant relationship, which is based on blood, also required circumcision. It is clear that, in Israel, blood relationship was never totally determinative.[15] Even in the initiation of the covenant, covenantal status was extended to anyone who was part of the household, including slaves.[16] "Both he that is born in your house and he that is bought with your money, shall be circumcised" (^Gn 17:13). Note that even in this extended application of the covenant, the family (household) is key. The critical factor was whether or not one was a part of Abraham's household and belonged to him, either through natural birth or through some other means. Once the covenant was initiated, being a part of Abraham's family *and* being faithful to the covenantal relationship with God were intrinsically linked through circumcision. Here, the concept of the covenantal household/family is both extended and restricted. It can go beyond physical descent, yet it always requires incorporation into Abraham through circumcision. In this sense, one

14. Genesis 17:10 states that circumcision is the actual covenant (זֹאת בְּרִיתִי / *zōʾt bᵉrîtî*), whereas Gn 17:11states that it is a sign of the covenant (לְאוֹת בְּרִית / *lᵉʾôt bᵉrît*). See Excursus 3 (pp. 000–00) for a discussion on the precise relationship of circumcision to the covenant.

15. Ben-Zion Dinur comments: "The words 'the men of Abraham's house' (Gen. 17:23), 'the souls that they had gotten in Haran' (Gen. 12:5) are understood by early commentators as referring to those whom Abraham had won over to his faith, i.e., proselytes" (B. Dinur, "Jewish History—Its Uniqueness and Continuity," in *Jewish Society through the Ages*, ed. H. H. Sasson and S. Ettinger [New York: Schocken Books, 1973], 16). Cf. A. Cohen, *Everyman's Talmud* (New York: Schocken Books, 1995), 64.

16. In Gn 17, which introduces the covenant of circumcision, the extension to those "not your offspring" is mentioned four times (Gn 17:12, 13, 23, 27).

could say that all males were "adopted" into the covenant by means of circumcision, since all were required to undergo this ritual.[17]

BLESSING AS GIFT

At the heart of the covenantal family is the fundamental reality of blessing. The task of carrying the covenant (as arduous as it may be at times) is always rooted in grace. But to be the carrier of this covenant can never be a self-determining reality. One cannot simply say, "I am going to establish myself as the covenant link with God." *The initiative always remains with God.* The family must first be given the divine gift of the promised blessing. This is not something one can create for oneself; it can only be received. It is only by the choice and election of God that the covenant has entered into history and, then, it was bequeathed only to one person and his family. One can enter into the covenant with God only by being inserted into that chosen, salvific family.[18]

ABRAHAM: TEACHER OF THE FAITH

The above sets out the parameters of the covenantal call of Abraham. However, it is only in Gn 18:19 that the *raison d'être* for the covenantal family is revealed. The primary function of the covenantal fami-

---

17. This lays the groundwork for the Christian experience of baptism, by which *all* are adopted as sons of the living God. See Rom 8:15, 9:4; Gal 4:5; Eph 1:5. See Excursus 3. It is important to note that Abraham received the covenant in Gn 15 but only in Gn 17, at least thirteen or more years later, does he receive the sign of circumcision. This would seem to indicate that one enters the covenant, but, to remain faithful to it, one of the requirements is circumcision for males.

18. But what happens to the Abrahamic family in the New Testament? In Romans 11, Paul shows that both a continuity and a discontinuity exist. The Abrahamic family has to be completed in Christ, who radically transforms the original covenantal family (discontinuity). But this is the working out of the original blessing given to Abraham, so that the NT reality of the Church is organically tied to Abraham (cf. Rom 4:16), who is said to be the father of us all (continuity). The Church is the family of Abraham having reached its destiny in Christ. Paul makes this point in Rom 11, by comparing Gentile believers to wild olive branches that have been grafted into the natural olive tree (Abraham's family), which has been brought to completion in Christ (Rom 11:24).

ly is tied up with education, understood as the passing on of covenantal truth.

כִּי יְדַעְתִּיו לְמַעַן אֲשֶׁר יְצַוֶּה אֶת־בָּנָיו וְאֶת־בֵּיתוֹ אַחֲרָיו

For I have chosen to know [יְדַעְתִּיו] him, in order that he may command his children and his household after him [to keep the way of the LORD by doing righteousness and justice]. (•Gn 18:19)[19]

The preposition לְמַעַן (lᵉma'an) is derived from מַעַן (ma'an) and has the basic meaning of "for the sake of."[20] Hence the sense is that Yahweh *knew* Abraham for a purpose. יָדַע (yāda'—to know) is the usual Hebrew term used to depict marital intimacy between husband and wife. In this verse, the same verb יָדַע is used but translated as "chosen." (This intimate knowledge and exclusive choice of Abraham on the part of Yahweh was to result in Abraham bringing up his children and household in the ways of the LORD.) J. H. Hertz, in the *Pentateuch and Haftorahs,* supplies the following comments on this verse:

> An important doctrine is here taught in connection with the word "command" yṣwh, which has played a conspicuous part in Jewish life. It is the sacred duty of the Israelite to transmit the Jewish heritage to his children after him. The last injunction of the true Jewish father to his children is that they walk in "the way of the LORD."[21]

This passage sets up a cause and effect relationship. The Lord knows Abraham. This knowledge will result in the establishment of the covenantal family, whose purpose will be the formation of the children and the household in the ways of Yahweh. The family is the original cell of the covenant community, which in time will grow larger (into the tribe and then the nation), but the foundational principle always remains: any larger entity will always be predicated on the basic covenantal fam-

---

19. The verb translated here as "chosen" is יְדַעְתִּיו (yᵉda'tiv), which means "to know" and is also used of sexual intimacy.

20. Ludwig Koehler and Walter Baumgartner, *The Hebrew and Aramaic Lexicon of the Old Testament,* trans. and ed. M. E. J. Richardson, vol. 2 (New York: E. J. Brill, 1995), 614. Also see B. Davidson, *The Analytical Hebrew and Chaldee Lexicon* (London: Samuel Bagster and Sons Ltd., 1959), 606.

21. Hertz, *The Pentateuch and Haftorahs,* 64.

ily unit. There is simply no way to replace the value of the family in the covenant.

The importance of this educational function can be seen in Deuteronomy. In Dt 6:4, Israel is given its creedal existence:

שְׁמַע יִשְׂרָאֵל יְהוָה אֱלֹהֵינוּ יְהוָה אֶחָד:

Hear, O Israel, the Lord our God, the Lord is one. (+Dt 6:4)

At the heart of the creed is the command to love the Lord God. In Dt 6:5, the Israelite is commanded to love (אָהֵב / 'āhēḇ) God with his whole heart, soul, and strength, which in essence means that the individual Israelite is instructed to love Yahweh with the whole of his being. From this flows the command to form his children in the ways of this covenantal love:

> You shall teach them diligently [שִׁנַּנְתָּם / shinnantām] to your children, and shall talk of them when you sit in your house, and when you walk by the way, and when you lie down, and when you rise. And you shall bind them as a sign upon your hand, and they shall be as frontlets between your eyes. And you shall write them on the doorposts of your house and on your gates. (^Dt 6:7–9)

The whole atmosphere of the Hebrew's daily life was conducive to the passing on of the content and reality of the faith revealed to Israel. The care with which this was to be carried out regarding to children is indicated in the verb שִׁנַּנְתָּם/shinnantām which is used here. Its root, שָׁנַן/shānan, means "to sharpen" and, in the form found here,[22] means "to inculcate, to teach diligently."[23]

THE ROLE OF EDUCATION

In his study of education in the ancient world, William Barclay noted three hallmarks of Jewish education. The first was that Hebrew society understood that the child and his education were of the utmost importance to the community's existence. As Barclay commented, "No

---

22. This is the Piel form.
23. Davidson, *The Analytical Hebrew and Chaldee Lexicon*, 731.

nation has ever set the child in their midst more deliberately than the Jews did. It would not be wrong to say that for the Jew the child was the most important person in the community."[24] This view is clearly confirmed in the Talmud (*Babylonian Shabbat* 119b), which states: "Perish the sanctuary, but let the children go to school."[25] This is breathtaking when one considers what the Temple represented, the place where God dwelt with His people. The presence of God was concentrated in this one place. But in this saying, the formation of godly offspring is even more important. How can that be? Without offspring formed in the ways of the Lord, there would no longer be another generation of God's people through whom the covenant would pass. Hence, the education of the child becomes an essential link in the continuation of the covenant.

The second hallmark was that the content of Hebrew education was completely religious in nature. "There was no text-book except the Scriptures; all primary education was preparation for reading the Law; and all higher education was the reading and study of it."[26] For the ancient Hebrews, education focused on the formation of the child in the wisdom and intricacies of the Word that had been given to Israel.[27] Without this learning, without this centering on God's revelation, there would be no covenant. Such ignorance would deprive Israel of its informing principle and she would consequently descend into a state of

24. William Barclay, *Train up a Child: Educational Ideals in the Ancient World* (Philadelphia: Westminster Press, 1959), 12. On a certain level, this valuation can be seen in Jesus' reaction to the children in Mt 18:1–5.

25. Barclay, *Train up a Child,* 12.

26. Barclay, *Train up a Child,* 13. Morris Joseph notes that "of secular education there is scarcely a trace. All the ordinances dealing with education deal with it in its larger aspects as a preparation for the moral and religious life, as a means of developing character." Morris Joseph in *Encyclopedia of Religion and Ethics,* ed. J. Hastings (Edinburgh, 1915), 5.194, quoted in Barclay, *Train up a Child,* 14.

27. Köstenberger examines the formation of the child in the OT and shows the extent to which specific instruction for the teaching and training of a child is given in Proverbs. They are to grow in the wisdom necessary to live life properly and successfully. Giving specific references, he lists 21 positive attributes (diligence and industriousness, justice, kindness, generosity, righteousness, truthfulness and honesty, discretion in choosing friends, caution and prudence, gentleness, etc.). See Andreas J. Köstenberger, *God, Marriage, and Family* (Wheaton, Ill.: Crossway Books, 2004), 104.

non-being. Thus, knowledge of and commitment to the precepts and teaching of the covenant (i.e., revelation) were essential if the community was to survive.[28]

Barclay relates a third hallmark: "However high [was] the Jewish ideal of the school, the fact remains that to the Jew the real center of education is the home. For the Jew education is not education in any kind of academic or technical knowledge; it is education in holiness."[29] The family in Israel was conceived of as the pre-eminent place of personal formation. The commandment to the fathers in the Torah makes it clear that they were responsible to educate and form their children in faith.[30] As Barclay said, "The responsibility of teaching the child is something that the parent cannot evade, if he is to satisfy the Law of God."[31] Education was mandated by the Law, itself.

Thus, the Hebrew family was the place where education and formation in the covenant took place on a formal level. This pedagogical role was divinely willed and became constitutive of the identity of the covenantal family.[32] In fact, the whole atmosphere of the home lent itself to bringing to ever greater consciousness the covenant with its joys and its demands. Our next task will be to examine how the structures of family life oriented all the family members toward a deeper encounter with God and how this educational process was carried out through the rituals and the structures of daily life.

---

28. A clear expression of this pedagogical process and its reasoning is best found in •Psalm 78:5–7: "God set up a decree in Jacob, established a law in Israel:/What he commanded our ancestors, they were to teach their children;/That the next generation might come to know, children yet to be born./In turn they were to recite them to their children,/that they too might put their trust in God,/And not forget the works of God, keeping his commandments."

29. Barclay, *Train up a Child*, 14.

30. Cf. Miller, *Biblical Faith and Fathering*.

31. Barclay, *Train up a Child*, 17.

32. It is important here to see the contrast between the natural family, which is a part of the created order, and the covenantal family, which came into existence with the call of Abraham. This covenantal family was called into existence by God with the express purpose of being the vehicle by which the covenant would be passed on and the contents and faith appropriated by each new generation.

CHAPTER 4

FAMILY AS THE CARRIER OF THE COVENANT

If the family was to carry out its function of transmitting un-impaired the covenant from generation to generation, it had to ensure that both the ethos of the covenant and all its specific details were faithfully "handed over" to the next generation.[1] To do this, the family had to acquire a precise form and structure by which this task could be accomplished. Within the covenant, human sexuality and the family played a significant role which would ensure the survival of the covenant. They were no longer merely the instruments by which human life was physically continued. Rather, as the well-known Jewish philosopher Hirsch noted, the nascent human life born to the family had to be shaped and formed so that the person would be conformed to God. This required that the family be structured by informing principles which were derived from the covenant itself. In

1. It should be noted that the word "tradition" comes from the Latin wood *traditio* meaning to "hand over." The purpose of *tradition* in the Biblical and ecclesiastical sense is to guarantee the *unimpaired* transmission of truth from one generation to another. It is a principle of conservation by which the original data and their meaning are preserved from distortion. It also prevents subjective interpretations from being passed on which would usurp the place of objective truths that have been acquired.

this chapter we will examine how the structures of family life enabled the child to encounter the reality of God and to realize more fully the *imago dei*.

FAMILY AS "SANCTUARY" AND
THE HALLOWING OF TIME

The family in the Old Testament can be seen as the sanctuary in which the covenantal life was experienced by each child through the *hallowing of time*. Abraham J. Heschel brings out the importance of this concept of "hallowed time":

> To understand the teaching of the Bible, one must accept its premise that time has a meaning which is at least as equal to that of space; that time has a significance and sovereignty of its own.... Judaism teaches us to be attached to *holiness of time,* to be attached to sacred events, to learn how to consecrate sanctuaries that emerge from the magnificent stream of a year.... On the Sabbath we try to become attuned to *holiness of time.*[2]

It is increasingly difficult to understand this concept because time has been thoroughly instrumentalized in the modern period. It is something to be controlled and used to achieve specific goals and enhance productivity. The *hallowing of time* is a concept foreign to the modern understanding, which sees time as a possession, totally at the disposal of the individual. But with the loss of the sacredness of time, the consequences are predictable. Inevitably, the loss of the sense of hallowedness is extended to both place and person, something which is easily witnessed in the contemporary world. A process of instrumentalization takes place in which all three (person, place, and time) are seen merely as objects to be used.

In contrast, Israel's understood that life (and time) was fundamen-

2. A. Heschel, *The Sabbath* (New York: Farrar, Strauss and Young, 1951), 6–10, quoted in *Judaism,* ed. A. Hertzberg (New York: George Braziller, 1962), 119. As the emphasis on the distinction between "different seasons" and/or "different times" has all but collapsed in the modern world, even within the Christian community, there has been a wholesale loss of the sacredness of time, which ultimately has resulted in the loss of sacredness in other spheres (including the sacredness of life itself).

tally a gift that was informed by the laws of God. This is the essential point of the creation narrative. As a contingent creature, Israel was called to remember and rejoice in her Creator through specific periods in which she relinquished her time and offered it back to the Lord. To be in covenant with Yahweh required that the whole of life be shaped by His commands. Essential to this was the structuring and hallowing of time. The experiencing of hallowed time within the home would present the child with the understanding that his very life was always to be lived within the matrix of God's design. The very fact that time was fundamentally a gift oriented towards God would bring the child into contact with the covenant at deep and unconscious levels. To begin with, the rhythm of family life was determined by the cycle of Shabbat and festivals. It would be hard to overestimate the importance and effect of these festivals and, in particular, the Sabbath, which provided a weekly renewal of Israel's faith. "Six days you shall work, but on the seventh day you shall rest; in plowing time and in harvest you shall rest" (^Ex 34:21).[3]

No child could help but see how different the Sabbath was from all other days; the child, in turn, would himself be differentiated from all his pagan contemporaries. Life changed on Shabbat; not only was there no physical work but certain other conditions obtained. "You shall not even light a fire in any of your dwellings on the sabbath day" (•Ex 35:3); "do not bear a burden on the sabbath day" (^Jer 17:21); not even sticks were to be gathered (Nm 15:32–36).[4] In the Mosaic code, the consequence of violating the Sabbath was death.[5]

Through these divinely appointed temporal periods of holiness, the spiritual sense of time was transmitted to all Israel. Each person saw, on an experiential level, the ordinary rhythm of time being penetrated by the appointed times of holiness. It was the divine *intersecting* common reality. The most influential of these holy days was Shabbat, which was the weekly commemoration of the creation, instituted as the unique holy day in seven. As the command to keep this day holy was observed,

3. Compare Ex 20: 8–11.
4. The man who gathered sticks on the Sabbath is put to death.
5. ^Ex 35:2: "Whoever does any work on it shall be put to death."

secular time was regularly *invaded* by the holiness of Shabbat, which had been instituted as a "sign between Me [God] and the sons of Israel forever" (+Ex 31:17). This could not help but form the child's spirituality.

Similarly, the regular rhythm of life was interrupted by the obligatory pilgrimages to Jerusalem. These feasts were central to the Mosaic Law and provided a means by which the communal/covenantal identity of Israel could be regularly re-affirmed. "Three times in a year all your males shall appear before the LORD, your God, in the place which He shall choose: at the Feast of Unleavened Bread, at the Feast of Weeks, and at the Feast of Booths" (+Dt 16:16).[6] It is difficult for us to envision the disruption these annual pilgrimages must have wreaked on the ordinary schedule of life. All the adult men had to leave their home, their work, and travel to Jerusalem in obedience to God's command.

Nothing had priority over obedience to the Law, not even the economy of the land. In this way, the identity of Israel was reinforced regularly throughout the year and this would have had a profound unconscious effect upon young children. Here, the unity of the nation was periodically displayed. This provided psychological space for fathers and sons to be alone, as well as for the mothers and daughters along with the younger children. Psychologically, this afforded time for bonding which further strengthened the relational bonds within the family and its identity. Thus, through Shabbat and through the pilgrimage feasts, the very ebb and flow of Israelite life was determined by God and effected the hallowing of time.

PARENT-CHILD RELATIONSHIP

As noted above, it was within the family that the contents of the covenant were taught to the child. In Scripture, the responsibility for teaching the faith was clearly a parental one. "All this law which I set before you this day...make them known to your children and your children's children" (^Dt 4:8–9). This same injunction to teach one's children the Law of God is enjoined in three other passages (Ex 10:2; 13:8. 13:14). The

---

6. Cf. Ex 23:14–17.

context is telling: all three passages are contained in the account of the Exodus out of Egypt. God, on the verge of miraculously forming a people, commands Israel to teach her children the Law.

As already noted, education for the Hebrew meant only one thing: religious training in the covenant. Nowhere is the religious and educational formation of children relegated to anyone other than the parents. Thus, the relationship between the parents and children was vital to the covenant and its continuance. The critical importance of this relationship is shown by its inclusion in the Ten Commandments and by the reference to parents in relationship to the coming of the Messiah in the prophetic literature.

The Ten Words given in Exodus 20[7] set out the basic requirements for the survival of any society.[8] Listed among these essential elements is the command to honor your father and mother (20:12) which, as noted in the New Testament (Eph 6:2), is the first commandment with promise. The healthy relationship of children to parents is essential for the health of any society.[9] This is further emphasized by a mention of the parent-child relationship in Malachi. In his final prophetic section (3:23–24 MT / 4:5–6 ET), Malachi announces that Yahweh will send Elijah before the coming of the day of the Lord, i.e., the coming of the Messianic age. His task will be to establish proper relationships between fathers and their children. He shall "turn the heart of the fathers to the children and the heart of the children to their fathers" (+Mal 3:24). If this healing does not take place, then Yahweh "shall come and smite the land with a curse/destruction" (+Mal 3:24). To prepare for the coming of the Messiah, the relationships between children and parents need first to be healed.

---

7. The Hebrew text refers to the Ten Commandments as the ten words (עֲשֶׂרֶת הַדְּבָ־ רִים / 'ăseret hadd°bārîm) in Ex 34:28.

8. See J. David Pleins, *The Social Visions of the Hebrew Bible* (Louisville, Ky.: Westminster John Knox Press, 2001), 52–54, which shows the concern of the covenant code for the disenfranchised and the poor. While the presuppositions of his argument are problematic in places, the reference to the poor is accurate.

9. See the insightful analysis of the commandment to honor one's parents in T. Dozeman *Commentary on Exodus* (Grand Rapids, Mich.: Eerdmans, 2009), 492–94. He shows how the commandment regarding the Sabbath (which is related to the world of worship) is linked to

PEDAGOGICAL PRINCIPLES

The educational process in Israel was informed by sound pedagogical principles. One of these was the concept of the *"teachable moment."* Often fathers are commanded in Scripture to wait until children become curious because of some external event in a ritual or due to some artifact they see. When they begin to ask questions about its meaning, the father is then to give the explanation which will take the child deeper into the faith of Israel. In Exodus, there are explicit instructions concerning the pedagogical dimension of the Passover: "When your children ask you, 'What does this rite of yours mean?' you shall reply, 'This is the Passover sacrifice of the LORD,'" (•Ex 12:26–27).[10] This same method of giving the explanation when the child initiates the discussion is prescribed in Ex 13:14, which deals with the practice of the redemption of the first born. A third example can be seen in the passage concerning the memorial stones set up by Joshua at the Jordan River. "When your children ask in time to come, 'What do those stones mean to you?' Then you shall tell them…" (^Josh 4:6–7).[11]

The wisdom here is that education is not an artificial construct that is imposed upon the child, but rather it grows out of the concrete expe-

---

the command regarding parents (the world of ethic) and how this linking further reinforces the thematic relationship that is established between God and parents. "The power of creating can be attributed to both. Malachi 3:17 makes the analogy explicit when God states: "I will spare them [the Israelites] as parents spare their children" (p. 493). As well, the honor (כָּבוֹד / *kābōd*) is required for both God and one's parents. Thus there is conjunction between parents and the cult (ibid.).

10. In later Jewish tradition, this question and answer took on a ritual form in the Passover meal where the youngest child is instructed to ask the questions as to the meaning of the different actions and items on the Passover table. This ritualizing did not take place with other such "teachable moments," for example, with the redemption of the first born or the stones in the Jordan.

11. Other examples of these "physical reminders" of the faith include the instructions in Dt 6 which are set in the context of teaching the faith to the children of the family. Here, the Israelite is commanded to write the word of God on his doorposts, on his hands and forehead. In later Israel these reminders took the form of a box containing a Scriptural verse(s); the box was attached to the doorframe or wound with leather thongs around the head and arms. Children would normally, at some point in their lives, be curious as to the meaning of all these things. At this point, a child would be receptive to hear an explanation of the faith.

rience of the child and waits for the moment when the child is psychologically engaged with the subject. The environment of the child should
contain "icons" of the faith, material expressions of the covenant both
in rituals and in objects, which give witness to the reality of God. In
this way, the child regularly encounters the faith on a multitude of levels, both consciously and unconsciously. These physical reminders also
become a primary means by which the child can be brought to a deeper
realization of the faith as the child begins to question the meaning of
both rituals and memorials.

SPIRITUAL PRINCIPLE: ORGANIC UNITY

The underlying spiritual principle of Hebraic education was the establishing of an *identity in terms of organic continuity with the past generations reaching back to the primordial founder, Abraham.* The child
(i.e., the next generation) was never understood to be some autonomous, separate entity. Rather, his existence was mysteriously and inextricably bound with the past generations from which he came. The
realism of this understanding was so vital that each generation was to
consider the experiences of Israel in the past as actually part of its own
experience. In some mysterious fashion each person too was present
at the founding events of Israel's life and shared in them. An example
of this dynamic interpenetration of the past and present is found in
^Dt 6:20:

> When your son asks you in time to come, "What is the meaning of the
> testimonies and the statutes and the ordinances which the LORD our
> God has commanded you?" then you shall say to your son, "We were
> Pharaoh's slaves in Egypt; and the LORD brought us out of Egypt with
> a mighty hand."

The key phrase in this instruction is "We were slaves of Pharaoh
in Egypt." Through this ritual answer each Jewish child was given his
identity. This answer told them *who* they were, regardless of when or
where they lived. All who composed the family of Abraham had a common identity, which was tied to the suffering in Egypt and to the deliverance by the mighty hand of God. This ritual provided the child with

a concept of family which organically related all members throughout the generations. This sense of corporateness (or organic interrelatedness) lay at the heart of the covenantal experience. Through this, the child discovered a way in which the limitations of time could, to some degree, be overcome. In some mysterious way he was present at the Exodus by which Israel experienced redemption. A certain sense of not being strictly bound by the present period was inculcated within the child.[12]

This key educational component eventually became ritualized within Israel and took the form of the Passover liturgy within the home. The *Haggadah,* the ritual book used during the Passover meal, provides the hermeneutic by which this event is to be interpreted and enunciates the principle of "generational solidarity."[13] During the meal, the youngest child asks why the Passover night is different from all others. The reply is telling:

> In every generation let each man look on himself as if he came forth out of Egypt.
>
> As it is said: "And thou shalt tell thy son in that day, saying: It is because of that which the Lord did for me when I came forth out of Egypt" [Exod. 13:8]. It was not only our fathers that the Holy One, blessed be he, redeemed, but us as well did he redeem along with them.[14]

---

12. This is a difficult concept to articulate. In a sense, what the child was partially experiencing was the fullness of time. That is, all time, both past and present, was in a small measure present to the child. The celebration of the Shabbat linked him to the act of creation; circumcision and the covenant with the person and blessing of Abraham; and the Passover with the events of the Exodus. This was not a mere psychological remembering of these things, but, for some of these events, there was a participation in them. Thus, the sharp demarcation between past and present was overcome at times.

13. The Haggadah probably took its present form during the Mishnah era (70–200 AD). The structure of the Seder meal is first presented in Mishnah Pesahim 10. It presumably is reflective of the centuries of celebrations that had preceded its emergence. Clearly, the principles of generational solidarity come from the Scriptures themselves.

14. Nahum Glatzer, *The Passover Haggadah,* rev. ed. (New York: Schocken Books, 1969), 49. He comments: "The text is based on Mishnah Pesahim X.5. A passage of central importance in the *Haggadah:* Exodus and redemption are not to be taken as happenings in days of long ago, but as a personal experience."

Each Jew was to feel as if he were present when the original Exodus took place. "We were slaves of Pharaoh." The solidarity and continuity of the generations were to be experienced by each child, by each generation. In this way their fundamental identity was formed which was shared by all. Somehow, every Jew of every generation was present in Egypt; they existed as one people extended throughout space and time.

FAMILY AS LOCUS OF THE CULT

Marshal McLuhan coined the phrase "the medium is the message." He wanted to establish the close and inextricable relationship between what one says (content) and how one says it (context). This phrase aptly describes how the family functions in relationship to the covenant. As we have seen, the family provides the *context* wherein the child experiences the covenant and is the means by which the child is formed. Through the family one is inserted into, and is connected with, the covenant, and in this way the family becomes the divine instrument of the covenant. In this case, the family becomes the place where the rituals of the covenant are lived out and participated in.

PRIESTLY FATHERHOOD

Part of the role of the family was that it was the locus for the cult, particularly at those moments when life and the covenant intersected. In earliest times, the priesthood was exercised by the father of the family.[15] This is particularly seen in the sacrifices offered by Noah (Gn 8:20), Abraham (Gn 12:7; 13:18; 15:9–18; 22:9) and Jacob (Gn 28:18; 35:14).[16] In

15. "Acc[ording] to the OT the priesthood before the age of Moses was patriarchal. The father sacrificed for the family (Noah, Gen. 8.20; Abraham, Gen.22. 13)" (F. L. Cross and E. A. Livingstone, *The Oxford Dictionary of the Christian Church,* 2nd ed. [New York: Oxford University Press, 1974], 1122 (hereafter ODCC). Also cf. Bolle's comment: "There was no official priesthood among the patriarchal groups. Heads of families performed acts of public worship in the shrines they visited (Gn 31.54; 46.1)" (K. W. Bolle, "Priest and Priesthood, Israelite," *New Catholic Encyclopedia,* ed. W. J. McDonald, vol. 11 [New York: McGraw-Hill, 1967], 772).

16. Cf. Cross and Livingstone, *ODCC,* 1122.

each case, the head of the family takes upon himself the priestly role of officiant at the sacrifice and offers the sacrificial gift to the Lord on behalf of the whole family unit. There were no previous ordination rites or rituals of consecration to empower the father for this role. Rather, by the very fact of his being a father, the founder of his house, each man stood before God as the representative of his family. Thus, within ancient Hebrew society, the very essence of fatherhood *implicitly* contained within itself the spiritual dimension of priesthood. Through the generation of life and by being the head of the household, each father, by nature, was a priest for his own organic family. Even when the institutional priesthood was instituted under Moses, this primordial sense of the father was never lost.[17]

This priestly, spiritual dimension of fatherhood is seen especially in the patriarchal blessings. Pedersen explains the perduring power of the father's blessing in terms of the *nephesh* or soul.

> In the *patriarchal legends* we read how the blessing came to Israel.... That the blessing is handed down from father to son is a consequence of its being a power of the soul. It must go with the family, because there is a psychic community in the latter.... It is the soul of Abraham that lives on in Isaac.[18]

Thus, the blessing which the father gives has real power which confirms the identity of Abraham in the soul of the next generation. While the power to *give* this blessing belongs to the father, it is not entirely under his control. First, the blessing must be received, as it does not originate within any human agent. We are blessed and then can give the blessing to the next generation. Second, as the case of Esau illustrates, one cannot retrieve the patriarchal blessing once it has been given (cf. Gn 27:36–38). The ability to bless is thus a power which passes *through* the father, yet the blessing possesses its own constitutive nature

---

17. This representative role, which derives from the organic understanding of the nature of the whole human race in general and of the marriage/family unit in particular, continues into the NT and underlies the Pauline concept of headship. See 1 Cor 11:3ff.; Eph 1:22, 4:15, 5:23ff.; Col 1:18, 2:10ff.

18. Johannes Pedersen, *Israel, Its Life and Culture I–II* (London: Oxford University Press, 1926; reprint, 1954), 190.

not derived *from* the father. What was received (i.e., from his father) is now passed on by the head of the family to his heir. The ultimate origin is the blessing originally given by God to Abraham as part of the covenant. *This blessing becomes a power in the soul and as such is received and then given as one generation succeeds another.* Both the father's priesthood and his blessing are essential aspects of the covenantal family and both familial priesthood and blessing protect and transmit the covenant from generation to generation. Both provided the structure and identity of the family and enabled the family to function as a covenantal community.[19]

Because it is of the nature of created man to worship, the family unit had to have some way by which to carry out this activity. Because in the ancient world the man was seen as the natural head of the family, it was logical for him to occupy the role of priestly representative of the family before God.[20] This "domestic priesthood," which proceeded out of the created order, therefore, existed before the ministerial priesthood instituted under Moses. As Aquinas taught, "the priesthood...existed before the Law among the worshippers of God in virtue of human institution."[21] For the Hebrew, priesthood would also be linked to the idea of representation. The first human being was the man from whom all others came. Hence, the one properly constituted to represent the human community before God would be the man. In terms of the family, the father would be seen as the point of origination, thus replicating the role of Adam. As all are incorporated in Adam, so the whole family is incorporated in the father. Consequently, he is the proper representative before God and would rightly assume the role of officiant at the family sacrifice.[22]

---

19. This section is indebted to (†) Father Benedict Ashley, OP, who kindly gave of his time and willingly discussed this topic with me.

20. See Thomas Aquinas, *Summa theologiae* I, q. 92, a. 1; II-II, q. 164, a. 2.

21. Thomas Aquinas, *ST* II-I, q. 103, a. 1. Here, he also mentions that the dignity of the priesthood was "allotted to the first-born" which probably had ties to the patriarchal blessing.

22. "Thus in patriarchal times the head of the family would normally have exercised priestly functions" (editorial comment, *Summa Theologiae* [New York: Blackfriars with McGraw-Hill, 1965], 235).

One of the primary functions of the priest's role is to represent God to the community. He acts as the mediator between man and God either by nature (the father) or through ordination (the Levitical priesthood).[23] As we have seen, in Hebraic culture, in the domestic sphere it was the father who assumed this role vis-à-vis his own family. On a number of levels he imaged forth God to the members of his household. Just as sexuality, and hence marriage, could be seen as participating in the primordial sacrament of creation,[24] the priesthood of every father can be considered in a similar way. In the patriarchal period, given that the family was itself the primary unit (rather than the nation or state), the role of priest-father was sufficient for all spiritual needs. But during the Exodus, Israel took on a broader identity as a nation and its structure was regulated by the provisions of the Mosaic covenant. Now, the needs of the individual extended beyond the nuclear family both in terms of the inter-relationships of large numbers of people (property rights and civil order) and in terms of national identity (national security and war). The emergence of the state necessitated the emergence of a supra-familial religious structure, including a ministerial priesthood which functioned for the whole community.[25] It is important to note that the ministerial priesthood does not abolish, eclipse, or absorb the priestly role of the father. Rather, the ministerial and the domestic priesthood complement each other.[26]

23. Aquinas defines "the characteristic function of a priest is to act as mediator between God and his people" (Aquinas, *ST* III, q. 22).

24. "Man appears in the visible world as the highest expression of the divine gift.... And with it he brings...his masculinity or femininity.... A reflection of this likeness is also the primordial awareness of the nuptial meaning of the body.... Thus in this dimension, there is constituted a primordial sacrament" (John Paul II, *Original Unity of Man and Woman: Catechesis on the Book of Genesis* [Boston: Daughters of Saint Paul, 1981], 143). There is a specificity to each gender, which, in the case of the man, is intrinsically tied to fatherhood. John Paul II brings out the uniqueness of the male's role in *Familiaris Consortio* 25, where he shows how the man is to relive the fatherhood of God.

25. Wellhausen comments: "Speaking generally, however, the priesthood has distinctly consolidated itself as compared with its former condition, and gained not a little alike in number and in influence; it has become an important power in public life, *without which the nation cannot be imagined*" (Wellhausen, *Prolegomena*, 134) (emphasis added). Cf. also Cross and Livingstone, *ODCC*, 1122, and Bolle, "Priest and Priesthood," 772.

26. In the NT there is also the recognition of a relationship (even if at only the notional

CRISIS IN FATHERHOOD

Certainly, within ancient Israelite society, the father was still the primary transmitter of the covenant.[27] In fact, the same Mosaic legislation that established the ministerial priesthood also specified the (priestly) role of the father in the family. Besides his specified duty as teacher of religious truths for his family, the father presided over the most critical rituals in the establishment of the covenant, each of which can be described as a *home liturgy*. It was specifically through these rituals that the father carried out his priestly role within the family sphere.

John W. Miller, in *Biblical Faith and Fathering*, rejects the modern notion of the non-relevance of the father, and convincingly shows how, within the Israelite covenant, the role of the father is essential to the well-being of his children, his family, and the covenant itself. In a brilliant analysis Miller shows how the Hebrew revelation radically differentiated Yahweh from the pagan conception of the divinity. As shown above, the divine sphere in pagan minds was thoroughly sexualized, licentious, and arbitrary. The older father-gods were seen as weak, senile and ineffective. Violence, intrigue, and murder ensue as the younger gods seek to overthrow the older ones, and this wrecks the divine homes until a new order is eventually set up. Consequently, these myths would have had a profound effect upon the understanding of human fatherhood. Ultimately, the image of the father present in these pagan myths was one of ineffectiveness, weakness, and irresponsibility.

An excellent example of this fatherhood crisis is found in the *Enûma Eliš*, the Babylonian myth of creation which unfolds in two acts.[28] The

---

level) between the leadership in the church (i.e., bishops/*presbyteroi*) and leadership in the home (i.e., biological fathers). The Pauline teaching is that leaders of the "household of God" (Eph 2:19) were explicitly to be modeled after the image of the father in household of the family (1 Tim 3:1–5). While the exact relationship between the two is not clearly worked out, there is a tacit acknowledgment that the two are related. The more important question is whether or not, because of the understanding of the Church and the nature of salvation, the father's role is either absorbed or abolished in the new covenant. This issue needs further research.

27. This section on fatherhood is indebted to Miller's *Biblical Faith and Fathering*.

28. In this section, I have incorporated Miller's insightful comments on the aspect of fatherhood in the ancient pagan myth called *Enûma Eliš*.

primeval gods, Apsû, the father-god and Ti'âmat, the mother-goddess, are conceived of as two bodies of water which intermingle to form the next generation of deities who in turn form other gods (*Enûma Eliš*, 1:2–14).[29] However, these generations of children were troublesome and noisy; their actions were considered "loathsome" and "mutinous" (*EE* 1:27, 49). The father-god, Apsû, is so disturbed by the noise that he proposes murdering his own progeny (*EE* 1:39,49). Ti'âmat is deeply grieved and rages against killing her own children. Apsû, however, is convinced by an adviser to pursue his course of action and "grew radiant" with the thought of murder (*EE* 1:51). News of the upcoming slaughter is revealed to the younger gods, whose shock renders them incapable of action. It is the all-wise Ea who designs a master spell to cast over the father-god, Apsû, divests him of his symbols of authority and power, and slays him (*EE* 1:60–69). Ea then proceeds to build his dwelling place and sanctuary, using the corpse of Apsû as a foundation.

Here we see the crisis in fatherhood. In the mythological stories, the father is not committed to his children, is not caring or sacrificing for them. Instead, he is weak, indulgent, and violent; his power is subjected to nothing other than his own whims. He is essentially out of control. Sons rise up in rebellion against him, rendering him powerless, in order to overcome the father and steal his authority, position, and power. This becomes the Babylonian paradigm for fatherhood.[30]

The second act of creation begins when Ea begets Marduk, the powerful storm god, who will eventually be the one to form the universe. He has a "double godhead" (*EE* 2:91). Ti'âmat, the primordial mother is distressed by this and seeks to avenge the death of her husband, Apsû, by killing the rebellious younger gods. She makes a pact with others (presumably who were not involved with the murder) and creates an army of monsters to carry out her will (*EE* 2:124–31). Ti'âmat's plan is revealed to Ea, who goes to his forebearer, Anshar. Each of the father-gods is asked

---

29. The text of *Enûma Eliš* (hereafter, *EE*) is taken from Pritchard, *ANET*, 60–72. The first number refers to the specific tablet (the epic poem consists of 7 tablets), and the numeral following the colon refers to the line of the poem.

30. As Miller says, it would appear that during the second millennium, the ancient Near East "was experiencing a fathering crisis of sorts" (*Biblical Faith and Fathering*, 35).

to confront Ti'âmat, but all are too fearful (see Tablet II).[31] Finally, the assembly of the gods is convened and Marduk is asked if he will lead the fight against Ti'âmat and save them. He agrees, so long as they will "proclaim supreme my deity" (EE 2:125). Battle is finally engaged, with the resultant victory over Ti'âmat.

> Then joined issue Ti'âmat and Marduk, wisest of the gods.
> They swayed in single combat, locked in battle...
> He released the arrow, it tore her belly,
> It cut through her insides, splitting the heart.
> Having thus subdued her, he extinguished her life.
> He cast down her carcass to stand upon it.[32]

The household of the gods was conceived of as a place of intrigue, where one struggled to establish dominance and where one resorted to violence to establish authoritative leadership. The children could rise up in rebellion, as there was no authority to stop them. There reigned a form of controlled chaos. It is within this context of battle and destruction that the created universe emerges. Marduk takes the corpse of Ti'âmat, the mother-goddess, and splits it in two to form the dome of the heavens.[33]

> The lord [Marduck] trod on the legs of Ti'âmat,
> With his unsparing mace he crushed her skull.
> When the arteries of her blood he had severed,
> The North Wind bore (it) to places undisclosed...
> Then the lord paused to view her dead body,
> That he might divide the monster and do artful works.
> He split her like a shellfish into two parts:
> Half of her he set up and ceiled it as sky...
> In her belly he established the zenith.[34]

All of this graphic detail is important for several reasons. First, it shows that the pagan conception of the gods, their lives, and the creation of

---

31. A typical response on the part of the fathers is shown by Anu: "But when Anu was near enough to see the plan of Ti'âmat, he was not able to face her and he turned back" (EE 2:81–82). Cf. Miller, Biblical Faith and Fathering, 37.

32. EE, 4:93–104 .

33. Presumably, the bottom half became the earth.

34. EE, 4:129–38; 5:11.

the universe (and the principles which inform it) are radically different from Israel's. Secondly, there is a profound difference also between the understandings of fatherhood. The assumption that the God of Israel is simply a continuation of the patriarchal gods of the surrounding pagan cultures is false, according to Miller. Rather, he sees that a revolutionary understanding of fatherhood emerged in Israel because of their experience of Yahweh as the Redeemer-God, the all-powerful creator who protected and took care of His chosen ones. He perceptively asks "whether biblical faith in God as father ... may not instead have arisen on the wings of an emotional spiritual revolution,"[35] wherein the understanding of fatherhood was fundamentally reconceived. Our thesis is that this, in fact, is what did occur.

Israel stood in complete contrast to the pagan world in her understanding of the fatherhood of God. In pagan mythology, the gods were sexualized and creation emerged from their sexual activity. But in Israel the creative activity of God is separate from sexuality. Tasker uses Dt 32 as a prime example of this. As he notes, although God is presented as a personal father, it is in terms of a "rock". There is no sensuality here. As Tasker concludes: "The unusual contrast between the obvious fertility/virility symbol of a bull, seen so often in the ANE, and the non-sensuous rock, distances the biblical description of God's fatherhood from the notion that the Father-God is the great progenitor."[36]

For Israel, the fundamental character of Yahweh derived from His salvific role in the Exodus. Here, the God of the Hebrews showed Himself to be a father deeply involved with His family, protecting His children, and doing whatever was necessary to bring them to safety. He was a father who had sworn absolutely fidelity to His people by means of the Abrahamic covenant. Because the revelation to Israel was monotheistic, there could be no fundamental conflicts within the divine sphere. Yahweh has absolute power, but uses this power to protect and defend His children, to rule and to guide, and this is pre-eminently revealed in the Exodus account. It is appropriate to say (analogously) that Yahweh

---

35. Miller, *Biblical Faith and Fathering*, 35–36.
36. Tasker, *ANE Fatherhood*, 86.

(in some fashion) subordinated His own life to the welfare of His children. That is, He is not the god of the Deists; He is not a watch-maker god who, having created the universe, winds it up and walks away. No, the Biblical revelation is that God continues to care for His creation and directly intervenes in the lives of His people to bring them to safety and to enable them to carry out the divine plan. This, in fact, is the underlying meaning of the term *patriarchy.* It primarily means the rule (*arche*) of the father (*pater*), but this exercise of authority is ordered not to the benefit of the father but to the children and family.[37] In the Biblical context, it is Yahweh and His salvific acts which provide the hermeneutic by which fatherhood is to be understood. The father in the covenantal family, like Yahweh, (a) is the one who lays down his life for his family, (b) is concerned that each member comes into the fullness of being (particularly during the early years where educational formation is crucial) and (c) is the protector during times of danger.[38] *The divine fatherhood of Yahweh became the lens for understanding human fatherhood within Israel.* This becomes the Biblical understanding of patriarchy.[39] What is being established here is a life-sustaining order within the family, such that the welfare of each individual and of the family as a whole is secured by the authority of the father being subjected to the rest of the family.[40] Patriarchy within the Biblical paradigm is not

37. The father does not possess absolute power he can wield in any manner he wishes. As we have seen, the father must bring his sons into the covenant through circumcision (Gn 17); he must educate his children in the law of God (Dt 6:1–5); he must answer their questions so they can grow in faith (Ex 12:26). The husband has the obligation to provide his wife with food, clothing, and sexual pleasure (Ex 21:10) and he is commanded to not deal treacherously with the wife of his youth (Mal 2:14–15). Both husband and wife had rights to ensure for a stable home life, but the father/husband clearly did not have absolute control.

38. The children also had responsibilities, particularly when they had grown up and needed to care for elderly parents. This may be part of the meaning of honoring father and mother.

39. Daniel I. Block shows the genuine tenor of patriarchy when he states: "This emphasis on the responsibilities associated with headship over the household (as opposed to its privileges and power) is consistent with the overall tenor of the Old Testament, which views leadership in general to be a privilege granted to an individual in order to serve the interests of those who are led" ("Marriage and Family in Ancient Israel," in *Marriage and Family in the Biblical World,* ed. Ken Campbell [Downers Grove, Ill.: InterVarsity Press, 2003], 43–44).

40. Daniel I. Block gives an in-depth listing of the duties of the father who, *de facto,* must

father-centered but other-centered. In this way, the father, like Yahweh, serves his family by giving selflessly of himself and thus becomes the servant-leader.[41]

EXCURSUS 1: MOTHERS AND THE COVENANT

It is clear that the role of the father is clearly delineated within the legal structures of Israel. But does this mean that the role of the mother was marginalized? Given a) the specific requirement to honor mothers in the Ten Commandments, b) their salvific role in the narrative history of Israel, and c) the responsibility of the wife/mother regarding cultic purity, it should be evident that mothers also played a vital role within the covenant. Each family, *precisely as a family,* was the medium and instrument of the covenant; the constitutive members (fathers, mothers, and children) lived out their role within the God-given structures of the family.

A perspective that would marginalize mothers or children can only arise when one does not take into account Jewish hermeneutics when reading the OT. Laws are of fundamental importance but they are not the only source of the community's self-understanding. The Jewish communi-

---

yield himself to his family and its needs: "Whether the man was the head of the extended family (*rō'š bêt 'āb*) or of the nuclear family of within the *bêt 'āb,* he was obliged to serve the family by (1) personally modeling strict personal fidelity to Yahweh; (2) leading the family in the national feasts... (3) instructing the family in the traditions of the Exodus and of the Torah... (5) providing the basic needs of food, shelter, clothing, rest; (6) defending the household against outside threats; (7) functioning as elder... (8) maintaining the well-being of the individuals in the household... (9) implementing decisions made at the level of the *mispaha* [clan]" (Block, *Marriage and Family,* 47).

41. The father's authority is most clearly displayed in kingship. But Biblically, the king was not allowed to increase his wealth and power or to lord it over his fellow citizens, whom he was to regard as brothers (see Dt 17:14–20). He had to submit to theTorah and serve the kingdom. Kingship (the authority of the father) is given its Christological form (whence it originally derives its power) in the Passion. Here we see the battered body of Jesus stretched out on the Cross dying to atone for the sins of mankind. Above His head, the plaque read: "Jesus of Nazareth, King of the Jews." Here is the quintessential meaning of kingship, of fatherly authority. One is to become a suffering servant. This is the foundation for the Biblical understanding of patriarchy. (Cf. Eph 5:22ff.)

ty looks at both *halackic* (legal) texts and *haggadic* (narrative) texts in order to grasp what is truly going on in Israel. Each makes its own invaluable
contribution.

The halackic material in the Torah sets out the various commandments
required for Israel to be faithful to God and that were essential for the nation's continued existence. There is a large legal framework which specifies
the father's role. But, also, of great importance to the family were the purity laws of Israel which were essential for Israel to carry out her mission.
These laws enumerate the specific duties of husbands and wives and included cleansing after emissions of bodily fluids, menstruation, issues of
blood, etc. While complex, these laws also witness to the crucial role of
the mother, who, like the father, played a key role in being a "carrier of the
covenant." The wife's/mother's responsibility for ritual purity was essential in securing sanctified sexual relationships (see Lev 12 and 15). In menstruation, the woman was in an "unclean" state (טָמֵא / *tāmē'*) because of
the issue of blood and had to wait for a period of seven days before sexual
relationships could be resumed (Lev 15:19). In childbirth, again because of
blood emissions, the mother was in an "unclean" state until she brought
the proper offering to the Temple (Lev 12:1–8), which she was commanded to do (Lev 12:6). To remain in impurity was to "defile the Temple"
(Lev 15:31) and, therefore, was a grave offense against the covenant. Thus,
the mother/wife, like the father, was an active agent in maintaining family
purity and the covenantal relationship of the family with God. Both father
and mother were "carriers of the covenant."

While the haggadic material is more difficult to analyze precisely because it is in narrative form, it also shows the essential role played by
mothers. For example, Ex 2:1–10 describes the actions of Moses' mother. It
was she who saved Moses; his father is not mentioned. In the narrative sections of Scripture, we see that the fate of Israel often in the hands of mothers (Sarah, Rebekah, Deborah Esther, etc.). Within Judaism's own self-
understanding, its law of membership shows that the very identity of a Jew

is bound up with the mother. Jews are Jews because their mothers are Jewish, not because their fathers are. It is the mother who created the home in Israel. The Shabbat meal, which was central to the observance of the Shabbat, was the creation of the mother. The home she created provided the context in which the Torah was lived out. Because of the profound interiority of the home and the role of the mother, it may be more difficult to articulate the mother's role in legal terms. But this does not make it any less real or of less importance.

We should also note that the NT also witnesses to the vital role of mothers (and grandmothers) in the Jewish community in passing on the faith. The early Christians were all Jews and thus carried with them the religious discipline that obtained within Judaism at that time. In 2 Tim 3:15 Paul makes reference to Timothy and how he knew the Scriptures from infancy. Then we learn from Acts 16:3 that Timothy's mother was Jewish and his father was Greek. Therefore, it can be assumed that it was his mother who taught the Scriptures to Timothy and perhaps his grandmother, Eunice, who was also a believer. See 2 Tim 1:5.

It is precisely within the God-given structures of the family that the covenant is lived out and passed on from generation to generation. It is both father and mother who play indispensable roles in the transmission of the covenant, being carriers of this divine grace.

FATHER-LED RITUALS

In ancient Israel, there were several specific home rituals, led by the father, which provided the constitutive structure for family life, involving the man as the principal agent for the transmission of the covenant.[42] Fathers and these family rituals were inextricably bound together, and both were essential for the continuance of the family and the Hebrew covenant. Miller comments:

---

42. This section leans upon Miller, *Biblical Faith and Fathering*, 69–87.

One soon becomes aware of the striking fact that among the most important biblical rituals are several having to do with family, and with the *father's* role in the family in particular.... These rituals are rites of the *family*...and of the *nuclear* family specifically—not rites of the sanctuary or the community as a whole. In other words, these oldest and most enduring religious ceremonies are *nuclear family* affairs.... Furthermore, and equally important, I suggest (and this point too is not usually sufficiently noted or emphasized), they are family rituals in which the *father* plays the leading role. Finally, all of these father-family rituals have to do with the father's role as caretaker and guardian of his *children* above all.[43]

This is in radical contrast to the pagan myths and their conception of divine fatherhood.

This intersection between fathers and home rituals is decisive for Israel's identity and the identity of children. It is clear in Israel that fathers and mothers had a privileged position. This is substantiated by the fact that one of the ten *debarim* (commandments) is devoted to how children must honor their fathers and mothers. This means that the way in which parents were treated in the family setting was an essential element in God's covenantal relationship with Israel and reflected the degree to which the Hebrews were living out their faith. In other legislation concerning the home rituals, the father's unique role as teacher and transmitter of the faith was highlighted. While both father and mother are essential and are at the center of the covenantal experience, there was, nonetheless, a unique role played by the father which was critical for the formation of the children in the faith.[44]

43. Ibid., 71–72.

44. This unique role of the father is well attested in psychological literature. See Don Eberly, ed., *The Faith Factor in Fatherhood: Renewing the Sacred Vocation of Fatherhood* (Lanham, Md.: Lexington Books, 1999). This is a unique compilation of essays from an ecumenical viewpoint that examines the indispensable role of the father in the development of the child, including his role in faith formation. See also *Josephinum Journal of Theology* 9, no. 1 (Winter/Spring 2002), which was devoted to the issue of fatherhood, especially P. Vitz's essay, "The Fatherhood of God: Support from Psychology," 74–86. This indispensable role that the Hebrew father played can perhaps be linked to the manner in which John Paul II describes human fatherhood in *Familiaris Consortio*: "In revealing and in reliving on earth the very fatherhood of God, a man is called upon to ensure the harmonious and united development of all the members of the family" (*FC* 25).

Despite modernity's penchant (for political reasons) to deemphasize any substantial distinction between fatherhood and motherhood, the fundamental differences cannot be eradicated. Because of biology and the fact that the child develops within the womb for nine months, the mother normally forms a bond with the child. The mother of a child is changed through the process of pregnancy and birth, and this bonding is achieved primarily on a biological-emotional level for the woman which is extended to the spiritual dimension as well. This is not true in the same way for the father. The very process of conception is a process in which the man momentarily engages in intercourse with a woman and then is fundamentally left outside the process, which takes place wholly within the woman's body. He remains an outsider until the child is born, when he can see and touch the child. Psychologically, bonding between father and child is achieved only when some events or set of events intervene and a societal framework is provided that will enable this to take place. It is not a guaranteed reality but is a fragile societal achievement.[45] Miller shows why the problems that we have seen in the last half of the twentieth century have emerged:

> Due to the marginality of males in the reproductive process, fathering is a cultural acquisition to an extent that mothering is not. Hence, when a culture ceases to support a father's involvement with his own children (through its laws, mores, symbols, models, rituals) powerful natural forces take over in favor of the mother-alone family.

These are valuable psychological insights but they need to be properly modified by a Biblical theology of creation and of the body. It is clear that fatherhood resides innately within the male, waiting for fulfillment.[46] This requires not only sexual union with a female but also

45. See the comment by Peter Wilson: "An adult female will be naturally transformed into a social mother when she bears a child, but there is no corresponding natural transformation for a male," in *Man the Promising Primate: The Conditions of Human Evolution*, 2d ed. (New Haven, Conn.: Yale University Press, 1983), 71, quoted by Miller in *Biblical Faith and Fathering*, 11.

46. Miller's insights are excellent but need to be better situated within the principles of creation. An example of this approach is the theology of the body as developed by John Paul II who establishes the sacramental principle which shows that the human body is revelatory of the person. Masculinity and femininity are not accidents of the human person (like

a process of socialization that affirms the reality of the man's paternity and directs him towards the full acceptance of it. For this to be achieved on a societal level, rituals are necessary which acknowledge the necessity of fatherhood for the child's well-being; also required are social structures that punish those who reject the primary responsibility for their own children.[47]

In ancient Israel, *three* important father-rituals served to establish and reinforce the father-child bond and helped to define the nature of fatherhood within the covenant: *redemption of the first-born, circumcision,* and *Passover.*[48] Each ritual is directly expressive of Yahweh's covenant with Israel, mirrors that relationship, and has a formative impact on the father-child relationship.[49] These three rituals were central

---

hair color) but are, in fact, what constitute the being of the person. Each gender is ordered to a teleological purpose which is fulfilled in the light of the other. The unique specification of masculinity (being a husband and father) and femininity (being a wife and mother) are consequently not accidents either, but are derived from the essence of each person's nature and are, therefore, not interchangeable. Men and women are ontological realities, not merely manipulable biological matter. Their biological specificity is intrinsically tied to who they are (their nature) and to their final end (*telos*). Their very bodily structures are, therefore, revelatory of who they are. Their mission (as father and mother) proceeds out of who they are (as masculine and feminine persons) and this is historicized in their bodily structures which must always be respected.

47. Miller's basic thesis (that fatherhood is a cultural achievement) is well argued and a major contribution to the modern discussion on fatherhood. However, one major criticism of his presentation is that fatherhood could be construed as an extrinsic reality to the psychobiology of the man, that is, being only a societal construct which has been agreed upon (in a positivistic manner) which is then superimposed on the males in a given society. This we would strongly argue against, and, in fact was not Miller's intention (as he confirmed in private conversation with me). Within the Judeo-Christian framework, masculinity is a created reality ordered within the divine will towards fatherhood and designed to reflect the divine fatherhood. This ordering guarantees that the psycho-biological structure of the man is apt for, and fulfilled in, fatherhood. The nature of the male is *intrinsically* linked to the reality of fatherhood.

48. Miller identifies these father-led rituals and provides insightful commentary on them in *Biblical Faith and Fathering*, 55–70.

49. The blessing of children is not part of these three father-led rituals. Scripturally it is differentiated from the three primary home rituals, which specifically condition the covenant and the community of Israel in a way blessings do not. The three home rituals are God-given commandments, having a specific form, and are constitutive of the structure of the Israelite community. To disobey would wreak incalculable damage on the covenantal

to the family's structure and enabled it to become the medium and matrix of the divine covenant. This is well expressed in McLuhan's phase: "the medium is the message." The following analysis will show how the family, the rituals, the covenant and fatherhood were all intrinsically bound to and dependent upon each other.[50]

The Redemption of the First-born

The first ritual to be examined, the redemption of the first-born, is directly related to the actions Yahweh performed to secure the safety and rescue of Israel as recorded in Exodus 13. The meaning of the rite is linked to the final redemptive act by which Yahweh brought Israel out of Egypt, that is, the death of the first-born of Egypt. This ritual memorializes that sacrifice which was the direct cause for the liberation of the Hebrews.

> When Pharaoh stubbornly refused to let us go, the Lord slew all the first-born in the land of Egypt, both the first-born of man and the first-born of cattle. Therefore I sacrifice to the Lord all the males that first open the womb; but all the first-born of my sons I redeem. (^Ex 13:15)

Accordingly, the ritual associated with this event dealt only with the first-born son or the first-born of animals. The Lord's instructions in +Ex 13:2 states: "Consecrate to me all the first born, all that first opens the womb." Throughout their succeeding generations, the Israelites would never forget the cost of their freedom. Every first-born, whether or man or beast, had to be offered to the Lord with the proviso that

---

community. Blessings, per se, do not have the same form, nor are they related in the same way to the formal structure of Israel. But the physical blessings by the father were of vital importance as they were the means of transferring the Abrahamic blessing from generation to generation (see Gn 27:30ff., dealing with the blessing of Isaac).

50. This did not mean that mothers did not play a valuable role as well. Köstenberger examines the specific contribution that mothers made to the home. It is clear, he states, that "the wife and mother were functionally subordinated to her husband and male head of the household." But there is clear evidence of dignity and influence in the home. His analysis points to complimentarity of relationship, mothers naming children and coming to the defense of their daughter's questioned virginity, mother's wisdom being paralleled with the father's, and women influencing their husband. Proverbs 31 is said to show that a woman is not subservient. See Köstenberger, *God, Marriage, and Family*, 97.

the first-born son had always to be redeemed by a substitutionary sacrifice. In this reenactment of the original redemption, the core element of Israel's salvation was transmitted anew to each generation. Here, as noted above, the educational principle of the "teachable moment" came into play. As children saw only the first-born animals being sacrificed,[51] their curiosity would be aroused on seeing a special ritual associated with the first-born son. Then an explanation for the redemption ritual could be given "when your son asks you in time to come, 'What is this?'" (+Ex 13:14). Within the rite of redemption of the first-born son, the events of the original redemption would be narrated, effecting a type of *anamnesis* during which the grace of Yahweh's redemptive act in the Exodus would now be applied in the concrete here-and-now to the contemporary family. Like his ancestor in Egypt, this child was being redeemed. Today this ritual takes the following form:

> As the father approaches the rabbi with his child, he is asked whether he wishes to redeem his child or leave him at the altar. The father in reply expresses his desire to redeem and keep his son, hands over the redemption money as a substitute, and then recites two benedictions.... The rabbi then solemnly pronounces three times: "Your son is redeemed, your son is redeemed, your son is redeemed."[52]

This ritual has several profound psychological effects. First, there is the awareness of the absolute value of human life: the child must be redeemed and cannot be allowed to die. Secondly, each family (precisely because this is a family ritual) and the whole community are renewed each time by this reliving of the central redemptive act by which Israel was delivered. The action of Yahweh was not just an historical narrative. Rather, through the ritual re-telling of the first redemption of the first-born son, it was lived out in the present moment. Thus an organic link was forged afresh between the generations by each re-enactment. Never could Israel move away from this decisive event or substitute something in its place.

51. See Matthew Henry's commentary on Ex 13:1-16 in *Commentary on the Whole Bible*, Vol. 1 (Genesis to Deuteronomy) (Old Tappan, N.J.: Fleming H. Revell Company, n.d.), 324–26.

52. Miller, *Biblical Faith and Fathering*, 73–74.

On a psychological level, this ritual act effects a strong bond between father and child, and the relationship is objectively proclaimed before the community.[53] In this rite the father is confronted existentially with the choice which he alone must make. *On a symbolic level, the true meaning of fatherhood is revealed.* The man is faced with a life or death decision. He can walk away from this new life, maintaining his independence and personal freedom, or he can accept responsibility. Existentially, this means that the father is willing to take on the responsibility for forming this child in Torah, which means subordinating his own desires to the child's needs. *Symbolically,* this is a moment of existential crisis; the consequences of his decision are clear: his rejection will result in the death of the child, while his acceptance will result in the flourishing of the child's life. Such is the importance and meaning of fatherhood. This is the existential question facing a man *qua* father. This is the drama of fatherhood. Will he accept responsibility for this child and do what is necessary to save and redeem his life or will he let the child die? In consciously accepting the responsibility for his son, he acknowledges the child as his own and establishes a primary bond with him.[54] As Miller has shown, such rituals are needed to enable a man to embrace fully his fatherhood consciously.[55]

For the child, the ritual provides a foundation for his self-understanding. First, through this ritual enactment, the child's father has been identified to the community, thereby providing the child with his own identity, fundamental security, and a "place of belonging." Secondly, through the ritual, the father proclaims how valued his son is to him.[56] This rite of redemption witnesses to the incalculable value the

53. In the ancient world, and until the invention of DNA testing, one could never be certain of the paternity of a child; one could be certain only that a specific woman was the parent of a specific child. The *rite of redemption* provides an instrument by which the father would accept responsibility for a specific child and proclaim, in an objective and binding manner, his paternity, thus strengthening the family bond.

54. It is easy to see how this type of ritual confirms the man in his identity as father and provides instruction (in an explicit manner) as to where his duty lies.

55. See chapter 2, "Origins of the Father-Involved Family," in Miller's "The Idea of God as Father," in Eberly, *Faith Factor in Fatherhood,* 208.

56. Cf. Miller, *Biblical Faith and Fathering,* 74. There is a second aspect to this ritual as

community placed on children and their essential role in the covenant.

This father-led ritual provided the hermeneutic by which father-hood was understood in Israel. The redemption of the first-born ritually imaged forth what Yahweh had done for His son, Israel.[57] In this way, and precisely because of the terminology used, fatherhood in Israel was meant to reflect the fatherhood of God. As Miller noted, "To redeem and care for children in this manner was spiritually motivated; since this was what Yahweh himself had done in redeeming *His* children from Egypt, this is only what human fathers can be expected to do with their children as well."[58] Through these rituals and the recitation of the Exodus narrative, a religious consciousness of Yahweh as a *caring* and protective Father was developed and experienced, especially in the family. Because of this, the family came to be the instrument through which each generation encountered the salvific activity of God. As such, *the family became the carrier and medium of the covenant.* The medium was the message.

Circumcision

Circumcision was the second major father-led ritual. It was an essential part of the salvific covenant given by Yahweh to Abraham and was to be practiced in every generation (Genesis 17). A careful analysis is necessary here because, while circumcision is a symbol deeply tied to the meaning of the covenant, this meaning is not readily grasped. A key requirement for all males in the Abrahamic household was that they be

---

well. Psychoanalytical literature shows that there can often be a rivalry (albeit unconscious) between a father and his sons, particularly with the first-born son, who is seen as a primary antagonist, seeking to overthrow the father's authority (cf. the Oedipus complex). One could speculate that this ritual goes a long way toward resolving this discord by having the father affirm his love and care for the son in such an objective manner.

57. This link becomes eminently clear in the sacrifice of Jesus, the Lamb of God who is also the first-born. Within the narrative of salvation history within Judaism, the cost of freedom for the enslaved Hebrews was the life of the first-born of all Egypt. Pharaoh continually refused the Lord's command, and it was only when God brought about the death of first-born of man and beast (which is central to the original Passover experience) that Pharaoh finally agreed to let Israel go. Freedom cost the life of the first-born, all of which now are sanctified to the Lord.

58. Miller, *Biblical Faith and Fathering,* 74.

circumcised in accordance with the terms of the covenant. If not, they would be cut off (נִכְרְתָה / *nikrʾtaʰ*) from God's people (Gn 17:14). Being a member of Abraham's household demanded circumcision. This was true for those naturally born into his family, foreigners wishing to be incorporated into Abraham, and for those who were purchased as servants. Thus, while biological descent was important,[59] it was never fully determinative of continued covenantal membership. Something else (circumcision) was always required for males, which, in some ways, opened up the boundaries of the covenant beyond biological membership.

Sometimes, mistakenly, circumcision is understood only horizontally and is seen as "the mark of this paternal covenant between father and son."[60] While undoubtedly a profound link is formed between father and son through this ritual, it is important to interpret exactly what the father is doing here and whom he represents. Rabbi S. Raphael Hirsch provides a corrective to this restrictive interpretation in his exegesis of Genesis. He shows that in the rite of circumcision the father is acting not primarily as a father, but as the representative of the community/family of Abraham. One must understand that, when he enters his sons into the covenant, his individual fatherhood is enfolded into, and participates in, the primordial fatherhood of Abraham. He is doing what Abraham did.

Hirsch begins by establishing the fact that the very existence of Israel is predicated on the grace of God. Israel exists *only* because God intervened in the life of the aged Abraham and Sarah and made it possible for her to conceive (see Gn 15). After God had chosen Abraham and established the covenant with him, Yahweh had to directly intervene to enable the family line to proceed physically from Abraham's own aged body and Sarah's barren womb. This gratuitous act of God, *and this alone*, allowed Israel to come into existence. Thus, both the covenant and the Abrahamic family are predicated completely on God's grace.

59. In the case of Isaac, it was necessary that the heir to the covenant come from the body of Abraham (see Gn 15:3–4).

60. Miller, *Biblical Faith and Fathering*, 62. It is important to see the father as not only the individual but also the representative of the Abrahamic community.

The covenant is not earned but received. Consequently, for the natural born Jew, the covenant is the very basis of his existence.

> This duty [to keep the covenant] is incumbent on all of Abraham's descendants. These descendants have to thank this duty undertaken by Abraham not only for their spiritual and moral calling *but even for their very physical and material existence.* Their whole existence proceeded from this duty undertaken. Without it no Isaac would have been born. They only came into existence under this condition, and only breathe as the children of this covenant. Their very existence itself makes them in duty bound to keep this covenant.[61]

Circumcision represents more than the establishment of a father-son relationship, important as that is. There is always the communal dimension which goes beyond the individual family. Even within the giving of the command to circumcise, Hirsch finds a relational progression between the family and the nation:

> First of all the command is given in three sentences.... First the command to the nation...the nation is to be responsible that...everyone who belongs to you becomes circumcised. This then has the result...that everyone of us has the Mila [circumcision] performed on himself...so that it can be a sign of the covenant with God for him.... Only in verse 13 is the command given to the father, *and the duty placed on him to perform the Mila on his children, and indeed, highly significantly, not as a father on his son, but as the representative of an Abrahamitic house on those born to his household.* Every child of such a household is born to, and acquired by, the Abrahamitic community, and every representative of an Abrahamitic house has to see to it that the Mila is preformed on every male member of his house for that community.[62]

It is evident that within the covenant there is a mutual interdependence between the family and the nation; both are essential. In the constitutive rite of circumcision, the father acts both as father for his own child and as a father of the community (acting, as it were, in the *persona* of father Abraham). The father, by virtue of the covenant of circumcision which he has received in his own body, is now the transmitter of

---

61. Hirsch, *Genesis*, 298–99 (emphasis added).
62. Ibid.

that tradition. He is responsible for the covenant, and hence acts as the representative for the whole Abrahamic community in history.[63] This he does, not only for his own children, but for everyone in his household.

Bearer of Spiritual Traditions זֵכֶר / זָכָר (zāchār / z'hor)

Without an understanding of Hebrew anthropology, the fact that only the male receives the sign of the covenant would seem to deny the covenant to everyone in the family. At best, such a practice would seem to be the remains of an obscure and antiquated religion. Further study shows that this practice was not arbitrary but reflective of the Semitic understanding of the human person. As in creation, there is an originating single point from which the many come but which ensures the organic relationships among all the different members; the many can be consolidated into a single entity. Hence, there is always a corporate dimension of the person that is in deep contrast to the modern atomistic constructs of the person and family.

Hirsch, in commenting on Gn 1:27 sought out the differentiation between male and female by philologically exploring the two Hebrew terms zāchār (male) and n'qēbāh (female).

> Zākār [is] from zākār to remember, [and is] related to skr, sgr,—the spiritual "keeper" of godliness, and of human traditions. The male sex forms the perpetuators, the links of the chain of traditions. Nĕqēbāh [is]—from nqb to determine, decide, fix—the "fixed" one...it is only in conjunction with the man and in joining his efforts that woman finds

63. By Jewish law (*Tractate Kiddushin* 29A), it is the father's responsibility to have his sons circumcised. This is called *berith milah* in Hebrew. In Gn 17:9 God commands Abraham to keep his covenant and in Gn 17:10 the covenant is defined as having all the males in his household circumcised. Abraham, as head of his house, is responsible for this and this is a primary responsibility that devolves upon every father of each Abrahamic household. While fathers in ancient times carried this duty out themselves, gradually the office of *mohel* developed, which consisted of men trained to carry out circumcision safely. But always, the responsibility lay with the father. That the father acts as a representative of the Abrahamic community is shown in that, if a father refuses to carry out this duty, the responsibility to see that the child is circumcised is not the mother's, but devolves to the *beth din* (the authoritative Jewish council). The community must ensure that a Jewish son is faithful to the Abrahamic covenant.

the decision for the particular direction and particular sphere in which she is to carry out her share in the common joint mission of mankind.[64]

Hirsch saw that within the covenantal structures, the man and woman (because of their different natures) possessed differentiated roles. He observed that the words for "male" and "to remember" have the same root, *zāchār*. Thus, for Hirsch the *zāchār*-ness of the male (i.e., his maleness) is rooted in his mission to remember. As such, within the covenant, the fundamental function of *zāchār*/male was that of "bearer of the spiritual traditions of mankind."[65] In this way, the male is obligated to remember the covenant; he becomes the spiritual link between the generations.[66] Hence, "the perpetuation of the fundamental condition of the Abrahamitic covenant of God is to be performed on the body of that sex."[67] This resonates analogously to some degree with Aquinas's thought that, as natural head of the family, the father would be the one to preside at cultic functions. In each case, the male becomes the link between the generations in terms of covenantal knowledge and practice. Hirsch directly connects this understanding of *zāchār* maleness with the covenant of circumcision, "the special Abrahamitic tradition."[68] It is the man who, having the obligation *to remember* the covenant, carries its mark in his body and, in turn, inscribes it on the bodies of *his* sons.[69]

64. S. R. Hirsch, *Genesis*, 33. The complementarity of these roles is expressed by M. Kaufman: "The Jewish idea is that marriage brings a couple to the complete state in which they can establish proper communion with God. It creates out of two individual complementary entities a single, transcendent superentity of mystical significance through which, in the words of the Sages, 'heaven and earth embrace'" (Michael Kaufman, *Love, Marriage, and Family in Jewish Law and Tradition* [Northvale, N.J.: Jason Aronson Inc., 1996], 8).

65. Hirsch, *Genesis*, 301.

66. This idea is explored and given validation in the essays found in Eberly, *Faith Factor in Fatherhood* (see note 44).

67. Hirsch, *Genesis*, 301.

68. Ibid.

69. See A. Murtonen, *Hebrew in Its West Semitic Setting: A Comparative Survey of Non-Masoretic, Hebrew Dialects and Traditions: A Comparative Lexicon* (Leiden: E. J. Brill, 1986), 165, the entry for *zkr*: "The Bed entry may be a loan from Arab, and so the root is limited to Sem. On the other hand, I do not see reason to divide it into two, as both the concept of memory…and masculinity share the salient characteristics of active nature, virility; both are also represented in all the major Sem subdivision."

The male is considered as "the 'remembering one', so that the duty of... studying the Law, devolves primarily on him." The woman has another sphere in which to carry out her mission. She "is given the great task of forming and directing the earthly home as a place in which the godly spiritual, joined to all the earthly material, lives a life of blossoming and development."[70] Both aspects are essential and complementary to each other.[71] The rite of circumcision would be of no effect if there were no home environment in which the covenant could be lived out and transmitted through the generations. On the other hand, *the home would not be effective if there were no authority or organic continuity with the Abrahamic community.* The key principle here is that one cannot invent the covenant. One can only receive and transmit it. Thus, both the man and the woman, and the differentiated male and female roles and spheres of influence, are essential.[72]

Circumcision as Covenant

The rite of circumcision is particularly useful to help us understand how the family is both "medium" and "message." In Gn 17:10–11, circumcision is called both a covenant (בְּרִיתִי / b⁰rîtî) and a sign of the covenant (לְאוֹת בְּרִית / l⁰'ôt b⁰rît). While at first this text may appear contradictory, it nonetheless holds in tension two truths about circum-

---

70. Hirsch, *Genesis*, 301.

71. Köstenberger examines the role and responsibilities of women in ancient Israel in *God, Marriage, and Family.* He is clear that, while there is differentiation, it does not mean that women become some form of chattel. There were certainly threats to her dignity, such as divorce and polygamy. While there is a subordinate role, it did not mean that she was subservient. See Köstenberger, *God, Marriage, and Family,* p. 97. He approvingly refers to the thorough study by Daniel Block, extensively quoting him: "to view women in ancient Israel as chattel of their husbands and fathers is to commit a fundamental fallacy: the failure to distinguish between authority and ownership, legal dependence and servitude, functional subordination and possession" ("Marriage and Family in Ancient Israel," 64–65.)

72. It is important to grasp the fundamental meaning of עֵזֶר ('ezer) in this connection. This is the appellation used of the first woman in Eden. The Lord was seeking to provide an 'ezer (helper) suitable for the man to help him carry out his life project. This includes the bringing forth of the next generation and forming it in godly ways. For this, the woman is indispensable. It must be remembered that the word 'ezer does not imply something negative. It is properly translated as *helper* and is also applied to Yahweh in His relationship with Israel. (See 2 Kgs 14:26; Ps 30:10; 54:6.) He enables Israel to realize her mission.

cision, both of which are important to grasp. As Hirsch astutely comments:

> In a striking manner the Mila [circumcision] itself is first called *brît,*
> so that the performance of it itself seems to be fulfilling the covenant,
> and then, in the following verse it is declared to be *'ôt brît*...the sign of
> the covenant, as a symbol to represent *brît* so that the fulfillment of the
> covenant itself must be something transcending the mere act of the circumcision.[73]

Thus, at one and the same time, circumcision is identified with the covenant but also is the sign of something greater than itself. There is a sense in which circumcision does contain the meaning of the covenant and, therefore, *is* the covenant. On the other hand, one is never to forget that the covenant *transcends* this physical act and contains a reality which is always greater. Likewise, the family appears to function on two levels vis-à-vis the covenant. On one level, the family is the instrument by which one is taught about and introduced to the covenant. But at the same time, the family and its rituals are the very matrix in which the covenant is lived out historically. The first covenant-as-family (and conversely, family-as-covenant) was established in and through the person of Abraham (see Gn 12:3: וְנִבְרְכוּ בְךָ /*v'nikr'hû b'kā*—in you shall be blessed). The covenant was cut into the flesh of the sons through a familial ritual led by the father. To not be circumcised would cause one to be separated from the covenantal community in father Abraham.

The identity and, therefore, the existence of the family were grounded in this covenant. This prevented "family" from being reduced to the immediate, atomistic present. Instead, the family extended back through time to the origin of the covenant and forward into the future to comprise all those who were of Abraham's household and circumcised. The extension of the covenant through time was achieved through the family generations; hence the covenant and circumcision were bound up together. Therefore, it can equally be said that the iden-

---

73. Hirsch, *Genesis*, 299. Within the Christian context, Paul saw that baptism was the fulfillment of circumcision. (See Col 2:11ff.)

tity and, therefore, the existence of the covenant are grounded in the family. In the Abrahamic family, the two are *inextricably* linked.

Passover

The third father-led ritual was the Passover. This is the ritual meal that commemorated the salvific experience of the Jews when they were delivered from Pharaoh and were formed into a nation. For our purposes, it is important to note that this event and its commemorating rite were focused on the individual family. The Exodus narrative makes clear that the family is the basic unit in God's salvific design. The father of each family was commanded to take a lamb into his care and then slaughter it on the fourteenth day of the month. "Tell all the congregation of Israel that on the tenth day of this month they shall take every man a lamb according to their fathers' houses, a lamb for a household" (^Gn 12:3). While God is saving Israel as a nation, the salvific action is confined to the individual homes and the actions of the fathers of these homes; individuals are saved in and through their own personal family structure.[74] The dramatic action of the narrative had two foci. Outside, the individual homes were marked with blood, while inside, a ritual meal connected with the salvific actions of Yahweh was eaten as a family meal (Gn 12:4).

The Passover is of essential importance for Christians because Jesus, Himself, links His Passion to the Exodus-Passover complex. We will, therefore, draw out some of the key correspondences. From the New Testament perspective, these two historical events, the Passover and Passion, are understood to be differentiated points in the same continuous trajectory of God's salvific will. They interpenetrate each other. What began in the Exodus is taken up and reaches its teleological fulfillment in Christ. Thus, for the early Church, the symbolic density of the Exodus was revealed *in* the light of Christ. Jesus situates His own salvific mission within the Passover and, strikingly, Moses and Elijah

---

74. Thomas Dozeman captures the corporate nature of the paschal act in the Exodus ritual: "The point of emphasis in the slaughter of the Passover victim is on the houses, not on the individual Israelites.... Instead, the blood of the Passover victim protects each Israelite house" (*Commentary on Exodus*, 267).

speak about Jesus' Passion in terms of his exodus (ἔξοδον αὐτοῦ) when they meet Him during the Transfiguration (Lk 9:31). The houses during the original Exodus were to be marked with blood from the sacrificial lamb in a specific manner (Ex 11:9). Dozeman notes the symbolic significance of the door in the home and shows how the use of blood unites the home and the Temple:

> The doorway is the point of vulnerability, the threshold into a home. Each Israelite house must be protected from the ensuing plague of death by placing the blood of the Passover victim on its frame, including the doorposts and the lintel. The blood on the doorpost invites comparison to the tabernacle altar.[75]

The home now becomes the locus of the cult, the place where blood is ritually manipulated in obedience with God's law. In this way the Israelite home becomes associated with the Temple. The divine cult is to be exercised not only in the sacred space of the Temple; now the family becomes an extension, to some degree, of that same sacred space. Dozeman shows not only the liturgical importance of the home in the Jewish experience but also its spiritual importance:

> All light, including fire, has been eliminated in the plague of darkness (10:21–29). The absence of light indicates a cosmological battle.... Death is on the horizon. It has enveloped the land. The only oases from the consuming darkness are the individual Israelite houses. Each is lit up in the sea of darkness (10:23). They now become the setting for the drama of the Passover.[76]

According to the instructions given to Moses, the blood was applied to the lintel (top bar) of the door and then the two side posts. On a midrashic level, this can be understood as forming a cross of blood which

---

75. Dozeman, *Exodus*, 267.

76. Ibid. This view of the Israelite home and its relationship to the cult and its role in salvation history captures in Old Testament terms the ecclesial nature of the home. This theological vision sees the cosmic battle that continues from the Fall until the consummation of history and understands the covenantal home of believers to be the place where the chosen people of God gather out of the darkness and into the revealed light of God. Within this covenantal home, this ecclesial matrix, as it were, a person is protected and begins to experience the powerful action of God.

covered the houses in Egypt with the blood of the sacrificial lamb.[77]

The New Testament bears witness to this intrinsic connection between Christ's Passion and the Passover as noted in Luke (9:31). The NT records that Jesus, before His death, took the unleavened bread (*matzot*) and wine, the principal elements of the Jewish Passover meal, and transformed them into His Body and Blood during the Last Supper with His disciples. Paul in 1 Cor 5:7 refers to Christ as our Passover. It is clear that both Jesus and the NT writers directly connected the Hebrew meal of liberation with the work on the Cross that would introduce final freedom into the created order. In Christ, the salvific meal of the chosen family of Abraham reached its fulfillment by being transformed into the salvific meal of the universal Church.

It is important to note that it is the family that provides the context for experiencing the mighty redemptive work of God. The angel of death passed over those who stayed within the confines of the family, observing the Passover ritual in homes marked with the blood of the lamb. The meal became the pedagogical means by which the salvific event of the Passover was participated in and transmitted from one generation to another. "When your children ask you, 'What does this rite of yours mean?' you shall reply, 'This is the Passover sacrifice of the LORD'" (•Ex 12:26–27). The family was the only means by which this event continued in the religious consciousness of the Jewish people throughout history. The family Seder meal linked Israel with God's salvific activity in Egypt.

Conclusion

In the Old Testament, the covenant and the family are inextricably bound together. It was the divine will to link salvation with the cove-

---

77. Note that this analysis is speculative: one can propose that this application of blood might result in a stylized cross being marked on the homes. The blood was applied using a hyssop branch and, as a liquid, would streak the top bar (the lintel) of the door frame and then drip down. It is plausible that the father would have put the blood in a bowl and, using the hyssop branch, applied the blood to each of the side posts with a sweeping motion. In effect, he would be tracing out a rude cross of blood. This, of course, is speculative. The key, which is not speculative, is that the homes of the faithful were covered with the blood of the Passover lamb.

nantal family. Concisely put, the family in the OT becomes *the carrier of the covenant* in history. It must be remembered that for the family to be assumed into this salvific process, it had to be created with a nature that could receive and fulfill this covenantal mission. Hence, while the family is certainly a sociological phenomenon, it also possesses a profound theological meaning that needs to be comprehended. Grounded in creation, it received a divinely appointed mission to be the carrier of the covenant. Having established these parameters, the third area of investigation will examine the theological *functioning* of family in the OT. In the following chapter, our examination will show that the family takes on an iconic role and *images forth* the reality of the covenant in several key areas and in this fulfills its destined purpose.

CHAPTER 5

FAMILY AS
IMAGE OF THE
COVENANT

SYMBOL AND SIGN

Although the differences between a sign and a symbol are not always clear, one general distinction is that the symbol inwardly participates in the reality and shows forth what it represents, whereas the sign is of an arbitrary nature vis-à-vis the object represented.[1] As we have seen, the family is an intrinsic part of the Hebraic revelation and plays a symbolic role in the cov-

---

1. "The symbol is closer to the thing signified, and is less arbitrary than the sign.... The symbol in the sense so defined stems from man's essential constitution as a spirit-body.... Hence the symbol does not refer to something else. A reality appears in it—in "the other of itself"—which is there and present but not fully exhausted by this appearance" (Jörg Splett, "Symbol," *Sacramentum Mundi*, ed. Karl Rahner, vol. 6 [New York: Herder and Herder, 1970], 199). One has to be careful when entering into a discussion on symbolism. Usually, the understanding stated in the above text obtains, but there are authors who reverse this understanding and thus have the sign as participating in the reality more than the symbol. Another problem can arise when the word "symbol" is used in a sacramental context; it can convey the idea of unreality or non-identification. It is important to realize that there are various degrees of symbolic participation, ascending all the way to the Eucharist. Whenever "symbol" is used in the sacramental context, it is used in its most profound sense. Here the distance between that which is symbolized and that which is used as symbol is collapsed and there is an identification between the two. The bread becomes the Body of the Lord.

128

enant. The Abrahamic family not only carries and transmits the covenant but also inwardly participates in it. There are two critical questions that flow from this fact: What within the created nature of the family allows for this role? And, in what specific ways does the family image forth the covenant?[2]

To begin with, it is important to recognize that the covenant relationship in the Old Testament between Yahweh and Israel is *explicitly* depicted in familial terms. Ontologically, this begins with the initiation of the covenant with Abraham. The salvific design of God is centered on one person (Abram) and is extended to his family. The covenant is inextricably bound to the person of Abraham and all who are organically united to him as family. It is grounded in the family of Abraham and can have no other form than a familial one. Though Abraham's organic family provides the medium for the covenant, it is not until the experience of the Exodus that family-specific terminology begins to be applied to the covenant per se.

The God who frees Israel from the slavery of Egypt reveals Himself to be a Father to His people: "Is He not your Father who bought you?" (+Dt 32:6).[3] In this experience of deliverance, the sonship of Israel is also revealed: "And you shall say to Pharaoh, 'Thus says the Lord: Israel is my son, my firstborn son, and I say to you, 'Let my son go'" (+Ex 4:22–23). Deuteronomy goes further and establishes a *causal* relationship between the call to holiness (and all its specific demands) and the status of Israel as sons. This is clear in those prescriptions of the Law where the regulation and their rationale are both given: "You are the sons of the Lord your God; you shall not cut yourselves..." (^Dt 14:1).[4]

---

2. I have devised and use this compound phrase "image forth" to indicate the symbolic nature of created reality (keeping in mind the limits of the *anologia entis*) so that nature and the structure of specific things can have iconic value pointing to greater realities beyond themselves which at times involves some form of participation. Thus, human fatherhood can be an image of the fatherhood of God and, therefore, can be said to "image forth" God's fatherhood in an analogous manner. Human sonship becomes an image of how we relate to our heavenly Father. As well, human sonship becomes a way of expressing the relationship of Jesus to the Father that requires an ontological participation.

3. See Miller, *Biblical Faith and Fathering*, 50.

4. This concept of God, as Miller noted, sharply contrasts with that of the pagan cultures

Thus, within the earliest strata of the revelation, the covenant is perceived as a familial reality, both ontologically and terminologically.

Later, this understanding grows and receives even greater clarity and depth of meaning within the prophets. When Israel is faced with the inevitable consequences of her apostasy, the prophets arise to witness to the concept of divine paternity. Hosea reveals the tenderness of Yahweh's paternal concern: "When Israel was a youth, I loved him, and I called my son out of Egypt" (+Hos 11:1). In Jeremiah, Yahweh declares His fatherly care for Israel: "I will make them walk by brooks of water, in a straight path in which they shall not stumble; for I am a father to Israel, and Ephraim is my first-born." (^Jer 31:9) The prophecies of Isaiah both begin and end with the statement of Yahweh's paternity.[5]

Most importantly, it is also within the prophetic canon that marital terminology is used with greater intensity and clarity, revealing Yahweh as the "husband" of Israel. Isaiah develops his theme of creation within a specific nuptial paradigm: "For your Maker is your husband [בֹעֲלַיִךְ / bōʿălayiḥ], the LORD of Hosts is his name" (+Is 54:5). Jeremiah applies this same marital language to the redeeming actions of God as far back as the Exodus: "They broke my covenant, and (though) I had married [בָּעַלְתִּי / bāʿaltî] them" (+Jer 31:32). This is powerful language which, on one level, could be easily misunderstood because of the surrounding pagan cults, which had assumed sexuality into their worship and had used sexuality as a means of manipulating the divine realm.[6] Thus it would seem there was a need for a trajectory within the biblical witness that developed the language of the covenant with God first in the less problematic familial terms; only at a later stage did it include the fuller nuptial dimension.

---

surrounding Israel. God is truly Father and not a mother-figure. As well, Yahweh, as Father, demands His people "shall serve him exclusively and alone" (Ex 20:3; Dt 5:7) (Miller, *Biblical Faith and Fathering*, 50).

5. "Sons have I reared and brought up" (^Is. 1:2) / "But, You, O LORD, are our Father" (+Is. 64:8).

6. The sexualizing of the gods and the existence of cult prostitution resulted in human sexuality itself being mythologized and becoming an instrument by which to obtain favor from the gods. As has been demonstrated, Israel's faith was constructed on a totally different basis.

But underlying this pagan concept was an authentic *intuition* that somehow our sexuality is related to the divine reality. Unfortunately, the ancient pagan faiths misconstrued this relationship and engendered their gods and made a direct correlation between the human experience of sex and that of their gods. Israel's long history of monotheism and its effect of demythologizing sexuality acted both as a corrective to this pagan paradigm and as a protection against confusing and intermingling the nature of Yahweh and human sexuality. But what was the relationship between human sexuality and the divine sphere? Although it would not be fully resolved until the appearance of the Bridegroom in the New Testament, the resolution of this problem had begun to be articulated by the time of the prophets. For the moment, Yahweh could at least identify Himself as husband without any possibility of the Hebrews sexualizing the divine sphere.

In a similar fashion, Hosea extends the use of familial language to express the fundamental nature of Israel's covenant with Yahweh. In his prophetic work, the marital relationship (along with family life and particularly the birth of children) is used analogously to graphically portray the present condition of the covenant. The marriage and family life of the prophet Hosea are purposely used by God (albeit in a negative fashion) to show the covenantal status of the people of Israel. Not only does Gomer, the unfaithful wife-prostitute (זְנוּנִים אֵשֶׁת / 'eshet z'nûnîm),[7] illustrate the apostasy of Israel in dramatic terms, but the children brought forth from this union also played a prophetic role in imaging forth what the destructive future of Israel was to be. Yahweh instructs Hosea: "Go, take to yourself a wife of harlotry and have children of harlotry.... She [Gomer] conceived and bore a son. And the LORD said, 'Call his name *Not my people* [(עַמִּי לֹא / lō' 'ammî], for you are not my people and I am not your God'" (+Hos 1:2–9).[8] Thus, Ho-

---

7. אֵשֶׁת זְנוּנִים ('eshet z'nûnîm) means "wife (אֵשֶׁת / 'eshet) of fornications (זְנוּ־ נִים / z'nûnîm)." The word for fornication is used in the plural and is the intensive mode of זְנוּת (z'nût). This phrase can be translated as "wife of harlotry."

8. In Hebrew, the word עַמִּי ('ammî) is the word for people. Here it is modified by the negative particle (לֹא / lō'). In this context, the name of Hosea's child is announcing Israel's loss of the covenant.

sea's life as a husband and father becomes a living image of how Israel lived out her covenant with Yahweh. As James Limburg comments:

> For no other prophet were professional calling and personal life so closely linked as for Hosea.... The three children who grew up in the village and played in its streets also shared in the prophet's task, as walking audio-visual aids in the service of the prophetic message of doom. For Hosea there was no separation between office and home, vocation and family life.[9]

Thus, the family structures are clearly used as a means by which the divine covenant with Israel can be expressed. But the question is, to what extent is one to take this language? Revelation is "essentially a dialogue in which God addresses man."[10] Consequently, revelation has to be couched in human terms taken from human experience in order to be understandable. One can easily see how marriage, because of its very communitarian nature, "became the means of revealing the covenant."[11] Is the relationship between the covenant and marriage merely extrinsic (which would render marriage and family arbitrary signs, used to help explain the covenant because of an accidental, surface resemblance)? Or do marriage and family have an intrinsic relationship to the covenant and somehow interiorly participate in it? Put another way, is this prophetic use of familial language only metaphoric or is something greater going on?

Schillebeeckx's analysis of biblical imagery can help us as we grapple with the theological functioning of family in such imagery. He points out that for any structure to be able to image forth the reality of the covenant, one of two things must be present. It must include "an intrinsic objective reference to the saving mystery of the covenant of grace, or at least be inwardly receptive and open to a reference of

9. James Limburg, *Hosea-Micah in Interpretation* (Atlanta: John Knox Press, 1988), 9. Cf. also Schillebeeckx's comment: "Hosea had three children by this marriage, two sons and a daughter. Their names, and especially the names of the two youngest children, show clearly that the curse of the worship of Baal was upon them" (Schillebeeckx, *Marriage*, 36).

10. Schillebeeckx, *Marriage*, 31.

11. Ibid., 32. "The married life of human beings, with all its ups and downs, its certainties about the past and its uncertainties about the future...all this forms the prism through which the prophets saw the saving covenant of God with his people" (ibid.).

this kind... (or) gain the inner reference from the revelation itself."[12] In his study on marriage, Schillebeeckx concludes that while marriage is used to express the covenant in the Old Testament, the fullness of its essential meaning is never revealed there. He makes the point that whenever "the connection between human marriage and the covenant is established... what is at issue is not marriage but this saving covenant, itself."[13] He is correct in that in Hosea and other places marriage is grasped in the OT as an effective medium to express the relationship of Yahweh to His people. But how far are we to take this? Is this mere metaphor or does this relationship have a more ontological sense to it?[14] It would seem that it is only with the arrival of Jesus, the Bridegroom, that marriage's intrinsic relationship to the covenant is fully understood.[15] As Schillebeeckx noted, there is no explicitly developed theology of marriage in the OT. Only in the revelation of Christ is the true nature of marriage fully united to the truth of salvation (cf. Eph 5).

On the other hand, it is possible to argue that in the OT the concept of *the family* was already assumed into the covenant to a much greater degree than marriage. The nuptial imagery does not clearly emerge in the Scriptures in any sustained fashion until the prophetic period, especially with Hosea, and then in a negative way. The concept of God as Father and Israel as His son(s) is found in the Torah (e.g., +Ex 4:22: "Thus says the LORD, 'Israel is My son, My first-born'"; +Dt 32:6: "Is he not your Father who bought you?"). It was the family, and specifically the Abrahamic family, which had already *become* the covenantal community from its inception. The covenant depended on the continued existence of this family line in which the promises would be fulfilled.

12. Ibid., 33.

13. Ibid., 31.

14. It is clear that all language used of God has to be analogous. According to the decree of Lateran IV, "For between creator and creature there can be noted no similarity so great that a greater dissimilarity cannot be seen between them [*maior dissimulitudo in tanta similitudine*] (Decree: *On the Error of Abbot Joachim*).

15. It should be noted that the intrinsic relationship is not denied, but neither is it grasped fully. What we have in the OT is the privileged use of marriage and family to express the covenant, which takes on greater and greater density as the trajectory of salvation history moves towards its conclusion in Christ.

Most important is the fact that Yahweh directly refers to Himself as "Father" and calls Israel His "son." These terms seem to be more than mere poetic speech. The use of such familial terminology would appear to define the nature of the participants in this covenantal relationship, and the familial nature of the covenant itself.[16] Though all terms must of necessity be analogical, they can, at the same time, represent something more than mere metaphor.

Although there could be different degrees of participation, it is clear from the biblical witness that both marriage and the family are expressive of the covenantal relationship that Yahweh has with His people. The relationship of marriage and family to the divine covenant was not an artificial construction. It was precisely because of their created natures and their prior ordination towards communion that marriage and family were able to receive the mission to image forth the reality of the covenant within the created order. Precisely because of their constitutive natures, they are vibrant images of the covenant, reflecting and participating in the divine, salvific reality.

FAMILY AS HOLY

While the family functions theologically as the image and carrier of the covenant, its *raison d'être* can be summed up in one word: "holiness." The family was to be the ordinary sphere of holiness, while the Temple was to be the extraordinary sphere. It is perhaps this theme of holiness which will prove the most fruitful in our search for the roots and meaning of "domestic church" in the Old Testament.

Given our modern mentality, the first question for us is whether holiness can in fact be attributed to the corporate entity of the family per se, or is holiness attributable only to a righteous individual. This problem arises because the ancient (Hebraic) and modern worlds conceive of holiness differently. As A. Vanhoye points out in *Old Testament Priests and the New Priest*, "as we understand it, holiness is almost syn-

---

16. In the NT, those baptized in Christ are called "sons of God." See Rom 8:14, 19; Gal 3:26, 4:6.

onymous with moral perfection; it suggests an assortment of eminent virtues.... The ancient mentality did not think of tying sanctity to perfection. For the ancients, 'holy' was not the opposite of 'imperfect' but of 'profane.'"[17]

In the modern context, this fundamental understanding of holiness has receded from our consciousness. Within the Old Testament the essence of holiness was understood as separation. In Genesis, the dynamic of separation is critical to the creation process. "God separated the light from the darkness...and separated the water which were under the expanse from the water above the expanse.... Let there be lights...to separate the day from the night" (Gn. 1:4ff.). Finally, after all is created, God separated the seventh day from the other six. "God blessed the seventh day and sanctified it" (Gn 2:3). It is the separating out of this one day from the others that causes it to become holy. The day does not become holy because it is morally good but rather because it has been separated out for God's special purposes.

What should be noted is the *locus* of holiness. Ultimately only God is holy and whatever is made holy is willed by Him to participate in this holiness. Robert Hodgson concludes, "Holiness is not inherent in creation but comes by God's dictates."[18] In the Old Testament, God chooses parts of His creation for specific purposes and sets them aside, creating them as markers of His presence within the created order. He makes them holy by orienting them towards Himself. This includes different elements within various spheres of human experience: (a) time [the Sabbath and festivals]; (b) geographical areas [city, hill, holy place, mountains, ground]; (c) sociological units [nation, people and fami-

17. Albert Vanhoye, *Old Testament Priests and the New Priest according to the New Testament*, trans. J. B. Orchard, Studies in Scripture (Petersham, Mass.: St. Bede's Publications, 1986), 27. Unfortunately, all these terms are misunderstood in the modern context. The ancients understood people and things to possess a status that was changeable. Most of reality simply existed in the ordinary state which was termed "profane." It was essentially a neutral state. When something was dedicated for the use of Yahweh, it went through rituals so as to be moved from a common state into the sphere of holiness. Neither was intrinsically tied to morality.

18. *The Anchor Bible Dictionary*, ed. D. N. Freedman (1992), s.v. "Holiness," by Robert Hodgson Jr.

ly]; (d) status [the firstborn]; and (e) objects [the Temple implements].[19] What has been separated from the ordinary is no longer part of the "profane" (i.e., ordinary) sphere and is consequently accorded a special status. The ordinary sphere is, as it were, invaded by God's will and parts of it share in the holiness of God. These will be the places where the divine and the secular meet. Through these actions of God the ordinary becomes a vehicle for divine holiness.

It is critical to observe that holiness is tied to the nature of God and, in fact, is one of the self-definitions of God. The term "holiness" is first applied to the Sabbath and expresses the hallowing of time. God sanctified the day and made it holy (וַיְקַדֵּשׁ/ vayᵉbāreḥ). It is to be noted that holiness here emerges within the *covenantal* framework of the Sabbath day: "The sons of Israel shall keep the Sabbath, observing the Sabbath throughout their generations, a perpetual covenant" (+Ex 31:16). The next occurrence of קֹדֶשׁ (qōdesh—holiness) is again in a covenantal context. In Ex 3:5, when Moses is called by God at the burning bush, the ground he is standing on is said to be holy ground (אַדְמַת־קֹדֶשׁ/ ʾadma-qōdesh). Once the exodus from Egypt is accomplished, Yahweh reveals to Moses His plan for Israel; they are to become "a kingdom of priests and a holy nation (וְגוֹי קָדוֹשׁ/ vᵉgôy kādōsh)" (+Ex 19:6). They are to be separated from all other nations so as to be "a treasured possession" (+Dt 14:2). In each case, something is separated out from the regular reality and becomes closely associated with God. To touch these realities is to touch something of God Himself.[20]

Leviticus makes clear that the holiness of created things is grounded in the holiness of Yahweh Himself. This is particularly evident in those sections which enumerate the laws by which Israel was to live and be differentiated from the world. In this section, called the Holiness Code (Lev 17–26), this self-revelation of the nature of the Lord ("I am holy")

---

19. Some of the many references here include, for *Time:* Gn 2:3, Ex 12:16, Lev 23:4; *Geographical:* Ex 3:5, Ex 28:35, Ps 87:1, Neh 11:1, Ps 2:6, 3:4; *Nation/Family:* Ex 19:6, Dt 7:6; *Status:* Nm 6:8, 2 Chr 23:6; *Temple and Objects:* Ex 26:33, 28:2, 29:37, 30:25, Lev 2:10, 16:33, 26:33, 27:30, Ps 11:4.

20. Cf. Zech 2:12, where the prophet reveals the uniqueness of Israel: "the one touching you [Israel] *is* the one touching the apple of His eye."

and its concomitant requirement that God's people be holy is reiterated on five separate occasions.[21] These narratives are critically important because Yahweh makes His own nature (i.e., His holiness) the ground for Israel being holy. "I am the LORD your God, consecrate yourselves and you shall be holy because I am holy…you shall be holy because I am holy" (+Lev 11:44–45).

In this and the other four corresponding verses, two critical points emerge. One is that "(t)he existence of God, and the Holiness of God, are identical."[22] God is intrinsically holy. The second point deals with how this relates to God's command to Israel to be holy. As Hirsch observed, in the second part of these verses, "we are referred to the Holiness of God as being the source of our ability to attain holiness, and as the reason for our duty to attain it."[23] Israel is to be holy because God is holy.[24] This interplay which defines the existence of Israel is well expressed by Hirsch's summary of the teaching in this part of the Torah: "We are only *qdwšym* [holy], if we belong to God with every fibre of our being; we only belong to God if we are *qdwšym* [holy] with every impulse of our being."[25]

Thus, Israel is not only to be separated out *from* the surrounding nations but is also separated to God. She is become like Him in holiness by conforming her behavior and her attitudes to the revealed Torah in order that they be compatible with God's nature of holiness. For this

21. "I am holy" (Lev 11:44, 45; 19:2; 20:26; 21:8).

22. S. R. Hirsch, *Leviticus*, vol. 3 of *The Pentateuch: Translated and Explained*, 2nd ed., trans. I. Levy (Gateshead, England: Judaica Press, 1976), part 2, 584.

23. Hirsch, *Leviticus*, 584. This can be seen to be analogous to Jesus' command at the Last Supper when He said: "A new commandment I give to you, that you love one another; even as I have loved you, that you also love one another" (^Jn 13:34). We are commanded to love with a specific type of love (the same as Jesus'). As Jesus loved us, so we are to love one another. In experiencing the love of Jesus, we are then abled to love others in the same way. So the command and the power to carry out the command are part of the same reality, the divine love of Christ.

24. Gammie sees that the separation of Israel from the pagan nations required in Deuteronomic theology is "derived from the notion of the oneness of God and of the divine election of a people and of a particular place for worship" (John G. Gammie, *Holiness in Israel* [Minneapolis: Fortress Press, 1989], 110).

25. Hirsch, *Leviticus*, 584 (*qdwšym*—holy ones).

to occur, a process of separation had to occur that removed Israel from her pagan environment, which in turn allowed her to be then dedicated to the Lord. This process of separation was always understood to have two movements: to be set apart *from* the common in order to become consecrated as holy *for* the Lord's use.

SPHERES OF REALITY: DEGREES OF SEPARATION

One aspect of ancient Semitic thought that is difficult to grasp is its classification of all things as existing within one of the four different spheres of existence: clean, unclean, holy, common. Some of these categories were contagious; thus, to touch something unclean, such as blood, made one unclean as the contagion spread from the blood to the person. Also, things that were holy were highly contagious and their holiness was also communicated by touch. A person who did not have the proper status (of holiness) would die (cf. 2 Sam 6:6–7).[26] This dynamic system was essential to the cult of Israel and was premised on the principle that no confusion was allowed between the different spheres of life. Confusion between these states threatened the very existence of Israel.[27] This principle of separation, which is not a valuation of morality, was evidenced in the process of creation. The Genesis narrative presents the earthly creation as an explicit series of separations from a common source. The more things become differentiated, the more creation comes into the fullness of being. Lines of demarcation (between light and darkness, water and land, etc.) are fundamen-

---

26. See J. Milgrom, *Leviticus 1–16* (New York: Doubleday, 1991), 45. "In the earliest traditions of the Bible, the sancta communicate holiness to persons, the sanctuary's inner sancta more powerfully so—directly by sight (if uncovered) and directly by touch (if covered), even when the contact is accidental."

27. One sees this operating within the NT. Luke 8:43ff. presents us with the woman who had had an issue of blood for twelve years. Hence, she is in a continual state of impurity. She touches the hem of Jesus' garment and is healed. Her reaction is a bit puzzling. She is afraid to tell that it was she who had touched Jesus when He asks. The reason lies in the fact that she knows that she, being impure, should not touch another person, as that renders the touched person impure as well.

tal to the structuring of the created order. To reject or transgress these boundaries would be to enter a process of de-creation. Thus, any confusion between the spheres of reality would be understood as a fundamental rejection of the order of creation.[28]

Many of the laws in the Torah are involved in keeping these boundaries intact and not allowing them to be overcome or, once they have been transgressed, to provide the ritual means to restore order and prevent confusion from reigning. This is critically important when dealing with the spheres of existence (holy, profane; pure, impure). *To maintain the created order, the different and opposing spheres must not penetrate each other permanently but must be kept separate.* When there is a violation, the community is in danger and ritual means must be used to restore order. Many of the laws in Leviticus deal with those who have impurities (e.g., menstruants) and consider them to be impure until they undergo a water ritual to be restored properly to the community. Only then are they able to worship again in the Sanctuary. Till then, they were not to touch anyone or anything until they had become clean or they would render the touched person/object impure. If they persisted in their impure state, they would ultimately defile the Temple: "You shall warn the Israelites of their uncleanness, lest by defiling my Dwelling, which is in their midst, their uncleanness be the cause of their death" (•Lev 15:31).

As Thomas McComiskey states in his article on קֹדֶשׁ (qōdesh—holiness), "A basic element of Israelite religion was the maintenance of an inviolable distinction between the spheres of the sacred and the common or profane."[29] This is evidenced within the life of Israel, where fundamental distinctions are made. For example, one day is separated

---

28. This principle can be see within Gn 1, in which the creation gradually emerges into its fullness. There are clear boundaries between the different created spheres that must be respected for creation to flourish. The Flood can be understood as the punishment for sin in which those boundaries are no longer respected and disaster follows. Leviticus is a textbook of laws and regulations used by the Israelite priests to determine what offenses were culpable and what rituals had to be carried out. Impurity had to be purged from individual people and from the community as a whole so that each could return to a proper relationship with God. See Lev 16, which provides the ritual for the Day of Atonement.

29. Thomas E. McComiskey, "qadosh" in *TWOT*, vol. 2, 787.

out from the others and made holy, and becomes the special symbol of the covenant between God and His people (see Ex 31:17). Within the people, one tribe (Levi) is set apart and consecrated to the Lord to deal with cultic worship.

But the sphere of life that is perhaps most hedged around with laws and regulations to preserve its holiness is the family. Kaiser, in *Toward an Old Testament Ethics,* explains how the laws of holiness and purity are intrinsically a part of the understanding of the family within the covenant. He draws attention to the Holiness Code in Leviticus 17–26 and shows how this block of legislation can be considered a separate unit, which in some ways parallels the giving of the Law in Exodus 20.

> The features that attract our attention...in these chapters is the introductory formula of Leviticus 18:2: "I am the LORD Yahweh your God" (a feature that is almost identical to the one that introduces the Ten Commandments, Ex 20:2; Dt 5:6), the formula "Be holy, because I, the LORD your God, am holy" is repeated four times in this section (19:2; 20:7, 26; 21:8...), and the words "I am the LORD your [or their] God" occurs nearly fifty times in these chapters.[30]

The purpose of this biblical narrative is to articulate clearly for Israel the demarcation line between that which is holy and that which is not. What is most important for our discussion is the fact that two thirds of this Holiness Code is concerned with limiting behavior that directly affects the family. A key text is ^Lev 18:3: "You shall not do as they do in the land of Egypt, where you dwelt, and you shall not do as they do in the land of Canaan." To remain as the holy people, Israel's behavior had to be holy. The first third of this code is given over to defining acceptable/holy sexuality (e.g., "you shall not have carnal relations with your neighbor's wife" [•Lev 18:20]). This disciplining of the sexual instinct would help to stabilize both the home and society. The overall effect of this circumscribing of sexual behavior was to cause Israel to behave differently than her pagan neighbors and to eschew their practices. To become holy, Israel had to be thus separated out from all other nations.

This process of separation continued within the confines of the com-

30. W. C. Kaiser, *Toward Old Testament Ethics* (Grand Rapids, Mich.: Zondervan, 1983), 115.

munity of Israel herself. Even within the properly determined Israelite home, there were times when sexual relationships were further delimited. ^Lev 18:19 limits when a couple may have intercourse: "You shall not approach a woman...in her menstrual uncleanness." In this case, the issue of blood during a normal bodily process (menses) renders the person impure and, therefore, incapable of having sanctified sexual relations. This impure status would then have to be rectified before proper sexual relationship could be resumed. In fact, much of Israel's cultic life was centered on the maintenance of this state of purity, which alone allowed a person to approach and share in the holiness of God.

The last third of the Holiness Code deals with punishments meted out for violations of the code. As Kaiser notes: "Leviticus 20 is mainly that, a penal code. It can be divided into two sections: the penalty for Molech worship...(vv. 1–8, 27), and penalties for sinning against the family (vv. 9–26). Both sections conclude with a strong exhortation for holiness of life."[31] It is interesting to note, as Kaiser pointed out, that the death penalty was required for a number of these transgressions, including adultery, incest, homosexuality, and bestiality.[32] For engaging in sex with a menstruant (which rendered sexual intercourse impure), the punishment was to be cut off from the community, which was another form of death. Thus, *to sin against the family was, in effect, to visit a form of death upon the community* and called for drastic measures.

The law which Kaiser did not identify and comment on (and which would make his case even stronger) is that cursing either father or mother required the death penalty.[33] It is particularly noteworthy that this penalty comes before any of the sexual transgressions are listed and follows immediately upon the punishments for apostasy. Parents are the source of life for each child and to curse them is to curse life itself. The consequence of this type of behavior is death on a number of levels. The law simply reflects this reality.

It is clear from the above analysis that in Leviticus there is an overwhelming concern for family purity. Kaiser concluded:

31. Ibid., 124.   32. Ibid.
33. Lev 20:9.

The issue at stake in every one of these crimes is the holy status of the family. Every assault against an individual here is simultaneously an attack on the very existence of the family. Said Kellog, "Where there is incest or adultery, we may truly say the family is murdered.... The gravity of the punishment ought, instead, to indicate the importance and the significance of the family in any kind of holy living."[34]

In Israel, the holy status of the family had to be maintained if Israel was to continue as the covenantal people of Yahweh. Consequently, the behavior of the family, particular in the sexual realm, had to be minutely controlled by legislation.

What is interesting is the conflicting opinion von Rad and Schillebeeckx have concerning some of these laws. The latter maintains:

> Yet there is one question in connection with this fundamentally healthy Old Testament conception of marriage which remains unanswered, namely the laws of cleanliness in relation to all sexual matter, such as menstruation, the nocturnal emission of semen, and so on. From these laws it would certainly seem as if sexual life was subject to all kinds of religious taboos which cast a certain shadow on Israel's essentially healthy view of marriage.[35]

Schillebeeckx sees no value in these laws but conceives of them as some form of atavistic tendencies that have been remanded over from Israel's past. By contrast, von Rad, while struggling to understand their meaning and purpose, nevertheless admits they may have some purpose.

> Without question, early Israel as well was spellbound by this "dynamistic" view of the world. Indeed, she clung so persistently to the idea of the material force of what was holy or unclean, and to the possibility of its transmission, that we are faced with the question whether this was only a matter of survival of a way of thinking virtually long overcome, or whether it was something much more important for Israel.[36]

---

34. Kaiser, *Old Testament Ethics*, 124–25 (emphasis added). This is perhaps a sober reminder for a society which no longer seeks to protect the family but increasingly allows destructive tendencies to be legalized, turning a blind eye to the eventual corruption that these practices have on family life and on the nation as a whole.

35. Schillebeeckx, *Marriage*, 88–89.

36. Von Rad, *OTT*, vol. 1, 34.

Schillebeeckx's analysis is problematic, because it would require that the laws on purity, and especially sexual purity, were only peripheral to Israel's identity. However, the contrary is true. These laws still form the basis of Orthodox Judaism.[37] They are imbedded in the Holiness Code, which is central to Israel's identity and existence, and these laws define the way in which Israel is to be holy. These laws form a large part of this narrative. As well, violation of them provoked some of the severest punishments. For example, the penalty for violation of *nidda*[h] (the menstruant) was separation from the community, which meant spiritual death. In the traditional Jewish understanding, the Levitical passage where these laws (including those on *nidah*) are located is called *K'doshim* (Holy Ones). Michael Kaufman relates: "This all-encompassing scriptural passage which introduces the section dealing with *nidah,* is understood to contain the fundamental purpose of Judaism. It provides the Jew with a basic guideline for the conduct of his entire life: to elevate himself to the level of godliness."[38]

Being at the heart of Jewish identity, the laws on purity can hardly be understood as mythological constructions which were better left in the past. As Kaufman noted, "The laws of Family Purity are considered *gufei Torah,* among the most fundamental directives of the Torah, and their observance distinguishes the practicing Jew from the nonobservant one."[39] This is as true today for the Orthodox Jewish community as it was in the time of Moses. While these laws seem strange to non-Hebraic sensibilities, they are at the heart of the rationale for the covenant. In addition, when their underlying meaning is properly understood, these laws on purity help us understand better the holiness of the domestic church.[40] The case of the menstruant and the requirement of the *mikvah* illustrate the need for the domestic sphere to continually

37. See Aryeh Kaplan, *Waters of Eden: The Mystery of the Mikvah* (New York: NCSY Union of Orthodox Jewish Congregations of America, 1976). See also Kaufman, *Love, Marriage, and Family,* 195–96.

38. Kaufman, *Love, Marriage, and Family,* 196.

39. Ibid., 195.

40. This point was developed at length in my doctoral dissertation, "Mystery of Water, Mystery of Holiness," John Paul II Institute for Studies on Marriage and Family, Washington, D.C., 1999.

safeguard its holiness and to eliminate from its borders all that would endanger this status. Only by preserving its holiness can the family be an instrument of a holy God.

MIKVAH

When a woman enters into her time of menses, the issue of blood renders her impure and she must not have sexual relations with her husband. After a period of separation and once the issue of blood has stopped, the woman then needs to remove her status as a *nidda*[h] (i.e., being in the state of impurity) by a ritual immersion in a *mikvah*.[41] *Note that this state of impurity is not a moral determination.* The *mikvah* is critical to the immersion process by which one's status is changed; it can be interpreted along several lines.[42] Kaiser believes that the command to refrain from intercourse while the wife is in *nidda*[h] status shows that "no husband has sovereignty over his wife or her body, but that ultimately all is owed to God."[43] M. Kaufman explains: "Judaism understands that the ritual, properly observed, elevates conjugal relations from an act of self-gratification to a meaningful, blessed *mitzvah* devoted to the service of God—a joyous, sacred physical-spiritual union of body and soul."[44] By maintaining the proper spheres of existence (purity/impurity), by not confusing boundary lines, and by walking in obedience to God's laws, sexuality is elevated from a mere physical reality and is infused with profound spiritual meaning.[45]

41. This state of *niddah* (being impure) is dealt with in Lev 15:19–24. The rabbis compared Leviticus 15 with similar texts dealing with impurity and concluded that a menstruant needed to immerse before her impurity was removed. For example, the issue of a continual blood flow is likened to menstruation and immersion is explicitly required (cf. •Lev 15:25ff.: "she shall be unclean, just as during her menstrual period"). See the section "Immersion by Implication" in Atkinson, "Mystery of Water," 325ff.

42. The *mikvah* is in fact the place where the ablutions take place. The first instance of the biblical word *mikvah* is in +Gn 1:10 and means "a gathering of waters." Gn 1:10 and Ex 7:10 cited in Kaufman, *Love, Marriage, and Family*, 196. An excellent theological interpretation of the *mikvah* is given in Kaplan's *Waters of Eden*.

43. Kaiser, *Old Testament Ethics*, 199.

44. Kaufman, *Love, Marriage, and Family*, 197. See Kaplan, *Waters of Eden*.

45. It is this type of understanding of sexuality which is fulfilled in Christ and which becomes the ground for the understanding of the family as the domestic church.

This practice of ablution in the *mikvah* is, therefore, constitutive of the holiness of marriage in the Old Testament. To understand its role we need first to grasp what is taking place in this ritual:

> Ritual immersion prior to participation in a religious act denotes both a rebirth and an elevation in status. The original biblical consecration of Aaron and his sons as *kohanim* (priests) involved, as a first step, their immersion in a *mikvah* through which they were both "reborn" and had their status elevated. Immersion in a *mikvah* is also used to signify the "rebirth" and change of status of a convert.... When the married woman immerses herself in the *mikvah*, she, too, becomes like a person born anew.[46]

Kaufman draws two comparisons here. He first states that "the bride's act of immersion in a *mikvah* is analogous with the immersion of the Israelites[47] prior to their symbolic 'marriage' with God at Sinai[48] during the giving of the Torah."[49] Then he draws the link between the marital *mikvah* and the immersions of the OT priests:

> Hirsch compares the married woman's immersion in the natural waters of the *mikvah* prior to resuming marital relations to the *kohen*'s immersion in the *mikvah* prior to entering the Sanctuary for the Temple service in Jerusalem. On Yom Kippur, the climax of the Temple ritual was the entry of the *kohen gadol*, the High Priest, into the *Sanctum Sanctorum*, the Holy of Holies. Five times during the day, before each major service, he would immerse himself in a *mikvah*. The immersions were symbolic acts of purification which had the effect of raising his spiritual status to allow him to enter the Holy of Holies, a place to which entry ordinarily was strictly forbidden.[50]

Both the bridal bath and the immersion of the priests before carrying out sacrificial Temple duties are powerful images.[51] Once again, we are confronted with the question: how realistically are we to understand this imagery? Rather than being remnants of a mythological past, these rituals image forth a fundamental understanding about

---

46. Kaufman, *Love, Marriage, and Family*, 197.

47. Here Kaufman references *K'ritot* 9a.

48. Here Kaufman references Ezek 16:8, 9.

49. Kaufman, *Love, Marriage, and Family*, 165.

50. Ibid., 197.

51. See the *CCC* 1617 and its interpretation of Eph 5 on the bridal bath.

marriage and the family that we need to grasp.[52] Kaufman noted: "Both of these acts are of a consecrated nature and thus require prior *mikvah* immersion: the Jewish woman preparing for marital relations and the *kohen* preparing for participation in the Temple service."[53] As Jewish reflection deepens following the prophetic period, the connection between marriage/family and the Temple is more firmly grasped and it is this which promises to prove theologically rich for the understanding of the domestic church.

Yisroel Miller's *In Search of the Jewish Woman* develops the concept of the home being the *mishkan,* that is, the Holy Tabernacle in Jerusalem. This idea is clearly within the Jewish tradition, but it is very difficult to trace down. Miller, however, does make the point (through Ramban's commentary)[54] that "the greatness of the *mishkan* is that it approximates the true Jewish home. Abraham, Isaac, Jacob, Sarah, Rebecca, Rachel and Leah—they all created a dwelling place for the *Shechina*" (i.e., the Presence of the Lord).[55] It is to be remembered that their homes existed long *before* the Temple was built in Jerusalem. In other words, the homes of the covenantal family, the marriages of believers and the families they created, were to be little sanctuaries where one experienced the Presence of God. We need to explore this claim by examining the Scriptures to see if such a connection is made within the Old Testament.

MARRIAGE AND FAMILY AS ICONS
OF THE TEMPLE

In this section we will establish that the matrix of marriage and family was theologically meant to be a reflection of the Temple, the sanctuary of God's Presence amongst His people; that is, the family was meant to be a micro-sanctuary. This temple-family connection,

52. See note 2 in the present chapter.

53. Kaufman, *Love, Marriage, and Family,* 197–98.

54. Ramban, a famous Jewish exegete, was born in 1194.

55. Yisroel Miller, *In Search of the Jewish Woman* (New York: Feldheim Publishers, 1984), 28.

if true, provides a strong foundation for asserting that the family is a micro-church (a domestic church) through baptism. We will establish this intrinsic link between the family and the Temple by examining Genesis 2 and showing that this text, which primarily provides the description of the male-female relationship, is replete with cultic and sanctuary imagery pointing to the intrinsic connection between marriage and the covenant with Yahweh. The text itself explains with precision the exact relationship that exists between man and woman. But the deeper meaning of this relationship is grasped when we see that there is a subtext operative in Genesis 2 that presents the Garden of Eden as the prototypical Temple. This subtext reveals that the man-woman relaitonship is not only a social phenomenon but also possesses a covenantal structure that is ordered towards the Temple. In Genesis 2, the covenantal imagery is the context in which the male-female relationship is worked out and becomes the lens through which the meaning of the text is grasped. Marriage, and, therefore, family, are reflected in the Temple and are linked to it; they are meant to be covenantal and, like the future Temple, are to be the means for experiencing the Presence of God. If this is correct, then there is a relationship of mutual illumination between the family and the Temple. Michael Fishbane, in *Biblical Interpretation in Ancient Israel,* has worked out a compelling hermeneutic for interpreting the Hebrew Scriptures. He suggests that Israel had developed a "typological imagination" that allowed primordial events (such as Eden) to provide paradigmatic structures for subsequent developments.[56] That is, by recovering the symbolic significance of certain original experiences (Eden, the Exodus, etc.), the fuller meaning of later events or institutions (in our case, marriage and family) can be grasped:

> Another aspect of the typological imagination in ancient Israel is the tendency to identify diverse loci of sacred geography. In line with the phenomenon widely known from the history of religions, foundational events and institutions are located at a "sacred center"—an *axis mundi* where the powers of heaven and earth conjoin—which provides the pro-

56. Michael Fishbane, *Biblical Interpretation in Ancient Israel* (Oxford: Clarendon Press, 1985), 368.

totype for later events and institutions.... Particularly notable in this
regard is the typological reapplication in different biblical genres of the
archaic imagery of Eden to Canaan, Zion, and the Temple in Jerusalem.[57]

SANCTUARY SYMBOLISM IN GENESIS 1–3

The Israelite sanctuary and its ritual system can be understood in
varied ways. However, the most fruitful approach is to see it as the historical realization of the archetypal Garden in Eden. That is, the Temple replicates the Garden of Eden in a fallen world; it becomes the one
place where we can uniquely experience the Presence of God. The Temple, seen in this way, is an icon of Eden. To see this, one must read the
first chapters of Genesis with a renewed sensitivity towards symbolism.
As Alonso-Schökel has written: "If we want to overcome a minimalist
reading and recover part of the Biblical wealth, we need a mental conversion that may make us attend to the world of symbols. We must read
with a new attitude, that of a hunter: alert, ready for the surprise."[58]

57. Ibid. In an earlier work, Fishbane states that the understanding of Israel's sanctuary as
"a sacred place of renewal...is related to a mythic image that is widespread among world religions and those of the ancient Near East in particular; namely, that the creation began at and
unfolded from a specific center point. This primal place was regarded as the paradigm of all
origins, the point where heaven and earth met" (Michael Fishbane, *Text and Texture: Close
Readings of Selected Biblical Texts* [New York: Schocken Books, 1979], 111). Fishbane not only
develops the Edenic imagery but provides an insightful analysis of his typological hermeneutic which confirms the direction taken in the present work: "A 'reading' of the Bible through
the refracted shapes which this archetypal intuition of spatial harmony has assumed spon-
sors a unique mode of literary inquiry. For it regards the Bible not simply as composite textual phenomena, but as a closed system of texts.... Indeed, by tracing the recurrent recompo-
sition of Eden-imagery around core moments in biblical history, a unique dimension of that
history is brought into view.... The historical oscillations of Eden-imagery disclose the coor-
dinates of a deep and persistent religious reality in the Bible" (ibid., 111).

58. L. Alonso-Schökel, "Marriage Symbols in the Bible," ed. Joseph Atkinson (unpublished), 12–13. In chapter 2, Schökel deals with the wedding at Cana and shows that, though
the text is demonstrably dealing with a real village wedding, it is acting (within the structure of John's Gospel) as a filigree (*en filigrana*), a conceptual framework "beneath which
one can catch 'a glimpse of the groom, Jesus, and the bridegroom's mother, Mary'" (ibid., 9).
In a similar manner, one can read Gn 1–2 and see the significant symbolic structure which
points to the sanctuary.

This, of course, is not an entirely new approach. Fishbane, Eliade, Cassuto, and Wenham have made significant contributions in recovering the symbolic structure of Genesis 1 and 2 as it relates to the sanctuary.[59] Our task at this point is to uncover the parallels between Gn 1–3 and Israel's Temple. We will discuss the most pertinent ones and then provide a detailed exegesis at the end of the book for those seeking to study this aspect in greater technical detail.

Sabbath Structure of Creation

As Westermann points out, creation is not finished on the sixth day of creation.[60] Time, like the rest of creation, is affected by the principle of separation. Hence, there are two kinds of days, ordinary and holy. But it is precisely in the holy seventh day that the other ordinary days find their meaning and fulfillment:

> The sanctification of the seventh determines the time which begins with creation as structured time. And within which one day is not just the same as another. The days each have their goal in a particular day which is different from the rest—a day which is holy and apart.... [Hence] a new dimension is introduced with the sanctification of the seventh day: to give the holy a special place in the stream of events is to indicate the goal of creation...a holy day set apart.[61]

---

59. Wenham states: "The garden of Eden is not viewed by the author of Genesis simply as a piece of Mesopotamian farmland, but as an archetypal sanctuary, that is a place where God dwells and where man should worship him. Many of the features of the garden may also be found in later sanctuaries, particularly the tabernacle or Jerusalem temple. These parallels suggest that the garden itself is understood as a sort of sanctuary" (Wenham, "Sanctuary Symbolism," 399).

60. Westermann has carried out a careful and exhaustive analysis of Genesis, examining the various possible interpretations of the text. However, in the case of the Eden texts, not only does he not mention the parallel with the sanctuary, but he does not mention authors who do recognize these parallels. This is particularly surprising since he is familiar with the work of Cassuto. Westermann does see the Sabbath as having cultic dimensions, but that is all. One is reminded of Schökel's remark about how few exegetes today have a sensitivity towards symbolic reality. Nevertheless, Westermann's analysis is helpful, for though he himself does not draw the parallel, his work makes it possible for those who are aware of these dimensions to do so.

61. Westermann, *Genesis*, 171. This point is a development of a point made in an earlier work: "There is an order established for mankind according to which time is divided into

The commentary of Cardinal J. Ratzinger succinctly sums up the theological meaning of the text: "Creation exists for the sake of worship."[62] The principle that emerges here is that worship is the *telos* (end point) of all things. Thus all things, including the human person, find their sense of being and purpose to the degree that they worship. This principle will become critically important as we attempt to develp an adequate theology of marriage and family. Ultimately we will see that only to the degree that marriage and family are assumed into worship can they fulfill their destiny.

Westermann shows that the phrase "and he sanctified it" (וַיְבָ֖רֶךְ / *vay*ᵉ*bāreḥ*), used in conjunction with the seventh day, has cultic connotations and must refer to some sort of human observance of this hallowed time period. As he says, "A holy period of any sort can only be concerned with the person who celebrates it."[63] Given the sequential structure of Gn 1, it is clear that creation is moving towards the goal of worship as expressed in the Sabbath. But this revelation of the Sabbath was more than the establishment of a holy day; it would also include the means by which a people were to keep this day holy. Von Rad specifically ties the Sabbath to the Tabernacle/Sanctuary, while Westermann brings in the cultic dimension. The latter comments that "the verb 'to sanctify' expresses a cultic idea and cannot be referred to a day

the everyday and the special, and the everyday reaches its goal in the special.... The work which has been laid upon man is not his goal. His goal is the eternal rest which has been suggested in the rest of the seventh day" (Claus Westermann, *Creation*, trans. J. J. Scullion [Philadelphia: Fortress Press, 1981], 65).

62. J. Ratzinger, *In the Beginning...A Catholic Understanding of the Story of Creation and the Fall*, trans. B. Ramsey (Grand Rapids, Mich.: Eerdmans, 1995), 28. Cf. Ratzinger's comment: "The Bible declares that creation has its structure in the sabbath ordinance" (ibid., 29). Indeed, the compact yet profoundly theological phrase used for the heading of the present section comes from ibid., 30. He states: "In the creation account the sabbath is depicted as the day when the human being, in the freedom of worship, participates in God's freedom, in God's rest, and thus in God's peace. To celebrate the sabbath means to celebrate the covenant" (ibid., 30–31).

63. Westermann, *Genesis*, 170–71. Von Rad confirms this insight and explicitly ties it to the cult: "Nothing of that is apparent to the people...but once a community and a tabernacle are present, they will be bound to observe this rest of God.... Thus at creation God prepared what will benefit his people in this life" (von Rad, *Genesis*, 62, cited by Westermann, *Genesis*, 171).

destined for God himself, but must in some way or other signify something related to people."[64]

"He Finished His Work"

This connection with the cult is even further strengthened by comparing the conclusion of the creation account with the finishing of the Tabernacle by Moses:[65]

God finished His work—מְלַאכְתּוֹ ... וַיְכַל אֱלֹהִים / *vay°kal °ĕlōhîm m°-la'k°tô* (+Gn 2:2)

Moses finished the work—וַיְכַל מֹשֶׁה אֶת־הַמְּלָאכָה / *vay°kal mōsheh °et-hamm°lā'kāh* (Exod 40:33)

The same phrase כָּלָה מְלָאכָה (*kālāh m°lā'kāh*—he finished the work) is used in both texts to express the completion of both the creation and the Tabernacle. The repetition of this phrase led Westermann to conclude that "the sentence 'so Moses finished the work' is an echo of Gn 2:2."[66]

There is a further paralleling between creation and the Israelite cult in the use of the seven-day cycle. In creation, the cycle culminates with the divine institution of the Shabbat. Similarly, in Exod 24:16 Moses waits six days on the mountain and on the seventh he encounters the glory of God and is given the instructions that become the basis for the cult. Strangely, Westermann finds a conflict between sacred time and sacred place, believing that Gn 1–3 contains the archetypal sacred time (the Shabbat) but not the archetypal sacred space, which he sees being inaugurated only with the Sanctuary:

> The context here is very significant. Ex 24:15b–18, which is a continuation of the priestly description of Ex 19:1, 2a, is the basis of Israel's cult and worship. According to this passage the holy place, the holy period of time, the mediator of the holy are basic to the structure of the cultic event. Though it is only in this event that the holy place is founded (Sinai and the tent of the meeting which derives from it and which prefigures the temple in Jerusalem), the holy period is nevertheless already

---

64. Westermann, *Genesis*, 170–71.   65. Ibid., 170.
66. Ibid.

there ("six days…and on the seventh day"). P is pointing out here that the holy period of time as a basic part of the cult has a strongly universal character, while the holy place has a strongly particular character…[and] receives its function only with the beginning of the history of the people.[67]

But the concept of holy space is actually present in Genesis 2 and is just as archetypal as that of holy time. Westermann is misled by an approach to Genesis 1–3 that fails to account for the symbolic substructure that is clearly present. If, as Schökel urges, one develops an openness to symbolic realism, then the reader will see that *both* these archetypical realities are present in the text. The Sabbath (Shabbat) is the institution of the holy rhythm of time, while Eden is the primordial expression of that place where God and man meet, the *place* of holiness.[68] Eden is indeed that archetypal sanctuary. Hence, the sanctuary (later, the Temple) is to image forth this primordial reality. If the theme of the first three chapters of Genesis is creation and alienation, then it is reasonable to assume that the structure of the narrative would also reflect, at some level, the corrective response to this situation. In particular, we should not be surprised to see some adumbrations of the future cult that was instituted to deal with specific effects of the Fall (namely, sin and impurity).[69] Thus one can see that (a) the theology of Gn 1–3 makes worship the end (*telos*) of creation, and (b) the thematic structure of these chap-

67. Ibid., 172. Westermann, here, analyzes the text along the higher critical lines initiated by Wellhausen, which breaks the text down into isolated and separate sources. "JEDP" are the traditional letters attached to these hypothetically constructed sources. Umberto Cassuto, on the hand, rejects the JEDP theory. See Cassuto, *Documentary Hypothesis.*

68. While Eden is not itself called holy in Genesis, we see the process of differentiation going on here which can be associated with holiness (for example, the seventh day is separated out from the others and made holy). Eden is separated out from the rest of the creation and made a special place wherein man is placed. That this place is holy is greatly reinforced when the covenantal and temple imagery of Gn 2 is recognized. Further evidence may possibly be found in Ez 28:13–14 which associates the king of Tyre with Eden and seemingly calls Eden the holy mountain of God (28:14).

69. This concept of the Fall has Jewish roots. As Westermann notes, Paul's understanding of Gn 3 as the Fall "is rooted in late Judaism." Westermann substantiates this by citing ^2 (4) Esd. 7:118 (48): "O Adam, what have you done? / For though it was you who sinned, / the Fall was not yours alone, / but ours also who are your descendants" (Westermann, *Genesis*, 275).

ters would lead one to expect the inclusion, at some level, of symbolism associated with the Temple and cult. This points to the covenantal (and cultic or sacramental) nature of marriage and, by extension, the family which are critical themes in these chapters. In this case, the structure of the text gives the clue as to the real meaning of the male-female relationship. Again we are reminded of McLuhan's famous dictum, "the medium is the message." The sanctuary substructure of Genesis 3 provides the hermeneutic by which we can more fully understand the interior nature of both marriage and family. This substructure becomes even clearer when we examine man's purpose within the Garden and key components of Eden which are described in the narrative.

"To work and to keep it"

And the Lord God took the man and put him in the Garden of Eden to work it [לְעָבְדָהּ / l°'obdāh] and to keep it [וּלְשָׁמְרָהּ / ûl°shomrāh] (Gn 2:15)

Here we see that another reference to the sanctuary emerges when we examine why man is placed in the Garden (Gn 2:15). In this text the two cultic terms 'obdāh (עָבְדָהּ) and shomrāh (שָׁמְרָהּ) appear together. 'obdāh is associated with the liturgical work of the cult and shomrāh is thematically linked with keeping the covenant. Philologically, each verb ends with ה, which is the feminine object marker. The problem, however, is that garden (גַּן) to which the suffix is normally taken to be referring, is masculine.[70] To what then does the object marker refer? It cannot be to the garden, because it is the wrong gender grammatically. If the verb שָׁמַר (shāmar) has the sense of "to guard or protect," it makes no sense that the land needed protection, because there was no danger before the Fall (which had not yet occurred). Thus, keeping or guarding the land would make no sense. Nor can it refer to tilling the ground (here, in the sense of difficult toil), since this type of ardu-

---

70. Cassuto has done a thorough analysis of this verse. "In most texts the final *He'* has a *Mappiq*, which creates a difficulty, because the word גַּן / *gan* ['garden'] is invariably masculine. Nor is the suggestion…that the pronominal suffix refers to אֲדָמָה / *adamah* [a feminine word, meaning 'ground'] acceptable, since this noun [in v. 9] is too far away from our verse" (*From Adam to Noah*, 122).

ous work "was not imposed upon man till after his banishment from the garden."[71] The feminine object marker הָ (ha) may, however, have a cultic sense. If this is true, then it may be "a means of exploiting the allusion to the Torah (feminine) which is to be kept and cultivated."[72] If this is true, then the Garden of Eden is indeed a prototype of the Temple, which is associated with the Torah and Temple imagery that secures the link between marriage and family and the sanctuary. The implication is that the family has some fundamental association with the covenant and with the cult. and as such it is an instrument by which the (salvific) presence of God can be experienced.

As Cassuto mentions, the *Midrash Rabbah* on Bereshith (Genesis) suggests that each of the two words שָׁמַר (shamar—keep) and עָבַד ('ābad—work) is related to the activities of the Israelite cult and is "an allusion to sacrifices."[73] This connection finds substantial support in the Scriptures. The *Midrash* cites Exod 3:12, in which God tells Moses, who is to lead Israel to the mountain of God, "You shall worship/do cultic service (תַּעַבְדוּן / ta'abdûn)[74] to God on this mountain." This midrash also refers to Nm 28:2. Here, God is instructing the Israelites to remember to safeguard (תִּשְׁמְרוּ / tishm°rû—you shall keep)[75] the presenting of the offerings to Him. The manner in which these verbs are employed and the context confirm that they carry a cultic connotation.

A study of OT terms shows that the verb לעבד (to work) and its noun עבדה (work) are technical terms for cultic activity.[76] Two examples will suffice. First, in Josh 22:27, an altar is built as a witness to re-

71. Cassuto, *From Adam to Noah*, 122.

72. See Cassuto, *From Adam to Noah*, p. 122. Also cf. a paper by F. Martin, "Material on Genesis One–Three." Martin mentions that this idea is expressed in the targumic texts such as *Neophyti* I. This targumic text states: "And the Lord God took Adam and had him dwell in the garden of Eden to toil *in the Law* and to observe its *commandments*" (*Targum Neofiti 1: Genesis*, vol. 1A: *The Aramaic Bible: The Targums*, ed. K. Cathcart, et al., trans. M. McNamara, [Collegeville, Minn.: Liturgical Press, 1992], 58).

73. H. Freedman, ed. and trans., *Midrash Rabbah*, vol. 1: *Genesis* (New York: Soncino Press, 1983), 130.

74. The root of תַּעַבְדוּן (ta'abdûn) comes from 'āvad and means "work." The work of the Temple is sacrifice.

75. The root of תִּשְׁמְרוּ comes from *shamar* meaning "to keep" or "to observe" and is specifically used in a covenantal context when "keeping the Law" is mentioned.

76. Cassuto examined the phrase "to work" (לעבד) in contemporaneous Mesopota-

mind future generations of the obligation to "carry out the work/worship of the Lord" (עֲבֹדַת יְהוָה / *ăbōdat YHWH*). Second, in reference to the celebration of the Passover, Ex 12:25 commands the Israelites to "keep" (וּשְׁמַרְתֶּם / *ûsh°martem*) his "work" (אֶת־הָעֲבֹדָה / *'et-hā'ăbōdāʰ*) when they enter the Promised Land. In this phrase, we have the two terms "to work"(*'ābad*) and "to guard" (*shāmar*) that appear in Genesis 2 coming together and clearly referring to cultic religious activity.[77] These and numerous other examples show that the root עבד / *'obdah* can have clear cultic connotations.[78] If this is correct, then the feminine pronominal suffix (ה) at the end of both verbs in Gn 2:15 could refer to some cultic activity that the man is required to do. This (unspecified) activity is a part of the cult or somehow related to the divine relationship.[79] The idea that there may be a subtext here is heightened by the fact that there is no feminine object in the sentence to which these pronominal suffixes can refer. This fact lends credence to the idea that the suffixes may be referring to the Torah, which is feminine, and that it is the covenant (of which the Torah is a critical part) which provides the substructure and the hermeneutical key to interpret this passage.

"To Walk in Your Midst"

Eden represents the place where God and man are in perfect communion with each other, a sphere of existence which is marked by peace and wholeness. It is the archetypal expression of perfect human existence.[80] H. N. Wallace says the central motif of Eden is the "unme-

---

mian texts and noted: "The rabbinic explanation...explains the term to refer to the sacrificial service, corresponds to an ancient tradition of the Orient...according to which man was created for the express purpose of *serving God*" (*From Noah to Adam*, 122).

77. The word "work" (עבד / *ăbōd*) is a common noun used in many different contexts. The key here is that within the semantic range of meaning, it can be demonstrably shown to refer to cultic activity at times.

78. Further examples are Ex 13:5, 30:16; 1 Chr 23:27–28, 26:30, 28:20; and Ezek 44:14, 16. *TWOT* notes under עבד: "The same concept is used of serving Yahweh with the Levitical service (Nm 3:7–8; 4:23, 30, 47; 8:11, 19ff., etc.)" (*TWOT*, 639).

79. Grammatically, עבדה (*ăbōdāʰ*), which is feminine, can be the object of the two verbs in Gn 2:1.

80. It is interesting to note that Philo of Alexandria developed the idea that the cosmos itself was a form of the Temple of God. See his *De specialibus legibus* 12:66.

diated access to the deity."[81] One of the key experiences of Eden is the nearness of Yahweh Himself. The Garden is the place of divine communication and the place where God is found:

> And they heard the sound of the Lord God walking [מִתְהַלֵּךְ / *miṯhallēk*] in the garden (בַּגָּן / *baggān*) in the breeze of the day." (+Gn 3:8)

This theme is reiterated after the Fall in terms of the covenant and the sanctuary:

> I will walk [וְהִתְהַלַּכְתִּי / *v'hiṯhallakktî*] among you [בְּתוֹכְכֶם / *b'ṯôk'kem*] and will be your God, and you shall be My people. (^Lev 26:12)[82]

God's intention *to be with* His people is even further specified in the Exodus narrative when God brings Israel out of Egypt: "They shall make a sanctuary [מִקְדָּשׁ / *miqdāsh*] that I shall dwell [וְשָׁכַנְתִּי / *v'shāḥantî*] in their midst" (+Ex 25:8).[83] Thus, just as God dwelt with His people in Eden, so He desires, within the terms of the covenant, to dwell with His people by means of the sanctuary.

EDEN AND
THE ESCHATOLOGICAL
SANCTUARY

Finally, water is a constitutive part of Eden, of the sanctuary, and of Ezekiel's eschatological Temple. In examining the texts of Gn 2:1–25, the thing which is most striking is how the narrative is broken up by a large, seemingly irrelevant, section devoted to a description of the rivers of Eden. The question must be asked: Why this intrusion into the narrative? By careful analysis, one sees in fact, that the river is not an

---

81. Howard N. Wallace, *The Eden Narrative* (Atlanta: Scholars Press, 1985), 79.

82. Cf.+ Dt 23:14 [H:23:15]: "Because the Lord, your God, is walking about [מִתְהַלֵּךְ] in the midst of your camp."

83. Levine also notes the importance of the term *mishkan* and how it conveys the sense of "residence" and shows its connection with the Hebrew phrase "to walk about in your midst." However, he does not connect it directly with Eden. See Baruch Levine, *Leviticus: The Traditional Hebrew Text with the New JPS Translation*, JPS Torah Commentary Series (Philadelphia: Jewish Publication Society, 1994), 184.

intrusion, but rather a central motif of the Eden story. In Eden there arose a paradisal river which flows out of the Garden and nourishes the whole world. Thus, the paradisal water becomes a source of life.[84]

This river is the link between Eden and the outside world.[85] The story has not yet unfolded, but we already see two spheres: Eden, where man experiences perfect communion with God, and the world outside of Eden, which initially is barren. This is where man will be exiled to live in a diminished reality. Between these two states there already exists a link. In his study on the *mikvah* (the baptismal-like Jewish water ritual), Kaplan develops the symbolic value of this Edenic river. He mentions the rabbinic commentary here that teaches that "all the water in the world ultimately has its root in the river that emerged from Eden."[86] From this, he concludes: "In a sense, this river is the spiritual source of all water. Even though a person cannot re-enter the Garden of Eden itself, whenever he associates himself with these rivers—or with any other water—he is re-establishing his link with Eden."[87]

Determining the exact interpretation of any symbolic reality is difficult precisely because it goes beyond the normal analytical categories. But water, as a link with Eden, seems resonant with what we have discovered to date. If Israel's sanctuary is indeed the cultic experience of Eden, then the water of the cult will be linked at some level to the primordial waters of the Garden.[88] In Gn 2, life-nourishing water flows from the environs of Eden. In the later Israelite Temple, it will be water ablutions which allow one to remove death-like impurities and enable one to have contact with the holy. As Kaplan explains:

---

84. It should be noted (vv. 5–6) that rain had not yet been sent by God to nourish the world.

85. I wish to acknowledge Aryeh Kaplan's work in this area, on which the following analysis is based. See Kaplan, *Waters of Eden*.

86. Ibid., 35. He cites *Bechoros 55a* and suggests comparison with Malbim on Genesis 2:10.

87. Ibid.

88. This thought persisted in Jewish thought. Kaplan tells how in the *Pirke DeRabbi Eliezer* (20 [47b]) there is the story that "after Adam was driven from Eden, he repented by sitting in this river. Although he had been permanently barred from the Garden itself, he tried to maintain a link through this river" (ibid.).

Ultimately, all uncleanness is a result of Adam's sin.... This explains why a person who has been defiled by something unclean was not allowed to enter the grounds of the Holy temple. The Temple represents a miniature garden of Eden.... But how does man purify himself and remove himself from this state of uncleanness?... This purification is primarily through water, through immersion in the Mikvah. Water is the primary connection that we have with the Garden of Eden.[89]

Thus, from Eden there is a single river. In the cult there are numerous water rituals, which seek to reunite man to his holy state, and then, finally, there is the promise in Ezekiel 47 of a single river flowing, not out of another garden, but out of the eschatological Temple. Like the river from Eden, this river brings life wherever it goes, even reversing the effects of death in the waters of the Salt Sea. On its riverbanks are trees whose fruit will continually bring healing (Ezek 47:9, 11–12). Thus, at both the primordial beginning and the eschatological conclusion of history, it is water coming from a center of holiness that gives life to the world.

Cassuto, commenting on the river of Eden, hears echoes of this theme of healing sanctuary waters in Joel 4:8, Zech 14:8, and Ps 46:40.[90] In this context he also mentions the theme of "the Divine river which is destined to bring blessings in the days of the Messiah."[91] He concludes that these prophecies of the Divine Messianic River may "refer to the renewal of the bliss of the Garden of Eden by means of the stream that will flow from the site of the Temple."[92] As Wenham notes: "In every case the river is symbolic of the life-giving presence of God."[93] This

89. Ibid., 35. Kaplan's scholarly analysis is rooted in the scriptural texts and is supplemented by the historical (and organic) development of these ideas in rabbinical Judaism. However, one has to be careful not to read the specific Second Temple's institution of the *mikvah* back into the earlier periods. It can, however, be shown that the *mikvah* did develop organically out of the biblical ablution and purification system.

90. Cf. Cassuto, *From Noah to Adam*, 76–77.

91. Ibid., 115.   92. Ibid., 117.

93. Wenham, *Genesis*, 65. There is a further, but more obscure, connection between Creation, Eden, and the Temple. This concerns the *'eben sh'tyyah*, the Foundation Stone. Helmut Ringgren notes that, although it occurs only in late sources, there is a reference possibly in Isa 28:16 to "a foundation stone laid by Yahweh in Zion." Ringgren connects this to the stone that was in the Holy of Holies in the Second Temple. The ark was no longer there. Later Jewish writings said that when God was creating the heavens and the earth, He created

meaning of water will become important for the New Testament and can be understood as a ground for baptism.[94] This will be examined more thoroughly in subsequent chapters.

CONCLUSION

Beneath the surface of Genesis 1–3 lies a whole symbolic world which, in various ways, creates a resonance between the primordial garden and the later cult of Israel, especially as practiced in the Temple. The dynamic of sin, separation from the holy, precious stones, cherubim, the "walking presence" of God, the menorah/tree of life, the cultic service of *working* and *guarding,* and, above all, the divine waters are present in various modes in both Eden and the sanctuary cult. Most important for our study is the fact that in Gn 2 this cultic/sanctuary setting is the context in which God reveals the nature of marriage (and, by extension, the family). This is clearly not accidental but points to the fact that marriage and family are assumed into the covenantal and cultic life of Israel, participate somehow in the Temple and are meant to be vehicles, not only for the covenant, but also for the Presence of Yahweh in the life of Israel. The context of cult and Temple enables us to understand the inherent meaning of marriage and family. Kaplan writes:

> The reason for the Sanctuary was because the entire world had become intermingled with evil as a result of Adam's sin. When God chose Israel, He told them to build one Sanctuary where this evil would not enter. This Sanctuary was to be like a miniature Garden of Eden, devoted totally to the service of God, where everything pertaining to man's fallen state would be excluded.[95]

---

this stone to act as a lid over the deeps to keep the waters in check. It was this stone which was removed to cause the Flood. "Thus the foundation stone of the temple holds the chaos waters in check" (Helmut Ringgren, *Israelite Religion,* trans. D. E. Green [Philadelphia: Fortress Press, 1966], 162).

94. This meaning of water and the water rituals in the OT becomes fulfilled for the Christian in baptism, in which the individual becomes a new creation (2 Cor 5:17). All his relationships are affected, such that marriage becomes sacramental (Eph 5:32), and within the familial unit holiness is conveyed amongst the members (1 Cor 7:10ff.).

95. Kaplan, *Waters of Eden,* 34. Rabbinic sources cited are *BaMidbar Rabbah* 13:2; *Shir HaShirim Rabbah* 5:1; *Pesikta Rabosai* 5 (18b).

This, on the national level, takes form as the Wilderness Tabernacle and later the Temple. But, as we shall see, this understanding of a place where the effects of the presence of God could be felt will also be extended to the more personal realities of marriage and family, such that the covenantal family will come to be understood in terms of Eden as well. In fact, in later rabbinic writings the family becomes known as the *miskan katan,* the little sanctuary. Here, within the covenantal family, the effects of man's fallen state were to be mitigated, holiness was to prevail, and a sphere of sanctity was to be created so that the covenant could be experienced and passed on throughout the generations.[96] Theologically, this becomes foundational to understanding the baptized family as the "domestic church."

96. A parallel is seen between the Sanctuary/Temple and the home. Only certain types of foods were allowed to be consumed or used in each. The family table was like the Temple's altar; laws of purity surrounded the activities appropriate to each, etc. Later rabbinic writings teach that the presence of the Shekinah (God's glory) is present in a godly Jewish home.

CHAPTER 6

HEBRAIC ANTHROPOLOGICAL PRINCIPLES

Corporate Personality

To understand the organic structure of marriage and family and why they are capable of their function within the divine covenant, it is necessary to grasp the basic principles informing Hebraic anthropology. Earlier, the Semitic concept of corporate personality which lies at the heart of Old Testament anthropology was briefly examined. Having investigated the structure of the Hebrew family and its purposes, we will now more fully examine the structure of corporate personality and see how it provides the fundamental informing principle of both the individual person and the family.[1] This concept

---

1. While in some ways this material could have been presented earlier, it seemed best to study the structure of the family first with only minimum reference to corporate personality and then examine this concept as the family's informing principle. Within the academic community there is a debate whether or not corporate personality is fundamental to the Semitic viewpoint. Our procedure has been to establish the raw evidence of what constituted the family in terms of its nature and purpose, and then examine this data in terms of an organizing principle. Our thesis is that the Semitic category of corporate personality is this informing principle, that it is clearly in evidence in ancient Israelite thought, and that it explains the value and functioning of the individual and family within the covenant.

alone allows the family to have an organic nature so that the family can extend throughout the generations and yet preserve its fundamental unity. The role that the family does in fact play in the salvific will of God is predicated on this constitutive corporate dimension of both the individual and the family and ultimately is what allows the family to function as the carrier of the covenant. In this section, we shall critically examine this concept, investigate the fundamental contributions of Pedersen, Robinson, de Fraine and others who have helped in the recovery of this Biblical concept and show, by way of contrast, the limitations of modern anthropological principles.

THE FAMILY: AN ORGANIC IDENTITY

On examination, there appears to be active in Hebrew thought a construct which is foundational to and permeates the Israelite understanding of family. Like many underlying factors, it is not obvious and, perhaps because it is not obvious, it is all the more powerful. In any consideration of the OT understanding of family, the sense of an "organic" dimension begins to emerge. There is a vital organic link between the generations; the common ancestor-father provides the very identity for the later generations of the tribe. Abraham and his family, who together form the basis for all of Israel, provide the prime example. This comprehensive corporateness is seen in the Passover exhortation, where all generations are to consider themselves present during this formative event. Secondly, on a personal level, the individual is always situated within the larger social context, the family or tribe. The family is conceived of as an organic entity; both blessings and curses are visited on the whole family because of the father's actions. Noah, Abraham, and Achan are but a few examples of this. As A. Causse stated: "A certain organic solidarity uniting the group and a very great dependence of the individual on the community characterizes the primitive organization of the Chosen People."[2]

---

2. A. Causse, *Du groupe ethnique à la communauté religieuse. Le problème sociologique de la religion d'Israel* (Paris, 1937), 20, quoted by Jean de Fraine in *Adam and the Family of Man* (New York: Alba House, 1965), 16.

THE MODERN MIND:
AN OBSTACLE

In the modern view, which is atomistic, the individual is the primary point of reference and is autonomous and self-determining. Consequently, the organic dimension of the family is very alien to the modern mind. De Fraine, in *Adam and the Family of Man,* is very blunt about what must take place if we are to grasp Biblical reality. "In order to understand the content of the concept under study, it will be necessary to divest oneself of the ordinary philosophical categories and create a new Semitic or biblical mentality."[3] The task before us is to see the world through Semitic eyes.

In relation to the present theme, therefore, we need to carry out a preliminary study which will take us into the workings of the Semitic mind and uncover what allows for the family to function as it does in the OT. At the center of this study is the relationship between the individual person and the family (taken in both its smallest and its largest sense).[4] Given the profound organic sense that is expressed in OT anthropology, the most promising principle which would help to explain the theological nature of the family seems to be that of "corporate personality."

3. Jean De Fraine, *Adam and the Family of Man* (New York: Alba House, 1965), 11. Pedersen echoes the same sentiment, "Israelitic psychology seems near and familiar to us...but it is not to be taken for granted that the words mean the same to us as to them.... The Israelitic view of life is determined by other factors than ours" (Pedersen, *Israel I–II,* 99). Cf. also Chapter 3, "Primitive Mentality," in J. W. Rogerson, *Anthropology and the Old Testament* (Atlanta: John Knox Press, 1978), 46–65. Also, see H. Wheeler Robinson, *The Christian Doctrine of Man* (Edinburgh: T & T Clark, 1911), 5: "We may repeat the same words, but we cannot easily recall the same attitude in saying them, and it is attitude that says the last word as to meaning."

4. As de Fraine says: "The problem of the relationship between the individual and the collectivity is taken for granted in human speculation. Man has always been interested in determining the correlation between his individuality and his membership in the social group. Far from finding a contradiction between the two, he has always realized that there is rather an undeniable affinity between the two" (de Fraine, *Adam and the Family of Man,* 13). Arguably, this has been true up until the modern period, when the sense of the individual and of individual rights has grown to become an absolute value over and against any sense of the collective. This manifests itself in modern laws regarding life issues (e.g., abortion, cloning, euthanasia) and in the modern understanding and definitions of marriage.

ROBINSON'S CORPORATE PERSONALITY

The doctrine of corporate personality was first articulated by H. Wheeler Robinson in 1907 and 1911.[5] It seems clear that at least some of his thought is based on the work of both Sir Henry Maine and L. Levy-Bruhl.[6] Our contention is that his intuition is fundamentally right and that this principle helps to explain the dynamics of the family in salvation history. However, in its classic form as proposed by Robinson, the theory is not without its problems. It is interesting that Kaiser, who has little regard for Robinson's proposal,[7] succinctly summarizes the three basic tenets of corporate personality that Robinson developed, namely organic unity, representative figure, and the many/one oscillation.[8]

Organic Unity

The idea of "corporate personality" gives clear expression to the organic unity that is apparent in Biblical thought. Robinson cites the example of "being gathered to one's fathers."[9] Another example is Rachel. Robinson says we must not "think of a merely ideal or figurative existence of Rachel, when the prophet depicts her as weeping for her children by the family graves. Rachel weeps because she dies in her children."[10] Robinson explains this phenomenon in terms of a single group consciousness. "The group possesses a consciousness which is distributed amongst its individual members."[11] In other words, this unity and identification was not metaphoric or symbolic but had a vibrant

5. Kaiser, *Toward Old Testament Ethics*, 67.

6. J. W. Rogerson states this in his article "The Hebrew Conception of Corporate Personality: A Re-Examination," *Journal of Theological Studies* 21 (1970): 1–16.

7. Kaiser, *Toward Old Testament Ethics*, 68–72.

8. Ibid., 69–70. He actually makes these into three categories. But for our purposes the last two can be combined.

9. H. Wheeler Robinson, "The Hebrew Conception of Corporate Personality," in *Werden und Wesen des Alten Testaments*, Beihefte zur Zeitschrift für die alttestamentliche Wissenschaft 66 (1936): 50.

10. Robinson, "Corporate Personality," 52.

11. Ibid.

and important realism to it. Somehow, the generations were organically one, as if they were a single body extending throughout time and
space.[12]

The Representative Figure

Here, one individual "often embodies the whole group."[13] Robinson mentions the interpretation of the "I" in the Psalms and of the Servant in Isaiah. An analysis of the OT will show that the community
can be, and was, embodied in an individual.[14] Robinson saw that the
dimensions of "community" and "individualism" were thoroughly in-
tertwined. "If the collective sense is so much a part of the person and of
his outlook as it was with the Israelite, then he can never wholly detach
himself from the social horizon."[15]

The Many-and-the-One Oscillation

Corporate personality also refers to the principle of the "one" representing the "many" and the many being in the one. As Herbert G. May
noted, this is well illustrated in the Psalms by the fluidity with which
the speaker represents himself and the whole community.[16] Robinson
suggested that the Hebrews did not see the individual and the community as being "sharp antitheses" of each other.[17] Rather, "in the ancient
world they were much more closely and subtly blended than in the
more self-conscious modern, and so it was possible to combine both,
or to pass easily from one to the other."[18] The classic example Robinson

12. See Paul Merkley's comments in *The Greek and Hebrew Origins of Our Idea of History*, Toronto Studies in Theology 32 (Queenston, Ont.: Edwin Mellen Press, 1987), 89: "The
Biblical view is that absolute confidence in the unity of human destiny depends on dogmatic
confidence in the unity of human *beginning*, expressed in the story of our common deriva-
tion from one human couple."

13. Kaiser, *Toward Old Testament Ethics*, 69.

14. See Pedersen, *Israel I–II*, 110, regarding the Moabite representing "Moabithood." See
also de Fraine, *Adam and the Family of Man*, 29–31.

15. Robinson, "Corporate Personality," 58.

16. Herbert G. May, "Individual Responsibility and Retribution," *Hebrew Union College
Annual* 32 (1961): 108.

17. Robinson, "Corporate Personality," 53

18. Ibid., 54

uses is the punishment of the whole of Achan's family for his sin (Josh 7). Also, it should be noted that Achan's one sin implicated the whole of Israel in his guilt and suffered consequently.[19] Here, as Kasier pointed out, "the group was treated as an individual."[20]

In his doctrine of corporate personality, Robinson enunciated an important principle of Hebrew anthropology. Although his intuition was right, he began to read a modern viewpoint into the data. In speaking of "corporate personality," Robinson says, "whether in relation to man or to God, the individual person was conceived and treated as merged in the larger group of family or clan or nation."[21] This particular viewpoint is further corroborated by his contention that in the "primitive" Hebrew mind, the collective mentality repressed any understanding of individualism. In *The Cross in the Old Testament,* Robinson cites with approval McIver's comment: "To the primitive man the group is all. He finds himself in the group, but he never finds *himself.* He is not a personality, but one of the bearers of a type-personality."[22] Earlier, Robinson had made reference to J. B. Mozley's depiction of corporate personality as a "defective sense of individual personality."[23] But this view does not accord with the evidence of Hebrew thought or the witness of Scripture and has been rightly challenged by a number of scholars. Ironically, Robinson did not grasp fully how the Hebrew mind worked. As de Fraine said:

> More than any other mentality, whether ancient or modern, "the Israelite genius tends to incorporate the destiny of the people (chosen) in a representative person." There exists a biblical personalism which proclaims the integrity of the individual person in relation to the group, while at the same time admitting that the individual person can, under proper circumstances, represent the entire group. This is in opposition to an exaggerated individualism which sees in the individual the

19. The same principle of the "many" being affected by the "one" and vice versa is active in the New Testament. All Christians are members of the Body of Christ and affect each other. (See •1 Cor 12:12–27: "if [one] part suffers, all the parts suffer with it.")

20. Kaiser, *Toward Old Testament Ethics,* 69.

21. Robinson, *The Christian Doctrine of Man,* 27.

22. H. Wheeler Robinson, *The Cross in the Old Testament* (London: SCM Press, 1955), 76.

23. Ibid., 76.

supreme unit of the social structure, the only solid basis and the only driving force of the group created by him, as well as an exaggerated collectivism which looks upon society as the driving power and basic norm of the individuals governed by it.[24]

CRITICISMS FROM PORTER
AND ROGERSON

Robinson had imagined that ancient Israel operated within the paradigm of corporate personality until the prophetic movement caused individual responsibility to emerge in Hebrew consciousness. Both J. R. Porter and J. W. Rogerson took issue with Robinson on this point. They contended that the sense of the individual was never absent. Porter closely examined this issue and found Robinson to be wanting in his explanations. Specifically, Porter does not find this lack of individualism in early Israel. As he noted, concerning the "Book of the Covenant" found in Exodus 20–23, "the individual wrongdoer is consistently made responsible in his own person, while his family is not touched."[25] Porter challenged Robinson on the basis of the legal codes and pointed to the fact that "at any stage of a developed Hebrew legal system...the law is rooted firmly in the responsibility of the individual and of him primarily, if not solely."[26]

J. W. Rogerson follows up on Porter's initiative and articulates several problems he has with Robinson's position, beyond the legal codes. He makes the following astute comment:

> It is important to ask how Robinson was able to maintain at one and the same time that the corporate personality was a primitive survival in Hebrew thought that was gradually superseded by individual moral responsibility, and that in the first century A.D., the idea was still operative in Hebrew thought.[27]

24. De Fraine, *Adam and the Family of Man*, 14–15. The quote is from A. M. Dubarle, in *Melanges Lebreton*, RSR 39 (1951/52), I, 59.

25. J. R. Porter, "The Legal Aspects of the Concept of 'Corporate Personality' in the Old Testament," *Vetus Testamentum* 15 (1965): 365.

26. Ibid., 366.

27. Rogerson, "Hebrew Conception," 6.

This is clearly a problem for Robinson, because the Semitic worldview always held both the personal and the corporate aspects of the person in a dynamic, positive tension. Neither dominates at the expense of the other, for each is constitutive of the individual, of the nation, and of the covenant, *and* they actually inform each other. In any adequate anthropology, both aspects must be accounted for and given proper balance.

Rogerson also has difficulty with Robinson's proposal that the innocent member of a group could be punished *"because he was not regarded as an individual."*[28] Rogerson's critique of Robinson on this point is hindered by his own inability to grasp how the sense of individualism and corporate identity can co-exist or mutually penetrate each other in the Israelite mind. The better critique of this problematic part in Robinson's presentation is Porter's work in which he had already demonstrated Robinson's error on this point. The early legal codes in Israel give ample proof of the already existing value of the individual in ancient Hebrew society; in many instances, it was only the individual who was addressed by the Law (e.g., the Ten Commandments) and not the community as a whole. The community comprised individuals who had to be responsible for their own conduct.

Basic Intuition

But although Robinson's understanding was flawed, it was not fatally so. His basic intuition was correct. There is an organic, corporate dimension which permeates and is at the basis of Hebrew thought. Though the criticisms by Rogerson and Porter are valid, they go too far in rejecting the concept itself.[29] Porter tries to dismiss the corporate nature of the sin and punishment meted out to Achan's family on the basis of a holy contagion that required blotting out.[30] But he does not grasp the underlying reality that Achan's sin did affect the whole community of Israel. As the Holiness Code stipulated, God's people had to

28. Ibid.

29. "In the interests of clarity it would, therefore, be best to drop the term corporate personality completely, and at the same time to abandon any attempt to explain Old Testament phenomena in terms of primitive mentality." Rogerson, "Hebrew Conception," 14.

30. Porter, "Legal Aspects," 372.

be holy because God was holy. His holiness could not tolerate the presence of sin. Because of Achan's sin, the Lord no longer walked before Israel.

Porter also cites Lev 21:1–9, again without fully grasping its corporate dimension. In this text, a priest is said to be unclean if his daughter becomes a prostitute.[31] This is another example of the organic personality that exists within the family. All the members of a family were seen to participate in the family's *nephesh* or soul. Thus, while they were differentiated from each other, they nonetheless were organically connected and, therefore, affected each other. The priest, called to minister in the sanctuary, had to have a level of holiness that would have conflicted with the impurity of prostitution. If his prostituted daughter had been an autonomous individual, her status would not have affected her father. They would simply be autonomous individuals. But the Semitic mind saw the intrinsic connection between family members. Thus, the unholiness of one would make the whole family unholy.[32] Rogerson, in like manner, goes too far in demanding that the term *corporate personality* be dropped. Both critics are helpful in pointing out the misconstructions in Robinson's proposal, but they lack an appreciation of how foundational this principle was in OT understanding.

The corporate sense is always an underlying current in Hebrew thought. H. H. Rowley illustrates this in his comment about the emphasis on the emergence of individualism in Jeremiah: "Moreover, the New Covenant of which he prophesied, while it was to be written on men's hearts, and thus to be an individual covenant, was at the same time a covenant with the house of Israel, and thus a collective one."[33] Rowley correctly sees that the collective and individual spheres are not antithetical to each other but rather complementary.[34] "In no period of

31. Ibid., 370.

32. Cf. 1 Cor 7:10, where the baptized believer makes the pagan spouse holy, and 1 Cor 5:5 and Gal 5:9, which use the analogy of leaven affecting the whole batch of dough.

33. H. H. Rowley, *The Faith of Israel* (Philadelphia: Westminster Press, 1956), 105–6.

34. Herbert G. May makes the same observation: "It is a distorting of the picture to affirm that in pre-Exilic Israel Yahweh was the God of Israel and *only secondarily* the God of individual Israelites. He could be equally both at the same time." May, "Individual Responsibility and Retribution," 108.

the life of Israel do we find extreme collectivism or extreme individual-ism, but a combination of both."[35] These two realities coexist; this is the genius of Hebrew thought.

SCRIPTURAL EVIDENCE

The Individual and Personalism

In the Hebrew Scriptures there is an obvious regard for the individual. The first human creation was originally a single individual. In fact, the creation account in Genesis is the antithesis of an impersonal production of a mass of humanity and is in contrast to some of the pagan myths.[36] The account in Gn 2:7ff. shows the special and individual care that Yahweh takes in creating the individual man and woman. Beyond this, man is given the dignity of being bearer of the divine image in creation. Hence, the value and dignity of the individual is indisputable. It is important to note that God did not create several initial progenitors for the different nations. Nor did God make two separate creations, man and woman, and then bring them together. Instead He formed one man.[37] Indeed, the man's very singularity is expressed in his ensuing loneliness. "It is not good for the man to be alone" (2:18). In creating woman, God does not again turn to the ground for fresh material, but instead brings forth woman from the already existing man: he took one of the man's ribs הַצֵּלָע / ḥaṭzēlāʿ (Gn 2:21).[38] Again, the sense of singularity is conveyed by the emphasis on the one distinctive rib (הַצֵּלָע). With this, God then builds (וַיִּבֶן / vayyiben) the woman. It is at this point that Adam finally recognizes there is another creature similar to himself:

וַיֹּאמֶר הָאָדָם זֹאת הַפַּעַם עֶצֶם מֵעֲצָמַי וּבָשָׂר מִבְּשָׂרִי

The man said, "Finally, this is bone of my bones and flesh of my flesh." (Gn 2:23)

---

35. Rowley, *The Faith of Israel*, 100.

36. See *Enûma Eliš*, Tablet VI, lines 29–40, in Pritchard, *ANET*, 68.

37. "and the Lord God formed the man"—וַיִּיצֶר יְהוָה אֱלֹהִים אֶת־הָאָדָם / vayyîtser YHWH ʾělōhîm ʾet-hāʾādām (+Gn 2:7)

38. הַצֵּלָע אֲשֶׁר־לָקַח מִן־הָאָדָם / hatstsēlāʿ ʾăsher-lāqaḥ (Gn 2:22)

The purpose of this is so that:

וְדָבַק בְּאִשְׁתּוֹ וְהָיוּ לְבָשָׂר אֶחָד

He will cleave to his wife and they shall become one flesh. (Gn 2:24)

God did not create two principles, the male and female, which were then brought together. Rather there is already an interior ordination of one to the other; one comes from the other and together they form a unity, בָּשָׂר אֶחָד (bāsār 'eḥād—one flesh). In this way, the loneliness of man is overcome and he is brought to peace.[39] The unity here is not achieved through mutually compatible personalities but has a more profound, ontological basis. The account portrays their unity as something that already existed within the original "one" and was then differentiated. The unity is constitutive of both the male and the female. *They become one because they are one.*

Conversely, while there is an emphasis on the individual and on unity, there is also another principle operative in the OT which can be described as the "unfolding-in-differentiated-unity." This is illustrated in Gn 5:3: Adam "had a son in his own likeness, in his own image." This is a clear reference to Gn 1:26. From man had come woman, and in their unity, another comes forth. He is differentiated from them, yet he is not an independent entity. Like man from God, like woman from man, Cain proceeds from a prior source, from the union of his parents. The idea of absolute independent existence has no place in Hebrew thought. Everyone is dependent on others in profound ways. Only Yahweh is self-existent.[40]

---

39. This idea of *shalom* is important to the concept of the corporate personality. As Schillebeeckx noted: "Because it [the relationship between man and woman] was always authentically human in the full sense of the word it was expressed as a *physical blood-relationship*. In this expression—as in the expression *básár ehádh* (one flesh)—three elements are fused together. The first is the idea of blood-relationship, seen as an extension of the idea of peace (*shálôm*) in the life of the clan and the solidarity of the family" (Schillebeeckx, *Marriage*, 19).

40. This is one of the explanations for the name of God in +Ex 3:14: אֶהְיֶה אֲשֶׁר אֶהְיֶה/'ehye^h 'ásher 'ehye^h, which means "I am who am." It is essentially a form of words based on the verb "to be" and has the sense that all reality comes from the being of God. See Roland de Vaux's article "The Revelation of the Divine Name YHWH" in *Proclamation and Presence*, ed. John I. Durham and J. Roy Porter (London: SCM Press, 1970), 48–75.

Corporate Identity

The idea of being vitally linked to others (incorporation) has a further dimension. This anthropological principle is operative (and essential) throughout the New Testament as well and is explicitly used to underscore the validity of Christ's priesthood in Hebrews 7. To prove its point, Hebrews refers back to an incident in Genesis 14. Abraham, in returning from rescuing Lot, encountered Melchizedek and paid him a tithe of the plunder (Gn 14:18–20). The line of argument in Hebrews is that there is a greater priesthood than the one exercised by the Levitical priests. This is proved by showing how the Levites, who as priests do not tithe, actually paid a tithe to the founder of this other priesthood, namely Melchizedek.

> One might even say that Levi, who collects the tenth, paid the tenth through Abraham, because when Melchizedek met Abraham, *Levi was still in the body of his ancestor.* (Heb 7:9–10)[41]

Here is expressed the idea that somehow, within the very body of the ancestor (Abraham), the future generations already existed; hence it illustrates the idea of incorporation. Consequently, when Abraham gives the tithe to Melchizedek, it is not only he who is giving it but also the future generations, who are somehow present within his being.[42] This type of dynamic organic unity is difficult for the modern mind to understand but it plays a key role in Hebrew experience.[43] Laban, upon meeting his nephew Jacob for the first time, cries out:

אַךְ עַצְמִי וּבְשָׂרִי אָתָּה

Surely you are my bone and my flesh. (Gen 29:14)

---

41. Emphasis added.

42. This is similar to H. W. Robinson's explanation of Rachel as noted above: "Nor must we think of a merely ideal or figurative existence of Rache...Rachel weeps because she dies in her children" (*Corporate Personality*, 6).

43. There is a parallel here with the modern claims of genetics. Through advances in the study of genetics, we thoroughly accept the fact that each of us is the product of the genetic contributions of our ancestors.

But we need to be careful to realize that corporate identity, for the Hebrew, was something much deeper than mere personification or imagery.

HEBREW CONCEPT OF THE SOUL

Another construct essential to the Biblical understanding of the human person is the Semitic concept of the soul (*nephesh*). The way in which it was conceived allowed for the dynamic of corporate personality to pervade Hebrew thought. To begin with, it is essential to see that there is a fundamental difference between the modern and the Hebraic conceptions of the soul. Modernity sees the soul as something that is infused into the body of man, resulting in a dichotomy between the body and the soul. In the Hebraic account of creation a different conception is revealed:

$$\text{וַיְהִי הָאָדָם לְנֶפֶשׁ חַיָּה}$$

> [And He breathed into his nostrils the breath of life;] and the man became a living *nephesh* [soul or being]. (+Gn 2:7)

As Pedersen noted: "It is not said that man was supplied with a *nephesh*, and so the relation between body and soul is quite different from what it is to us. Such as he is, man, *in his total essence*, is a soul."[44] It is rather difficult to grasp this concept of the totality of the soul. In essence, it seems to mean that the individual we see before us exists only as part of a much greater reality, which is determinative of his existence and of which he is a concrete representative.

> Therefore, the soul is at the same time something visible and invisible. Instinctively one senses only individual parts of the man one meets. One perceives a figure with a certain expression, certain movements, a certain manner of speech, etc. This momentary impression only becomes the idea of a soul when the whole of its background is imagined, so that it finds its place in the whole.[45]

---

44. Pedersen, *Israel I–II*, 99 (emphasis added).
45. Ibid., 101.

That is to say, the reality of a man before you is not just the momentary impression standing before you but the whole history and context which has given rise to this individual and which he incarnates in this point of time.[46] Thus, a man does not exist by himself but only in the context of his history, which is present in him.

> If they met a man whom they do not know, they ask who he is, in order to know to what totality they must refer the impression which they receive of him. If he answers: I am Saul, the son of Kish, then they have the totality image. They know Kish...they are aware of his importance...they are familiar with the history of his kindred...they know his soul.[47]

This understanding helps to clarify the dynamics of family relationships. Pedersen draws the conclusion that "*mishpaha* [families/clans] are those who are of common flesh and blood...it is the expression of a common character, of a psychic community."[48] In particular, the contemporary father and the common ancestor are essential because they become "the bearer of the unity."[49] The family can be understood as an organ designed to perpetuate the race and faith. These ideas were all predicated on a specific understanding of the father. As Pedersen says, "Round the man the house groups itself, forming a psychic community, which is stamped by him. Wives, children, slaves, property are entirely merged in this unity."[50] But it must also be remembered that the individual father is never an absolute entity. As Pedersen shows, he is the representative of the original ancestor whose soul (*nephesh*) marks the whole clan. The *bèth ʿâb* (the house of the father) is a primary unit in ancient Israel, and all Israelites share in the household and blessing

---

46. Ibid., 101–2. The case of Adam is unique, of course, inasmuch as he is the first man. He is the prototype of all that will come after him, and the manner of his creation, and that of the first woman, show that there was meant to be an original "one" that is differentiated into a plurality. There is *always* an organic/intrinsic link between all human beings going back to the first man, such that all can be seen in the "one" and the "one" in the all. Thus, all future generations are a further differentiation of the beginning ground. All participate in him in some manner. This principle is at work in the creation of Israel. They do not self-determine what their identity is to be. Rather, as Pedersen shows, to be a Jew is to participate in the *nephesh* of Abraham, because all Isreaelites come from his being (*nephesh*), which was marked with the covenant.

47. Ibid., 101–2.
49. Ibid., 54.

48. Ibid., 50.
50. Ibid., 63.

of Abraham.[51] An Israelite is a father only to the degree that he has received this blessing and passes it unto his children. As we saw in the rite of circumcision, the father of the family was acting not only as an individual but on behalf of the whole Abrahamic community, of which he is the sole representative at a specific moment.[52]

Again, it must be emphasized that the personal identity of any member is not denied. Rather, the function of the family consisted in "imbuing him with the common character and spirit of the community."[53] This is particularly evidenced in the OT phenomenon of corporate representation in which one person could represent the whole community or the whole community could be seen in a single person. In this understanding, individuality is enhanced, because the individual is provided a foundation rather than being cut off from his roots. As Pedersen described it: "The whole is entirely in the individual and *vice versa*."[54] It is this principle which lies at the heart of the Old Testament understanding of family.

EXTENSIONS INTO PAST
AND FUTURE

This concept of corporate personality extends both into the past and into the future. As J. L. McKenzie noted, "the present moment could be conceived as recapitulating the whole past just as it could be conceived as pregnant with the whole future."[55] Pedersen illustrates this critical dimension by a further example.[56]

---

51. Compare the role of Abraham in Isaiah. He is called the "rock" and "one": "Look to the rock from which you were hewn, and to the quarry from which you were digged. Look to Abraham your father and to Sarah who bore you; for when he was but one I called him, and I blessed him and made him many" (^Is 51:1–2).

52. See ibid., note 262. It is interesting to note that all the males were circumcised in Abraham's household, even Ishamael. But Yahweh makes it clear that the covenant will only pass through Isaac, the son who is the fruit of Abraham and Sarah's bodies.

53. Ibid., 57.   54. Ibid., 55.

55. J. L. McKenzie, "Royal Messianism," *Catholic Biblical Quarterly* 19 (1957): 25–52, 50, quoted in de Fraine, *Adam and the Family of Man*, 24n30.

56. I thank Fr. Francis Martin of the Dominican House of Studies, Washington, D.C., for suggesting this example.

[The Hebrew] takes hold of the essential, that which more particularly characterizes the idea, and lets the details subordinate themselves to that, and so his thought is ruled by the general idea. If, for instance, he calls up the image of Moabite, then it is not an individual person with a number of individual qualities, which also include the fact of his coming from Moab. The features which make the specially Moabitic character, create a *type* which is the sum and substance of Moabitic features. This type is called *mō'ābh* and the individual Moabite, *mō'ābhī*, is a manifestation of it.[57]

This runs completely counter to the modern emphasis on individualism. Today, the attempt has been made to create societal equality and uniformity by disregarding the actual histories of people. In the Semitic worldview, the whole of one's past was vitally determinative of each person and it considered the personal and the corporate dimensions as inseparable. One is not an isolated individual but a person who emerged out of a context. It is this totality which the person embodies, but the historical context also now takes on a personal embodiment. Pedersen makes this point clearly: "This is the relation between the individual and the family. The individual Moabite is not a section of a number of Moabitic individuals, but a revelation of 'Moabitehood.'"[58] The distinctive essence of the Abrahamic family was the covenant. Thus, each member of that family carried the covenant, which was impressed upon his *nephesh* (soul). He is the manifestation of the covenant.

De Fraine, relying on Pedersen's analysis, rightly concludes that this understanding resulted in a profound corporate identification. "It follows that the individual never acts solely for himself; all that he does, the family does. For together they form an organism so closely united that no part can be separated from the others as an independent entity."[59]

ORGANIC STRUCTURE

It is extremely difficult for the modern to perceive the organic dimension of anything beyond the individual.[60] However, without an acute

57. Pedersen, *Israel I–II*, 109.
58. Ibid., 110.
59. De Fraine, *Adam and the Family of Man*, 32.
60. Like the modern scientific worldview, our psychological/religious worldview has be-

grasp of corporate personality, our basic reading of the Old Testament will be distorted. To help better understand the sense of organic unity that is operative within Hebrew thought, let us review again Joshua 7. It borders on the impossible for the modern mind to understand this text, which centers on the battle to capture Jericho. After the Israelite victory, everything was commanded to be destroyed. But Achan secretly stole something, and his act jeopardizes the continued advance of the fledgling nation. This story presents the modern mind with two incomprehensible things. First, why should the actions of one son of Israel, Achan, threaten and affect the well-being of all the tribes of Israel who had acted properly. Not only Achan, but the whole of Israel becomes unholy. We are told that not Achan but "Israel has sinned [sing.], *they* have transgressed [pl.] my covenant" (+Josh 7:11). Here, the *one* clearly represented and affected the *whole* community. But secondly, it is even more difficult to understand the punishment: Achan's entire household is destroyed (Josh 7:24–26). This totally goes against the modern sense of individual responsibility and the question of culpability. It is only when this text is understood within the Hebraic worldview that it begins to make sense. Within the Semitic mind, there existed a genuine organic unity between all members of a family, forming, in reality, a single organism.[61] "The individual never acts solely for himself; all that he does, the family does."[62] While this clashes with the modern perspective, it nonetheless does underscore the realism and importance of the vital organic connection within the family. Our task is to recover the truth of this corporate dimension and wed it to the personal dimension so that they enhance each other. To reject this will only encourage a rampant subjective individualism that is bereft of the corporate dimension which is equally destructive as a collective sense without any genuine personalism.

---

come atomistic. It is forgotten that atoms exist to be bonded with other atoms to form specific entities.

61. In modern times, Israel had used the procedure of sealing off and destroying family homes of known terrorists as a measure of self-defense. (However, a military commission has concluded that this procedure is ineffective as a deterrent.) The basis for this practice is the principle of corporate personality. See the Israeli newspaper Haaretz.com, April 10, 2009, http://www.haaretz.com/hasen/spages/1077080 (accessed April 21, 2009).

62. De Fraine, *Adam and the Family of Man*, 32.

EXCURSUS 2: THE SIN OF ACHAN

The sin of Achan (Josh 7:1–26) is always a difficult text to understand. Part of the problem can be resolved by situating the text in its proper context and by identifying its specific genre and *sitz im leben* (life setting). These go a long way in helping us understand the text correctly. The text is one of a small number of texts which involve the divinely ordained ban (חֵרֶם / *hērem*) which causes the military actions of Israel to become a virtual extension of the cult itself. All that is captured must be offered up to God as a holocaust. The word *hērem* is specifically mentioned eight times in Josh 7:1, 11, 12, 13, 15). Thus, this is *not* a normal situation and it *cannot* be taken as prescriptive. The prescriptive texts dealing with theft (which is the sin of Achan) are found in the legal corpus of the Torah (Exodus, Leviticus, and Deuteronomy). The prescribed punishment is codified under the concept of *lex talonis* ("an eye for an eye…"), meaning that a punishment may not exceed what was taken or lost. The episode involving Achan is something other than the "normal"; otherwise, Achan would simply have returned the stolen goods.

Modern sensibilities emphasize the personal and individual aspects. But this was not lost in ancient Israel. In fact, the prescriptive legal texts emphasize the *individual* responsibility of the guilty party. For instance, Dt 24:16 states: "Fathers shall not be put to death for their children, nor children for their fathers; only for his own guilt shall a man be put to death." This was normative; Achan's situation was not. Achan's stealing of the goods of Jericho was an act of desecration. Several times the texts states that Achan's sin is, in fact, the sin of the whole community (Josh 7:1, 11, 12, 13). The principle is this: the one is in the many and the many is in the one. When dealing with the cult, there is always the principle of "contagion." That which is holy can makes things holy; that which is unclean can make things unclean (Ex 29:37; Lev 11:32). With Achan, this principle of cultic contagion works in reverse. He is made "unholy," as it were, by his act of desecration and all that he is organically a part of (Israel, his family) is affected as well.

There remains the question of the degree to which Achan's family shares his fate. There are two ways of reading this text. The Hebrew text first states that Achan was stoned (Josh 7:25) and then they "burned *them* with fire." It is not clear if "them" refers to the members of Achan's family. Josh 7:26 says Israel raised a heap of stones over *him* (and not *them*) when they were finished. Given the insistence on individual responsibility in Dt 24:16, Josh 7 can be read as possibly meaning that only Achan and his household goods were destroyed.

The other reading is that the phrase "and all that was his [which was to be destroyed]" refers to the other family members. The reality may be that the family members were complicit in Achan's action. This would seem to be substantiated by Josh 7:11 which states, "*They* have stealthily taken goods subject to the ban, and have deceitfully put them in their baggage." Whatever interpretation is given to the text, it is not prescriptive about justice in normal situations. The invoking of the *hērem* makes this a highly unique circumstance, as such an invocation causes all things to be taken up into the cult.

BLOOD-TIES, ANCESTORS, AND THE COVENANT

What is the basis of this organic unity? Robinson concluded that for the Semite the basis was "the common blood-tie, whether real or fictitious (as by a blood covenant or some form of adoption)."[63] De Fraine, in investigating this idea, shows its implications for the understanding of family.

The concept of "corporate personality" always implies in one way or another the influence of a great personality who stands at the origin of the group and who "actualizes" it through the course of history.... The Isra-

63. Robinson, "Corporate Personality," 52.

elite mind is so convinced that the community grows out of the expansion of an individual that it tends to conceive of the group—the family, the clan, the nation—as the participating extension of an initial concrete personality.[64]

It is the originating point of the ancestor that is critical for the idea of corporate personality. This, in turn, is crucial to the covenant that is predicated on this dynamic principle. There are two aspects to this covenantal/corporate experience. First, there is, at the source, the initial ancestor, Abraham, who was chosen by God and given the covenant. The experience of the living God determined and defined Abraham's whole person. His status, like that of a priest within the Christian *ecclessia*, was changed forever, his *nephesh* (soul) was indelibly marked, and he became the one salvific point in the created order.[65] This election was indelibly marked in his flesh through circumcision. The second aspect deals with how this initial Abrahamic experience was actualized afresh in each new covenantal family. In each specific family, the father, like Abraham, had received circumcision from his father and, in turn, will circumcise his son and mark him with the sign of the covenant. If the child is not circumcised he is cut off from the Abrahamic community. The critical link with God, through Abraham, is forged afresh by each new father and a *covenantal family* is formed each time, which, if faithful, will convey the covenant to the next generation. The role of the father is crucial. In his own body the covenant is marked and he is responsible to hand the covenant on bodily to the next generation of his family.

De Fraine rightly shows how this combats any criticism that corporate personality debases individuality. On the contrary, it should heighten our awareness of it.

> It must be noted that at the center of the idea of "corporate personality" one exalts the worth of the concrete and living individual, the preeminent

---

64. De Fraine, *Adam and the Family of Man*, 23.

65. The purpose of this section is to show how malleable the soul *nephesh* (soul) is. It could receive into itself, by way of experience, a power which marked it and gave it a specific character or orientation or blessing. In the OT, the priest was taken from men, separated out, and given a degree of holiness. Concerning the priest, +Lev. 21:15 states: "For I am the LORD who sanctifies him." ^Lev 21:8 states that the priest is to become holy as he offers up the bread of God: "You shall consecrate him, for he offers the bread of your God; he shall be holy to you; for I the LORD, who sanctify you, am holy."

embodiment of the center of influence of a given community. In both cases, the "corporate personality" assumes the character of a "father"; he is either the royal *paterfamilias* who rules over an existing group or he is a patriarchal ancestor whose life is prolonged in a number of generations.[66]

This has a direct bearing on covenantal theology and is foundational to it. The individual is not a mere cog in an impersonal massive structure. Rather, the value of each person is recognized as an indispensable link between the generations. Each person is the contemporary instantiation of the covenant and must be formed and developed in the image of God. The individual is indispensable.

It would be easy to conceive of the covenant passing through Abraham because of his election by God. He could be seen as the instrumental conduit for the covenant. But Abraham is more than a conduit, because the covenant is cut into his own body through circumcision. The covenant is incarnated, as it were, in his body. All who wanted to enter the covenant had to become organically part of Abraham, to share in his covenantally marked *nephesh*. This, as has been shown above, not only could occur through blood-relationship but could be formed through other means of adoption and incorporation.[67] The key was to belong to Abraham and become part of his house. But this, in the Semitic mind, was not like joining a fraternal organization. As W. Robertson Smith said:

> A kin was a group of persons whose lives were so bound up together, in what must be called a physical unity, that they could be treated as parts of one common life. The members of one kindred looked on themselves as one living whole, *a single animated mass of blood, flesh and bones,* of which no member could be touched without all the members suffering.[68]

---

66. De Fraine, *Adam and the Family of Man,* 24.

67. De Vaux makes this point as well. He shows that the principle of the common ancestor or bloodline is still safeguarded, for "the newcomer is attached 'in name and in blood' to the tribe: this means that he acknowledges the tribe's ancestor as his own, that he will marry within the tribe and raise up his family inside it. The Arabs say that he is 'genealogized' (root *nasaba*)" (Roland de Vaux, *Ancient Israel,* trans. John McHugh [New York: McGraw-Hill, 1961], 6).

68. W. Robertson Smith, *The Religion of the Semite,* 273–74, cited by de Fraine in *Adam and the Family of Man,* 25 (emphasis added).

This is particularly realized in the family unit. The underlying structure which enables the family to be this expression of physical unity is the role of the father.

> The sacred bond of common origin is expressed by the term *baith*, "the household." The close cohesion of the family group is due to the "father of the family," who guarantees the unity of the home, for the term used for "the family" is precisely *bét 'âb*, "the household of the father."[69]

The covenant is predicated on the principle of corporate personality. Each generation actualizes afresh the covenant of Abraham; each generation is the organic unfolding of what was already present in Abraham.[70] Each father who forms a covenantal family is not just a representative of Abraham; rather, that family participates in Abraham himself and his covenant with God.

PSYCHIC UNITY

What seems to be key in all this is the concept of a psychosomatic unity. R. Aubrey Johnson, in *Sacral Kingship in Israel*, notes:

> The individual is regarded as a center of power which extends far beyond the contour of the body and mingles with that of the family and the family property, the tribe and the tribal possessions...to form a psychical whole, and, what is more, such a psychical whole has an extension in time as well as in space, so that the mystic bond which unites society may be conceived retrospectively as regards its ancestors and prospectively with regard to future generations.[71]

This dynamic organic unity is critical to the well-being of the individual for "it is precisely this union with the group which enables the

69. De Fraine, *Adam and the Family of Man*, 53.

70. This understanding of the organic connection between the generations and their identification with a primordial figure is witnessed to in the NT as well. This is clearly seen in Hebrews 7, which applies the Semitic understanding of corporate personality to Abraham and the Levis (and hence all priests) who are considered to be present in a certain fashion in the loins of Abraham when he gave tithes to Melchizedek. The audience of the Letter to the Hebrews were Jewish, and this type of reasoning was certainly not foreign to them or they would have rejected the argument of this epistle.

71. R. Aubrey Johnson, *Sacral Kingship in Israel* (Cardiff: University of Wales Press, 1955), 2, cited by de Fraine, *Adam and the Family of Man*, 29.

individual to assume his proper role."[72] In other words, one finds one's identity and purpose by identification with the group. This becomes particularly important in the Hebrew experience of the covenant, because one is incorporated by birth/adoption and circumcision into the salvific family of Abraham. By being a member of Abraham's house, one begins to participate in the covenantal stream in history. Basing some of his thought on G. E. Wright's *Biblical Doctrine,* de Fraine shows how corporate personality and salvation intersect:

> It is certain that the formation of the Chosen People is the central act of God in the Old Testament. God revealed to the community of the "children of Israel" its election, its task, and its destiny. *The individual finds his true life when he accepts his vocation in this community.* This presupposes that the individual hears the Word of God addressed to the group as addressed to him personally.[73]

By being an organic member of Abraham, one participates in the covenant that God established in him. The family becomes the context and the purveyor of this covenant precisely because the family in each generation is organically linked to, and is a part of, Abraham. This is why the stories of the patriarchs and the genealogies are of such great importance. Their histories are the unfolding of the primal and salvific event grounded in Abraham, only differentiated over time into successive covenantal families of the one chosen family of Abraham.

But while the individual is situated in the covenant by virtue of family line and circumcision, the individual must appropriate to himself what is being offered to him. It is precisely in the context of the family that one is given identity and is formed as a member of the covenant community, particularly through Torah teaching. The family is the fundamental matrix for appropriating the covenant. The individual and family cannot exist without the community or the community without the individual and family. All are dimensions of the same covenantal reality. Hence, the identity of any individual is inextricably tied to the experience of community and family. The family is the most fundamental

---

72. De Fraine, *Adam and the Family of Man,* 29.

73. De Fraine, *Adam and the Family of Man,* 45, in which G. E. Wright, *The Biblical Doctrine,* 1.c. p. 18 is referenced (emphasis added).

of all communities. In a primary way, it actualizes the principle of corporate reality; it is "the type (*analogatum princeps*) for every other kind of group."[74] The power of the family to so deeply form and "mark" the child in the covenant is primarily related to the Hebraic concept of soul, which is fundamentally a pliable reality involving the whole person that is awaiting powerful influences to determine and guide it.

THE SOUL'S RELATIONSHIP TO CORPORATE REALITY

Pedersen's extensive analysis of the soul provides a vital clue in the understanding of "corporate personality". It is perhaps the Hebrew understanding of *nepeš* (soul) that will prove most fruitful for grounding the doctrine of the family as the "domestic church." In the following we will examine Pedersen's descriptions, draw upon the thought of Martin Buber, whose understanding of the soul and human relationships appear to have affinities with corporate identity, and make some tentative suggestions as to how this may help ground the doctrine of "domestic church."

Pedersen sees that the soul in Hebrew thought is pliable and oriented to being formed and stamped with a character. Consequently, the interactions of people can have profound effects on those involved, particularly when the relationship is close.

> A human being cannot be isolated, as this is contrary to its disposition. It must act, *i.e.,* act on others and itself be acted upon by others; in that manner the souls are brought into real contact with each other. This openness towards other souls, or this pliability is part of the fundamental character of the soul, and for that the soul is created; when being born it exists only as a link in an organism, the family. And life consists in constantly renewed combinations with souls.[75]

Obviously, not every encounter with another produces change in a person's character. But people are profoundly and organically united in family and marriage. It is these relationships which provide the opportunity for deeply affecting another person's soul. As Pedersen observes:

74. De Fraine, *Adam and the Family of Man,* 65.
75. Pedersen, *Israel I–II,* 165.

Every time the soul merges into a new entirety, new centers of action are formed in it; but they [that] are created by temporary situations, only lie on the surface and quickly disappear. There are other entireties to which the soul belongs, and which live in it with quite a different depth and firmness, because they make the very nucleus of the soul.[76]

Thus, the soul can be affected in differing degrees, but at the center is a nucleus which deeply influences and helps shape the personality of the individual. When the husband and wife become one flesh (and when their union issues forth into children), they have created a new "entirety" in which they will live and by which they will be fundamentally shaped. In these relationships, in this oneness-of-flesh of both marriage and family life, each person profoundly affects the soul of the other.[77]

APPLICATION IN THE NEW TESTAMENT

Given that all the early Christians were Jews, it is not surprising that this idea of the *nephesh* and the principle of corporate personality continued to play a key role in the New Testament's understanding of person and of the personal structures of marriage and family. We see evidence of this particularly in the Pauline teaching on marriage.

76. Ibid., 166.

77. This is not to deny the free will of the individual. The genius of the Hebrew conception of the individual is that it keeps the personal and corporate dimensions in healthy tension. Both are absolutely necessary for a proper understanding of the person. The person (i.e., the individual) can never be understood in isolated terms but must always be understood within a communitarian context (the family, the nation, and the covenant). On the other hand, the corporate dimension must never collapse the absolute value (and responsibility) of the individual person. This is particularly demonstrated in the Ten Commandments, which lie at the very foundation of Israel's covenant with God and her identity as a community. It is clear that this is a communitarian covenant. As noted above, the actual laws are addressed to the individual Israelite (second person singular). The individual, whether man or woman, is responsible for his own actions, but it is also true that his actions affect the whole community. The individual receives his identity from the community and, in turn, forms and shapes the community. Thus, there is always a profound personalism which is evident in individual responsibility, but it is always within a corporate context. This is precisely the corrective that is needed in Western culture today.

The believing partner, united to his spouse, deeply affects that person, even to the point of sanctifying the spouse (1 Cor 7:14). Examining this text in terms of Semitic categories, the dynamic of which Paul is speaking in a Christian-pagan marriage can be expressed in the following way. In accepting Christ as Lord, the believer is baptized and receives Christ as a new dynamic power within his life; Christ becomes the new informing principle of the soul (*nephesh*). The person, though, is never just an isolated individual but always has an effect upon the people around him, especially those of whom he is an organic part. Thus, each member of the one-flesh entity now comes into contact with Christ.[78] The basic principle can be stated as follows: as there is already an organic unity and a corporate reality to the family, that is, the one-fleshness, it will be in the family that people will be most affected by changes in other people, because they form a psychosomatic unity.[79] As Pedersen observed, "When our souls are united, they get a common will and thus form a psychic unity."[80] When Christ becomes Lord of one of those souls in a family, an eschatological dimension is added to the *whole* household, because *all* are organically one body.[81]

78. Although Paul does not articulate his teaching in this way, it nonetheless shows how the Semitic worldview could be seen to be operating within the NT situation.

79. From this perspective, household baptisms in the NT (Acts 11:14; 16:15; 16:31; 1 Cor 1:16) are a natural progression from the rite of circumcision in the OT and its understanding of the familial structure of the covenant. Household baptisms would make no logical sense if the Church had considered that only adult believer's baptism was valid. A theology of covenant initiation, which denies the inclusion of children, rejects both the corporate and familial dimensions of the covenant that are present in both the Old Testament and the New. This topic will be examined at greater length in the New Testament section.

80. Pedersen, *Israel I–II*, 165.

81. Pedersen is not talking about moral responsibility but rather the "character" that is formed. The point here is that future generations proceed from an initiating point which has effect on the each person who is organically a part of that group. This is clearly seen in original sin, wherein, through no actions of their own, all generations who proceed from the original couple share in the same nature, which is now fallen. Their "character" has been inherited. The moral dimension enters into the decisions that the individual makes within the context of that inherited nature. Abraham provides a second example. His experience with God and the initiation of the covenant "marked" his *nephesh*, his soul. The covenant became the formative principle within the personality of Abraham. He became the critical point of the covenant and the friend of God. While this shaped his personality, it was not in essence a moral category. It is clear from the Genesis narrative that Abraham had to learn to become

This idea may become clearer if we remember the Hebrew understanding of house. As Pedersen points out, "The family is not merely a *bēth 'ābh,* the father's house, but also a *bēth 'ābhōth,* the house of the fathers. A great and strong man like David introduces an entirely new blessing into his family and thus founds a new house."[82] This means that there can be a starting point for something new which is added to the family (in this case, the Davidic promise), in which all the members of the present and future generations participate. In the greatest Old Testament example, the whole family of Abraham and Sarah, including future generations, participate in the divine covenantal promise. The pagan Abram experiences the Lord and receives the covenant. The divine blessing is a new power within him, marking him, changing him. The Semitic understanding is that all succeeding generations are connected to Abraham and share in his *nephesh,* which is now marked with the divine covenantal blessing. One can begin to see the consequences of this understanding once it is applied to the early Church's experience of incorporation into Christ. As with Abraham, each time a person came to Christ and was baptized into Him, his soul was marked by the indwelling of Christ, who then became the new center of power within the man's soul. As with Abraham, a new beginning point was made. When that person was married and had a family, all those to whom he was *organically* bound and with whom he was one-flesh were now also affected. Their organic unity was a reality, not a metaphor. Their oneness-of-flesh now was experiencing Christ. Analogously, as with the beginning of the covenant with Abraham, a new house was established, one in which the Lord was the informing principle.[83]

---

faithful to this election. He became morally culpable in his responses to the initiative of God. Finally, in the new covenant, Christ becomes the informing principle for Christians. Their *nephesh*/soul is marked with Christ and they are indwelt by Him. This happens to such a degree, that they are said to possess a new nature and become a new creation. But this does not take away personal responsibility. Each person—whether man, woman, or child—must work out his own salvation (see Phil 2:12) and, thus, is morally culpable for what he does with the grace of new life that has been given to him.

82. Pedersen, *Israel I–II,* 53.

83. This is the definition of the "domestic church": a family in which Christ is truly present and of which Jesus is Lord through baptism and in which all the baptized have the responsibility to live out Christ's ecclesial mission (as prophet, priest, and king) corporately. This will be taken up in greater detail in the next two chapters.

BUBER AND CORPORATE
PERSONALITY

Modern thought is characterized by an obsessive focus on the autonomous, self-determined individual and has little sympathy for the corporate dimension in human life. However, that is not universally the case, and it would be helpful to discover those corporate ideas or concepts which some modern thinkers propound and which will help overcome the atomistic sensibilities of the modern worldview. They can be used as a starting point in the rediscovery of a more Biblical understanding of the human person, of marriage, and of family.

While contemporary anthropologies do not express themselves in OT terminology, there are some instances in which traces of Biblical corporateness can be detected. In parts of the anthropology of Martin Buber, the Jewish philosopher, we can find three concepts that seem to resonate with the Biblical category of corporate reality: (1) man: relational and impressionable; (2) relationship between the collective and the individual; and (3) the communion of marriage/the household.

Relational Man

Buber's understanding of human nature, like Pedersen's, sees the person as being impressionable at his center—indeed, ontologically oriented to being affected by the other. Grete Schaeder's analysis of Buber's Hebrew humanism succinctly reveals the latter's similarity with Pedersen:

> Only from the standpoint of Buber's religious presuppositions can we fully understand the concept of "ontic participation" as the participation of creation in the life of God and the product of its creaturely interdependency. In the larger context of creation the soul is "that tender surface of personal life which longs for contact with other life"; and a dialogic relation, although hardly perceptible, makes for an ontic "between," a sphere of being common to two people, which "has its being between them, and transcends both."[84]

---

84. Grete Schaeder, *The Hebrew Humanism of Martin Buber*, trans. N. J. Jacobs (Detroit: Wayne State University Press, 1973), 435.

While the terms used are different, this is similar to the Biblical understanding of man. There is a unity to which man is always oriented and which has the capacity to profoundly mark his character. Man has that "tender surface of personal life" which is oriented towards the other. This idea resonates with Pedersen's understanding of the pliability of the *nephesh*.[85]

Collectivism and the Individual

Secondly, as in authentic Hebrew thought, Buber avoids the Scylla and Charybdis of individualism versus collectivism; instead, he suggests a third way, which he calls the "between." His articulation of this idea is quite different from that of the Biblical "corporate personality," yet there is sufficient resonance between the two to suggest they may have a common basis. Again, the human soul is deeply impressionable and, consequently, a sphere exists in a person's life that desires authentic community.

> The fundamental fact of human existence is neither the individual as such nor the aggregate as such.... The individual is a fact of existence in so far as he steps into a living relation with other individuals.... The fundamental fact of human existence is man with man.... It is rooted in one being turning to another as another...in order to communicate with it in a sphere which is common to them.... I call this sphere...which is still conceptually uncomprehended, the sphere of "between"...it is a primal category of human reality.[86]

Here Buber expresses the idea that man is not a solitary individual nor is he a collective animal. Instead, man finds his identity in *community*. Our beings are fundamentally oriented to being in relationship with the "other." The genius of this modern Hebrew mind is that it weds the community and the individual together, bringing them into a fruitful tension.[87]

85. See the section above: "The Soul's Relationship to Corporate Reality." See also Pedersen, *Israel I–II*, 165.

86. Martin Buber, *Between Man and Man*, trans. R. G. Smith (New York: MacMillan, 1965), 203.

87. The communitarian dimension to man is also found in Aristotle (see, for example, *Nicomachean Ethics*, bk. 8, ch. 9, and *Politics*, bk 1).

Corporateness in Marriage

Finally, Buber's understanding of marriage has strong similarities with the Old Testament sense of corporate and organic identity. While using different categories, he articulates how the husband and wife share in each other's being in a fundamental way:

> He who has entered into marriage, has taken in earnest, in the intention of the sacrament, the fact that the other *is,* the fact that I cannot legitimately share in the Present Being without sharing in the being of the other, the fact that I cannot answer the lifelong address of God to me without answering at the same time for the other…as one who is entrusted to me.[88]

Buber's understanding of the marital community is predicated on its being a privileged place where the encounter of husband and wife participates in the greater encounter of man with God. He bestows upon this space a spiritual character and describes it as sacramental. He has an intuitive grasp of the profound implications of the corporate and organic dimensions of this fundamental human experience. In all three examples, we find Buber wrestling with the mystery of the human person, who is at once a personalized individual but also is called to a fundamental communion with others which must be realized if he is to be fully human. His Hebraic background enables him to intuitively combine ancient Semitic categories with modern sensibilities. Schaeder's conclusion about Buber's perspective (in *The Hebrew Humanism of Martin Buber*) shows perhaps the problem that we face in trying to translate the truths of a Biblical worldview into the modern context:

> Buber's world image had always retained something of the dynamic of a religious myth that could not be rendered in the language of modern philosophy. A coherent presentation of the theme What is man? was not possible starting with such presuppositions, and Buber had to be content with elaborating the basic principles of his dynamic "ontologism" as contributions to a philosophical anthropology.[89]

---

88. Martin Buber, "The Question to the Single One," in *The Writings of Martin Buber*, ed. Will Herberg, trans. R. G. Smith (New York: Meridian Books, 1956), 83.

89. Schaeder, *The Hebrew Humanism of Martin Buber*, 436.

Nonetheless, Buber has provided us with an excellent example of how ancient categories and understanding, imported into the modern context, can enable us to understand the human person and his relationships.

CONCLUSION

We are able to see that the family's role in the salvific process did not begin in the NT but has strong roots in the experience of the Hebrew people, where it is intrinsically connected to the covenant. Because of the saving acts of Yahweh and the knowledge of His nature, Israel's understanding of sexuality and the family were radically differentiated from that of the surrounding pagan culture. It was Israel who understood their true nature and was able to recognize their rightful place in the created order and provide their meaning. Like creation itself, sexuality and family have been assumed into the will of God and have become the instrument of His salvation.

As the carrier of the covenant, the family in Israel is aptly suited to its task, not only because of the educational opportunities and the parent-child relationships that enhance this process, but also by the intergenerational organic bonds that are at the heart of the family. Our study shows that the structure of the family possesses the interior disposition to portray symbolically the covenant. Because the realities of marriage and family interpenetrate each other and are ordered to each other, the essential structures of both resonate with, and image forth, the covenantal relationship with God. The covenant is experienced and lived out in the familial context, which is a concrete expression of the relationship of Yahweh to Israel (see Hosea 1–3, 11). Hence, the family is called to be a *sphere of holiness*.

This theological function of the family is predicated on the reality of corporate personality. This term expresses the organic and corporate understanding of life that allows the community to participate in the *nephesh* of Abraham and allows the generations to have a vital identification with each other.

Implications: Given this salvific and corporate dimension of the family, it would be strange for the New Testament, which understands itself to be the fulfillment of the numerous theological trajectories in the Old Testament, to formally jettison it. Indeed, what happens in the New Testament is precisely what one should expect. It incorporates, while also extending, the Old Testament's corporate understanding of reality. The NT family is considered an organic whole and a vital sphere of eschatological activity, a dynamic which is only possible because of the reality of corporate personality.[90]

Thus, any fruitful construction of a theology of the domestic church has to be grounded in the OT principle of corporate personality. The first part of this study has provided a framework by which to analyze the theological nature of family in the Old Testament and has unearthed the foundational principles that inform the covenantal family; the task that remains is to explore to what degree these realities are integrated in the New Testament's vision of the family. To be adequate, any theology of the domestic church must take into account the OT roots of the family. As Schillebeeckx reminded us earlier: "The fact remains that it pleased God to reveal himself within Semitic society and in the course of a Semitic history.... We can ignore this history and civilization only at our peril, for it is impossible to grasp the word of God...divorced from its human expression."[91]

---

90. It can be argued that the proclamation of the gospel, itself, and the Eucharistic community are more fully spheres of eschatological activity. This insight, however, does not deny the real ecclesial identity of the baptized family. In fact, it is a subset of the full Eucharistic community, the Church. That is why the appellation "domestic church" is so apt. The gospel is particularly lived out in the home within the day-to-day familial relations that make up our lives. The grace received in the sacrament of the Eucharist enables us to live Christ's life in our marriages and families. It is true that all these activities are places where the Holy Spirit is actively bringing about the eschaton. But one of the profound insights the Church provides in describing the family as the domestic church is its *ecclesial* identity. The primary activity of the family is the bringing of the eschaton into the world. In this, the family is not unique, for it primarily shares in this mission of the Church. What is new is that few have acknowledged or understood that this eschatological dynamic was also present in the family.

91. Schillebeeckx, *Marriage*, 9.

PART 2

FOUNDATIONS OF THE FAMILY IN THE NEW TESTAMENT, EARLY CHURCH, AND VATICAN II

> If anyone is in Christ, he is a new creation. The
> old has passed away, behold the new has come.
>
> 2 Corinthians 5:17

THE WITNESS OF THE NEW TESTAMENT

In analyzing the New Testament texts in terms of the domestic Church, it is important to recognize that there is no fully developed theology of the family within the New Testament. This is accounted for by the fact that the entire early Church was initially Jewish. Indeed, Christianity was considered as emerging from within Judaism and was called "the Way" (cf. Acts 9:2). For the early Church it was not a question of repudiating the Hebrew covenant; rather, early Christians believed that in Christ the covenant with Abraham had reached its teleological conclusion.[1] In

---

1. The phrase "teleological conclusion" is not a tautology, but is used to prevent misunderstanding. What is meant here is that the Abrahamic covenant has

effect, this meant that the first Christians brought with them all the OT understanding of the family and, therefore, would see it as a critical element in the new covenant.[2] In other words, theologically there was not a break between the Old and the New Testament family; rather, there was a fulfillment of the former by the latter. This dynamic of fulfillment was already announced by Christ in His Sermon on the Mount: "I have come not to destroy but to fulfill (πληρῶσαι)" (Mt 5:17).

Several New Testament texts testify to this dynamic of continuity with the OT, but there was also a radical newness to Christianity. With the Incarnation and the Passion of the Lord, a decisive act of God in history had been accomplished and the eschatological moment inserted into chronological history; the kingdom of heaven had definitively begun. Thus, though a radical continuity is clearly evident, there is also a radical discontinuity in the NT that must be accounted for.[3]

One form which this radical newness takes is the experience of being inserted into Christ through baptism. It is within this sacramental reality that one becomes a new creation and the eschaton begins (in some form) within the believer's own personal life. Because Christ has become the new informing principle of a person's soul (*nephesh*),[4] those who are organi-

---

reached its conclusion but not in the sense that it has ended per se. Rather, there was an original teleological design inherent in the covenant that has now been realized.

2. The very first "cell" of the Church was composed of Jews who had come to see Jesus as the promised Messiah and were baptized into Him. Although the Gentile world did not share this inheritance, St. Paul shows us that the Gentiles do not stand in isolation from this foundational Jewish influence but "when the fullness of time came" (Gal 4:4) they were called to be incorporated into it and to become sharers in these same promises to Abraham. ("Remember that at one time you, Gentiles...were...without Christ, alienated from the community of Israel.... But now in Christ Jesus you...have become near" [Eph 2:11–12].) As Paul shows in Romans 11:24ff., the Gentiles are grafted into the natural olive tree of Israel, which is the main root. Thus, the Hebraic understanding of family was formative for the whole Church. Ultimately, the Church is the family of Abraham reaching its "teleological conclusion," towards which it was always moving inherently.

3. Henri de Lubac, *Sources of Revelation*, trans. Luke O'Neill (New York: Herder and Herder, 1968), 143–47.

4. +Gal 2:20 expresses the new state of the believers in these terms: "And no longer do I

cally part of him, that is, his family, have also become affected by this new Presence in the family. The family still retains the *function* of being the carrier of the covenant, but now it is transformed into *the sphere of eschatological activity.* The power of Christ and His salvation are present within the baptized family and everyone within its orbit is affected—even those who are not yet believers (cf. 1 Cor 7). This understanding of the effect of grace is predicated on the corporate nature of the human person and logically results in the practice of household baptisms (see Acts 11, 16). This Semitic view of human nature is evident not only in this practice but also in the Pauline understanding of mixed marriage and the consequences that flow from the corporate nature of marrige (see 1 Cor 7). In fact, the Corinthian teaching on marriage is incomprehensible without an understanding of corporate personality.[5]

Our need in the next part of our study is to discover the fundamental principles that inform the understanding of the family as the "domestic church" in the New Testament. Our first task is to establish the continuity between the two Testaments (through the use of genealogies and the primary figure of Abraham). The second is to examine the evidence to determine the extent to which the Semitic idea of corporate personality continues to operate in the New Testament. It will be within this context that the effects of baptism on marriage and the family will be studied. The third task is to carry out a philological study of the term domestic church as it appears in the texts and to determine to what degree this term provides Scriptural foundations for the theology of the domestic church. Follow-

---

live, but Christ lives in me." To express this in terms of the Semitic categories we have considered, it would be possible to say that Christ had become the new informing principle within the person and is a new source of power with his *nephesh.*

5. This passage will be examined later. The important point here is that, in contrast with certain modern trends, the individualistic understanding of salvation is not operative within the NT. While salvation is always deeply personal, it is always grounded in the corporate dimension; an individual person is baptized, but the ground of his baptism is always in the corporate reality of Christ. In baptism, the state of isolation caused by sin ceases as the person is grafted into the *corporate* body of Christ.

ing this, we will focus on how the Church Fathers appropriated and understood the theological meaning of the family in terms of the domestic church. In particular, we will see how they explicitly thought of the Christian family not only in terms of its ecclesial mission (i.e., its participation in the life of the Church), but also how they conceived of the family as having ecclesial structures. We will see that they situated the structures of the Church analogously within the ecclesial reality of the home.

CHAPTER 7

THE FAMILY OF
ABRAHAM IN THE NEW
TESTAMENT

From the beginning of Christianity there has been a tension between the revelation in Christ Jesus and its relationship to the covenant with the Hebrews. It formed the basis for the first major theological struggle in the Church, when the relationship between circumcision and baptism had to be worked out. Later, Marcion championed the idea that the Christian revelation was so radically different from the Old Testament that it necessitated a rejection of the older Semitic understanding of God. While this teaching was determined to be heretical, it nonetheless underscored the problem of the relationship between the two testaments. Even today, the Old Testament remains a closed book for many Christians. However, in Romans 11 Paul teaches that the Gentiles were grafted into the natural olive tree of Israel and hence the reality of Christ and the Church is predicated upon and grounded in the revelation to the Jews.[1] St. Augustine pithily caught the essence of this relationship between the old and new covenant by writing that

---

1. "But if some of the branches were broken off, and you, a wild olive shoot, were grafted in their place and have come to share in the rich root of the olive tree, do not boast against the branches. If you do boast, consider that you do not support the root; the root supports you" (•Rom 11:17–18).

"the new is hidden in the old and the old is revealed in the new."[2] As Christ himself taught in the Sermon on the Mount, not one jot or tittle of the Law would pass away until the Law had been fulfilled (Mt 5:17–18). In fact, instead of repudiating the Law of Moses, Jesus presents Himself as the new Moses who reveals the deeper intentionality of the Law and raises it to a new level.

Our study will now examine the intrinsic linkage between the teachings and realities of the Old Testament and their appropriation within the new covenant. We will show the fundamental continuity between both testaments, especially in the meaning and function of the family. This can be done, in the first place, by an examination of the use of genealogies. We will see that the *tôldôt* of the old covenant are extended into the New Testament and reach their fulfillment there. Secondly, we will see that the early Church did not perceive of the new covenant as something completely original. Rather, the NT writers took great pains to show the continuity between the new creation in Christ and the unconditional covenant that was given to Abraham (which, it must be remembered, was the beginning of the salvific process). Hence, Abraham figures largely in both testaments and becomes *the father of all the faithful—both Jew and Christian.* This teaching has been largely ignored within the Christian context, but in fact, it is part of the foundation of the Christian faith. This chapter, therefore, will analyze the role of Abraham as the father of faith for the new covenant. The use of the genealogies and the foundational role of Abraham establish the continued importance of family within the Christian economy and provide the foundation for the theology of the domestic Church.

GENEALOGIES

The concept of historical time that emerged in Hebraic consciousness introduced not only an absolute beginning point for creation but also a teleological conclusion towards which history was moving.

---

2. "Ut Novum in Vetere lateret et in Novo Vetus pateret" (*Dei Verbum* 16, which references *Quest. in Hept.* 2, 73: PL 34,623.)

Within this context, human sexuality, which hithertofore had magical connotations and was used to manipulate the gods, became thoroughly demythologized. Concretely, the meaning of each human reality (sexuality, the family, marriage, etc.) becomes comprehensible to the degree that it is related to the end (*telos*) for which all were created. Specifically with the Abrahamic covenant, the family is assumed into the salvific process and becomes a part of the covenantal process by which the creation was to be restored to the Creator. Thus the generations (*tôldôt*) became an essential component of the covenant, and the family became the means of transmitting the salvific covenant from one generation to the next.

For the modern reader who is unfamiliar with the Old Testament, the recitation of the OT genealogical tables at the beginning of the gospels is somewhat perplexing and their purpose is somewhat incomprehensible: "The book of the generation of Jesus Christ, the son of David, the son of Abraham."[3] To grasp their meaning it is important to note that this NT genealogy is the final ancestral recitation in Scripture and provides the *terminus ad quem* for all the Hebrew genealogical lists (the *tôldôt*). These genealogies, now stretching from Adam to Christ,[4] form the bridge between the two testaments and guarantee that the gospel is radically grounded in the Abrahamic covenant and not a departure from it. In fact, the genealogy of Jesus specifically secures the organic continuity between Christ and the primary realities of Adam, Abraham, and David. Their location at the opening of Matthew and Luke is dictated by the theological necessity of having to establish Jesus as the teleological conclusion of all preceding genealogical lists.[5]

This critical dependence on the family lines shows the intersection of history and the covenant and the essential importance of the family (and the family line) to salvation history. In Christ, the family has reached its final and proper form. It is through the family that God is working out His purposes in history. The family is not extrinsic, ac-

---

3. "Βίβλος γενέσεως Ἰησοῦ Χριστοῦ υἱοῦ Δαυὶδ υἱοῦ Ἀβραάμ" (+Mt 1:1).

4. See Mt 1 and Lk 3.

5. The lack of any further development of the *tôldôt* is an indication that this terminal point has indeed been reached.

cidental, or voluntaristic but is rather an essential part of God's plan, even up to and including the New Testament period. Within the Hebrew mind, both the personal with its emphasis on the individual, and the corporate with its emphasis on the family, tribe, or nation have always been present in positive tension.[6] This understanding carried over into the Church, which has always accepted the corporate dimension of salvation and understood the covenant in personal *and* corporate terms.

While it is evident that the use of these genealogies in the gospels is derived from the Hebraic conception of narrative revelation, the New Testament uses the genealogies in a specific way so as to give them their own *theological* form.[7] To understand the purpose and functioning of the genealogies in Matthew and Luke, it is necessary to see that they are structured around three divine initiatives found in the Old Testament: the creation, the covenant with Abraham, and the establishment of the messianic Davidic line. Each of these is necessary to understand the nature of the Messiah and His mission, which in turn, structure the Church, of which the Christian family is an integral part. We will investigate each aspect so that the fuller Christological dimensions of the family become apparent.

EXCURSUS 3: THE MESSIANIC FAMILY

Jacob Neusner, in *A Rabbi Talks with Jesus,* understands profoundly the implications of the claims of Jesus and clearly shows both the radical continuity and radical discontinuity of His claims. Unlike many scholars today who posit an opposition between the (simple) miracle-working prophet, Jesus, found in the Gospels and the (complex) Christ created by Paul, Neusner sees that if one understands the claims of Jesus in the Gospel,

---

6. Contrary to some interpretation of the prophetic movement where individual responsibility is emphasized, Israel never substituted individualism for corporate reality.

7. The NT did not invent the use of genealogies to structure its message; that was clearly a Hebraic mode of revelation. But Mt 1 and Lk 3 use this genealogical form to established specific theological points.

they are in fact the same as those presented in the early Church! ("The distinction between the one and the other…strikes me as not well founded" [68–69].) Neusner also realizes that Jesus is saying something fundamentally different about family than had hithertofore been understood in Israel. Jesus reveals that we must love Him *more* than our families (see Mt 10:34–37). The Torah places great emphasis on the family; in fact, Neusner claims that it makes family parallel with one's obligations to God and provides the numerous passages where these parallels occur (66–68). For example, "Honor the Lord with your substance…. Honor your father and mother" (67). Within Israel, the community of Torah sages has urged loyalty to family as a form of loyalty to God. However, Neusner recognizes that even these sages developed the idea that Torah knowledge took precedence over the unlettered father of family and cites Tractate *Baba Mesia* 2:11 of the Mishnah to that effect. But as Neusner points out, the contrast is not strictly Torah versus family (i.e., father representing natural genealogical relationship) but is between Torah knowledge and a father who does not know the Torah. If the family is Torah observant, then the "claim of the father, based on both Torah and genealogy, outweighs the claim of the sage [who knows Torah]" (65). Jesus, in His radical claim to our first love (we must love Him more than all others), is making a much greater claim. In fact, Neusner correctly identifies exactly what Jesus is revealing here and asks the Christian, "And is your master God? For, I now realize only God can demand of me what Jesus is asking" (68).

For Neusner, in the Torah God brings about salvation in terms of the family (of Israel) which is eternal (28, 36, 45). For him, Jesus speaks only to the individual but not to the collective family of Israel. He believes that Jesus is thus rejecting the place of the covenantal family and requires, in its place, a loyalty to Himself. Neusner asks: "But then, is everything in your torah's fulfillment of the Torah to speak only to my conduct as a person? Is there no torah for me as part of a family, as part of that Israel that existed before Sinai and assembled at the foot of Sinai: children of Abraham and

Sarah, Isaac and Rebecca, Jacob and Leah and Rachel? I am of the family of Israel. What have you to say to me in that family?" (70). The answer to that question is at the heart of what Christianity is. What the Apostles and early Christians (all of whom were Jews) saw was that Jesus was not rejecting the covenantal family but taking that Abrahamic family and forming it into the messianic family of the Church, born out of His own Body. This family was the fulfillment of the Abrahamic promise which began with the giving of the covenant in Genesis 12. It was not disassociated from this original family. Paul clearly makes this point in his analogy of the olive tree in Romans 11. However, a radical change had been effected through the Incarnation and Passion of Christ by which the family of Abraham becomes the Body of Christ. This sense of radical "newness" was already witnessed to in Jeremiah's prophecy that a "new" covenant (בְּרִית חֲדָשָׁה) was coming (Jer 31:31). Jesus is the seed of Abraham (Gal 3:16) and as He dies, His life is now multiplied in His members (i.e., the Church). The Akeda or near sacrifice of Isaac (Gn 22) is perhaps instructive here. Abraham was called to be the only salvific family in creation. This promise passes *only* through Isaac and yet God calls Abraham to sacrifice him. Abraham walks in obedience and goes to Mount Moriah to offer up Isaac. No value, even the family itself, can be greater than obedience to God. In this case, Abraham is tested and found to be faithful. God provides a ram, and Isaac is set free. But the Akeda is typologically fulfilled in Christ who, as the beloved Son, dies on the Cross. For Him, there is no substitute. What God did not require of His people, He requires of Himself. The Christian claim is that by this sacrifice of the Messiah, He becomes the grain of wheat (Jn 12:24) which, having fallen, now will become "many." All who are baptized into Christ become His Body, brothers and sisters of each other, and form the Messianic family. It is the salvific family of Abraham, having received its Christological basis. Christ does not reject the importance of the mediation of the salvific family but brings it into full existence.

FAMILY AS STRUCTURE
OF CREATION

The creation account in Genesis establishes the fact that all people are fundamentally interconnected and have an originating point in the first personal creation of God, namely Adam. The precise point which the narrative makes is that there are no autonomous individuals;[8] rather, the whole of humanity (extending both into the future and into the past) is ultimately viewed as a single organic reality.[9] Since the Hebrew genealogical lists are ultimately grounded in the creation, they act as potent witnesses to the interrelatedness of the whole human race and to the corporate dimension of the human person. In Luke's gospel, the *terminus a quo* for the Messiah is found in Adam and as such this genealogy links the reality of Christ with the structures of creation. The messianic reality is not totally extrinsic to our human reality but, in some mysterious fashion, it emerges from within the created order as well. It will be through the flesh and blood of the Messiah, through the matrix of human relationships (i.e., the family) and the organic interconnectedness which this affords (and which a corporate creation in Adam secures), that salvation will be procured and experienced.[10] Thus, the Incarnation, which the genealogies safeguard, demonstrates

8. This is true even of the first *'ādām* because he was created already oriented towards another which was necessary for his existence. Hence, he experiences loneliness until the appearance of the "other" (Gn 2:23).

9. C. S. Lewis gives an excellent description of this phenomenon in *Beyond Personality*: "They (human beings) look separate because you see them walking about separately but then we are so made that we can see only the present moment. If we could see the past, then of course it would look different. For there was a time when every man was part of his mother and (earlier still) part of his father as well: and when they were part of his grandparents. So if you could see humanity spread out in time, as God sees it, it wouldn't look like a lot of separate things dotted about. It would look like one single growing thing—rather like a very complicated tree. Every individual would appear connected with every other and not only that. Individuals aren't really separate from God, anymore than from one another.... When Christ becomes man...it is as if something which is always affecting the whole human mass begins, at one point, to affect that whole human mass in a new way. From that point, the effect spreads to all mankind" (London: Geoffrey Bles, 1952), 30.

10. Docetism was an early heresy that affirmed only the spiritual reality of Christ and denied the reality of His humanity. Again this points to the importance of the genealogical

that our bodily reality (including marriage and family) is not extrinsic to but fundamental to the salvific event. The earliest strata of revelation give evidence of this connection between flesh and salvation. We see in Gn 3:15 (known as the *protoevangelium*) that in the cosmic battle with Satan, salvation comes through humanity (the seed of the woman) and not by some extraneous force parachuting into creation to bring about its healing.[11]

ABRAHAMIC FOUNDATION

The second divine initiative that is emphasized in the genealogy of Christ is the call of Abraham. Up to Genesis 12, all the genealogies had universal scope inasmuch as they applied to the whole of humanity. However, with Yahweh's establishing the unique covenant with and through Abram (Gn 12, 15, 17), a critical distinction is made which divides humanity into two spheres.[12] This is the formal beginning of the salvific process by which the creation will be restored to the Father (see Col 1:15–20), a process which can be seen as being continuous with the promise in Gn 3:15.[13] Abram *alone* becomes the salvific contact point

---

lists, because they affirm the humanity of Christ and show that it is precisely in the material realities of creation (i.e., *our* bodily life) that salvation is procured and lived out.

11. Gn 3:15 was recognized as early as Irenaeus as a key text announcing in subliminal terms the work of Christ. Critical methodologies usually reject this interpretation because they take "seed" as being in the plural and not referring to a final individual (see Westermann, *Genesis*, 26off.). But given Paul's use of the singular meaning of "seed" in Gal 3:16, in which he shows that Jesus is the final "seed" of Abraham and the fulfillment of Gn 12:1–3, the traditional interpretation is quite plausible within a biblical worldview. In the midst of the Fall, God announces the plan of salvation (again, in veiled terms), which is portrayed as a cosmic battle, the seed of the serpent fighting and wounding the seed of the woman; the woman's seed will in turn crush the head of the serpent. In Rv 12:9, the serpent is revealed to be Satan. Note, already in Philo there was the understanding that the serpent referred to evil powers (see Westermann, *Genesis*, 261). The crucial point here is that it is precisely someone who comes in and through the flesh who will gain the world's salvation—not an angelic spirit.

12. This is why the call of Abraham can be seen as parallel to creation. See Dumbrell, *Covenant and Creation*, 57–58.

13. There are some modern exegetes who reject the trajectory proceeding from creation; they connect the Abrahamic covenant with David (see Dumbrell, *Covenant and Creation*, 50n5).

between God and creation. While there is an emphasis on particularity (the covenant is established only with Abram and his family), there
is, surprisingly, even at this initiating stage, an opening towards a uni-
versalism that will be realized at a later date.[14] But once the covenant
is established, the genealogies will now only focus on the Abrahamic
family line.

When Abram was initiated into the covenant (Gn 15), Yahweh revealed to him the future of his family: they would go down to Egypt,
endure servitude, and then be delivered by the mighty acts of Yahweh.
The historical realities of his own family were caught up in the salvific
purposes of God. Their suffering and deliverance become part of the
vocation of the covenantal family, which alone was the sphere of salvific activity within history.[15] Consequently, given the importance of the
Exodus in salvation history, one would expect the insertion of a genealogy once the Hebrew descendants of Jacob/Israel had been delivered.
This is precisely what happens in Nm 1:1–2:34, which provides the genealogical records of the people who were rescued from Pharaoh. As is
evidenced in each of the OT covenants (whether with Noah, Abraham,
or Moses), the covenant is clearly a familial reality.

The covenant with Abraham is both unconditional and foundational to Judaism. It is God alone who bestows it upon Abraham, who
is simply called to follow God.[16] Jesus, in His humanity, shares in the
nephesh of Abraham and is thus linked to this primary covenant which

---

14. וְנִבְרְכוּ בְךָ כֹּל מִשְׁפְּחֹת הָאֲדָמָה / *v'nir'ḥû b'ḥā kōl mishp'ḥōt hā'ădāmāh*—"and in you all the families/tribes of the earth shall be blessed/find blessing/bless themselves" (+Gn 12:3). Because the covenant is established only with Abraham and his descendants, he be-comes the unique source of blessing for the entire world. See Dumbrell, *Covenant and Creation*, 70ff.

15. This is not to say that God is not concerned about the rest of creation. The very fact that the election of Israel is meant to serve the rest of the world and to become the means of its blessing proves that God's concern is universal. As well, there are numerous references in the prophetic literature that attest to God's oversight of all the nations. But there is a unique-ness about Israel, who becomes God "special possession"—סְגֻלָּה / *s'gullā*ʰ (Ex 19:5–6). It is clear that the salvific trajectory is initiated and continues only within the structure of the Abrhamaic family. See Jesus' remarks in +John 4:22, where he points to the uniqueness of Judaism ("for salvation is from the Jews"/ ὅτι ἡ σωτηρία ἐκ τῶν Ἰουδαίων ἐστίν).

16. Dumbrell, *Covenant and Creation*, 53ff.

He is meant to fulfill. Christ does not establish something totally new but acts within the structures of (salvation) history. Consequently His death and passion do not establish an utterly new reality in contradistinction to the Abrahamic family; instead, they transform that original covenantal family so that it is informed by the Holy Spirit and becomes the Body of Christ, the Church.[17] In Christ, the covenantal family of Abraham is not annulled but reaches its teleological conclusion and becomes the universal Church. Thus, by directly grounding the genealogy of Jesus in the person of Abraham, the New Testament establishes an organic connection to Abraham and his family that can never be dissolved. The family, either as carrier of the covenant or in its eschatologized form, plays a central role in God's salvific will.

MESSIANIC DIMENSIONS OF THE FAMILY

The third focus of the NT genealogies is the messianic promise, which is founded in David and his household. Christ's messianic claims are grounded in the covenant established with David. This is not an independent covenant but rather a subset of the covenant with Abraham. While Israel's demand for a king was an ultimate rejection of God's original plan for Israel, this rejection is finally resolved by the establishment of the royal line of David.[18] The importance of this covenant becomes clear only when the kingship runs its course and ends in national apostasy, which ushers in the exilic period. Only within the prophetic period, as the prophets begin to show how God will redeem

17. The theology of fulfillment is based on Jesus' teaching in the Sermon on the Mount and requires both continuity and discontinuity with the old covenant. From this perspective, one can better understand the parable of the householder who legitimately brings out from his storage treasures both old and new. (+Mt 13:52—"Jesus said to them, 'Every scribe who has become a disciple of the kingdom of heaven is like a man, a householder, who brings out of his storehouse new and old things.'")

18. 1 Samuel records the fact that God's intention for Israel was that it should take the form of a theocracy. Her demand for a king was understood to be a fundamental rejection of the rule of God (see 1 Sam 8:7). The Lord allows this development but works it into His own salvific design when He inserts the messianic dimension into the (Davidic) kingly line (see 2 Sam 7:13–14). Thus, the rejection of the rule of God ultimately becomes the means by which the kingdom of the Messiah will enter into human history.

the unfaithfulness of Israel, do the messianic dimensions of the Davidic line become clear.[19] Ezekiel gives us an excellent example of this process. In his writings, there is a growth of messianic ideas and imagery that become associated with the future leadership of Israel which becomes identified with God Himself. Narratively, this reaches a particular density in Ezekiel 34 with Yahweh's condemnation of the evil "shepherds" of Israel.[20] The Lord declares that He Himself will come to shepherd His people (Ezek 34:11).[21] Then in verse 37:24 He reveals that His servant David will be king over them.[22] Here we have the prophetic announcement of the direct rule of Yahweh over His people, and the restoration of the Davidic line. This is echoed in several other prophets including both Isaiah (with the development of his Davidic branch theology)[23] and Hosea (with the restoration of David as king).[24] Later, this prophetic announcement that Yahweh will shepherd his people becomes the backdrop to Jesus' declaration that He is the good Shepherd (Jn 10:11),[25] thereby revealing both His divine identity and His mission. Because of the organic identification of Christ with the Church (which is His Body),[26] the Church shares in His messianic mission, as

---

19. Dumbrell, *Covenant and Creation*, 139, 150. See Abraham Heschel, *The Prophets* (Philadelphia: Jewish Publication Society of America, 1962), 660ff.

20. "Son of man, prophesy against the shepherds of Israel.... Thus says the Lord GOD: Woe to the shepherds of Israel who have been pasturing themselves!... You did not strengthen the weak nor heal the sick nor bind up the injured. You did not bring back the strayed nor seek the lost" (•Ezek 34: 2–4).

21. כִּי כֹה אָמַר אֲדֹנָי יְהוִה הִנְנִי־אָנִי וְדָרַשְׁתִּי אֶת־צֹאנִי וּבִקַּרְתִּים—"For thus says the Lord GOD: Behold, I, I myself will search for my sheep, and will seek them out" (^Ezek 34:11).

22. וְעַבְדִּי דָוִד מֶלֶךְ עֲלֵיהֶם/—"My servant, David, *will be* king over them" (+Ezek 37:24). While some question the direct connection between messiah, kingship, and Jesus, the early Church saw that the different prophetic trajectories converged on Jesus and identified him with those passages which developed the idea of the messianic kingship and the suffering servant (particularly Is 53). It is not accidental that John's gospel specifically draws attention to the sign on the Cross above Jesus' head which read: "Jesus, the Nazarene, King of the Jews" (+Jn 19:19).

23. Is 11:1.

24. Is 11:1; Hos 3:5

25. "I am the good shepherd. The good shepherd lays down his life for the sheep" (+Jn 10:11).

26. This is dramatically shown in Saul's encounter with the living Christ in ^Acts 9:5, in which the voice responds to Saul, "I am Jesus, whom you are persecuting."

do all those baptized into Christ along with their baptized families.[27]

As we have noted, there is no fully developed theology of the family in the New Testament. In the Old Testament the critical role of the family as the carrier of the covenant is well established, and the genealogies, which structure the OT, are evidence of this. In the NT, everything is relativized in relationship to Christ. What is critical is our personal relationship with Him. This can lead one to assume that the family plays no role in the salvific plan in the NT. But there are several indicators that the idea of the covenantal family continues to be a factor in the salvific process, even in the new covenant. The first link between the Old and New Testaments is a genealogical one. Matthew begins by presenting us with the genealogy of Christ, which connects with the *tôldôt* of the OT. The purpose of those earlier genealogies is now realized fully in Christ, the Messiah. The family, which is the carrier of the covenant, has now "delivered" the messiah into human history. But is that the end of the functioning of the family within God's design for salvation? This certainly has not been true of other critical aspects of the old covenant. Realities such as the Passover and circumcision are not simply rejected to be replaced by some totally new reality. Rather they are radically transformed by Christ, finding their fulfillment in Him. This dynamic of fulfillment is what underlies the relationship between the Old and New Testament realities. For example, in the new covenant sacraments of Eucharist and Baptism, Passover and circumcision are transformed. All they pointed to is now realized in and through the actions of Christ, which are *effectively* made present in these new sacraments. One can posit that the same dynamic happened

27. It is very difficult for the modern (Western) mind to grasp the actual role of the family in the New Testament covenant. We tend to think of the individual as an absolutized individual who encounters Christ and makes a unique act of faith that only affects him, as if all his relationships (both those from which he came or which he has helped to create) are entirely extrinsic. Therefore, he is hermetically sealed off from those around him. By way of contrast, the Old and New Testaments witness to the intense personal relationship that each person has with God, but they never see this in solely individualistic terms. Always, there is an accompanying corporate reality that *grounds* the person's experience. Thus, while an individual is profoundly affected by his encounter with Christ, so too are those with whom he is intrinsically connected. This becomes the foundation for such NT concepts as the Body of Christ, household baptisms, the communion of saints, etc.

to the family. It is transformed from being the carrier of the covenant to now becoming the place where the salvation wrought in Christ is being effectively worked out. Marriage now becomes imbued with sacramental grace (see Eph 5:22ff.), and within the organic structure of family itself (i.e., the oneness of flesh) the members experience the power and presence of Christ (see 1 Cor 7:12ff.). The individual family is now inserted into the larger family of the Church. Just as Christians are sons in the Son, so baptized families now become salvific families (the domestic church) in the Salvific Family (the hierarchical Church).[28] In this way, the genealogies in the NT act something like a bridge or conduit which establish the radical connection between the two covenants and allow a continuity of the OT understanding and functioning of the family within the NT. In effect, to read the NT correctly, we need to affirm that there is both a radical continuity between the testaments and also a radical discontinuity. The roots within Judaism can never be rejected (see Rom 11:17ff.), but it is also true that something totally new has taken place in Christ. The introduction of a genuine new principle (i.e., Christ) effects a radical transformation of all things; including the family. This new principle does not destroy things but fulfills them so they can effectively operate within the design of salvation, but now in a Christological manner.[29] The carrier of the covenant becomes now the eschatological sphere of activity, i.e., a place where the Holy Spirit is active in a unique way to bring about the salvation of the world.

ABRAHAM: FATHER OF US ALL

The centrality of Abraham in the New Testament is one of the greatly neglected themes in New Testament studies. As noted above, Abraham plays a pivotal role in the genealogical development that culminates

28. The "hierarchical Church" refers to fullest expression of the Body of Christ, the Church united under Peter. The "domestic church" refers to is specific expression in the baptized family.

29. This means, for example, that the Passover now becomes filled with the sacrificial life of Christ, which is received in the Eucharist. The Passover becomes something which it could never have become on its own. Only the presence of Christ can fulfill it and transform it into the Eucharist.

with the birth of the Messiah. Without this grounding in the person of Abraham (and thereby all the promises that were made to him), the New Testament would have no fundamental connection to the Hebraic covenant and the claims that the early Christian church was the heir of the Abrahamic covenant would be questionable at best.[30] Therefore, in Matthew's Gospel the *terminus a quo* for the genealogy of Jesus is precisely situated in the person of Abraham.

But the role of Abraham goes well beyond that of structuring the genealogies.[31] In fact, Abraham plays a pivotal role in the development of Pauline theology. In both Romans and Galatians, Paul reveals the intrinsic connection between the Christian experience of salvation in Christ and the faith of Abraham, and demonstrates that the latter informs and fundamentally structures the former. The two are seen to be a single reality, organically linked to each other. In chapter 4 of Romans, Paul tackles the difficult theological problem of justification and its relationship to faith and works. This was a major theological problem in the early Church, the solution to which would determine the Church's understanding of the nature of salvation. Is one made right with God (δικαίωσις/justified) by obedience to a set of commands or is justification predicated on a personal act of faith?[32] One party in the NT Christian community argued that the believer in Christ had to uphold the Jewish law (including circumcision) in order to be then justified through faith in Christ. This position maintained that salvation was predicated on the observance of the Law which was then augment-

30. See both Rom 4:16 and Gal 3:29, where Paul states that those in Christ have Abraham as their father.

31. Luke's genealogy (3:34) establishes the genealogy of Christ back to Adam and God with no particular emphasis. The importance of Abraham in Luke comes out more clearly in the rest of the gospel, where Luke mentions Abraham thirteen times (five times in Chapter 16 in the periscope concerning Lazarus and the rich man.) The importance of the relationship to Abraham is seen in 19:9 when Jesus says to Zacchaeus, "Today salvation has come to this house, because he, too, is a son of Abraham."

32. This is a complex topic and a major theological theme in recent years within Pauline studies. There are widely differing analyses which emerge from differing understandings of Paul's theology and the nature of Judaism. The above presentation, in general, follows the Pauline argumentation articulated in Romans and Galatians. For Paul, the role of Abraham is central to the working out of this problem.

ed by the grace of the Cross.[33] However, Paul showed that the foundational covenant (which was established in and through the person of Abraham) came long before the giving of the Mosaic law, and the Scriptures speak of Abraham as being justified (reckoned as righteous) by his act of believing (in what Yahweh had told him). Thus, he was justified by faith apart from the Law.[34]

Paul's theological argumentation reveals an underlying tension between the Abrahamic and the Mosaic covenants. While these two are clearly integrally and organically related, a differentiation must be made between them. Precisely because Jesus is the God-Man, He is able to raise the mode of living (and of being) beyond the Mosaic norms.[35] By the insertion of the new principle of Christ into the created and covenantal order, a new creation was effected.[36] Paul showed that, by way of contrast, the Law was to bring mankind to the point of realizing its need of God; it could not bring about righteousness through its own power.[37] The Mosaic covenant had been broken but the Abrahamic covenant would continue and finally be fulfilled in the Person of Christ. At the heart of the covenant of God with Abraham was the experience of faith (Gn 15). Like Abraham, the Christian also makes an act of faith, only now the object of this faith is clearly revealed in the definitive salvific act of Jesus on the Cross. With this, the covenant (and the covenantal family) reaches its proper end.

33. The NT records the two opinions that were operating in the early Church, represented by Paul and by what came to be called the Judaizers. Paul believed one experienced salvation through the work of Christ and that one was called to have faith in what Jesus has done on the Cross. The Judaisers had faith in Christ, but also one had to enter into the Abrahamic covenant and keep its requirements, including circumcision.

34. "For we consider that a person is justified by faith apart from works of the law" (•Rom 3:28).

35. In the Sermon on the Mount, by the setting, the teaching, and the language used, it is clear that Jesus is presenting Himself as the new Moses ("You have heard that it was said.... But I say to you..."; cf. Mt 5:27, 28, 31, 32, 34, 38, 39, 43, 44).

36. Bernard J. F. Lonergan, *Method in Theology* (New York: Herder and Herder, 1972), 241. See also Atkinson, "Mystery of Water," 69ff.

37. Paul speaks of the Law as being a tutor that would teach the need for something other than law, since the law could never perfect the human person. In ^Gal 3:24, Paul writes: "So that the law was our custodian until Christ came, that we might be justified by faith."

ABRAHAMIC COVENANT
PERDURES

In the Sermon on the Mount, Jesus Himself enunciated a process of fulfillment within the salvific design of God. "I came not to destroy but to fulfill" (+Mt 5:17). As well, this hermeneutic of "greater fulfillment" was employed by the first Christians to explain how the covenant in Christ was related to the Hebrew covenant(s). See Rom 11:17ff., where it is said that the Gentiles are grafted into the natural olive tree. What gave this typological understanding credence was that this genre developed from within the OT itself.[38] Even within the revelation to Moses, there was already the indication that one like unto Moses was to come, implying that the Mosaic covenant was not the definitive reality for God's people.[39] Of particular note is the insistence that the new prophet would emerge from within the people of God: "The Lord, your God will raise up for you a prophet from your midst, from your brothers like me and you shall listen to him" (Dt 18:15). This serves to underline the developmental nature of the covenant.

Later, as Israel faced national destruction because of her apostasy, the prophets began to proclaim a future restoration, but this time the covenantal life of Israel was to be restored on a totally new basis. This is presented in two ways. First, there is the graphic witness of the prophets. In Hosea 1–9, the prophet's wife is a prostitute and his children's names reflect the dire situation of Israel: *Jezreel* which reveals the violence that is coming;[40] Lo-Ruhamah meaning "not pitied," which

---

38. See Michael Fishbane's *Biblical Interpretation in Ancient Israel*. In this book he shows how typological thinking was also present within the OT. In the NT, typology presents us with a person, a ritual, or an event, and then later its meaning is fulfilled by another person, ritual, or event. In the OT, Fishbane shows how the first Exodus under Moses becomes the foundation for later images/events. The meaning of these later events can be found in the former events. This is seen in the relationship between the Passover and Eucharist.

39. It is clear that the Jewish people at the time of Christ were expecting "the" prophet, which was an interpretation of Dt 18:15. In John's gospel (1:21) the Jews asks John if he is "the" prophet (ὁ προφήτης).

40.יִזְרְעֶאל / *yizrᵊ'e'l* (Jezreel). *TWOT* states that this name is a wordplay meaning both "to scatter" and "to sow." Israel will be scattered but later God will re-sow her in the Land

reveals that God will no longer have pity on Israel;[41] and, finally, Lo-ammi, meaning "not my people" which declares that Israel will no longer be God's people.[42] This follows the attested formula that effected a divorce in the ancient world. Because of her apostasy, a divorced is effected between Yahweh and Israel.[43] The Mosaic covenant was always understood to be conditional, necessitating Israel's obedience. God laid out the conditions for the continuation of the Mosaic covenant in ^Ex 19:5: "If you will obey my voice and keep my covenant, you shall be my own possession among all peoples."

Now that a break has occurred in the covenant, it is only because of God's faithfulness that there will be a future restoration (as prophesied in Hos 2). God, in forming His people Israel, had made an unconditional (and, therefore, enduring) covenant with Abraham. This vocation and calling will never be revoked. Yet the failure to fulfill the Mosaic covenant showed Israel's need for something further from God. As Hosea 2 intimates, this new covenant, which for Paul is intrinsically linked to the Abrahamic covenant, will be based on the gifts Yahweh will give to His people. These she could never provide for herself, and they will enable His people to be faithful. This is set out in nuptial imagery in which

---

of Promise. The name is also associated with bloody violence, including Jehu's slaughter of the remnants of Ahab's family and supporters (2 Kgs 10:11). See *TWOT*'s entry under מזרע (*mizrā'*), 582f.

41. לֹא רֻחָמָה / *lō' ruḥāmāʰ* is translated as "not pitied" and refers to the fact that the Lord will no longer have pity on Israel, because of her continued apostasy. This statement recognizes that by her unfaithfulness Israel has broken the Mosaic covenant, thus divorcing herself from Yahweh.

42. לֹא עַמִּי / *lō' 'ammî* is translated as "not my people" and can be understood as effecting a divorce between Israel and Yahweh. This is then followed by +Hos 2:2 [H:2:4], in which God mentions the prostitute who represents Israel: "Because she is not my wife and I am not her husband." This is similar to the legal divorce formulae that were found in the texts of the Jewish community at Elephantine. It would seem that some form of divorce has been effected in the relationship between God and Israel. See Brad E. Kelle, *Hosea 2: Metaphor and Rhetoric in Historical Perspective*, Academia Biblica Series (Atlanta: Society of Biblical Literature, 2005) for discussions of the Hosean text.

43. Paul's contention will be that the apostasy of Israel did not void the unconditional covenant made previously with Abraham, but Israel's apostasy did break the later and conditional Mosaic covenant. This distinction is essential to understanding how Paul works out the relationship between the old and new covenants.

the divorce of Israel ("you are not My people" [Hos 1:9]) is followed by a new betrothal with Yahweh which is said to be eternal.[44]

The *mohar* (bridal gift) which the Lord gives to Israel in Hosea 2 will enable Israel to remain faithful to Him. The Lord will give to Israel righteousness, loving kindness, compassion, and faithfulness.[45] Only at this point, *through the grace of God*, will Israel be able to maintain her covenantal relationship with Yahweh. Only then will Israel will be able to realize her appointed end, which is to "know" the Lord. Both the nuptial imagery and the time periods in Hosea are important to the New Testament. Hosea qualifies this new betrothal by stating that there will be a long period of waiting as the Lord conforms Israel to His will.[46] Consequently, it is not accidental that when John the Baptist reveals Jesus to the world, he refers to Him as the bridegroom. It is at this point that the Hosean nuptials are concluded and the marriage of the Lamb is about to take place.

The second way in which the prophetic literature points to the coming of a greater covenantal reality is found in the use of the term "new covenant"—בְּרִית חֲדָשָׁה / *b'rît ḥădāshāʰ*.[47] From this phrase, it is clear that the restoration of Israel following the Exile will not be a return to the status quo. Instead, there will be the introduction of another principle into the situation of Israel, such that the relationship between Yahweh and His people will be understood in terms of a *new* covenant. The covenant with Abraham was unconditional and, in some form, will perdure. However, when Yahweh fully restores His people there will be a novelty to the covenantal structure. Jeremiah 31 captures this novelty in the use of the term "new covenant"; and, in addition, the Lord highlights the difference that will occur:

---

44. וְאֵרַשְׂתִּיךְ לִי לְעוֹלָם / *v'ēras tih li l'ôlām*—"I will betroth you to me forever" (+Hos 2:21).

45. "I will betroth you to me for ever; I will betroth you to me in righteousness and in justice, in steadfast love, and in mercy. I will betroth you to me in faithfulness; and you shall know the LORD" (^Hos 2:19–20).

46. Hosea 3:3–5.

47. הִנֵּה יָמִים בָּאִים נְאֻם־יְהוָה וְכָרַתִּי אֶת־בֵּית יִשְׂרָאֵל וְאֶת־בֵּית יְהוּדָה בְּרִית חֲדָשָׁה—"Behold, days are coming says the LORD and I will make a new covenant (בְּרִית חֲדָשָׁה / *b'rît ḥădāshāʰ*) with the house of Israel and with the house of Judah" (+Jer 31:31).

"Behold, days are coming," declares the LORD, "when I will make a new covenant with the house of Israel and with the house of Judah, not like the covenant which I made with their fathers in the day I took them by the hand to bring them out of the land of Egypt, My covenant which they broke, although I was a husband to them." (+Jer 31:31–32)

In several places in the NT Paul takes up the relationship between the old and new covenants, i.e., the relationship between the Mosaic Law and the Christian revelation of grace, and shows how there exists between them both a radical discontinuity as well as a radical continuity.[48] Only because he is able to differentiate between the Abrahamic and Mosaic covenants is Paul able to properly work out the tension between faith and works and understand the reliance of both upon grace. While an analysis of this topic is beyond the scope of this work, it does point to the importance of the Abrahamic covenant and how it must perdure into the new covenant (if it is to be consistent with the initial revelation to Israel) and yet be radically transformed by the presence of Christ to account for the novelty of His grace.

ABRAHAM AS PARADIGMATIC

This perduring of the Abrahamic covenant becomes critically important to the theology of the domestic Church and shows why there is no developed theology of the family in the New Testament. The covenantal family, which was operative within the Hebraic covenant, continues to be operative within the New Testament. But just as the Passover is informed (and transformed) by the insertion of Christ into the salvific order, so too the essential functioning of the covenantal family found in the OT continues in the church but now takes on an eschatological dimension. This means that the function, meaning, and structure of the OT family and the fatherhood of Abraham are assumed into Christ and become paradigmatic for the baptized family. Analogously, just as a full understand-

48. The phrasing here is precise. "Radical" comes from the Latin word *radix* which means root. An adequate accounting of Christianity must show that, on one hand, there is a continuous relationship with Judaism that goes to the very root, while, at the same time, something new has been added (i.e., Christ), which changes and fulfills things in a way the OT realities could not do on their own.

ing of the structure of the Eucharist is not possible without reference to the Passover, so too, the meaning of the family in the new covenant can be grasped only with reference to the Abrahamic prototype.

ROMANS 4:16 AND GALATIANS 3:29

Paul's use of Abraham in Romans is critical to the theology of the family, precisely because it points to Abraham as being paradigmatic for all Christians. The original covenant, which was initiated in Genesis 12 with Abraham, established him and his family as the single salvific point in the created order. This scandal of particularity (i.e., that God makes the salvific covenant with the Jews alone) reaches its conclusion only in the work of Christ, in which the fullness of grace and the salvific order are then opened up to the whole human race.[49] The first controversy that erupted in the early Church concerned the nature of salvation. Paul believed that the gift of salvation was based on one's having faith in Christ alone. Another group, known as the Judaizers, believed that salvation was predicated on following the Mosaic Law (including circumcision). One had to first become a Jew for the work of Christ to be effective. Was one justified before God (i.e., the initial step in salvation) because of the work you did (i.e., reliance on the Mosaic Law) or was one justified by having faith in Christ because no one could secure his own salvation by means of works. One side held to a salvation by works; the other to salvation by grace alone. A struggle ensued over which interpretation was correct. Paul's solution to this problem was to make a distinction between the Mosaic covenant, with all its laws and regulations, and the Abrahamic covenant, which was an unconditional covenant of promise.[50] In Romans 4, Paul shows how Abra-

---

49. The promise to Abram was that *in him* (בְּךָ / *b°ḵā* [Gn 12:3]) all the families of the earth would be blessed. This is finally realized in the birth of the Church, in which the whole human race is invited to enter into the fulfilled family of Abraham by way of Christ. Even the early disciples were not aware that all the Gentiles were to be included in the Messianic people. This only became clear as the Church recognized that the Gentiles had also received the promised gift of the Abrahamic covenant (i.e., the Holy Spirit) and were now being grafted into the people of God (see Acts 15:7–8 and Rom 11:15ff.).

50. See Gn 12, 15, 17 for the development of the covenant with Abraham.

ham comes to be justified with God—that is, made right with Him—not through his obeying of laws, but through his faith in what God has said to him. Paul refers to the encounter that Abram had with God in Genesis 15. "'Look up at the sky and count the stars, if you can. Just so,' he added, 'shall your descendants be.' Abram put his faith in the LORD, who credited it to him as an act of righteousness" (•Gn 15:5–6). Abram (i.e., Abraham) trusted in what God said He would do and thereby was considered righteous by God, which passage is quoted in Rom 4:3.

Paul establishes the priority of the Abrahamic over the Mosaic covenant by showing that Abraham was justified before God through an act of belief which occurred *before* the giving of the Law to Moses. Paul interprets this to mean that God was using Abraham to show the priority of faith, and that Abraham, as the one who made an act of faith, was to become the father of all who are justified through faith.

> Now we assert that "faith was credited to Abraham as righteousness." It was not through the law that the promise was made to Abraham...but through the righteousness that comes from faith. For this reason, it depends on faith, so that it may be a gift, and the promise may be guaranteed to all his descendants, not to those who only adhere to the law but to those who follow the faith of Abraham, who is the father of all of us. (•Rom 4:9–16)

Paul uses the same argument and shows the importance of Abraham for all Christians when he deals with the Judaisers in Galatia. In the Christian community in Galatia the theological controversy over justification was particularly acute. Almost immediately after Paul's preaching and the Galatians' conversion to the faith, the Judaizers arrived preaching that one could not be saved unless he followed the Law of Moses and was circumcised. In his correspondence with the Galatians, Paul provides a theological analysis showing the difference between relying on works of the law and relying on the grace in Christ. He does not denigrate the Law, but sees that it was impossible to obtain righteousness (or be justified) through the Law.[51] Using the experience of Abraham in Genesis 15 (cf. Gal 3:6), Paul shows that it is *through faith*

---

51. In his letter to the Galatians, Paul directly states, "a man is not justified by works of the law but through faith in Jesus Christ" (^Gal 2:16).

that we are justified and therefore, all who have faith now become "sons of Abraham" (Gal 3:7).

At the end of the discussion Paul makes explicit the consequences of being in Christ: in Him, those things which had separated people are now overcome, distinctions removed, and the fundamental unity of those incorporated into Christ is achieved. But even further, those who belong to Christ are now said to be the offspring of Abraham. This is an astonishing statement and is possible only if one grasps the idea of corporate personality operative within the Semitic mind! The covenant with Abraham, which requires participation in the *nephesh* of Abraham,[52] now will be extended beyond the boundary of those who are physically descended from the patriarch. One who is greater than Abraham (Jn 8:53, 58) has now arrived, and whether we are Jew or Gentile, we must be inserted into His reality. The critical point to note here is that the covenant in Christ Jesus does not annihilate the covenant of Abraham but fulfills and radically transforms it. What was the essence of the covenantal relationship between Yahweh and Abraham (i.e., faith) now becomes oriented towards Christ and becomes the fundamental structure of the new covenant, which is now open to the whole human race. Whoever will put their trust in the completed work of Christ Jesus on the Cross can enter into His reality through baptism (Rom 6).

In the Old Testament it was only in the family of Abraham where that salvific will of God was being worked out. In the Incarnation, the family of Abraham is encompassed in a single person (remember the many-in-the-one oscillation) and appears substantially in the one person of Christ.[53] He becomes the *telos* (i.e., the end point) for the family

---

52. Gn 2:7 says that when God breathed into the first *'adam* he became a *nephesh hayyah*, a living soul or living being. *Nephesh* refers to the totality of the person. As is often quoted, in Semitic thought man does not possess a soul, man is a soul.

53. This refers back to the Semitic idea of the "many" being in the "one" and the "one" in the "many." See the quote in chapter 6 from H. Wheeler Robinson, "Corporate Personality." The basic idea is that a single person contains within himself all of his ancestors who have preceded him. He becomes their living representative (the instantiation of all those of the past). The "many" are present in the "one" in an organic and concrete manner. This idea is clearly operative in the NT. See Heb 7 where the one-many oscillation explains the

of Abraham. With this insertion of Christ into the historical order, the particularized covenantal family will begin to take on its universalized form in the Church. In the new covenant in Christ, all humanity, Jews and Gentiles, are called into the one family of God which is the Church (Eph 2:19). In its core identity, the Church is not primarily an institution, but ultimately, is the *organic* body of Christ.[54] Thus, properly understood, the organic body of Christ, which continues in history as the Church, is nothing other than the family of Abraham, now reaching its final form which it was destined by God to take. As the Passover, imbued with the life of Christ, becomes the Eucharist, so the covenantal family of Abraham in Christ becomes the Church.[55]

The Abrahamic dimension of the Church, along with its organic nature and familial structure, is essential to any adequate ecclesiology. But this is also true for the domestic Church. The Christian family must also be rooted in the reality of the covenant of Abraham, especially in the revelation of how the family functioned in the Hebraic covenant, and the importance of Abraham's fatherhood for the faith. We must remember that in the New Testament the experience of salvation in Christ always brought the believer into contact with *Abraham*.

---

encounter between Abraham and Melchizedek. Paul's argument in •Gal 3:16 is based on similar lines: "Now the promises were made to Abraham and to his descendant [lit: seed—τῷ σπέρματι]. It does not say, 'And to descendants' [seeds—τοῖς σπέρμασιν] as referring to many, but as referring to one [ἑνός], 'And to your descendant,' who is Christ."

54. See 1 Cor 10:17; 12:12–13. Cf. also ^Eph 1:22–23: "The church, which is his body, the fullness of him who fills all in all."

55. That is why Paul in Gal 3:29 states that Christians are Abraham's seed and, in Rom 4:16, shows that Abraham is the father of all believers in Christ.

CHAPTER 8

THE CORPORATE DIMENSION OF BAPTISM IN THE NEW TESTAMENT

CORPORATE PERSONALITY IN THE NEW TESTAMENT

The manner in which Abraham functioned in the New Testament is once again reflective of the Semitic understanding of corporate personality which is foundational to Hebrew anthropology. Each family, tribe, or nation had its originating point in a single father to whom was given the covenant. All that sprung from Abraham is organically connected to him and imprinted with his *nephesh* (soul). This meant that whatever fundamentally informed Abraham's being continued to structure the person, family, or nation that participated in him. Specifically, that meant that those who participated in Abraham's *nephesh* shared in his covenant and the promises that Yahweh had made to him.

But we can also see how deeply this concept of corporate personality and its emphasis on organic unity continues to inform other realities in the New Covenant. The highest expression of this is found in the complete identification of the believer with Christ. In both 1 Cor 12:27 and Eph 5:30, Paul teaches that the individuals who have come to faith in Christ now become integrated members of His body.[1] The variations in one of the manuscripts for Eph 5:30 attest to the realism and make it even more concrete:

αὐτοῦ ἐκ τῆς σαρκὸς αὐτοῦ καὶ ἐκ τῶν ὀστέων αὐτοῦ[2]

[For we are members] of his body, of his flesh, and of his bones.[3]

This concept of organic identification lies at the very heart of Pauline theology and is probably the result of his encounter with the resurrected Christ. In his misguided zeal, the Pharisee Saul (Paul) took upon himself the task of destroying the new converts of the Christian Church. On his way to Damascus, he encountered the resurrected Christ, who asked of him: "Saul, Saul, why do you persecute me?" (Acts 9:4). Clearly, Paul had never met the historic Christ, and the only people he was persecuting were the followers of Jesus, that is, those who were baptized into Christ. Jesus' question, therefore, revealed to Paul the radical identification of the believers with Christ and their incorporation into His body. The individual did not simply join the group of Christians but actually became a part of Christ's living, organic body. Paul will work out the implications of this in his later theology. For our purposes, it is important to note that the anthropology, soteriology, and ecclesiology of the New Testament are predicated upon this Semitic understanding of corporate personality. It is this dynamic concept of organic identity which allows for the family in both the Old and New Testaments to be the conveyor of the covenant and to be intrinsically related to it. Salvation means to become an organic part of the family of Abraham. That is why Paul describes the Church as the Israel of God (τὸν Ἰσραὴλ τοῦ θεοῦ) in Gal 6:16.

---

1. "Now you are the body of Christ" (1 Cor 12:27); "For we are members of His body" (Eph 5:30).

2. K. Aland, et al., *The Greek New Testament,* 2nd ed. (Stuttgaart: Wurttemberg Bible Society, 1968), 677n8.

3. This Greek is retained in the Authorized Version, whose translation is given here.

NEW TESTAMENT USAGE
OF MELCHIZEDEK

One of the most illustrative examples of corporate personality in the NT occurs in Hebrews, where the author is arguing for the superiority of the priesthood of Christ over the levitical priesthood of the Temple. One of the problems the early Church faced was to provide the theological basis for how Jesus, who was not a Levite, could supposedly offer a sacrifice. It was clear that in the Temple ritual the Aaronic priesthood and sacrificial system were set in place and ordained by God through Moses. It was never claimed that Jesus was a Levite. How then could He usurp the official priestly functions? How could His priesthood be greater than the ministerial priesthood instituted by Moses? But the burden for the early Church was to show that Christianity was not a new religion but somehow brought to completion the OT promises. The legitimacy of the new Christian order *depended* on providing a theological rationale that would allow for the newness of Christ while, at the same time, it safeguarded the continuity with the Hebraic covenant.

To resolve this issue, the author of Hebrews used the meeting between Abraham and the mysterious figure of Melchizedek in Gn 14 as the means to resolve this dilemma.[4] In the Genesis narrative, Abraham has just rescued his nephew, Lot, and is now on his way home after defeating Chedorlaomer (Gn 14:17). He is met by Melchizedek, whose name has strong messianic connotations, for he is both "king of peace" and "king of righteousness."[5] He is also a priest of the Most High God (אֵל עֶלְיוֹן / ʾēl ʿelyôn), who brings out the offering of bread and wine (Gn 14:18), which for the Christian community would have clear eucharistic connotations. Abraham takes a tithe of his war spoils and gives them to this mysterious priest, who then blesses Abraham (Gn 14:19–

---

4. There are only two times in the OT where Melchizedek appears: Gn 14, under discussion here, and later in Ps 110, which is understood to have a Messianic connotation: "you are a priest after the manner of Melchizedek."

5. "[Melchizedek] first, being translated King of Righteousness and then, also, King of Salem which is King of Peace" (+Heb 7:2).

20). These last two actions, the tithing by Abraham and the blessing by Melchizedek, become decisive in legitimizing the superiority of the priesthood of Christ.

The argument of Hebrews is developed through four premises. First, Melchizedek is a divine messianic *type*.[6] He is a mysterious figure because, by contrast with the major figures in the OT, he has no genealogy and thus appears to have no beginning or end.[7] This would seem to point to something other than of human origin. When the messianic hope came to be more clearly focused during the prophetic era, the messiah was understood as being a righteous king who would bring paradisal peace.[8] Coming back from the Exile in 532 BC, the Jewish community began to see latent messianic references in various parts of the OT. Within the pre-Christian Jewish tradition, the mysterious king-priest figure of Melchizedek was understood to be a type (τύπος) of the Messiah.[9] Though not the Messiah, Melchizedek prefigures this saving figure.

Second, Melchizedek is superior to Abraham as evidenced by his receiving the tithe from the patriarch. It is clear from the Genesis text that Abraham paid a tithe to the priest-king, but, in fact, it is the role of Levitical priests to receive tithes from their fellow Israelites.[10] In this case, a person who has no connection with Abraham and is not part of the Jewish community is given a tithe (see Heb 7:5–6). But, in Abraham the future generations of Levites are present in an organic fash-

---

6. Ps 110 was understood to be messianic in the rabbinic literature. E.g., "R. Yudan said in the name of R. Ḥama: In the time-to-come, when the Holy One, blessed be He, seats the lord Messiah at His right hand, as is said *The Lord saith unto my lord: 'Sit thou at My right hand'* (Psalm 110:1)." *Midrash on Psalms,* vol 1, trans. William G. Braude (New Haven, Conn.: Yale University Press, 1959), 261.

7. "Without father, mother, or ancestry, without beginning of days or end of life, thus made to resemble the Son of God, he remains a priest forever" (•Heb 7:3).

8. ^Is 11:6ff states that "the wolf shall dwell with the lamb," and ^Is 9:6 prophesies, "A child is born, to us a son is given; and the government will be upon his shoulder, and his name will be called…Mighty God, Everlasting Father, Prince of Peace."

9. See 11Q 13 from Qumran, which deals with the role of Melchizedek (especially verse 9 and 25), as well as the *Midrash on Psalms,* 205–7, noted above.

10. "The Melchizedekian Priesthood," by Gil Rugh at http://www.biblebb.com/files/gr295.htm (accessed February 19, 2010).

ion. Thus, what Abraham does, his descendants must be considered, in some sense, to be doing as well. This argument of Hebrews remains incomprehensible unless the Semitic notion of corporate personality is taken into account. All of the previous argumentation would be futile if the Abraham-Melchizedek exchange simply remained bound to its own historical moment. But the Hebraic mind had a different understanding of anthropology. At the core of the argument is the understanding that the descendants of Abraham ontologically participate in him and, therefore, are mysteriously present in him when he met Melchizedek. "One might even say that Levi himself, who receives tithes, paid tithes through Abraham, for he was still in the loins of his ancestor [father πατρὸς] when Melchizedek met him" (^Heb 7:9–10). Therefore, according to the Hebrew way of thinking, the Levitical priesthood was paying tithes to Melchizedek, which would mean that he possessed a greater priesthood.

Third, Melchizedek is superior to Abraham as evidenced by his giving a blessing to Abraham. The logic here is simple: the greater person always blesses the lesser. Yet, here we have the priest-king blessing Abraham, who must, therefore, be of an inferior position (see Heb 7:7). Thus, according to Semitic thought, Levi, who is the father of Jewish priests, was himself blessed by the mysterious Melchizedek and paid tithes to him because Levi was "present" in his forefather Abraham.

Finally, Hebrews concludes its argument by showing that the Old Testament itself reveals that the Levitical priesthood was not the final sacrificial ministry to be established. Hebrews draws attention to Psalm 110, which states that the Lord will raise up His servant who is a priest not from the house of Aaron but according to the order of Melchizedek.[11] This shows that the Abrahamic covenant is not a static reality but is situated within a trajectory that is moving towards ever greater fulfillment. This is echoed in Jeremiah 31:31 in the prophetic announcement of the future new covenant. If the old covenant was suf-

---

11. "If, then, perfection came through the Levitical priesthood, on the basis of which the people received the law, what need would there still have been for another priest to arise according to the order of Melchizedek, and not reckoned according to the order of Aaron?" (•Heb 7:11).

ficient unto itself, why was there a need for something greater? This is understood as a theology of fulfillment, which posits that the Abrahamic covenant would be fulfilled, but in a new mode that would go beyond the Mosaic law. Note that there is a distinction between the two. For the Christian community, Christ becomes the "new" Moses, who institutes the new law of agapaic love and establishes a new covenant with a new priesthood (according to Melchizedek) and a new sacrifice.

This argumentation based on the OT figure of Melchizedek is clear evidence that the Old Testament's concept of corporate anthropology extended into the thinking of the NT period. In fact, the corporate understanding of the person deeply affects the whole of Pauline theology and it becomes critical for the proper understanding of the family in the New Testament, particularly as the domestic church.[12] In God's covenantal economy, including the NT, the individual person is never understood as an autonomous, isolated unit. Rather there is at once a profound affirmation of the individual's deep personal existence, which is always grounded in the prior corporate reality from which he comes. The family, therefore, is not accidental to the design of the person (or consequently of salvation) but is of critical importance and the basic context of one's individual existence and of covenantal life. The human person is not an autonomous, self-determining entity, and neither is the family. The idea that a profound experience such as conversion to Christ could only affect the individual without affecting those with whom the person was ontologically connected (i.e., his family) is not possible within the Semitic mindset, which also was operating within the early Church.[13] If this is correct, then we should expect to see per-

12. In his encounter with Christ on the Damascus road, Paul comes to understand that the Church is, in reality, identified with Christ. This experience of the corporate reality of Christ is foundational to Paul's theological constructs.

13. One has to be careful here that a precision is made. With the advent of Christ, everything takes on a relative value as compared to Him and this includes both the family and the individual person. In ^Lk 14:26 Jesus teaches, "If anyone comes to Me, and does not hate his own father and mother and wife and children and brothers and sisters, yes, and even his own life, he cannot be My disciple." Jesus is not advocating hatred but is showing that no other value (our love of our family or even of our own life) can take precedence over love for Him. Only in Him is life. Thus, salvation is found only in Christ Jesus and in our rela-

sonal conversions having salvific effects also upon both marriages and families. These relational structures should be changed (raised up) inasmuch as they now experience the grace of Christ because at least one person in the family or marriage has Christ living within them. Just as the individual person realizes his final destiny in Christ, so too should marriage and families. If corporate personality is found in NT thought, then, through the baptized person, Christ would be inserted into a baptized person's primary relationships (precisely because he is an organic member of them). We will now examine the evidence of the New Testament to see if such salvific effects are recorded there.

NEW TESTAMENT UNDERSTANDING OF FAMILY

There are at least two critical points at which faith intersects with the family in the New Testament: the practice of baptism and the effect of faith on marriage. As we examine these areas, we will see a profound underlying sense of the organic nature of both the marital and the familial unit, which will allow, first, for the phenomenon of household baptism, which is parallel to the circumcision rite in the OT, and second, for the sanctifying effect of baptism, even on nonbelievers. This runs counter to the prevailing understanding in the West, which radically conceives of the person in terms of strict individualism and autonomy. To be absolutely clear: *it is only the corporate understanding of the human person that allows the family to become the domestic church.*

ANALYSIS OF NEW TESTAMENT BAPTISM

During the time of Christ, Second-Temple Judaism was marked by the emergence of the various Jewish groups which claimed to have a

---

tionship to Him. However, this does not force a reductionist view of either the person or the family, nor does it deprive them of their created natures. Rather, they now must be understood within the terms of Christ. The person and the family, as created by God with a corporate personal nature, now will find their proper purpose and function in terms of Christ and His Body, the Church.

perfected understanding of the law and to be the true sons of Israel. They believed they were the ones chosen to usher in the kingdom of God. Foundational to many of these groups, and what often differentiated them, were water rituals, which assured the purity of the group and its adherence to the law. The Essenes, for example, underwent a daily immersion before their communal meal in the evening. The excavations at Masada have shown that there existed *mikvot* within the compound. Carol Selkin has shown the importance of these water rituals to the identity of these groups.[14]

The water ritual that John the Baptist employed added something new. Previously, ablutions in water represented a change that the person had initiated. The potential new members, upon accepting the teaching of a specific religious Jewish sect, used immersion in water as a symbol of their changed status. John's own baptism is similar to this. His call was to "repent for the kingdom of heaven has come near" (+Mt 3:2). The human action of repenting led to the human decision to undergo a ritual that identified one as a person preparing for the coming kingdom.[15] But John's water baptism had a certain provisional aspect to it, coupled with the expectation of the imminent coming of the Lord. Consequently, he was conscious that his water ritual in itself was not sufficient to accomplish the will of God. This was not the final point. Even as he was baptizing, he announced: "I baptize you with water for repentance, but he who is coming after me is mightier than I, whose sandals I am not worthy to carry; he will baptize you with the Holy Spirit and with fire" (^Mt 3:11). His baptism was, in fact, pointing towards an eschatological event of which he was only the preparatory messenger.

In Christ, the Jewish water rituals were fundamentally altered and took on an altered meaning. They became the place where an ontological interchange took place between the person and the Presence of the divine. The Spirit of God "invades" fallen humanity.[16] Repentance is

14. Selkin, "Exegesis and Identity." This work provides an excellent historical and exegetical analysis of the development of ritual bathing, culminating in the *mikveh*.

15. John's ministry was understood to be the fulfillment of •Is 40:3: "A voice cries out: In the desert prepare the way of the LORD! Make straight in the wasteland a highway for our God!"

16. This particular language developed by C. S. Lewis is helpful inasmuch as it graphi-

the necessary prelude to this event. But it is the actual Spirit of God who will effect something which hithertofore had not been possible. The baptized person is now "re-created," becoming a new creation. There is, thus, a new form of humanity, which is informed by the Holy Spirit.

In John's Gospel, Jesus speaks of the *indwelling* of the Spirit within the person: "He who believes in me, as the scripture has said, 'Out of his heart shall flow rivers of living water.' Now this he said about the Spirit, which those who believed in him were to receive" (^Jn 7:38–39).[17] Earlier, in his discussion with Nicodemus, Jesus linked this rebirth (which he describes as being "born again" into the kingdom of God) with the Holy Spirit and water. Baptism now has a twofold structure, which includes both the water ritual and being "invaded by" the Holy Spirit. As in the narrative of creation (Gn 1:1–3), the Spirit of God and water are inextricably bound.[18] The teaching of Jesus in the Gospels clearly show that something radically new is being accomplished in His messianic mission. Created reality is being penetrated in a unique way by the Spirit of God, Who now becomes an abiding presence within the redeemed person.

---

cally portrays the dynamic that lies at the heart of salvation. The human person, fallen and alienated from God, is, by the grace of God, filled with the divine presence (i.e., the Holy Spirit) and given a new nature. See C. S. Lewis, *Mere Christianity* (San Francisco: Harper Collins, 2001), 40ff.

17. This passage can be interpreted in two ways. The rivers of living water can be located in Christ or in the believer. In John 4:14, Jesus states that the water He gives to the believers will become a fountain within them, springing up to eternal life (ζωὴν αἰώνιον). However, the phrase "the one who believes in Me" may go with the preceding verb "drink." The text would become, "if anyone is thirsty, let him come to me; the one who believes, let him drink." The remainder of Jn 7:38 then stands alone as a text which provides the reasoning for these unusual imperative declarations. People can come and drink because it was prophesized that one would be coming from whom "living waters" flowed. See John Marsh, *Saint John* (New York: Penguin Books, 1983), 340–44.

18. In Gn 1:2, there is the original act of creation which results in the formless earth (הָאָרֶץ / *hā'āretz*) which is awaiting the further word of God to become differentiated and assume its proper form. At this initial moment, the formless earth is covered with the primordial waters (תְהוֹם / *t°hôm*) and the Spirit of God (רוּחַ אֱלֹהִים / *rûaḥ 'ĕlōhîm*) is hovering over them. Thus, at the beginning of the creation, water acts as an interface or point of contact between the creation and God's Spirit. See Atkinson, "Mystery of Water," 135ff.

The teaching and life of Christ, including His Passion and Resurrection, are not complete until the disciples are "clothed with power from on high" (Lk 24:49). During His Eucharistic discourse in John's Gospel, Jesus reveals, "For if I do not go away, the Paraclete / the Helper will not come to you" (+Jn 16:7). He then reveals the work of the Spirit: "But when this one comes, the Spirit of truth, He will guide you in (into) all the truth" (+Jn 16:13). Finally, in Acts 1:5, the disciples are commanded to wait for the promise of the Father, and Jesus explicitly refers to the baptism of John and how His own baptism is greater because it is a baptism with the Holy Spirit. Fifty days after the Resurrection, the Spirit descends on the small group of disciples, and Peter explains that this is the fulfillment of the promise given in the Old Testament. "For the promise is made to you and to your children and to all those far off, whomever the Lord our God will call" (•Acts 2:39). This "promise" comes from the initial covenant of God with Abraham. This is in reference to the Abrahamic promise in •Genesis 12:3: "All the communities [lit., families, clans] of the earth shall find blessing in you." This universal dimension of the promise to Abraham is finally realized in the outpouring of the Spirit at Pentecost, where all families of the earth are included in the salvific work of God. It is interesting to see that in the call of Abraham the word "blessing" is used five times, seemingly to overcome the five times that "cursed" is used after the Fall. The Abrahamic covenant was intended to begin the reversal of the curse of the Fall.[19] This calling forth of Abraham can be seen as a form of re-creation. Just as different parts of the created order emerged in the narrative of creation by being called forth and then differentiated from an original unity, so too, Abraham is called forth and differentiated from the rest of humanity. He becomes the sole salvific point in creation. But within this particularity was the promise that the blessing of God would come to all people. This salvific blessing is now offered to all through the bestowal of the Holy Spirit.

This connection of the Holy Spirit and the removal of sins is high-

---

19. See Dumbrell, *Covenant and Creation,* 71ff. This work provides an excellent rationale for the emergence of the Abrhamic covenant and its being the antidote to the Fall.

lighted at the end of John's gospel. On Easter evening when He appears
to His disciples, Jesus breathes on them and says: "Receive the holy
Spirit. Whose sins you forgive are forgiven them, and whose sins you
retain are retained." (•Jn 20:22–23). Here, the ability of the Church to
forgive sins (and thus restore the person to God) is linked with the reception of the Holy Spirit. While they are two separate realities, they
are inextricably linked. The first step in the redemption of creation is
for the removal of sin. Once purified, it can then receive the abiding
presence of God in the Person of the Holy Spirit. Both steps are necessary for the recovery of order and the return to God, which explains
why the salvific order requires both the Cross and Pentecost.

BAPTISM IN ST. PAUL

St. Paul's encounter with the living Christ fundamentally shaped
his understanding of baptism. On his way to persecute the early Christian community in Damascus, Paul is addressed by a person in a vision. This person identifies Himself by saying, "I am Jesus whom you
are persecuting" (+Acts 9:5). But actually Paul had been persecuting the
members of the fledgling Christian group. Here, Jesus is revealing to
Paul that by touching these members, he was actually touching Christ
himself. The individual believers had been incorporated into the very
body of Jesus and became members of Him, so much so that to touch
them was to touch Christ. The realism of this incorporation pervades
the whole of Paul's theology.[20] When Paul wants to explain the nature
of the Church, he takes up this concept of the "body" and shows how
the Church is in fact the body of Christ, composed of many individuals who have received gifts from the Holy Spirit to carry out the work
of ministry.[21] "As a body is one though it has many parts, and all the
parts of the body, though many, are one body, so also Christ.... Now
you are Christ's body, and individually parts of it" (•1 Cor 12:12, 27).

---

20. See J. Atkinson, "The Foundation of Pauline Thought: An Investigation," in *The Incarnate Word* (forthcoming).

21. Paul gives a full explanation of this in 1 Corinthians 12.

For Paul, the nature of the Christian believer has been fundamentally altered. Writing to the Romans (in Romans 6), Paul shows how the old nature of Adam has now died by being united with the death of Christ in baptism, and the baptized person receives the nature of Christ. Paul goes so far as to say that "if any one is in Christ, he is a new creation; the old has passed away, behold, the new has come" (^2 Cor 5:17). Christ has come not merely to teach a new way, or even a better way. Rather Christ has come to effect a new creation. Graphically, in Gal 2:20, Paul shows that Christ has died and the new reality of Christ becomes the informing principle in the person. Revealing the deepest dynamic of Christian experience, Paul writes to the Galatians: "I have been crucified with Christ; it is no longer I who live, but Christ who lives in me" (^Gal 2:20). This is a radical understanding of what it means to be a Christian. The Christian faith is not a philosophy, or a moral code, but a fundamental exchange of natures effected between the adamic man and the divine Christ.[22] In some real sense, the believer has died and Christ now lives in him.

Paul takes this even further by showing, in his explanation of the Church, that the believer now has a Christological existence which determines his identity. While it is always deeply personal, that identity is also always corporate. Paul explains that the dynamic movement within the church is the *ever-increasing* corporate reality of that body. In +Eph 4:13 he shows that the Holy Spirit is working within the Church "until we all arrive at the unity of the faith and of the knowledge of the Son of God, into a perfect man, to a measure of the maturity of the fullness of Christ." Earlier in the same epistle, Paul states that Christ is "head over all things in the Church which is His body" (+Eph 1:23). It is clear that Christianity is not the mere following of teachings or laws of moral conduct. Rather, in its essence, Christianity is an encounter with the Person of Christ, who transforms the person, making the believer an organic part of Himself along with all other believers. In Christ, all continue to live and mature until they come to live and act as a single

---

22. This is echoed in +2 Peter 1:4, which states you "may become sharers of the divine nature."

organic person.[23] The corporate nature which man was endowed with in the beginning now finds its end (*telos*) in Christ, into whom they are being transformed.[24]

ROMANS 6—THE DYNAMIC OF
NEW TESTAMENT BAPTISM

Where does this fundamental exchange between life and death, the old nature and the new, and the emergence of a new creation, take place? Paul is clear that this dynamic transformation takes place in Christian baptism. In the early Church, whenever people were converted to Christ they were *immediately* baptized into Him. Baptism was the instrument of this salvific change and so was administered without delay, regardless of the circumstances or inconveniences. We see this particularly on the day of Pentecost, when three thousand were added to the Church (Acts 2:41), and in Paul's ministry to Lydia and the jailer in Ephesus. The latter, in particular, was baptized along with his whole family after midnight (Acts 16).

In Rom 6, Paul examines the dynamics of baptism. As part of his argument, he wants to demonstrate that Christians are called to no longer participate in sin. They are able to do this precisely because they have died with Christ, which means their old (adamic) nature of sin has died as well. For Paul, baptism is never an empty ritual nor merely a proclamation of what the individual has done or come to believe. Rather, it is the actual sharing in the crucifixion of Jesus Christ. "Or are you unaware that we who were baptized into Christ Jesus were baptized into his death? We were indeed buried with him through bap-

23. See note 9 in chapter 7 for the quote from C.S. Lewis's *Beyond Personality,* 30. Later Lewis shows how in Christ, God is making a new form of humanity: "God became man to turn creatures into sons: not simply to produce better men of the old kind but to produce a new kind of man" (p. 56).

24. The realism of the indwelling of Christ is often overlooked in New Testament theology. However, it is clear that Paul intended such realism, particularly when we examine the end of his Corinthian correspondence. He asks Christians to test themselves: "Test yourselves *to see* if you are in the faith; examine yourselves! Or do you not recognize this about yourselves, that Jesus Christ is in you—unless indeed you fail the test?" (2 Cor 13:5). This is the New American Standard translation, which more faithfully renders the Greek.

tism into death" (•Rom 6:3–4). He underscores this being united with Christ's death when he states that "our old self was crucified with him" and that "we have died with Christ" (•Rom 6:6, 8). The purpose of this death is so "we know that our old self was crucified with him so that the sinful body [lit.: the body of sin] might be destroyed, and we might no longer be enslaved to sin" (^Rom 6:6). This is the radical claim of Christianity. In Christ, our sinful nature is put to death. Since our old nature has died, it must be replaced with a new life we receive from our union with Christ. In Romans, Paul refers to this as being raised with Christ and living with Him (Rom 6:4, 8). But in other letters, Paul expresses what is at the heart of the baptismal mystery in other ways. In Galatians, Paul expresses this transformation of the person in terms of having Christ live in us. "It is no longer I who live, but Christ who lives in me" (^Gal 2:20). In 2 Cor 5:17 Paul explains that anyone who is "in Christ" is a new creation (καινὴ κτίσις). Each of these expressions points to the same reality: the baptized believer in Christ has received His nature and this new nature gives the believer the power to resist sin. The Christian now has the power to walk in the holiness of God.

There is a logical coherence to this presentation. If Christ had merely given his teaching to the world and died as an example of holiness, human nature would not have been altered, other than by a gain of intellectual knowledge. Man would still be alienated from the nature of God. Paul shows that what Christianity offers is radically different. The baptized person becomes organically connected to Christ, one with Him, and truly becomes a "son" in the Son. This is so radical: that the believer is said to be a new creation. Now, the Christian is the person in whom Christ is literally present. This will have a fundamental effect upon all his relationships, particularly those which are covenantal and organic (i.e., marriage and family).[25] What baptism reveals is that the whole of humanity finds its fulfillment by incorporation into Christ.[26] We see here the expression of the corporate nature of the human per-

25. This particularly becomes evident when Paul discusses the question of mixed marriages 1 Cor 7 and the nature of covenant of marriage (Eph 5), which will be discussed later.

26. This is particularly shown in Paul's letter to the Ephesians, where he shows that the mystery of God's will is that He plans "to sum up/recapitulate [ἀνακεφαλαιώσασθαι] all things in Christ" (+Eph 1:10).

son and the fact that it finds its completed expression when the person is "in Christ." Only in Him is the experience of alienation overcome, precisely as one becomes part of His Body. Baptism "works" because the human personality has personal and corporate dimensions. Man is called to a deeply personal relationship with Christ and at the same time is called to live out his redeemed existence in a corporate mode, within the Body of Christ. As has been shown, because of this fundamental corporate nature of the human person, the manner of redemption is always conceived of in corporate terms, including baptism. As we will see, this allows for the incorporation of whole families into the faith. This practice, referred to in the NT as household baptisms, forms the basis of the domestic church. After an excursus on the relationship between baptism and circumcision, we will examine the NT phenomenon of baptizing whole households.

<hr />

EXCURSUS 4:
THE RELATIONSHIP BETWEEN BAPTISM
AND CIRCUMCISION

What precisely is the relationship between circumcision and baptism? Often it is thought that the way of *initiation* in the old covenant was by way of circumcision, which was performed only on males. If that were true, then the NT would be presenting a novelty and advancement, because baptism replaces circumcision and is applied to both males and females. This would represent an equalizing factor vis-à-vis the genders that is new with Christianity. Put another way, circumcision and baptism are the entry points into the covenant, and whereas the former is only for males, the latter is for males and females.

However, the comparison between the two and their relationship to covenantal initiation is more complex than appears initially.[27] As well,

27. See J. Kaminsky's review of Matthew Thiessen's *Contesting Conversion: Genealogy, Circumcision, and Identity in Ancient Judaism and Christianity* (Oxford: Oxford University Press, 2011), in *Studies in Christian-Jewish Relations* 6 (2011). He makes the excellent point

the question of novelty (equal treatment of men and women in covenant-al initiation for converts) actually arose in *pre-Christian* Second-Temple Judaism. At that time, it was the practice that both men and women were required to undergo the water ritual using the *mikveh* (a specially con-structed immersion pool), which became the normative and required form for both genders to enter Judaism.

There is a fourfold trajectory which explains the relationship between circumcision and baptism: First, there is the *physical* rite of circumcision. Gn 17:14 states circumcision is both the covenant and the sign of the cove-nant. The male who is *not* circumcised is "cut off from his people" and "has broken the covenant." It would seem from this that the person was *already* in the covenant. How can you *break* a covenant if you are not already a part of it? Circumcision was only initiated in Gn 17, yet God had *already made a covenant* with Abraham in Gn 15:8.

The reality is that circumcision is practiced within an *already existing context.* It is not just any male who is circumcised, but every male who *already* belongs to the household of Abraham. This *belonging* is the foun-dational ground for circumcision. Normally, it was boys born to Jewish mothers who were eligible for circumcision. It is problematic to under-stand circumcision as the absolute and/or normative point of entry into the covenant. It is clear that the women of Israel belonged to the covenant; they were given laws to follow, they were not considered pagans; they were part of the holy Abrahamic community. Yet women were not circumcised. Circumcision, therefore, could not be the *normative* entryway into the

---

that circumcision by itself does not cause one to enter into the covenant: "Thiessen is correct that Genesis 17 (a text attributed to the Priestly [P] source) presents an enigma in that Ish-mael who is explicitly excluded from the covenant is circumcised along with all the foreign slaves in Abraham's household, people also not likely included in Israel's special covenant" (p. 1). Also see Michael Wyschogrod's *The Body of Faith: God in the People of Israel* (New York: Rowman and Littlefield, 1983). He states that "to become a Jew, a gentile must become seed of the patriarchs and matriarchs. The Talmud speaks of the convert as being born, or reborn, as a Jew" (p. xviii).

covenant, otherwise women would not have been part of the Abrahamic covenant. But, in fact, they were.

The point here is that *belonging* to the house of Abraham (in some organic sense) seems to be the normative foundation for circumcision and for membership in the covenant. In Judaism, Jews are Jews (whether men or women) because their mothers are Jews. From this it would seem to follow that both male and female children born into Abrahamic homes were, by their organic relationship to their mothers, part of the covenant in some basic sense.[28] However, the law of the covenant required males to be circumcised at eight days. Women also, particularly once they reached puberty, had specific rituals they carried out to maintain the viability of the covenant (see Lev 12 and 15). Although it is not explained, circumcision seems to point to something in the male that is not appropriate to the covenant and has to be removed. (This idea is taken up in Col 2:11–12.)

Secondly, during the OT period and within the OT text itself, there was a profound process of spiritualization that took place in regard to circumcision. The shift goes from the physical removal of flesh in the man to the spiritual removal of sins of the heart from all people. Jeremiah proclaims, "Be circumcised, remove the foreskins of your hearts" (•4:4). (See also

28. In *Old Testament Theology*, Routledge attempts to determine the relationship of circumcision to the covenant. If one takes the rite of circumcision as being definitive, then the role of women becomes ambiguous. He suggests that women possibly became part of the covenant by giving birth. "With regard to the female members of the community, the OT does not call for, or even suggest, female circumcision as the equivalent of male circumcision. If there is an equivalent, it is probably in giving birth" (Routledge, *OT Theology*, 168). But he acknowledges in a footnote that this does not take into account childless women. Beyond that, there is no biblical confirmation for this proposal. Instead, as offered above, the key is not giving birth but being born. Interestingly, just above this section, Routledge notes: "While the people can do nothing to earn or merit inclusion within God's covenant people, having been included, they are obliged to seek to live as members of it" (ibid., 168). This latter view would seem to cohere with my proposal. People become members of the community via their birth within an already covenantal family. The obligations of the covenant begin earlier for the male child (that they be circumcised) and later for the female child (the purity rituals). In each case, they are members through birth and are bound to the obligations of the Law.

Dt 30:6.) While physical circumcision refers to the male only, this spiritualized form of circumcision is not necessarily tied only to males, as all have sin in their heart.

Thirdly, in Second-Temple Judaism *prior to Christ*, there existed specific rituals that determined how a pagan could enter/be initiated into the Abrahamic covenant. To enter the Jewish covenant, faith in the covenant had to be professed and men had to be circumcised in accordance with the Law, but that was not enough. The definitive point of entering the faith was when one was totally submerged under water and then re-emerged from the *mikvah*. A modern Jewish commentator (Rabbi Creditor) explains the decisiveness of this ritual: "This is their defining moment. They enter the mikvah as a gentile and emerge from mikvah as a Jew."[29] One was incorporated into the Abrahamic community by this final step of water immersion, and this applied to men *and* women. Within the developed self-understanding of Israel, it is clear that circumcision is not considered the definitive means of entering the covenant for the *pagan* male.

Fourthly, there is only one passage in the NT (^Col 2:11–12) that associates circumcision with baptism: "In him [Christ] also you were circumcised with a circumcision made without hands, by putting off the body of flesh in the circumcision of Christ; and you were buried with him in baptism." The circumcision "made without hands" clearly points to a spiritual action, not a physical one. "Having been buried with Him in baptism" (+Col 2:12) indicates that baptism is the *locus* or place where this action takes place. Circumcision, which was first physical and then spiritualized, now is fulfilled in Christ. Several trajectories started in the OT (initiation, purity water rituals, status, etc.) find their completion in baptism. Now, physical descent does not determine one's membership in the newly dimensioned Abrahamic family. Rather, each person has to be incorporated

---

29. http://rabbigarycreditor.blogspot.com/2010/03/mikvah-part-three-conversion-to.html (accessed June 23, 2012).

into the person of Christ and is *re-born* by water and the Spirit, both Jew and Gentile (see Jn 3:1–8).

There is a novelty in baptism, but it needs to be understood within this fuller matrix of circumcision-covenant rituals outlined above. The novelty of men and women having the same specific ritual for entrance into the covenant emerged for the first time in *pre-Christian* Second-Temple Judaism, and this probably became the structural basis for Christian baptism. What is new in Christianity is that there are no longer any gender-specific rituals. In the OT, while there was an underlying belonging to the Abrahamic community derived from organic birth (a Jew is a Jew because his mother is Jewish), there were still differentiated rituals for both men and women (circumcision, ritual purity requirements, etc.). Now the meaning of all these rituals for both men and women is fulfilled in the Person of Christ. No longer is *physical* birth sufficient to ensure belonging to the New Israel in Christ. Physical birth is replaced with *spiritual* birth. This would seem to be the underlying thesis of Jesus' teaching in his encounter with Nicodmenus in Jn 3:1–8.

The prime novelty lay in baptism providing a new form of "birth" that initiates the people into the covenant and sacramentally re-creates each baptized person, making them all members of the Body of Christ. All now are brothers and sisters in Christ, showing the absolute dignity of men, women, and children. Differences are not collapsed, but each is now a full participant in the definitive covenant of God.

HOUSEHOLD BAPTISMS

In the New Testament there are five instances where whole households are baptized.[30] In each, the same corporate dynamic seems to be at work. The head of the house has an encounter with the gospel,

---

30. Acts 11:14, 44, 48 (Cornelius); Acts 16:15 (Lydia); Acts 16:33–34 (Philippian jailer); Acts 18:8 (Crispus); 1 Cor 1:16, 16:15 (Stephanus).

comes to faith in Christ, and then that person *and the whole family* are brought into the faith through baptism. The question becomes whether the whole family accepts the faith through individual, autonomous decision making or if there is genuine corporate dimension of the person and of salvation which must be accounted for and which would allow for a more organic and corporate response to the baptismal invitation.[31] In other words, does the faith of a principal member affect only that person or is the whole family unit affected through him as well? We will begin our investigation with a careful examination of the key texts themselves:

> Acts 11:14: "[Peter] will speak words to you [Cornelius] by which you and all your household [πᾶς ὁ οἶκός σου] will be saved."

> Acts 16:14–15: "One of them, a woman named Lydia...listened, and the Lord opened her heart.... After she and her household [ὁ οἶκος αὐτῆς] had been baptized..."

> Acts 16:31, 33 (addressed to the Philippian jailer): "Believe [πίστευσον— 2nd per. sing.] in the Lord Jesus and you [σὺ—2nd per. sing.) and your household [καὶ ὁ οἶκός σου] will be saved.... Then he and all his family [αὐτὸς καὶ οἱ αὐτοῦ πάντες] were baptized at once."

> •Acts 18:8: "Crispus...came to believe in the Lord along with his entire household [σὺν ὅλῳ τῷ οἴκῳ αὐτοῦ]...and were baptized."

> •1 Cor 1:16: "I baptized [ἐβάπτισα] the household of Stephanas [τὸν Στεφανᾶ οἶκον] also."

In each of these cases, baptism is a personal event, yet it is presented within the context of the family. Whatever the composition of the family was (i.e., whether or not it included children), it is clear from the text that the conversion and baptism of a principal member of a family affected the rest of that family. It would seem that whenever the head of a family came to faith in Christ, the whole family entered into the faith as well. This is expressed in the above examples by the phrases "and his

---

31. Nearly all of the reformers during the sixteenth century saw that salvation had this corporate dimension (with its evident link to circumcision, which was administered on the eighth day of an infant's life). This corporateness and the ability to bring one's whole family into the salvific reality of the Church were particularly important to Calvin's development of covenantal theology.

house" or "all that was his." If the decision to be baptized were solely a decision made autonomously and independently, and if this were
the *absolute* norm for baptism, then speaking of *household* as an object
of baptism would make little sense and, in fact, would be misleading.
Speaking of households in the context of baptism seems to allow for
whole families to come into the faith, following the conversion of the
head of the family to Christ, and this would include infants and young
children who could not make an autonomous decision. This household
language appears to assert that the OT practice of seeing the family as
the unit of faith and as the *entryway* into the covenant continued into
the NT period. This use of household in the baptismal context would
thus undermine the *absolute* autonomy of the individual and instead
point to an inherently corporate dimension to the person, as well as of
the structure of baptism itself. This would naturally follow from the OT
understanding of the human person and the covenant, and from the
practice of circumcision, which was a household rite administered to
an infants. If this interpretation is correct, then this use of household
terminology would argue for a place for the *family-as-a-unit* within the
scheme of salvation.[32]

Tellingly, this corporate dimension is confirmed in Peter's first presentation of the faith at the founding of the Church, when he intention-
ally linked the new status in Christ with the promise of Abraham. In
his sermon on Pentecost, Peter declared that the gift of the Holy Spirit (the promise) was linked to the family. In •Acts 2:39, he announces, "For the promise is made to you and to your children [τοῖς τέκνοῖς

---

32. A question can be raised here: how can the baptism of a believing member in a family affect others in the family who are not yet converted? It is clear that this is not through
faith, because the others are not yet baptized. Yet this is precisely where the dynamic realism of corporate personality comes in. The believing member of a family is not an arbitrary
individual but already "one flesh" with the other members because of familial bonds. They
are all organically one. Thus, when the head of this organic body begins participating in
Christ Jesus via baptism, Christ also begins to affect the others in that organic unit. That
does not mean they do not need baptism and conversion, but nonetheless, because of the
familial bond they have been brought into a sphere of holiness (i.e., into contact with the living Christ) and, in Pauline terminology, are said to be holy—even in their unbaptized state
(see 1 Cor 7:14).

ὑμῶν]." As we shall see, this language is similar to the οἶκος formula (οἶκος—family), which seems to underlie the understanding of how salvation operates in the new covenant.

While the practice of household baptisms (which would include the youngest children) would most fully cohere with the structure and experience of the Hebrew covenant, the terminology used in the NT does allow for some ambiguity. Those who would advocate for the "autonomous" position would argue that in texts mentioning household baptisms, each person in the household/οἶκος was already an adult (or had reached the age of autonomous reasoning) and, therefore, made his own personal decision to accept Christ.[33] If this were correct, only adults could be members of Christ. They would be acting as autonomous, independent agents with no reference to any other ontological relationships. If there were children or infants present within the family/οἶκος, they would be excluded from the salvific experience of Christ until they could make their own adult decision. In a theology that excludes children from the salvific covenant with Christ, the family can only be a sociological structure that remains extrinsic to the structure of the covenant itself and to the experience of salvation. Salvation then becomes a strictly individual matter. However, as we shall see, the evidence shows that there are serious problems with the "autonomous" position.

CONTINUITY

Primarily, there is the problem of continuity. It would seem rather odd to have the whole Old Testament witness to a corporate salvation, intrinsically tied to the family, overturned in the New Testament with the emphasis on the autonomous individual. This does not cohere with the Semitic mindset or underlying anthropology and, at best, would be an anachronistic overlay. In the OT, salvation is *never* just an indi-

---

33. The "autonomous" position is the belief that only an individual, having reached the age of reasoning, can make a decision to enter into a covenantal relationship with Christ and be baptized. Baptism is the public affirmation of the person's adult decision. This precludes any family context that would bring a child into the baptismal covenant.

vidualistic act. Rather, the anthropology of the OT attests to a fundamental communitarian aspect of man that fundamentally affects both his experiencing of good and evil *and* how he participates in salvation. By examining key points in salvation history, we see that redemption is always set in corporate terms: (a) the *whole* human race is negatively affected by the act of the first man, *prior* to each person's personal decisions and this negative result is passed on through the family line;[34] (b) the *whole* family of Noah is saved, not because of their own individual actions, but because of the righteousness of the one man, father Noah; and (c) the sons of Abraham enter into the salvific covenant, not through their own decision, but because of their father's faith. Having already themselves received the sign of the covenant through circumcision, they now act as representatives of the Abrahamic community when they circumcise their sons on the eighth day. Both the Fall and the redemption of man are experienced communally, *and the family plays a critical role in the transmission of the effects of both.* Consequently, since man's nature and the salvific process instituted in the OT are both corporate by nature, it is not surprising to see salvation in the NT also having a fundamental corporate and familial structure. Though there is a great difference between the old and new covenants, we see here that there is also a fundamental coherence between them as well. It could well be argued that it would be extremely difficult for Jews in the early Church to conceive psychologically of salvation expressed in absolutized individualistic terms.

EXCURSUS 5: BAPTISM AND INDIVIDUAL RESPONSE

Conversely, was the corporate dimension so dominant in the Semitic understanding of the person that it simply obviated the need for a personal response?[35] In household baptisms, did this corporate dimension overrule any sense of personal decision and responsibility? The problem is that the

34. See de Fraine, *Adam and the Family of Man*, 142ff.

35. Note that if this were the case, it would be in contrast to the evidence found in the OT, where both personal and corporate elements are kept in balance.

NT does not provide us with many specific details on baptism, and our reconstruction of NT baptismal practices has to be somewhat conjectural. But is the NT simply silent on the question of an adult personal response in areas of faith? It is true that the household baptism texts do not deal with the question of the personal response of adult members per se. However, by examining the household baptisms of Acts 16 in the light of Paul's discussion of faith within mixed marriages in 1 Cor 7:10–12, we can sketch out the probable "anthropological logic" that undergirded the phenomenon of household baptisms.

Household Baptism Texts

NT baptismal practices were informed by Semitic anthropological principles. The whole family was conceived of as a single organic reality. Thus, when the head of a family came to faith, the whole family was affected (•Acts 16:14–15; see above, with Lydia's conversion). The text witnesses only to Lydia's faith. The Lord "opens her heart" and from this she makes a personal decision of faith. Then the text jumps to record her baptism and the baptism of her household—but without any mediating steps. This is reminiscent of OT texts in which the faith of one person affects the whole household.[36] In line with Semitic anthropological principles, because Lydia has made a decision for Christ, her whole household was now brought into the sphere of Christ's influence. One of the determining factors in the whole household coming to baptism was the faith of this woman. Beyond this, we are not given details. The text simply does not confirm or deny that a personal response was required from each adult member of the household.

A few verses later, in Act 16: 25–40, we have the account of the conversion of the Philippian jailer and his household. The jailer asks how he is to be saved and Paul and Silas reply, "Believe [2nd person *singular*] on the

36. Jeremias has conclusively shown from the OT that the corporate sense is at play when the term "household" is employed, as in this text.

Lord Jesus and you shall be saved, you and your household" (+Acts 16:31). The text states unambiguously that the salvation of the jailer's household is predicated on his faith. This would certainly cohere with OT practice. The jailer's household becomes involved in faith through the faith of this one man. Once again, we are not given many details, only the outcome: the whole family is baptized. These texts do not deal with the question of personal adult response, but they do witness to the critical link between a man's or woman's decision for Christ and that of their household.

Marriage Texts

Despite a lacuna concerning personal adult decision in the household baptism texts, an examination of some of the Pauline texts on marriage can help us. In the early Church there was the problem of mixed marriages, in which one spouse was pagan and the other Christian. If the pagan spouse rejected the faith, what should a Christian do? Should the Christians spouse leave the unbelieving spouse? Paul's answer is predicated on the organicity of the family. Because of the oneness-in-flesh of the spouses, Christ's dwelling in the one spouse actually made the unbelieving spouse holy. This is then extended to the children.

> For the unbelieving husband is made holy through his wife, and the unbelieving wife is made holy through the brother. Otherwise your children would be unclean, whereas in fact they are holy (•1 Cor 7:14).[37]

In marriage, each person lives within an organic matrix (the one-flesh union, the family) that is constitutive of who he is. What happens to one profoundly affects the whole (see 1 Cor 12:26). But this corporateness *does not negate* the need of an individual response on the part of adults. The unbelieving spouse, in a mixed marriage situation, still needs to make a

---

37. This passage is not comprehensible unless we grasp the reality of corporate personality. Ultimately it is this principle that allows for infant baptism. An overemphasis on the autonomous, self-determining individual response forces the rejection of the baptism of children and the covenantal sense of family.

personal decision regarding the faith. If the pagan spouse does not resist the faith then, Paul states, the believing spouse must not separate from his unbelieving partner, because that person is made holy by the Christian spouse. This is equally true of husbands or wives.[38] As in the OT, holiness is a communicable reality within the family. Paul extends this principle when he states that because one of the parents is a Christian (and, therefore, has Christ living in him), the children of these mixed marriages are also holy. This provides a foundation for infant baptism.

But note that the critical factor is the personal decision of the unbelieving spouse. Both dimensions of the human personality are safeguarded and they mutually inform each other. The corporate dimension is recognized inasmuch as the martial union brings the unbelieving spouse into the sphere of holiness, which profoundly affects him. He is not within a neutral space. In marriage, he is part of an organic whole. But the personal dimension is equally safeguarded, inasmuch as this experience of Christ does not force the person to accept the faith. Possessing freedom, the unbelieving spouse can accept, tolerate, or reject the Presence of Christ. If he chooses to reject living with his faith-filled wife, his spouse is free (1 Cor 7:15). It is clear that the corporate encounter with Christ and holiness is in fact real but does not compel one to conversion, nor does it negate a personal response; in fact, it necessitates it.

Dynamics of Decision: Corporate and Personal

It is important to understand the nature of personal decision within the NT. Decision-making is *not* a neutral situation in which an autonomous individual is presented with certain truth claims, which are then adjudicated independently and autonomously solely through intellectual activity. This is the basic framework within which the modern concept of freedom operates. In contrast, the NT sees the person with a Christian spouse

38. "If any woman has a husband who is an unbeliever, and he is willing to go on living with her, she should not divorce her husband" (•1 Cor 7:13).

as *already* living within a context that profoundly affects him.[39] Through
the relationship, he is already encountering, and being ordered to, holiness. This relationship does not absolutely determine the person, but it
does profoundly affect him. Each person is a member of a family with ontological bonds that exist between the members. The individual is always
affected by the whole and vice versa. In this light, the autonomous, self-
determining person of modern thought is, in reality, a fictional construct.
By way of contrast, biblical anthropology accounts for the interplay between the personal and the corporate dimensions of the person.

Because someone (be it a Lydia or a jailer) has faith and is baptized, the
whole household is automatically affected, because all exist as an organic
unity. Christ, through the baptized member, has entered the whole household organism. No member is unaffected. But, as Paul shows in 1 Cor 7,
this presence of Christ is not irresistible. His presence is the presence of
divine love, and as the human soul is, by nature, already configured to
this love, there is a strong connaturality between Christ and the unbelieving members. But given human freedom (as can be seen in Gn 3) a person
can refuse this love, and *choose to separate himself from that eternal love
in Christ.* Given the Christo-centric nature of creation (Jn 1:1–14), we are
made already ordered to this love, that is, it is not a neutral situation. Giv-
en the ontological bonds within a family and this prior ontological ordering to Christ, it would seem natural to desire union with this divine love
and to accept Christ. But even this can be overridden by the exercise of our

39. This is closely aligned with the concept of divine election. This means, in essence,
that God has chosen us and not that we have (first) chosen Him. The truth is that we can do
nothing to earn our salvation, and so God chooses us while we are in rebellion against Him
(Rom 5:8), before we are even able to choose Him. The heart of all genuine Catholic theology is that *all* is grace; even our ability to respond to God is an act of God's grace working in
our lives. If a person relied on personal choice alone, or even as a beginning point, we could
never be saved. The initiative always remains with God. Our personal response in either the
old or the new covenant is critical, but it is never foundational. That rests on God's grace
alone; salvation is by grace alone. To rely on our own ability and decision for salvation is, in
essence, a form of Pelagianism.

free will when one chooses to be separate from Him. Even the salvific presence of Christ can never negate personal freedom.

This would seem to throw light on the question of adult decision/response in the context of household baptisms, particularly since the household is derived from marriage. By reading the household baptism texts alongside the Pauline marriage texts, we can *plausibly* construct the decisional dynamic within household baptisms. Given 1 Cor 7, it would seem that in all likelihood both the personal and the corporate dimensions of the human person were safeguarded in household baptisms as well. It is clear that the corporate dimension was secured because the person was never seen as an isolated and autonomous decision maker but as a member of a family formed through ontological bonds. The actions of one affect all. Thus, when Christ begins to live within one member, the whole body is affected and all begin to experience Christ. If one accepts that the anthropological basis of all these texts (marriage or baptism) is the same, then the personal dimension of the person would also be safeguarded, in that each adult, both men and women, had the freedom and responsibility to accept or reject the presence of Christ. But in rejecting, he separates himself from his baptized family. Thus one could plausibly conjecture that adult members of a family, both men and women, would probably be baptized unless they personally objected to the new faith and willed separation from Christ (and thus from their family as well). But given the solidarity of the family, the ontological bonds, and our ontological ordering to Christ, this would probably be rare. This understanding respects each person's freedom and decision making but it does not make the mistake of assuming that freedom is autonomous and that decision making is exercised in a neutral vacuum. We do possess freedom but we are not isolated, self-determining individuals. We always exist as part of a greater whole.

BAPTISM AND CHILDREN:
THE οἶκος FORMULA

Since the Reformation, the baptism of children has become a controverted question. If one posits some form of personal decision on the part of adults in the baptismal process (see Excursus 4), the question becomes: are children even candidates for this sacrament? As mentioned above, what is unusual in the NT texts is their frequent association of baptism with the reality of the household (οἶκος). To discern what was the actual baptismal practice of the early Church in regard to children we need to know what was the extent of the οἶκος. Did the οἶκος necessarily include children? Could children be excluded from it? One of the most insightful investigations into this area is the work of Joachim Jeremias.[40] What makes his work of particular interest is not only the profound scholarship he brings to bear on the subject but also the fact that he changed his position once he carried out his investigation and the evidence was established.

In *Infant Baptism in the First Four Centuries,* Jeremias shows how the concept of household (*beth*) in the OT can be used to understand the meaning and parameters of the term οἶκος/household in the NT. Basing his argument on E. Staufer's work,[41] Jeremias shows how the corporateness (the organic unity) of the Jewish family was fundamental to OT thought and was encapsulated in the term *"and his house."* He cites several texts which use the phrase as a kind of technical shorthand to be inclusive of everyone in the home, including infants:[42]

(1) 1 SAM 22:16. This text describes how Saul had all the family of Ahimelech murdered because they had offered refuge to David. In ^1 Sam 22:16, Saul addresses Ahimelech and says, "You shall surely die, Ahimelech, you and all your father's house [וְכָל־בֵּית אָבִיךָ / v'kol-

---

40. This and the following sections are indebted to the investigative work by J. Jeremias, *Infant Baptism in the First Four Centuries,* trans. David Cairns (Philadelphia: Westminster Press, 1961).

41. In *Infant Baptism* (p. 20ff.), Jeremias references E. Stauffer, "Zur Kindertaufe in der Ur kirche," *Deutsches Pfarrerblatt* 49 (1949): 152n2.

42. Jeremias, *Infant Baptism,* 20.

bêt 'ăbî hā].” Then, in verse ^22:19, the extent of this household is confirmed: it includes “men and women, children [מְעוֹלֵל / *mē'ôlēl*] and infants [וְעַד־יוֹנֵק / *v⁾ad-yônēq*].”[43] Both children and young nursing infants are particularly noted.

(2) GN 17:23. This passage provides the instructions for including children into the Abrahamic covenant by way of circumcision. Verse 23 describes the response of Abraham: “Then Abraham took his son Ishmael and all his slaves…every male [כָּל־זָכָר בְּאַנְשֵׁי / *kol-zāhār b⁾anshê*] among the members of Abraham's household [בֵּית אַבְרָהָם / *bêt 'abrāhām*]…and he circumcised the flesh of their foreskins.” Circumcision was the sign of the covenant and was a *household* ritual including all males, even infants who were only eight days old (see Gn 17:12).

(3) GN 45:18. This text is part of the Joseph cycle and describes how Jacob's family came down to Egypt to escape the famine in Israel. After the revelation that the Israelites were brothers of Joseph, the Pharaoh tells his brothers to go back to Israel and “take your father and your households [lit. houses: וְאֶת־בָּתֵּיכֶם / *v⁾et-bāttêkem*] and bring them down to Egypt.” The extent of these households can be determined from +Gn 45:19, which mentions that a wagon is to be sent for “your children [לְטַפְּכֶם / *l⁾tapp⁾hem*] and your wives.” When this same word for children is used in Dt 1:39, it appears to mean those who are young and vulnerable.[44] Also, the early age of these children may be indicated in Gn 45:19 by the fact that a wagon was needed, presumably for those too weak or too young to walk the whole way.

In each case, the use of the term בֵּית (*bêt*—house or household) is inclusive of both adults and children, even infants. It is not an exclusionary term but rather emphasizes the solidarity and organic integrity of the whole family. In fact, this term can be considered a technical formula precisely because it intends to indicate such inclusiveness. Jeremias quotes E. Stauffer's conclusion that “from early times there was a constant biblical 'οἶκος formula' which 'not only referred to the chil-

---

43. The term יוֹנֵק (*yônēq*) refers to infants who are nursing.

44. “Moreover your little ones [טַפְּכֶם], who you said would become a prey, and your children, who this day have no knowledge of good or evil…” (^Dt 1:39).

dren in addition to the adults but had quite *special* reference to the children and not least to any *small children* who might be present.'"[45]

It was this type of evidence that led Jeremias, following the lead of Stauffer in *"Zur Kindertaufe in der Ur kirche,"* to conclude that the use of the οἶκος/household formula in the New Testament was based directly on the use of the household formula in the Old Testament, particularly the association of the household with circumcision.[46] (This becomes clear when we realize that the Hebrew word for home/family (בַּיִת / *bêt*) is translated as οἶκος in the LXX.) This linkage helps to establish a continuity with the OT covenant and to posit that *baptism fulfills circumcision.*[47] Specifically, the use of the οἶκος formula indicates that, as in circumcision, all family members entered into the (baptismal) covenant—not just those who made personal decisions.[48] For circumcision and baptism to be so communal requires a concept of the person and of the family that is predicated on the idea of corporate personality, which guarantees the organic interrelatedness of all members.

> The New Testament *oikos* formula was adopted from the Old Testament cultic language (and in particular, we may say, from the terminology of circumcision) and introduced into the formal language employed in the primitive Christian rite of baptism; it has the same form and the same meaning as the old biblical ritual formula.[49]

This position is strengthened because the NT considers baptism as the fulfillment of circumcision.[50] Just as the Passover helps us to understand the structure and meaning of the Eucharist, similarly circumcision helps in regards to baptism. If a Jewish son was brought into the

45. Jeremias, *Infant Baptism*, 20.
46. Ibid, 20–21.
47. Paul explains baptism as form of circumcision in Col 2:11–12.
48. "If we grasp this, we shall have to agree with Stauffer's conclusion, that the New Testament οἶκος formula was adopted from the Old Testament cultic language…and introduced into the formal language employed in the primitive Christian rite of baptism; it has the same form and the same meaning as the old biblical ritual formula, i.e., it includes small children as well as others" (Jeremias, *Infant Baptism*, 21).
49. Ibid.
50. "In him you were also circumcised…. You were buried with him in baptism" (•Col 2:11–12).

Abrahamic covenant as an infant, it would seem strange to the Semitic mind to now exclude children from the new covenant until they could make their own profession of faith. Such a concept would totally undermine their previous understanding of the structure and meaning of the Abrahamic covenant, of the family, as well as of the human person. This interpretation would be anachronistic, as it would be reading eighteenth-century Enlightenment sensibilities back into first-century Jewish thought.

FATHER AS FOUNDATION

In a second line of reasoning, Jeremias shows how the concept of corporate personality was also grounded in the binding authority of the head of the family. Here he examines Acts 16:30–34 (the conversion of the Philippian jailer and his house) and Acts 16:11–15 (the conversion of Lydia and her house). In each case, the faith of the head of the house determines the faith of the whole household. As Jeremias rightly observes, "But when we consider family solidarity resting upon the authoritative influence of the head of the family it is scarcely conceivable that the baptism of a 'household' did not include all its members."[51]

The crucial point here is that the family was not seen as an assemblage of autonomous individuals but "was regarded as a unity in the sight of God"[52] upon which the grace of God was acting. On a psychological level, it would be virtually impossible for first-century Jews to reject the baptism of their children out of some regard for their autonomous rights or a novel belief in individualistic salvation. This would run counter to the Jewish experience of the covenant. The evidence leads us to conclude that the principle of *familial solidarity* lies at the heart of the New Testament understanding of the family and proceeds out of the covenantal experience found in the Old Testament.

51. Jeremias, *Infant Baptism,* 23.
52. Ibid., 24.

RELATIONSHIP TO PROSELYTE
BAPTISM

This organic view of the family is further corroborated by the practice of Jewish proselyte baptism during the Second-Temple period. During this period, Gentiles who had converted to the Jewish faith were required, as the final initiation into Judaism, to undergo a baptismal rite.[53] When the evidence for this ritual entrance into Judaism is examined, profound similarities with Christian baptism emerge which demonstrate that entrance into the (Jewish) salvific community was not only a personal decision for a pagan adult; his decision had familial consequences as well. In a manner consistent with how the Old Testament conceived of the person and salvation, proselyte baptism was extended to the infant children in the family. In this way, the organic integrity of the family and of salvation (a critical feature of the Semitic mindset) was maintained. Underlying this practice of proselyte baptism was an anthropology which was deeply personal but never individualistic (in the autonomous sense) and which always saw the individual intrinsically inserted into a familial context.

A comparison between Jewish proselyte baptism and Christian baptism shows that the similarities between the two are substantial. First, the preferential mode of administration for both was complete immersion into flowing water, which could be accompanied by a confession of sins. Second, there was a strong correspondence between the purpose and meaning of these two rites. In both, the person emerging from the renewing waters was considered to have been born anew in some fashion. The rabbinical literature states that "the proselyte in his conversion

---

53. Although there are no injunctions in the Torah to administer baptism, Jeremias has shown conclusively that the evidence indicates that proselyte baptism occurred within Judaism *prior* to the emergence of Christianity. He refers to the discussions of Hillel and Shammai (who lived in the first century B C), for whom proselyte baptism was an already established practice (see Jeremias, *Infant Baptism*, 22). Other evidence used to show the pre-Christian dating of this practice is the historical case of the High Priest's impurity during Yom Kippur in A D 17–18, along with a passage concerning purification in *Test. Levi* 14:6 (Jeremias, 19–20).

(to Judaism) is like a newborn child,"[54] while, in Christianity, baptism was understood as the rite of new birth (see John 3:5). Third, in each case, the rite represented a decisive break with the past and the initiation into a new form of life. This change was so radical that in both rites the person was considered to have experienced some form of *death*. The rabbis wrote that the new convert to Judaism had, in some form, been raised from the dead.[55] This closely corresponds to Paul's explanation of Christian baptism in Romans:

> Accordingly, we were buried with Him through baptism into death, in order that just as Christ was raised up from the dead through the glory of the Father, even thus we might walk in newness of life. (+Rom 6:4)

Fourth, in each form of baptism there was a connection with the remission of sins. Jeremias comments that for the rabbis the effect of this Jewish mode of baptism was a new state of existence for the convert, "all his sins being forgiven him (the proselyte)."[56] In Christian baptism, the grace of the Cross is applied to both original sin and the actual sins of the person in such a way that they are now forgiven. Fifth, in each rite, the baptized person acquired a state of holiness and is now oriented towards it. In both rites, the new status of the convert was often symbolized by the person assuming a new name.[57] The correspondences relating to the actual external rites and the theological understanding of Jewish proselyte and Christian baptism are so strong that Jeremias concludes: "The whole terminology of the Jewish conversion theology, connected with proselyte baptism, recurs in the theology of primitive Christian baptism. Here a chance coincidence and the possibility of accidental analogies is wholly inconceivable; the only possible conclusion is that the rites are related as parent and child."[58]

While it is impossible to *prove* causality between these two forms of baptism, the evidence is clear that there is a relationship of profound

54. Jeremias, *Infant Baptism*, 32n2, quoting b. Yeb 48b (Bar.) par. Ger 2.6 f. and referencing b. Yeb 22a, 62a, 97v; b. Bek. 47a.

55. See ibid., 33 quoting Qoh. R. on 8.10 (ed. Stettin, 1864, 1122).

56. Ibid., 33n8, quoting J. Bik. 3.65c. 61; Midr. Sam 17 § on 13:1.

57. Ibid., 36.

58. Ibid., 36.

influence between them. The dating of Jewish proselyte baptism is, therefore, of critical importance, because this can help determine the direction of influence.[59] Careful study shows that proselyte baptism existed before the Christian era, and consequently the former can be considered as the "ground" of the latter. If this is accurate, then the candidate who was allowed to receive proselyte baptism would show whether or not the Jewish community perceived baptism as an *autonomous* or an *organic* and familial rite. If *autonomous,* then the Gentile child could be admitted into the community of Israel only when he had made an adult decision to convert to Judaism, and his parents' decisions would have no effect upon them. If the *organic* understanding obtained, then male children of converts would be circumcised and both sons and daughters would undergo proselyte baptism along with their parents upon the conversion of the adults. On this point at least, the evidence is both clear and consistent. In the Tannaitic period (AD 70–200) a ruling was given that the son of a slave woman would be given immediate circumcision when she became a member of the Jewish household. However, once she had been made a member of the Jewish household, any other sons born to her would be circumcised on the eighth day as required of other Jewish children.[60] Thus, the proselyte baptism of the mother affected the status of the pre-born child.[61]

Jeremias also cites the rabbinic arguments concerning the legal status of a child of a Gentile woman who was to undergo proselyte baptism on her conversion to Judaism. It was resolved by Raba (AD 299–352), who states that "if a non-Israelite during her pregnancy becomes a proselyte, then her child does not need the baptismal bath." Conversely, this ruling means that any child born *prior* to the baptism would then need to undergo proselyte baptism themselves. The reasoning underlying this ruling demonstrates that (a) because of the *organic-familial* relationship, infants were proper candidates for admission into the salvific community of Israel by means of baptism, and (b) infants

---

59. See ibid., 24–29.

60. Ibid., 37–38 referring to the legislation recorded in b. Shab. 135 b. (Bar.). See n. 1, p. 38.

61. One is reminded here of the effects of the presence of Jesus (who was still within the womb of Mary) upon John the Baptist while he was still *in utero* (see Lk 1:41).

were affected by the decisions and actions of their mothers such that her status was given to the child while *in utero,* precisely because of their *intrinsic-organic* relationship.[62] After examining all the evidence, Jeremias concludes:

> We see that the oldest rabbinic sources, take it completely for granted that the children, even the smallest children, were admitted with their parents into the Jewish faith: the case is nowhere mentioned, and it is almost inconceivable for the feeling of the times, where on the admission of both parents the children who were minors remained Gentiles.[63]

It is clear that when Second-Temple Judaism had to deal with the question of admittance to the faith, they saw the conversion of a Gentile as a climactic experience in which the person spiritually went from death to new life. This was effected through proselyte baptism in which the person was, as it were, born again in the ritual waters. Children present in the family at the time of conversion also underwent proselyte baptism at the same time, showing that circumcision was not the *definitive* ritual for initiation into the covenant.

This practice is totally consistent with the corporate understanding of the covenant and its anthropological grounding in the Old Testament. In fact, it would require a major psychological shift in the Jewish and early Christian mindset to establish an autonomous understanding of salvation and the faith. Jewish proselyte baptism demonstrates that this did not happen. Given that virtually the entire membership of the early Church was Jewish, it would be highly unlikely that they would reject the familial nature of salvation which was their only term of reference and adopt the view that children were autonomous, outside the salvific community until they made an adult decision to join it. This would be incomprehensible to the Semitic mindset. And so here also, in the practice of proselyte baptism within Second-Temple Judaism, we see the family functioning instrumentally in the salvific order.

---

62. Jeremias, *Infant Baptism,* 39, quoting b. Yeb. 78a.
63. Ibid., 39.

HOUSEHOLD ORDER TEXTS

This corporate identity of the family is further corroborated by several Pauline texts, which have become known as the household order texts. Here, the whole family is addressed and given instruction on how to live "in the Lord" and how to work out their salvation within the concrete terms of their family life. The underlying assumption is that the family is an organic entity in which there is a real exchange of spiritual goods (i.e., a *communio*). Consequently, the family, as an organic whole, has been imbued with Christ, and, therefore, Paul properly addresses every member of this *organic* body, including minor children, as members of Christ. But if one takes the position that each member is autonomous (and, therefore, not fundamentally affected by the other members), then one can legitimately ask by what right Paul addresses the unsaved children of baptized parents since they would not be a part of the salvific community. Within the autonomous model, the only concern would be to introduce children to a saving experience of Christ once they had reached the age of reason; *growth* in the faith would not be possible until such an initiation had been effected. They remain outside the grace of Christ until such a decision is taken.

Under the "autonomous" model, since the early Church believed in the imminent return of Christ, then the primary concern of parents would be to secure the salvation of their children. However, we do not see in the New Testament any directive for parents to work towards the *conversion* of their children so they could be baptized into the faith. What we do find, however, is that *children* are already addressed as ἁγίοις or 'holy ones". The opening of Ephesians is addressed to τοῖς ἁγίοις τοῖς οὖσιν [ἐν Ἐφέσῳ]—"the saints [holy ones] at Ephesus." Later, in chapter 5, Paul addresses husbands and wives as to their Christian obligations and then in chapter 6, in a parallel fashion, begins to speak to the children (τα τέκνα). Given the opening salutation and the parallel structure of addressees, it is only logical to conclude that Paul assumes that children were part of the salvific community (i.e., the Church) and that they are numbered among the ἁγίοι (the saints). There is no evidence of a group within the early Church composed of young children, awaiting the age of reason, so they could make indi-vidualistic professions of faith. Rather, they were already seen as part of the salvific community.

This interpretation is particularly strengthened by Paul's admonition when he tells fathers, "Do not provoke your children to anger, but bring them up with the training and instruction of the Lord." (•Eph 6:4) It is a telling omission. Fathers are not instructed to bring about the conver-sion of their children but to bring them up in the Lord's teaching. The presumption here is that their children were already a part of the Body of Christ; otherwise the admonition makes no sense.[64] An analysis of 1 Cor 7 confirms this and can shed further light on the status of young children in the home and their relationship to the covenant.

FAMILY AS HOLY:
1 CORINTHIANS 7:12–16

This is a complicated passage, which contains Paul's teaching on mixed marriages and requires certain background knowledge if it is to be interpreted properly. It is arguably one of the most important passag-es in the whole New Testament for the theology of the domestic church, demonstrating as it does that the family (by virtue of its organic struc-ture and solidarity) has the capacity to *transmit* holiness. No other nat-ural structure has this potentiality.[65] For those who would hold to the "autonomous" position, this passage is impossible to interpret.

Key to this passage is the dynamic reality of baptism in the early Church. Baptism was not merely a rite by which one became a member

64. In the NT, salvation is by grace alone and is won for the human race by the work of Christ. Baptism is the moment at which one encounters Christ sacramentally and in which an exchange of natures takes place. Then, we need to work out this salvation (see Phil 2:12) which, for the child, requires growth in the knowledge and experience of the faith. Thus, once again, the family becomes the indispensable context in which the child comes to know ever more deeply the reality of the risen Christ.

65. Family here refers to the matrix of both the marriage of husband and wife and the family with children that proceed from this. For a discussion on OT rites and the concept of the different spheres of reality (including that of holiness), see Atkinson, "Mystery of Wa-ter," Section 3: "Purity and Holiness: Water in the Cult of Israel," especially pp. 293ff.

of an ecclesial organization. Rather, what baptism effected was nothing other than the baptizand becoming a totally new creation. In Paul's analysis, to become a new creation in Christ required the death of the old adamic (sinful) nature and the receiving of a new animating life principle. The most graphic portrayal of this is found in Paul's treatise on baptism in Romans 6, where he associates baptism with our dying with Jesus on the Cross:

> Or are you unaware that we who were baptized into Christ Jesus were baptized into his death?...For if we have grown into union with him through a death like his, we shall also be united with him in the resurrection. We know that our old self was crucified with him. (•Rom 6:3, 5–6)[66]

The only way of effecting a change in the fallen, adamic nature of man was that this nature should die. This was effected sacramentally through baptism, by which one is joined to the death of Christ. Hence, baptism was not primarily a subjective, personal act meant to provide a witness to the individual's experience. Rather, it was the *instrument* by which the exchange of natures necessary for salvation took place. Baptism by water was necessary to salvation. This critical (and nonnegotiable) requirement is witnessed to by Christ's insistence that one is born again by water and the Spirit (Jn 3:5) and also by the early Church's practice of immediate baptism for those who had come to faith (see Acts 8:36–38 and Acts 16). Salvation was intrinsically tied to faith *and* baptism.

The person emerging from baptism now becomes a new creation in whom the animating principle is no longer the fallen adamic nature, but instead is the very life of Jesus. For Paul and the early Church, this was not understood metaphorically; rather it was to be taken literally. It was precisely because Jesus now lived in believers that they became holy and were a part of the body of Christ. As mentioned above, this realism is given direct expression in Gal 2:20. Fundamentally for Paul, the Christian was the person whose sin-oriented nature was put to death through baptism and who had, in those saving waters, received

---

66. This is parallel in thought to +Gal 2:20: "I have been crucified with Christ."

the new life of Christ and became part of His body. For Paul, the eschaton had actually begun in the life of the believer.

In Paul's theology, baptism has a profound effect upon both marriage and family within the new covenant. Precisely because each member of a family is organically connected to the others and they form one body, when Christ begins to live in one, the whole organism of the family is affected. The great mystery is that when a husband or wife, mother or father, is baptized, all the members of a marriage or family begin to participate (at least to a certain degree) in the reality of Christ Jesus. Paul's teaching given in 1 Cor 7 throws light on the dynamic of personal decision within the corporate setting of the family. It is also critical because it is concerned with the holiness of the family and its communicability. In 1 Cor 7, Paul addresses the situation of a mixed marriage between a Christian and a pagan spouse. Paul teaches that Christian husbands or wives are not allowed to separate from their pagan spouse so long as that spouse is willing to live with the Christian partner. He sees that the ultimate destiny of the human person is salvation in Christ, and marriage can be instrumental in helping people to achieve this end.

The creation narrative in Genesis explicitly teaches that in any marriage the two spouses become one flesh (Gn 2:24). Their union effects a reality (the oneness of flesh) that heretofore had not existed. What they have bought into existence is a new psychosomatic, organic unity. This reality does not change in the New Testament. If one of the marriage partners is baptized into Christ, then Christ is not only living in a person, but He is also inserted into the one-flesh union. Because of this presence of Christ in one member, all enter into the sphere of holiness, even if they have not made a profession of faith.[67] This is the rather astonishing teaching of 1 Cor 7. Paul teaches that, as long as the non-

---

67. As Paul will indicate, this does not take place against the will of the pagan partner. If the pagan partner refuses to continue in the marriage (presumably because of the practice of faith) the Christian is free to leave. This would seem to mean that the pagan partner has rejected the faith and does not want to have anything to do with it. On the other hand, if the pagan partner decides to stay, then Paul says that the pagan spouse is ἡγίασται—sanctified or made holy. He still needs conversion and baptism, but it would seem that by the marital bond he is brought within the influence of Christ.

Christian does not object to and does not take action against this presence of Christ, the Christian partner must stay.

Paul explicitly states that the unbelieving husband/wife is made holy (ἡγίασται, from ἅγιος) through the believing spouse (1 Cor 7:14). *He can make this statement only based on an anthropology that takes seriously the corporate dimension of the human person and of the organic nature of the marital and familial bond.* If one maintained an "autonomous" anthropology, this teaching would not be possible. The passage then extends this corporate effect to the children of this union. Not only is the unbelieving spouse sanctified through the presence of Christ in the baptized partner, but the children who proceed out of this union are also said to be made holy: "Otherwise your children [from this mixed marriage] would be unclean, whereas in fact they are holy [νῦν δὲ ἅγιά ἐστιν]" (1 Cor 7:14). It is clear from this passage that children with at least one Christian parent begin to experience the effects of Christ and have entered into the sphere of holiness prior to their own autonomous decision. None of this denies the need for personal conversion and growth in the Lord. In fact, Paul shows that the unbelieving spouse still needs to grow in Christ and experience salvation: "For how do you know, wife, whether you will save [σώσεις—future tense] your husband" (•1 Cor 7:16).[68] There is a great mystery here; when even one part of the organic structure of the family is imbued with Christ, all the other members are brought into the salvific sphere of Christ's grace.

Thus for Paul, a Christian spouse actually brings the living reality of Jesus into the marriage structure. The family is the matrix where the Holy Spirit is working out the salvation of every family member, even those who are not yet conscious of the presence of Christ. Because there is a fundamental unity and organic relationship between all the mem-

---

68. See the discussion of this passage and the place of children within covenantal initiation in Oscar Cullmann, *Baptism in the New Testament* (London: SCM Press, 1950), especially chap. 2. He states: "1 Cor 10.1ff. [is] a passage which ought to be much more carefully observed in the discussion of child Baptism. It is here quite plain that the act of grace, which is regarded as the type of Baptism, concerns the covenant which God made with the whole people" (p. 45).

bers of the marriage and family, the introduction of any such dynamic presence affects all members.[69] In fact, it can be said that the family now becomes the "sphere of eschatological activity." This corresponds to calling the OT family the "carrier of the covenant." Just as the covenant is finally realized in Christ Jesus, so the family as the carrier of the covenant now reaches its proper function in Christ, who is the *telos* of the covenant. By virtue of baptism, the family now has the presence of Christ active within itself. The Holy Spirit is present, guiding the family, bringing about the salvation of its members and enabling the family to participate in the mission of the Church, of which it is a cell, and helping prepare for the Second Coming of Christ. Thus, the baptized family is a primary locus where God is working out His salvific will for the world. It is this understanding that provides the foundation for the theology of *the family as domestic Church*.

THE QUESTION OF TERMINOLOGY

We will now need to look at the evidence within the New Testament and the early Church to see how the concept of domestic church developed and what it implied. In the NT canon there are several instances where the ideas of household (*domestica*) and the church (*ecclesia*) are combined together. The term "domestic church" actually is derived from the Latin translation of the Scriptures. A cursory look at Jerome's Latin Vulgate would lead one to assume that the philological construction itself would give strong support to the contention that the Christian family has an ecclesial nature and is a subset of the Church. This is because Jerome translates οἶκος (household) and ἐκκλησία (church) when they occur linked together as the *domestica ecclesia*—the domestic church, the specific phrase in use today.

However, on closer examination of the original Greek, it is evident

---

69. Paul uses this same idea in reference to the Church as the Body of Christ. When one member is affected, the whole body is affected (1 Cor 13:27). To understand this properly, one should refer to Pedersen's work on the soul and especially its pliability. The soul absorbs dynamic influences which become formative for it; the stronger the influence, the greater the informing value (see Pedersen, *Israel I-II*, 99ff.).

that Jerome was not accurately reproducing some of the original texts syntactically, and, therefore, one cannot determine the connotation of this word combination (*domestica-ecclesia*) from the Vulgate. If prudence is not exercised here, one could claim more for the texts than they actually state. Thus, a critical area of research essential for the theology of the domestic church is determining the actual meaning of the οἶκος/ἐκκλησία linkage within the NT corpus. For us, the most initial question is whether or not the concept of the "domestic church" as it is now employed can be grounded in the NT's use of this term.

There are only four places in the New Testament where the words οἶκος (household) and ἐκκλησία (church) occur together. While there will be much overlap in the grammatical analysis of the texts, it is best to thoroughly analyze each one. Our task is to establish the precise relationship that exists between οἶκος and ἐκκλησία in each of these texts. Do these terms refer to two separate entities that are only extrinsically related, as when a Christian congregation (the ἐκκλησία) meets in a person's home (the οἶκος),[70] or is the reference to two realities that are intrinsically related and form an integral unit, as in the Christian family *being* a domestic church and having an internal ecclesial dimension. As will be shown, it is this latter understanding that was operative in the Church Fathers and prevails in the modern understanding of family as domestic church. The question, however, is whether or not, on a philological and contextual level, the New Testament allows for such an interpretation of this phrase. Because the Latin translation is critical, the texts of the Vulgate and the Greek, along with a literal English translation, will be provided to aid our analysis.[71]

Rom 16:3–5

Ἀσπάσασθε Πρίσκαν καὶ Ἀκύλαν... οἷς οὐκ ἐγὼ μόνος εὐχαριστῶ ἀλλὰ καὶ πᾶσαι αἱ ἐκκλησίαι τῶν ἐθνῶν, καὶ τὴν <u>κατ᾽ οἶκον αὐτῶν ἐκκλησίαν.</u>

---

70. It should be clear that this might include not just individuals but also, more typically, whole families. But even in this case, the sense of "church" is not intrinsically related to the nature of the family.

71. All English translations are by the author.

Salutate Priscam et Aquilam...quibus non solus ego gratias ago sed et
cunctae ecclesiae gentium <u>et domesticam eorum ecclesiam</u> salutate

Greet Prisca and Aquila...to whom not only I give thanks but also all
the churches of the Gentiles; and (greet) <u>the church at their house.</u>

In the Greek version, οἶκον is in the accusative case (governed by the
preposition κατ᾽), as is ἐκκλησίαν. But to what is ἐκκλησίαν grammatically related? Given the structure of the sentence it would seem that κατ᾽
οἶκον αὐτῶν—because it is placed between ἐκκλησίαν and its definite
article τὴν—should be taken as a phrase modifying ἐκκλησίαν. The Vulgate (Vg), by changing the noun οἶκον into an adjective (*domesticam*),
makes the house-church a more coterminous unit. It becomes the *domesticam ecclesiam* or "domestic church," but this changes the original
Greek text somewhat, which is semantically questionable. The question
is to what degree οἶκον is conceptually connected to ἐκκλησίαν. Is it really a single conceptual unit such that the family is a church? Or does
ἐκκλησίαν/church refer to a reality which is distinct from the household? Or is there some kind of overlap? C. E. B. Cranfield translates the
phrase thus: "Greet Prisca and Aquila...to whom not only I but all the
churches of the Gentiles are grateful, and the church in their house."[72]
Grammatically, Cranfield draws a parallel between "the church in their
houses", "I," and "all the churches of the Gentiles." But this would require ἐκκλησίαν (which is accusative) to be in the nominative case. The
more common translation of "greet the church in their home" (NASB,
NIV, NEB) takes οἶκον as the object of the verb "greet," which then has
to be supplied.[73]

Although Cranfield believes that grammatically this phrase might
refer only to what we would call "the nuclear family,"[74] he concludes

72. C. E. B. Cranfield, *A Critical and Exegetical Commentary on the Epistle to the Romans*
(ICC), vol. 2 (Edinburgh: T & T Clark, 1989), 751.

73. It may be the case that Cranfield is making "the church in their houses" the object of
the verb "greet" (Ἀσπάσασθε) and thus making it grammatically parallel to Prisca and Aquila.
The one advantage of this translation is that it follows the Greek order more closely. However,
this phrase is far removed from its verb ("to greet"), and so the translation is a bit conjectural.

74. C. E. B. Cranfield, *Romans: A Shorter Commentary* (Grand Rapids, Mich.: Eerdmans,
1985), 376. Even here, Cranfield shows that family would still include servants and other dependents and not merely father, mother, and children.

that the phrase more probably refers to the family, servants, and other neighboring Christians who met for worship. As he noted, there were no special liturgical buildings at that time,[75] and thus the large home of a recently converted (wealthy) Roman would be the logical meeting place for the nascent church.

In conclusion, grammatically the possessive αὐτῶν qualifies "house" (οἶκον), which follows the preposition κατ᾽ ("according to"). The meaning here is clear and should be translated as a unit, becoming "according to, of, or in their house." This then logically becomes attached to ἐκκλησίαν ("church"). The whole phrase should be translated as an objectival phrase, the verb "greet" being supplied. Thus, it would be rendered "[greet] the Church in their home."

1 Cor. 16:19

Ἀσπάζονται ὑμᾶς αἱ ἐκκλησίαι τῆς Ἀσίας. ἀσπάζεται ὑμᾶς ἐν κυρίῳ πολλὰ Ἀκύλας καὶ Πρίσκα <u>σὺν τῇ κατ᾽ οἶκον αὐτῶν ἐκκλησίᾳ</u>.

Salutant vos ecclesiae Asiae salutant vos in Domino multum Aquila et Prisca <u>cum domestica sua ecclesia.</u>

The churches of Asia greet you, Aquila and Prisca greet [vb. sing] you much in the Lord <u>with the church in their home.</u>

Grammatically, this text has fewer ambiguities. In the Greek manuscript, ἐκκλησίᾳ is in the dative case following σὺν ("with"), whereas οἶκον is in the accusative case following κατ᾽. Because there is a clear differentiation between the two terms in the Greek text, the phrase is properly translated "with the church in their house." However, the Latin text does not give each term its own separate identity but renders the Greek noun οἶκον adjectivally (domestica) and relates it to ἐκκλησίᾳ (ecclesia), thereby creating one conceptual unit: "with their domestic church." (Interestingly, this text, like the earlier one, refers to Aquila and Prisca—who are a married couple; see Acts 18:2.) Because this clearer Corinthian text parallels the one from Romans, it can help to

---

75. J. M. Petersen states that worship in the home came about due to danger and necessity. "There was no question of worshipping in houses in order to make religion part of daily life" (J. M. Petersen, "House-Churches in Rome," *Vigiliae Christianae* 23, no. 1 [1969]: 272).

interpret the text of Romans. Both should, therefore, be understood to be conveying the idea of "the church meeting in their home."

Col 4: 15

Ἀσπάσασθε τοὺς ἐν Λαοδικείᾳ ἀδελφοὺς καὶ Νύμφαν <u>καὶ τὴν κατ' οἶκον αὐτῆς ἐκκλησίαν.</u>

Salutate fratres qui sunt Laodiciae et Nympham <u>et quae in domo eius est ecclesiam.</u>

Greet the brothers in Laodice and Nympha <u>and the church in her home.</u>

Grammatically ἐκκλησίαν ("church") is parallel with Νύμφαν ("Nympha"), as both are objects of the verb Ἀσπάσασθε ("greet") and are consequently in the accusative case. Therefore, the phrase should be translated: "Greet…the church in her home." The Vulgate, by keeping οἶκον a noun (*domo*), maintains the separate identities of "church" and "home" and, for the first time, accurately translates the Greek text.

Philemon 1:1–2

Παῦλος…Φιλήμονι…Ἀπφίᾳ τῇ ἀδελφῇ καὶ Ἀρχίππῳ τῷ συστρατιώτῃ ἡμῶν καὶ <u>τῇ κατ' οἶκόν σου ἐκκλησίᾳ.</u>

Paulus…Philemoni…et Appiae sorori et Archippo commilitoni nostro et <u>ecclesiae quae in domo tua est.</u>

Paul…to Philemon,…and Aphia (our) sister and Archippus, our fellow soldier and <u>to the church in your home.</u>

Once again, the original Greek text does not allow for a conflation of οἶκος and ἐκκλησία as they are in different cases. The word for "house" (οἶκόν) is in the accusative case following κατ', while "church" (ἐκκλησίᾳ) is in the dative case. They have separate identities. If they were understood as intersecting realities, that would lead to the conclusion that the household and the church were the same reality. The Vulgate renders both terms as nouns in the Latin and puts them in differing cases, thereby following the Greek accurately. The phrase should be translated: "the church that is in your house." Again, the sense is "the church which is meeting in someone's house."

The critical question of how closely οἶκος and ἐκκλησία are related *philologically* in the New Testament corpus is clearly answerable from this grammatical study of the texts. In each of the above texts, οἶκος is preceded by κατα, indicating place.[76] This points to the house or home being the locus where something took place. In each case, the phrase should be rendered as "the church in their/her/your home."[77] The grammar of the texts does not allow the identities of the household and the church to interpenetrate and form a single entity. The church (ἐκκλησία) and the home (οἶκος) keep their own separate identities. The Vulgate in both Rom 16:5 and 1 Cor 16:16 renders the noun οἶκος adjectivally and hence forges a much closer association between "church" and "home" than the original Greek text does. This phrasing could be construed as allowing for the family itself to be seen as a church. As we shall see, that is what Augustine does. The Greek, however, does not appear to do this. The clearest sense of this phrase, therefore, is that it refers to a church which met in someone's home. This is the position taken by Cranfield, J. A. Fitzmyer, and G. R. Cragg.[78] It certainly doesn't exclude the family from being a part of the Church, but neither does it make the family per se a domestic church.

Moffatt, on the other hand, relates the two terms more closely. He rightly concludes that Judaism and the pagan religions were naturally "conducted on a family basis"[79] and so the church would act no differently. The ancient *familia* included not only the immediate family members but also servants and dependents (*clientes*). It is possible that because all Christians saw themselves spiritually as a family, the ancient *familia* would now be extended to include recent Christian converts. Moffatt notes how all of these people, forming a spiritual family,

76. Cf. *The Analytical Greek Lexicon* (London: S. Bagster and Sons, 1908), 213.

77. Cf. οἶκος in W. F. Arndt and F. W. Gringrick, eds., *The Greek-English Lexicon of the New Testament and Other Early Christian Literature* (Chicago: University of Chicago Press, 1960), 562–63.

78. J. A. Fitzmeyer, *Romans: A New Translation with Introduction and Commentary*, Anchor Bible Series 33 (New York: Doubleday, 1993); G. R. Cragg, *The Acts of the Apostles/The Epistle to the Romans*, vol. 9 of *The Interpreter's Bible*, ed. G. A. Buttrick (New York: Abingdon Press, 1952), 656.

79. J. Moffatt, *The Epistle of Paul to the Romans* (New York: Harper and Row, 1932), 236.

would have access to the familial burial ground. Interestingly, it can be shown that the Roman parishes (*tituli*) "may well have grown out of the domestic churches which used the family burial-places."[80] Thus, through this manner of association, the family and those converted to Christ became a united congregation.

Similarly, W. A. Meeks finds that Paul uses κατ᾿ οἶκόν not to designate a place, but probably "to distinguish these individual household-based groups from 'the whole church.'... The *kat' oikon ekklēsia* is thus the 'basic cell' of the Christian movement, and its nucleus was often an existing household."[81] However he explicitly states that this grouping was not "coterminous with the household"[82] but would comprise many others, including recent converts.

We must not superimpose our modern (atomistic) notion of family (the blood-related unit) on top of the ancient *familia,* which was a much wider social grouping, including servants and those helped by the family (*clientes*).[83] To this now were added the newly converted of the area who shared in the same faith, met together, and by that same faith formed one body, brothers and sisters of each other. Thus, within the New Testament canon there is little philological evidence that "domestic church" was applied solely to the individual baptized family. Nor did the term necessarily apply an essential ecclesial character to the family. It may be for these philological reasons that the above scriptural references were not used at Vatican II to support the concept of the "domestic church." It would seem that the house-church matrix (or the "domestic church" of the Vulgate) was probably the church that met in a particular person's home, the basis of which may or may not have been that person's own family but which, if it was his family, probably included members other than his own kindred. It was also probably a home that was large enough to accommodate the fledgling church.

---

80. Moffat, *Romans,* 236–37.

81. W. A. Meeks, *The First Urban Christians* (New Haven, Conn.: Yale Press, 1983), 75.

82. Ibid., 76.

83. Cf. *"Patria Potestas,"* in N. G. L. Hammond and H. H. Scullard, eds., *The Oxford Classical Dictionary,* 2nd ed. (Oxford: Clarendon Press, 1984), 789.

CONCLUSION

The philological evidence in the New Testament does not *ground* the concept of the domestic church. But that is not to say that the reality of the "domestic church" (the family having an ecclesial dimension and caught up in the salvific will of God) was not present in the New Testament. Indeed, the whole Semitic worldview and the organic, corporate understanding of salvation in the Old Testament and baptism in the New Testament would presuppose that the family was critical in some fashion to the new covenant in Christ. One also has to be careful not to confuse reality and terminology. For example, neither of the terms "Incarnation" and "Trinity" is present in the Christian canon, yet both realities have profound theological foundations in the text. Mere philological evidence does not secure the reality of something. To find the ground of the domestic church, we must look to the New Testament's theology of baptism, its understanding of the corporate and organic nature of the human person, and the intrinsic relationship between the old and new covenants.

CHAPTER 9

APPROPRIATION
BY THE CHURCH
FATHERS

We have seen that, in the New Testament, the Hebraic understanding of the person continued to play a critical role in the understanding of salvation in Christ. We have also seen through the phenomenon of household baptisms (Acts 10:1–48; 16:15, 31–34; 18:8, and 1 Corinthians 1:16; 16:15; cf. also with Heb 11:7 and 1 Tim 3:4) that the corporate nature of salvation, which is clearly evident in the Old Testament, is still discernible in the New Testament. In addition, Paul in 1 Cor 7:10ff. shows that even in the marriage between a pagan and a Christian, the influence of Christ, who is living within the baptized spouse, affects everyone in the family. *The family is, therefore, a privileged place where Christ in one member affects the many.* As in the OT, the NT family is not simply a social construct but is still used by God to further His salvific design. In this sense, one can call the family an instrument of salvation because, through baptism, the family becomes a sphere of eschatological activity. This means that the Holy Spirit is present and actively influencing all the members of the organic family unit. The early Church Fathers were particularly sensitive to this transforming effect of baptism on the whole family, its new identity in Christ, and its role in the order of salvation.

Our task at this point is to examine to what degree the early Church Fathers appropriated the concept domestic church, the meaning they gave to this term, and how they applied this ecclesial nature to the family.

Although the patristic evidence is limited, the concept of the baptized family household having an ecclesial identity clearly exists and is developed substantially by two of the most prominent fathers of the early period. The most important texts are found in the writings of Augustine and Chrysostom, whose writings played an important role at Vatican II. They were cited at the Council to validate the family having an ecclesial identity and were used:

- to confirm that *within the tradition of the Church* the Christian family was thought of in terms of church;
- to reveal the essential ecclesial structure of the home; and
- to establish marriage, and by implication the family, as a "state of life" in the Church. This would give the family an almost sacramental nature.[1]

This concept of the "state of life" is essential for the construction of a domestic church theology. The determination of a state signifies that a specific way of life has a specific form, which renders it a legitimate choice by which an individual can attain salvation. Although the Church had never formally denied that marriage and family were ways to holiness, consecrated celibacy had become, at least culturally, *the* recognized state in which the perfection of holiness could be attained. Marriage and family life were seen, at best, to be second-rate and the default choice of those who could not attain to the rigors of holiness required by celibacy. In Vatican II, the effort was made by the Council fathers to retrieve the authentic church tradition, which saw marriage (and thereby family) as reflective of the union of Christ and his Church, and, therefore, an instrument of holiness.

---

1. This is a critical point. There were many references in the Council debates concerning the status of marriage. It had to be firmly established that marriage itself was a holy and legitimate way of life in the Church. Only after this was acknowledged could the family, by way of extension, be conceived of as holy as well—i.e., a domestic church. The credit for achieving this goes to Bishop Fiordelli of Prato, Italy.

AUGUSTINE

One will look in vain for a developed theology of the family in St. Augustine.[2] For example, in the whole Augustinian corpus the term *paterfamilias* (father of the family) occurs only 43 times. However, Augustine plays a critical role inasmuch as he is the only Church Father to use the phrase, domestic church, directly.[3] His work is also essential to the theology of the domestic church because he situated both the nature and the structure of the Church *in* the family itself in such a concrete way that the reality of the Church became a tangible reality within domestic life. Both the *nature* and the mission of the Body of Christ are linked directly to the Christian family.

Domestica Ecclesia

One primary text, cited at Vatican II, was from Augustine's *De Bono Viduitatis* 29:

> Then, I beseech you earnestly through Him from Whom you have received this gift, and hope for the reward of this gift, that you shall remember to include me in your prayers with all your domestic Church [*cum tota domestica vestra Ecclesia*].[4]

Grammatically *domestica* and *ecclesia* are both in the ablative following *cum* and, because *domestica* is an adjective modifying *ecclesia*, the phrase represents an integrated unit.[5] It is clearly "your domestic/

2. This is confirmed by a statistical search I requested and which was carried out by Fr. Allan Fitzgerald of Villanova University, using the Latin database of the Augustinian corpus. Results (indicating number of occurrences): *domesticus*: 110; *paterfamilias*: 43; *materna*: 101; *proles*: 201.

3. Chrysostom preferred the term *micra ecclesia*, "the little church."

4. "Deinde, obsecro vos per illum a quo et hoc domum accepistis, et huius doni praemia speratis, ut me quoque orationibus vestris memineritis inserere *cum tota domestica vestra Ecclesia*" (PL 40:450).

5. This construction is similar to Jerome's Latin translation in the Vulgate. Augustine used a variety of Latin texts during his lifetime but chose Jerome's translation to correct his earlier usage of Scripture in at least some of his earlier work. See Hugh Houghton, *Augustine's Text of John: Patristic Citations and Latin Gospel Manuscripts* (New York: Oxford University Press, 2008).

home church" not the "church that happens to meet in your home." Thus, Augustine gives the family some sort of ecclesial identity, establishing an intrinsic link between the church and the Christian home. Here, the activity of Christian prayer is associated with this "home-ecclesia." The view that this letter is referring to a specific Christian family as a domestic church is strengthened when this letter is compared with a second letter (*Letter 188*) to the same woman. Both letters are addressed to the widow, Julia, who has a pious, celibate daughter. This daughter had received some of Pelagius's writings, and Augustine warns against them. In *Letter 188,* Augustine first quotes Lady Julia's own words: "all our family follow the Catholic faith to such an extent that never at any time has it [i.e., the family] fallen into heresy..."[6]

Here, the family is functioning in some fashion as a unit within the faith and is maintaining itself and all its members against erroneous teaching. Augustine conceives of this family that is animated by the Christian faith as a domestic church: "For we consider your home as not a small Church of Christ [*parvam Christi Ecclesiam*]."[7] The family in question is thoroughly Christian. The mother is living in holy widowhood, the daughter is a consecrated celibate, and the whole family follows the Catholic faith with no heretical leanings. This is an example of a domestic church.

Another key text is from his *Epistolae nuper in lucem prolatae.*[8] This text is important because it contains the only other direct Augustinian usage of *domestica ecclesia*:

> I have known how much you love Christ, even because your whole household is His family just as the apostle speaks of the domestic church [*domestica ecclesia*]. [I know] how much you wish the things of your house to belong to Christ and to be fruitful and increase.[9]

6. "Omnisque familia nostra adeo catholicam sequitur fidem, ut in nullam haeresim aliquando deviaverit." Augustine, *Epistola 188,* 3 (PL 33:849).

7. Ibid. "Domum enim vestram, non parvam Christi Ecclesiam deputamus."

8. These texts were only discovered in 1980, and therefore could not have been used as references at Vatican II.

9. Augustine, *De Epistolae Nuper in Lucem Prolate* (Corpus scriptorum ecclesiasticorum Latinorum, vol. 88, edited by J. Divjak [University of Salzburg, 1981]). "Novi quantum diligas Christum, et quia universa domus tua familia eius est et sicut apostolus dicit *domesti-*

Here we have the identification of the whole family with Christ and their becoming "His family," that is, a Christian family whose purpose is to see Christ increase in all its affairs. Thus, in all three texts, the domestic church is the family actively pursuing the Christian faith through celibacy, prayer, and discipleship. At the heart of each family is the reality of Christ, and they draw their fundamental identity from Him. This dynamic of being converted to Christ lies at the very heart of the experience of the family as "domestic church."

Ecclesial Structures

The texts from Augustine and Chrysostom were cited at Vatican II to show that the term (or conceptual idea) was used by the Church Fathers. But texts from these two fathers were also cited to show that even within the early Church the baptized family was understood to have an ecclesial structure. Because the family had a Church-like nature, it would follow that its structures would, therefore, reflect the structures of the Church in some recognizable manner. That is, the structures that define the Church would also be found in the family, but in a manner that was consistent with family life. This is vital, because only if such structures can be found operating within the family can the Christian family be legitimately called a "church." Without any such correspondence, the concept would simply be vacuous. It is in this area that Augustine makes a significant contribution. In particular, he teaches in several places that the function and role of the bishop is also operative in the domestic sphere. He does this with great boldness; so much so that for modern sensibilities it may be shocking.[10]

In his commentary on the Gospel of John, Augustine speaks to the fathers in the congregation and delineates the fatherly role clearly in terms of a bishop's duties:

---

ca ecclesia quantum que velis in possessionibus tuis possessionem christi fructificare atque crescere" (italics added).

10. Bishop Fiordelli thought that Augustine had gone further than the Council could accept, and in fact the Council fathers did delete the Augustinian references to the father having an episcopal-like role.

When, therefore, brothers, you hear the Lord saying: "Where I am, there will my minister be also," do not think of good bishops [bonos episcopos] and clergy only. You also serve Christ in your own manner by living well, giving alms, preaching/proclaiming His Name and doctrine as you are capable, so that every father of a family will, in this Name, acknowledge the paternal affection he owes to his family. On behalf of Christ and for eternal life, let him admonish, teach, exhort, rebuke, use benevolence, and exercise discipline for all who belong to him. In this fashion, in his own home, he will fulfill the ecclesial office and in a certain sense [quodammodo] the episcopal [office] [episcopale], ministering to Christ so that he may be with Him [Christ] in eternity.[11]

Here, the father's role is compared to fulfilling an ecclesial role. The very tasks Augustine assigns to him are specific episcopal functions. One could argue that Augustine is simply advocating the Roman concept of *paterfamilias,* but it is evident that Augustine understands the role of the head of the house in a thoroughly Christian manner, carrying with it specific Christian responsibilities:

- Fathers are called to minister to Christ *pro modo vestro.*
- Fathers, in particular, have a role to teach, preach, admonish, rebuke, etc., all *pro Christo* (on behalf of, for Christ), and thus are specifically charged with the spiritual welfare of all connected with them.
- In so doing, the father fulfills (*implebit*) the ecclesial (*ecclesiasticum*) and, to a certain degree, episcopal office (*episcopale officium*). While Augustine's use of *quodammodo* ("in a certain sense") qualifies the relationship between the two roles of bishop and father, nevertheless, the father is understood as fulfilling an episcopal-like function. One can draw a parallel between the bishop and the fa-

---

11. Augustine, *In Joannis Evangelium,* Tr. 51, 13 (PL 35:1768): "Cum ergo auditis, fratres, Dominum dicentem, Ubi ego sum, illic et minister meus erit, nolite tantummodo bonos episcopos et clericos cogitare. Etiam vos pro modo vestro ministrate Christo, bene vivendo, eleemosynas faciendo, nomen doctrinamque ejus quibus potueritis praedicando; ut unusquisque etiam paterfamilias hoc nomine agnoscat paternum affectum suae familiae se debere. Pro Christo et pro vita aterna, suos omnes admoneat, doceat, hortetur, corripiat; impendat benevolentiam, exerceat disciplinam: ita in domo sua ecclesiasticum et quodammodo episcopale implebit officium, ministans Christo ut in aeternum sit cum ipso."

ther; they both function in similar ways and for similar ends. The bishop within the hierarchical church exercises servant-authority for the good of the Church universal, whereas a father exercises servant-authority for the good of his own particular family.[12]

• Finally, Augustine points to the profoundly spiritual dimension of these paternal activities. They are oriented not only to the well ordering of the family in the temporal sphere, but also to the goal of eternal life, itself.

At the very least, the Roman concept of *paterfamilias* (father of the family) has become baptized in Augustine's understanding, and the father is now a bishop-like representative responsible for the spiritual welfare of his family and acting, as such, out of his faith in Christ. Through baptism, fatherhood has been assumed into the salvific process, and the manner in which a man exercises this role becomes part of the way in which he is working out his salvation.

Augustine's *Sermo 94* re-echoes this same teaching:

> Do our job/office [*vicem nostram*] in your homes. A bishop [*episcopus*] is so called because he supervises, because he has to watch over those in his care. So everyone of you in his own house, if he is the head of the household, the function of bishop [*episcopatus officium*] ought to apply to him, how his people believe, seeing none of them drift into heresy...keep a very watchful eye over the welfare and salvation of all your household.[13]

This is a clever, well-constructed sermon based on the parable of the talents (Mt 25:24–30). It was delivered in the presence of several neighboring bishops during the dedication of St. Stephen's shrine. The at-

---

12. In Scriptural terms, authority is meant for the development of the community and not for the aggrandizement of the person wielding the authority. See Dt 17:14–20, where the strictures concerning the Israelite king and his activities are carefully laid out. He becomes the servant of the community and bound to the Torah. This understanding is similarly reflected in the portrayal of the Suffering Servant in Is 52:13–53:12.

13. Augustine, *Sermo 96, 7, 9* (PL 38:588): "Agite vicem nostram in domibus vestris. Episcopus inde appellatus est, quia superintendit, quia intendendo curat. Unusquisque ergo in domo sua, si caput est domui suae, debet ad eum pertinere episcopatus officium, quomodo sui credant, ne aliqui ipsorum in haeresim incurrant...domesticorum vestrorum salutem omni vigilantia procurate."

tendant bishops had refused to help Augustine with the service and he reprimanded them for squandering their resources. Understandably, they had wanted to sit and listen to Augustine rather than lead in the liturgy! Using the reluctance of the bishops to act liturgically as a foil, Augustine turns to the congregation and shows them how they could "invest" wherever they happened to be (*potestsis ubicumque estis*). He then explained that the fathers of households were actually carrying out an episcopal function, having the care of souls under them (*domesticorum vestrorum salutem omni vigilantia procurate*). If a father carried this out, he would get paid for his investment. In this way, Augustine makes a play on the very words he used to condemn the visiting bishops! Strikingly, Augustine says "the job of bishoping ought to apply to fathers of families" (*debet ad eum pertinere episcopatus officium*) if they act in this manner. This extending of the episcopal office into the domestic sphere affirms a connection between the home and the church and, it could be argued, helps us to understand that the Christian family has some form of ecclesial identity.[14]

"Way of Life" in the Church

The greater part of the patristic texts referred to in the debates at Vatican II were used to establish marriage as a legitimate "state of life" in the church, on a level with, but inferior to, the states of celibacy and orders.[15] The problem that faced the Council Fathers was that the com-

---

14. *Vicem*, which means "to act in the place of someone," certainly strengthens this understanding. N.B.: *Familia* for Augustine, while primarily representing the blood-related kinship group, also included servants.

15. Prior to Vatican II there was sometimes a cultural assumption in Catholic circles that the real way to holiness was through celibacy. If you were unable to be truly dedicated to God and to choose celibacy, then you could choose marriage. Vatican II, with its doctrine of "the universal call to holiness," showed that there are several states of life that deal with holiness. That is, marriage is a true way of sanctification, as is celibacy. This did not reduce the different ways/states of life to a single way or confuse them. Ontologically, celibacy for the kingdom is an anticipatory sign of the eschaton. That is why it is superior and the Church has always recognized it as such. This is not because celibacy alone was the way to holiness, but rather because celibacy is configured to that end to which all will be conformed at the end of time. John Paul II writes in *Familiaris Consortio* (16): "The Church, throughout her history, has always defended the superiority of this charism [of celibacy] to that of marriage, by reason of the wholly singular link which it has with the Kingdom of God."

mon cultural assumption of the day (within the church) saw marriage and family as "second best" for those who did not have enough strength to follow consecrated life and this cultural assumption connected holiness with celibacy but not necessarily with family life.[16] This perception needed to be rectified; *both* celibacy and marriage (and the family) needed to be seen as ways of holiness, having their own proper sphere within the life of the Church. Consequently, the Council turned to the early Church Fathers to establish the legitimacy of marital (and thereby familial) life as a way of holiness in the Church.

The writings of St. Augustine contributed much towards establishing the essential holiness of Christian marriage. For Augustine, *Christian* marriage and (what he called) "conjugal chastity" were interchangeable. Within Christian marriage, sexuality is redeemed and is filled with, and directed by, the grace of Christ. This becomes the foundation of the domestic church: conjugal lives lived in and for Christ. It is clearly different from non-Christian forms of married life. It is for this reason that today we need to recover the idea of the vocation of marriage which can be differentiated from the vision of marriage presented by the secular culture.

Augustine applied very precise terminology to marriage. Though he does not call marriage a vocation, nonetheless the terms he uses to describe marriage help us to see that marriage for Augustine had much in common with what we today would call a vocation.[17] These terms include *professio, officia, vita, genus,* and *gradus.*[18]

The term *professio* is applied to something to which one willingly gives oneself and which is understood to be "a way of life." The term did not always indicate that a personal choice had been made because,

16. Unfortunately, culturally, the recognition of marriage and family as an authentic way of holiness (and a vocation) was lost with the rise of the monastic model for holiness.

17. The relationship of marriage to vocation in Augustine is perhaps somewhat analogous to the relationship of marriage to sacramentality in the saint's thought. Augustine does not conceive of marriage as a sacrament in the strict sense of the word. It would take the medieval period to work out the sacramental nature of marriage. But in Augustine there are already foundations for the sacramentality of marriage. Similarly, while he does not call marriage a vocation, he applies specific categories (*professio, vita,* etc.) to it that have a correspondence in the ecclesial understanding of vocation.

18. These were the primary descriptions used at Vatican II.

in Augustine's day, one did not necessarily choose one's way of life but inherited it from his father. In the Vatican II speech given by Fiordelli there is a footnote (8) that cites *Ennaratio in Psalmum 36*. The point being made is that Augustine saw marriage as a "profession" within the life of the Church (*status coniugatorum in Ecclesia apud Augustinum*), the implication being that married couples possessed some sort of state. But this connection may be somewhat tenuous to establish marriage as such a state, since Augustine is not answering that question directly. Rather, he states that in whatever varieties of lives that exist (*quocumque genere vitae*), amongst those which have some form of profession/avowal (*professionem*), there are both good and bad within them.[19] Nonetheless, Augustine does make a connection between marriage and *professio*.

Officium means "duties, official employment, dutiful action."[20] It carries the sense of obligation and can refer to a specific *office* that one has. *Sermo 96* gives an excellent presentation of Augustine's view of how the conjugal reality (and implicitly its attendant domestic life) is one of the states into which the Body of Christ is divided:

> "Whoever wants to follow me, he must deny himself." This is not for virgins only to hear but not the married…but the whole Church, the whole body, through the distinct and distributed functions proper to them ought to follow Christ.[21]

Augustine uses the word *officia* in this context and is clearly talking about the different states of life that exist in the Church, including celibacy and marriage. The comparison he makes between the different states of life is clear. The call to self-denial is issued to the whole Body of Christ, not just an élite. It is meant for all. Each state is joined with

19. Augustine, *Ennarationes in Psalmos* 36 1, 2 (PL 36:356–57). "Jam vero quia in quocumque genere vitae, quod habet aliquam professionem, non omnes inveniuntur probi, non omnes reprobi."

20. Cf. "*officium*," in D. P. Simpson, ed., *Cassell's New Latin Dictionary* (New York: Funk and Wagnalls, 1959), 410.

21. Augustine, *Sermo 96*, 7, 9 (PL 38:588): "Qui vult me sequi, abneget semetipsum. Non enim hoc virgines debent audire, et maritatae non debent…sed universa Ecclesia, universum corpus, cunctua membra per *officia* propria distincta et distributa, sequantur Christum."

the others and the duties/*officia* are distributed amongst them all as each follows Christ.

Gradus can mean "state" but it does not have the meaning of "associated privilege" that *status* has. This term is applied to the conjugal state in *Sermo 132* and *Sermo 192*. In the first, Augustine is addressing the married and requires the same level of purity in the man as in the woman. "Render what you demand. Man, you demand chastity from the woman; with an example, not words."[22] Thus, within the whole of marriage, there must be purity. Augustine repeats this advice in several different ways and then exhorts:

> Keep watch over your ranks/positions (*gradus vestros*): for God keeps watch over your honors/offices for you.... For in one way virginity shall shine there (in the resurrection), in another way conjugal chastity will shine there.... They shall shine in different ways, but all shall be there.[23]

Although the conjugal state and virginity differ, each is considered a *gradus*. There is thus a purity within marriage and a purity outside of marriage. In this case, there is a certain parallelism that exists between the married and celibate states, both being seen as states (*gradus*) within the Church.

This is particularly seen in *Sermo 192*, where Augustine employs the traditional typology of Mary, Anna, and Elizabeth as representing the states of virginity, holy widowhood, and conjugal chastity. In his text, he applies the term *gradus* to each of them: "All classes [*gradus*] of the members of the faithful have brought to the Head what they were able to contribute through His grace."[24] Thus, for Augustine there is no fundamental conflict between these states, and each contributes, in its own way, toward salvation of the person.

Genus is a descriptive way of differentiating one *type* from another;

22. Augustine, *Sermo 132*, chap. 2 (PL 38:735). "Reddite quod exigitis. Vir, a femina exigis castitatem, praebe illi exemplum, non verbum."

23. Augustine, *Sermo 132*, chap. 3 (PL 38:736) : "Servate *gradus* vestros: servat enim vobis Deus honores vestros.... Aliter enim ibi lucebit virginitas, aliter ibi lucebit castitas conjugalis.... Diverse lucebunt: sed omnes ibi erunt."

24. Augustine, *Sermo 192*, chap. 2 (PL 38:1012): "Omnes *gradus* fidelium membrorum capiti contulerunt, quod ipsius gratia confere potuerunt...."

it is applicable when something is taken and divided into parts. Its use in *Enarratio in Psalmum 36* was noted above.

In *Sermo 96*, Augustine goes beyond making a simple differentiation between being married or celibate; he clearly states that the married (and, implicitly, the family) have a legitimate place in the Body of Christ. They are a specific illustration of a *genus*, of which consecrated virginity and the clergy are the other examples, each being a unique way to follow Christ:

> Integral virginity has its own place there, chaste married people have their own place there.... Moreover, those members which have their place there are following Christ in their own particular way [*in genere suo*], their own place, and in their own manner.[25]

The word *vita* is used either alone (*Sermo 196*) or combined with *genus* (e.g. *Ennar. Ps 36*, see above). It is very close to the modern "ways or states of life." *Sermo 196* gives the clearest example of this concept by definitively stating that there are three ways of life in the Church:[26]

> In the Church of the members of Christ there are three ways/states of life [lit. "lives"—*vitae*]: the married, the widowed, the virginal. Because of these lives, these [forms] of chastity were going to be in the holy members of Christ; all these three states of life attest to Christ.[27]

What is astonishing here is the ease with which Augustine can combine the celibate and the married states and define them as instruments in the salvific process. Here, he gives clear witness that marriage (and thereby family) is a vocational calling, parallel with consecrated virginity and holy widowhood, all of which attest to Christ. This ecclesial nature of conjugal and familial life is further strengthened when Augustine goes on to say that these ways of life, including marriage, are

25. Augustine, *Sermo 96*, chap. 9 (PL 38:588): "Habet ibi locum suum integritas virginalis; habet ibi locum suum pudicitia conjugalis.... Ista autem membra quae hebent ibi locum suum *in genere* suo, et in loco suo, et in suo modo, sequantur Christum."

26. This makes the point clearly, yet it is surprising that it was not cited in the Vatican debates.

27. Augustine, *Sermo 196*, chap. 2 (PL 38:1020): "Tres *vitae* sunt in Ecclesia membrorum Christi: conjugalis, vidualis, virginalis. Quia ipsae vitae, ipsae pudicitiae futurae erant in sanctis membris Christi; omnes istae vitae tres attestatae sunt Christum."

"examples of salvation": "Each person should choose for himself which of these he wants.... All the models of salvation have been put before our eyes."[28] Thus, the terminology that Augustine applies to marriage and his frequent paralleling of it with the consecrated life and the celibate life show that marriage (and by implication the family) are not extraneous to the life of holiness and the Church but in fact are integral to it.

Augustinian Developments

Besides establishing the legitimacy of the conjugal way of life as a vocational choice, certain texts from Augustine can be used to show that conjugal chastity is a gift from God, just as continence is. In De Dono Perserverantia, Augustine interprets 1 Cor 6:7 and comments on the status of married life: "Whereby, it shows enough that not only is continence a gift [donum] of God but the chastity of married couples is also."[29] Thus, rather than seeing only celibacy as a gift from God, marriage is seen in the same light.

In Sermo 354 Augustine shows that there is a dynamic tension between celibacy and marriage and, though the former is superior, it is not absolutely so. While not denying the priority of the consecrated state, Augustine makes the point that married life is indeed something admirable and goes on to say that it is superior to the consecrated state if the celibates are full of pride: "For the conjugal life is praiseworthy and has in the Body of Christ its own place, and I dare to add those living a conjugal life, if they hold to humility, are better than the haughty chaste ones."[30] This is a much-needed corrective, and again shows the importance of having a proper disposition within these states. Here, there is no question of a second-class status in the Christian life.

Finally, in Sermo 267, Augustine notes that the activity of the Holy

28. Ibid. "Eligat sibi quisque de istis tribus quam voluerit.... Omnia exempla salutis proposita sunt ante oculos nostros."

29. Augustine, De Dono Perseverantiae, chap. 14, 37 (PL 45:1015): "Ubi satis ostendit, non tantum continentiam donum Dei esse, sed conjugatorum etiam castitatem."

30. Augustine, Sermo 354, chap. 4 (PL 39:1564–65): "Est enim conjugalis vita laudabilis, et habet in corpore Christi locum suum...et audeo dicere, conjugalem agentes vitam, si tenent humilitatem superbis castis meliores sunt."

Spirit is actually operative within both states of life. There can be no understanding of Christian marriage as a mere secular reality, because this reference to the salvific work of the Holy Spirit present within marriage shows it to have a holy nature. Appropriately, this sermon was given on Pentecost in AD 412; it shows how the Spirit works in each different way of life, and yet lives equally in all: "Thus is the Church of God:...in some holy ones he guards virginity, in other holy ones He guards conjugal chastity.... He works in each particular one, but all are equally living [alive]."[31]

Thus, for Augustine, Christian marriage was clearly one of the "ways of life" which was *situated* in the Body of Christ and participated in the salvific activity of the Holy Spirit. Christian conjugal life was predicated on the purity of both husband and wife, whose lives were shaped by Christ, the One who lived in them and directed the actions of their lives. This state, like chastity and holy orders, was equally a gift and, therefore, a calling from God. Conjugal life, as Augustine conclusively taught, was ordered to the procreation of children and, therefore, the establishment of familial life. A family which is so constituted in Christ, Augustine does not hesitate to call a small church, indeed, the "domestic church."

JOHN CHRYSOSTOM

Micra Ecclesia

Chrysostom does not use the phrase "domestic church." Instead, he prefers to call the Christian home a miniature or micro-church: "For the home (οἰκία) is a small Church (ἐκκλησία)."[32] Although his terminology is slightly different, Chrysostom's commentaries on Genesis confirm that his concept of domestic church is substantially the same as that of Augustine. In his shorter commentary on Genesis, Chrysostom writes:

31. Augustine, *Sermo 267*, chap. 4 (PL 38:1231): "Sic est Ecclesia Dei...in aliis sanctis custodit virginitatem, in aliis sanctis custodit pudicitiam conjugalem...singuli propria operantur, sed pariter vivunt."

32. "καὶ ἡ οἰκία γὰρ Ἐκκλησία ἐστὶ μικρά." Chrysostom, *In Epistolam Ad Ephesios*, Cap. 5, Hom. 20 (Patrologia Graeca [hereafter PG] 62, 143).

Therefore, all these things we should retain, my dear ones, and so we should put in [your] home both altars, one for food and the other for the sacred readings. Indeed, the man should repeat those things that are appointed; the wife, moreover, should learn thoroughly, the children should listen, nor should the servants be defrauded of these readings. *Make your home a church.* Indeed, the salvation [welfare] of both your children and your servants [must be rendered by you].[33]

In the longer commentary, similar concepts are expressed, but there Chrysostom adds: "Henceforth, make [your] home a church in order to put the devil to flight."[34]

It is clear from these texts that Chrysostom believed that the household could take on a definitive ecclesial structure.[35] In fact, Chrysostom is actively urging Christians to so structure their homes and domestic lives that their households are transformed into little churches. But this will require an effort on their part. The domestic church, here, is not seen as being automatically *derived* from the baptismal reality of the spouses and parents (which appears to be Augustine's position). Rather, the home becomes a domestic church to the degree that the husband and wife bring the activities normally associated with the church (such as teaching, reading the Scriptures, etc.) into their domestic sphere.[36] This is particularly appropriate because the baptized family is already

33. Chrysostom, *In Genesim,* Sermo 7 (PG 54:607): "Ταῦτα οὖν ἅπαντα, ἀγαπητοὶ, διακρατῶμεν, καὶ οἴκαδε ἀναχωρήσαντες διπλῆν παραθῶμεν τὴν τράπεζαν, τὴν τῶν σιτίων, καὶ τὴν τῆς ἀκροάσεως, καὶ λεγέτω μὲν ἀνὴρ τὰ εἰρημένα, μανθανέτω δὲ γυνὴ ἀκουέτω δὲ καὶ παιδία μὴ ἀποστερείσθωσαν δὲ μηδὲ οἰκέται τῆς ἀκροάσεως ταύτης. Ἐκκλησίαν ποίησόν σου τὴν οἰκίαν καὶ γὰρ καὶ ὑπεύθυνος εἶ καὶ τῆς τῶν παιδίων καὶ τῆς τῶν οἰκετῶν σωτηρίας...ἀπαιτεῖται."

34. "Καὶ ἐκκλησία λοιπὸν γενέσθω ἡ οἰκία, ἵνα φυγαδεύηται μὲν ὁ διάβολος." Chrysostom, *In Cap. 1 Genes.,* Homilia 2:4 (PG 53:31).

35. Paul Evdokimov gives us another passage from Chrysostom on the subject: "John Chrysostom taught this: 'Even at night...rise, kneel, and pray.... Your house must continually be an oratory, a church'" ("Conjugal Priesthood," in *Marriage and Christian Tradition,* trans. Sr. Agnes Cunningham [Techny, Ill.: Divine Word Publications, 1966], 86).

36. During the patristic period there were two ways of understanding the domestic church: (1) the domestic church emerges automatically from one's baptismal status, or (2) one makes his home into a domestic church. These two concepts are not ultimately in conflict. Rather, they can be understood in a Pauline manner, wherein there is a proper tension between being and doing. In his letters, Paul often exhorts Christians to become what they already are.

ordered to the ecclesial sphere. This activity is predicated on their baptismal status, which conforms them to Christ. By so transforming their family lives, they will "put the devil to flight." By conforming their home to its true ecclesial nature in Christ, the Christian family can help to establish the reign of Christ amongst themselves.

Scriptural Homilies

The precise nature of this structuring emerges through an examination of Chrysostom's homilies. One aspect that is constantly brought out is the centrality of the Word of God:

> I recommend you to have constant recourse to this remedy, and apply yourself diligently to the reading of Sacred Scripture...at home, taking the sacred books in your hands and earnestly absorbing the benefit of their contents. (*Homily 24*)[37]

> We will be able while relaxing at home...to take the sacred books in our hands and...provide spiritual nourishment for our soul.... If we defend ourselves in this way day by day, through reading...through spiritual discourse, we will be able to keep ourselves unharmed and render the devil's wiles ineffectual. (*Homily 10*)[38]

In both his commentaries on Genesis and in the above homiletic texts, Chrysostom shows not only that the Scriptures are to have pre-eminence in the Christian home, but that such an environment will help in the spiritual struggle. The Christian should be constantly nourished in his own home by the Word of God in order to defend his spiritual life from all harm.[39]

In *Homily 21* (which is based on Eph 6:1–3), Chrysostom treats of the educational dimension in the Christian family: "Bring him up in...the admonition of the Lord. Never deem it an unnecessary thing that he should be a diligent hearer of the divine Scriptures.... Make him a Christian.... Let us make them from the earliest age apply themselves

37. John Chrysostom: *Homilies on Genesis*, trans. Robert C. Hill, Fathers of the Church, vol. 74 (Washington, D.C.: The Catholic University of America Press, 1985), 8–9.

38. Ibid., 141.

39. This witness from the early part of the Christian era contravenes the commonly held wisdom that books (in whatever form) were not available to the general public. It would seem that some type of access was envisioned by Chrysostom here.

to the reading of the Scriptures."[40] Again, he is emphasizing the importance of Scriptures in the faith formation of children.

In commenting on Eph 6:5–8 (*Homily 22*), Chrysostom gives his own paradigm for the structure of the family:

> Every one's house is a city; and every man is a prince [ἄρχων—ruler] in his own house.[41] ...Because here too there are offices of authority; for instance, the husband has authority over the wife, the wife over the servants;[42] ...again the wives and husbands over the children. Does he not seem to you to be, as it were, a sort of king, having so many authorities under his own authority?[43]

For Chrysostom, the Christian home is to be structured around two principles: the centrality of Scripture and the proper ordering of authority.

In Homily 10 on 1 Tim 3:1–4, which deals with the office of bishop, Chrysostom explains the nature of authority and, in so doing, indirectly reveals the ecclesial structure of the home.

> *If a man desires the office of a Bishop,* I do not blame him, for it is a work of protection. If anyone has this desire, *so that he does not covet the dominion and authority,*[44] but wishes to protect the Church, I blame him not.[45]

A bishop of the Church does have genuine authority, but he must never seek to dominate others or seek authority for its own sake. Instead, the reason for such authority is that the bishop must seek to protect

40. John Chrysostom, *Homilies on Ephesians,* Homily 21 in Nicene and Post-Nicene Fathers (hereafter NPNF) series 1, vol. 13, ed. Philip Schaff (Peabody, Mass.: Hendrickson, 1994), 154.

41. "Πόλις ἐστὶν ἡ ἑκάστου οἰκία, ἄρχων ἐστὶν ἕκαστος τῆς ἑαυτοῦ οἰκίας." Chrysostom, *In Epist. Ad Ephes,* Cap 6, Homilia. 22:2 (PG 62:158).

42. "κρατεῖ τῆς γυναικὸς ὁ ἀνὴρ, ἡ γυνὴ τῶν οἰκετῶν." Ibid. (emphasis added in English translation).

43. John Chrysostom, *Homlies on Ephesians,* Homily 22, in NPNF Series, vol. 13 (Peabody, Mass.: Hendrickson, 1994), 159. The Greek text is found under Chrysostom, *In Epistolam Ad Ephesios,* Cap. 6, Hom. 22:2 (PG 62:158).

44. "ὥστε μὴ τῆς ἀρχῆς καὶ τῆς αὐθεντίας ἐφίεσθαι μόνον." Chrysostom, *In Epistolam 1 Ad Timotheum,* Cap. 3, Homilia 10 (PG 62:547).

45. John Chrysostom, *Homilies on Timothy,* Homily 10, translated by James Tweed in NPNF Series 1, vol. 13 (Peabody, Mass.: Hendrickson, 1994), 437.

that which he loves, the Church. Within this same homily, Chrysostom draws a parallel between the home and the Church such that the church can be said to be, as it were, a small home (μικρά οἰκία).[46]

> And if he that presides in the Church has partners in his power, so has the man a partner, that is, his wife. For the Church is, as it were, a small household, and as in a house there are children and wife and domestics, and the man [ὁ ἀνήρ] exercises [ἀνήρηται] the ἀρχή/the ordering principle of them all [πάντων]; just so in the Church there are women, children and servants.[47]

Chrysostom understands the wife as sharing in this role of presiding (τῆν ἀρχήν) with her husband as a partner within the home. The man carries the responsibility for the ordering principle in the home and his wife is a partner with him in carrying this out. This reflects the structure of Gn 2 where the woman is created as an ʿezer, a helpmate, for the man.[48] It is interesting to note the teaching of Ambrose, who lived

46. "Καὶ γὰρ τοῦτό ἐστιν ἡ Ἐκκλησία, ὡσανεὶ μικρὰ οἰκία." Chrysostom, *In Epistolam 1 Ad Timotheum*, Cap. 3 Hom. 10:2 (PG 62:519). It is interesting to note that Chrysostom here says the Church is a "small household." One would have expected that the hierarchical Church would be seen as a "large household." In the Migne Latin translation in Chrysostom's comments on 1 Tim 3, μικρά ("small") is changed to *magna* ("large"): Est enim Ecclesia velut domus magna.

47. Ibid., 550. Translation by author. A key word in this phrase is τῆν ἀρχήν (root ἀρχή). The meaning found in Lampe's *Patristic Greek Lexicon* is "beginning, source, principle" (p. 234). Ἀρχή has the sense of the beginning principle and conceptually is related to κεφαλή ("head") which Paul uses of the man in 1 Cor 11:3. The two meanings intersect in Gn 2, which shows the man being the ἀρχή ("the beginning point") for the human race and that from which the woman is created. But this is done in such a way that the absolute dignity of both man and woman is secured and yet the difference (the asymmetrical order) is safeguarded. Ἀρχή has the sense of "ordering principle." There is an order to all of creation (see Gn 1) which brings forth peace. This ordering principle is found in the family and the Church. For instance, the bishop exercises and is responsible for the ἀρχή over his diocese. The verb ἀνήρηται is from ἀναιρέω and is a middle/passive perfect, meaning something like "he has taken upon himself" and can be translated as "to exercise, take upon oneself, accept." Taken as a whole, the phrase would then mean something like "the man exercises or accepts responsibility for the ἀρχή [the ordering principle, the authority] of all [within the household]." This translation, which is more consonant with the full range of meaning of ἀρχή and ἀνήρηται, renders the deeper meaning of the text, without creating an inferior-superior nexus in relationships.

48. We should note here that ʿezer is also applied to Yahweh, who is the "helper" of Israel, yet this does not connote any sense of inferiority on the part of God.

during the same time as Chrysostom. He wrote to husbands: "Get rid of your obstinacy when your gentle consort offers you her love. You are not a master, but a husband. You have not acquired perchance a handmaid, but a wife."[49]

Chrysostom's development of the Church-family analogy is derived from one of the ways in which the New Testament presents the nature of the Church. In Gal 5:6–10 and Eph 2:19 it is seen as the household of God. Earlier, Chrysostom had presented the family in terms of the "small church"; now he reverses the order and presents the Church in terms of familial structures. By this process of mutual illumination, Chrysostom is demonstrating that there is a certain reciprocity between the Church and the family. In the modern context, this principle of reciprocity is crucial for understanding the nature of the domestic church. Not only can we now understand the true nature of the family by looking at the Church, but we can also understand the true nature of the Church by examining the baptized family.

Earlier, Chrysostom had determined the manner in which a bishop should rule and the servant-leader attitude he must take. Given the reciprocal relationship that exists between the home and the Church, it is possible now to locate this episcopal function in fatherhood. From Chrysostom's exegesis of 1 Timothy, it is clear that the man, acting as a bishop-like head of the home, like a bishop, should not covet having dominion or authority, but as head should seek to protect his family. Thus, the authority exercised in a family is always other-centered, exercised for the good of the other. From this it would seem that any sense of domination or self-serving would be a perversion of the God-

---

49. Ambrose, *Six Days of Creation,* trans. John Savage (New York: Fathers of the Church, 1961), 174. "Sed etiam tu, vir—possumus etiam sic accipere—depone tumorem cordis, asperitatem morum, cum tibi sedula uxor occurrit, propelle indignationem, cum blanda conjunx ad caritatem provocat, non es dominus, sed marius, non ancillam sortitus es, sed uxorem" (*Exameron* V, 19 in Corpus scriptorum ecclesiasticorum Latinorum, vol. 32 [University of Salzburg: 1886], 154). Chrysostom, in his commentary on 1 Tim 3:1–4, where he examines the nature of the episcopacy, concludes that the bishop, *qua* bishop, has the unique function to teach. However, in regard to certain other qualities (being sober, of good behavior, given to hospitality), "they [the Church] ought to be equal to those who 'rule' over them [i.e., bishops]." Thus, having a unique function (in this case teaching) does not make a person superior in being to others. But there is a differentiation of roles.

given role of the father. Chrysostom goes on to mention how Christ calls his followers to lay down their lives. Thus, the only type of authority that the Christian exercises is servant-authority. Chrysostom mentions this sacrificial attitude in enumerating the qualities of a bishop. In referring to John 10:11 ("the shepherd lays down his life for his sheep"), Chrysostom suggests that this sacrificial attitude should be especially found amongst the those who rule (i.e., the bishops), because Christ requires it of even those under authority. Thus, it would seem that any self-centered exercise of authority in either the Church or home would be antithetical to the true nature of authority.

Chrysostom further reveals the deeper ecclesial structure of the home in his commentary on Titus 2:2–5. In this analysis, he shows the underlying purpose of the home and reveals its teleological purpose:

> This is the chief point of all that is good in a household,[50] "a man and his wife that agree together" (Ecclus. xxv.i). For where this exists, there will be nothing that is unpleasant. For where the head is in harmony with the body,[51] and there is no disagreement between them, how shall not all the other members be at peace?[52]

One cannot fail to recognize the parallel between this passage and the Pauline concept of the Church being the Body of Christ, with the Lord being Head. This concept of harmony is reflective of the Old Testament concept of *shalom*. Though it is not worked out in detail, the concept nonetheless shows the critical function of harmony within the home and how *shalom* is predicated on a right relationship between the head and the body, the husband and wife. If this ordering is properly established, all members (including children) will be at peace. While important in its own right, this domestic peace also becomes an important witness to the Christological dimension of the domestic church. Christ, through His Passion, bequeathed to his fledgling Church the gift of His peace which the world could never give

---

50. "Τὸ κεφάλαιον τοῦτο τῶν κατὰ τὴν οἰκίαν ἀγαθῶν." Chrysostom, *In Epistolam ad Titum*, Hom. 4:2 (PG 62:683).

51. "Πῶς γὰρ, τῆς κεφαλῆς πρὸς τὸ σῶμα συννενευκυίας." Ibid.

52. John Chrysostom, *Homilies On Titus*, Homily 4, NPNF Series 1, vol. 13 (Peabody, Mass: Hendrickson, 1994), 532.

(Jn 14:27). This Christological peace, the *shalom* of God, is to reign also in the families of Christians.

Finally, Chrysostom also takes up the role of marriage as a "way of life" in the Church and confirms Augustine's teaching in this regard. In *Homily 30* of his commentary on 1 Corinthians, Chrysostom states:

> For in the Church also there are members many and diverse.... For example there are choirs of virgins.... There are fraternities of those who shine in holy wedlock;[53] in short many are the degrees of virtue.[54]

Although Chrysostom does not make the parallel between the married state and the other recognized "states of life" in the Church as clearly or as exhaustively as Augustine, yet the analogous relationship is still set up and marriage is viewed as one of the "degrees of virtue."

Summary

In Chrysostom's view, the Christian family is specifically ordered to ensure peace. There is a clear responsibility on the father's part to teach the children the faith. This catechesis is especially to be founded on the Scriptures. There is an obligation to make one's home a church, giving a central place to the reading of the Scriptures. Furthermore, because of the parallel between the Church and the home, one can determine that the father, being the center of authority, must not dominate or covet power, but use his authority to protect his family, even as a bishop would the church. In Chrysostom, the domestic church seems to emerge more from the efforts of Christian parents to Christianize their home than to proceed automatically from the spouses' own baptismal status.

---

53. "εἰσὶ τῶν ἐν γάμῳ σώφρονι λαμπόντων φρατρίαι." Chrysostom, *In Epistolam 1 Ad Corinthios*, Hom. 30 (PG 61:254).

54. Ibid., 179.

EXCURSUS 6:

THE PRINCIPLE OF ORDER (ἀρχή) AND

DIFFERENTIATION

Male and Female

It is important to safeguard the dignity of each person in the family so
that the capacity of each to act as an active and free agent is not compromised by the corporate nature of either the person or the family. But, on
the other hand, this personal dimension cannot devolve into the person
becoming an autonomous, self-determining agent. Some posit that exercising authority, even when other-centered and sacrificial, renders those
under such authority inferior and, in some respects, unable to be self-
determining. The crux of the question centers on one's understanding
of authority and the relationship of human freedom to it. Does the exercise of authority always leave some party inferior with a lack of self-
determination? Is the dignity of the person compromised by a differentiation within the family that allows for an ordering principle (which includes the proper exercise of authority) to secure the peace and order of
the home? Or is there an *inner form* to authority which, once it has been
redeemed from distorted expressions in the fallen world, becomes expressive of the ordering principle (ἀρχή) in creation, which in turn safeguards
the dignity of each person. This is, of course, a difficult and complex question to resolve, particularly in the modern context when words such as *order* or *authority* are almost always understood in terms of domination or
the reducing of another's autonomy or worth.

The narrative of creation, the New Testament, the teaching of the
Church Fathers, the Reformers, and numerous magisterial church documents over the centuries affirm that there is a real difference in creation
(the male-female axis), which is the ground for organic unity. Modern
magisterial teaching includes much from Pope John Paul II, who wrote
about the unique value of women in the family and in the Church, speak-

ing of the feminine genius. He devoted an Apostolic Letter (*Mulieris Dignitatem*) to the indispensable value of this genius of women. In *Familiaris Consortio* he stated: "Authentic conjugal love presupposes and requires that a man have a profound respect for the equal dignity of his wife." He then quoted the text from St. Ambrose that is quoted above. The unique dignity of the woman is not endangered or lessened because of the unique role of the father, which John Paul II describes in terms of oversight. "The place and task of the father in and for the family is of unique and irreplaceable importance.... In revealing and in reliving on earth the very fatherhood of God, a man is called upon to ensure the harmonious and united development of all the members of the family" (*FC* 25). Here the man, in "reliving the fatherhood of God," has a responsibility for oversight, making sure of the unity and harmonious development of the family. But this unique "reliving on earth the very fatherhood of God" does not relegate the wife to an inferior status. The father and mother are each unique, irreducible, and irreplaceable. The magisterium has constantly taught that this positive dynamic balance between the two must always be affirmed. This is important, as it safeguards against interchangeable egalitarianism in which men and women and their vocations are reducible to each other.

The Holy Family is also a paradigm for understanding the organic, differentiated unity of the family. In *Redemptoris Custos,* John Paul II points to the specific role St. Joseph plays as head and defender of his family: "Joseph was in his day the lawful and natural guardian, head and defender of the Holy Family." Then, like Chrysostom, he links this to the Church: "In the same way that he [St. Joseph] once kept unceasing holy watch over the family of Nazareth, so now does he protect and defend with his heavenly patronage the Church of Christ." Precisely because St. Joseph was "head" and responsible *in a fatherly manner* for his earthly family, he is now able to "protect and defend" the family of God, the Church.

But note that this does not infer any inferiority on the part of Mary. Her ability to respond to life is not lessened by Joseph being head of the Holy

Family. In fact, his protection allows Mary's "yes" to come to full fruition. Conversely, Joseph's fatherhood is predicated on the motherhood of Mary. Mary becomes who she is in response to and obedience to God. While there is an ordering principle within the Holy Family, Mary is not less self-determining because Joseph is head. He does not determine her, because, in fact, no one can do that for another person. The Church acknowledges that within the order of salvation Mary has a more preeminent place than Joseph, yet Joseph protects, defends, and is head. Both Joseph and Mary fulfill their vocations as husband and wife by working together, not antagonistically asserting their rights, but by being themselves in their own masculinity and femininity, not by diminishing their differences or collapsing their roles.

Neither the corporate structure of human reality nor the constitutive ordering principle (ἀρχή) can take away the freedom that each man and woman possesses to make personal decisions which determine the form of their existence. Conversely, personal freedom negates neither the reality of nor the need for an ordering principle. Nor can it be antagonistic towards the organic corporate nature of the human person. Rather, personal freedom works in conjunction with these *informing* realities so that the personal and corporate dimensions of the human person are always safeguarded. In fact, they are necessary to each other and relate in a circumincessive manner.

THE THEOLOGICAL NORM

We exist, but the meaning or *form* of our existence is obscured by sin. In *Meditations on Ephesians 5,* von Balthasar offers a profound insight into the question of the *form* (i.e., underlying reality) of the husband-wife relationship. He shows how Ephesians 5 draws the analogy between Christ-and-the-Church *and* the husband-and-wife relationship. He concludes that while there are limiting factors (e.g., the man is not divine and Christ is) "it is an analogy nonetheless; and this analogy allows us to acknowledge, even today, the truth contained in the statement that the husband is the head "of the wife." His point is that the differentiation of roles is *"not a norm patterned on the social customs of a particular time"* but rather is "a *theological norm.*" He concludes: "The norm of their sexual relationship is a *theological* one, namely, the relationship between Christ and the Church." Therefore, all aspects of the husband-wife relationship must be understood in terms of, and structured by, the sacrificial love of Christ.[55]

How can the Church respond to modernity's refusal to accept any real distinction (difference) especially when the modern world views such differentiation as always creating a nexus of superior-inferior relationships, regardless of how they are qualified? Given such presuppositions, the logic of modernity not only cannot understand the Church's perspective but now accuses it of being unjust. This has become particularly clear in the struggles over women being admitted to the priesthood and in the movement to legitimize same-sex union. Joseph Ratzinger recognized this problem in his *Collaboration of Men and Women.* The rejection of difference degenerates into a fatal uniformity, which ultimately urges interchangeability. Ratzinger wrote:

> Women, in order to be themselves, must make themselves the adversaries of men ... the answer for women is to seek power.... In order to avoid the domination of one sex or the other, their differences tend to be denied, viewed as mere effects of historical and cultural conditioning.... The obscuring of the

55. Urs von Balthasar, "Ephesians 5:21–33 and Humanae Vitae: A Meditation," in *Christian Married Love,* ed. Raymond Dennehy (San Francisco: Ignatius Press, 1981), 63, 66. "The husband, on the other hand, encounters his wife as a separate person, with her own freedom and her own act of surrender to him—a freedom and a surrender which he does not create. Nevertheless, it does not seem to me that this simply invalidates the statement about the husband being the head of his wife. Prescinding from any and every social system (patriarchal or matriarchal) and from all theories of procreation (ancient, scholastic or modern), it always remains true that in sexual intercourse it is the man who is the initiator, the leader, the shaper, while the woman's love—even if it is not passive, but just as active in its own way—is still essentially receptive."

difference...has in reality inspired ideologies which, for example, call into question the family, in its natural two-parent structure of mother and father, and make homosexuality and heterosexuality virtually equivalent, in a new model of polymorphous sexuality. [Section 2]

This impasse can be overcome only by seeing that the intended *form* of all order and difference is Christocentric. That is, the original meaning and structure of difference and of ἀρχή as the ordering principle of authority comes from Christ's relationship to the Father (on which the original creation is grounded) and Christ's relationship to the Church (which is of the salvific order) and must be configured to these primary relationships. Everything else is a distortion. Thus, the nature of any type of authority, be it exercised as the head of the home or episcopal authority in the Church, must always be other-centered, exercised in a spirit of service, and be sacrificial. It takes its nature from, and is grounded in, Christ and the Cross, and is an expression of Christ's love. Only in this way is the essential difference between man and woman safeguarded and the dignity of each man and women promoted. In this way, mutual antagonism is overcome, and the authentic collaboration between man and woman becomes possible. As Ratzinger writes: "From the first moment of their creation, man and woman are distinct, and will remain so for all eternity. Placed within Christ's Paschal mystery, they no longer see their difference as a source of discord to be overcome by denial or eradication, but rather as the possibility for collaboration, to be cultivated with mutual respect for their difference."[56] What is distorted in the Fall now becomes healed and restored.

The collaborative fulfilling of the distinct vocations of husband and wife does not blur difference, nor does it imply inferiority or superiority. It does not imply that one has a lesser degree of self-determination, for both are personal subjects. In fact, they come to know themselves (determine themselves) more authentically through this ordered relationship and the

56. Joseph, Cardinal Ratzinger, "On the Collaboration of Men and Women in the Church and in the World," Letter, May 31, 2004, Section 12.

sacrificial act of giving oneself over to the other. This is the meaning of the principle of order (ἀρχή), whether in the home or the Church, and it is governed by the theological norm of Christ's Passion.

Ironically, it is only by accepting the genuine difference of creation that one is able to make this profound personal and sacrificial commitment that is essential to self-determination.[57] This dynamic is at the heart of both the home and the Church. Only with the proper balance between individual freedom, personal decision, and absolute dignity (always operating within the reality of corporate identity) can a drift into destructive, autonomous, self-determining individualism be avoided.

ADDITIONAL PATRISTIC WITNESSES

There are a few other major witnesses to the reality of the domestic church in the first few centuries of the Christian era. Although they do not develop this concept at length, they nonetheless make a significant contribution, bearing witness to the fact that the family was indeed considered to have an ecclesial nature in this early stage of the Church's life.

Clement of Alexandria (AD 150–215)

Clement of Alexandria made an important contribution by his application of Mt 18:20 to marriage.[58] In his commentary, *Stromateis,* Clement attempted to contrast the Christian view of marriage against the false teachings of some of the gnostic sects and others of his day.[59] In particular, he showed how in the Christian family unit there exists the 2 or 3 people requisite for the Lord's presence to be made manifest

---

57. This act of sacrificial, self-giving seems to be the point of ^Jn 12:24: "Truly, truly, I say to you, unless a grain of wheat falls into the earth and dies, it remains alone; but if it dies, it bears much fruit.

58. "For where two or three are gathered together in my name, there am I in the midst of them" (•Mt 18:20).

59. Clement of Alexandria, *Stromateis,* trans. John Ferguson, The Fathers of the Church 85 (Washington, D.C.: The Catholic University of America Press, 1991), 256–63, especially 256n1 and 258n16.

amongst His people, according to the prescription found in Matthew. He asks, "Who are the two or three who gather in the name of Christ with the Lord in their midst? By three does he not mean husband, wife, and child?"[60]

From this it becomes clear that Christ is in the very midst of the Christian family. The Orthodox theologian Paul Evdokimov, in analyzing this text from Clement, makes explicit the ecclesial dimensions of the family baptized into Christ:

> One knows the saying from the Fathers: "Where Christ is, there is the Church." This fundamental affirmation is drawn from the word of the Lord: "Where two or three are united in My name, I am there in their midst" (Mt 18:20). A similar "union," in fact, has this ecclesial nature, because it is integrated into Christ and is placed in His Presence. Clement of Alexandria...places marriage in direct relationship with this word already cited and says, "Who are the two united together in the name of Christ?...Is it not the man and woman united by God?"[61]

Thus, for Clement, Christian marriages (and families) share in the reality of Christ. By their baptismal status as members of Christ, the Lord is present continually in the Christian family secured by the one-fleshness of the husband and wife, which issues forth in children.

Jerome (AD 347–420)

Jerome is the other Church Father who directly employs the phrase "domestic church," and his usage echoes St. Paul in Rom 16:5. In AD 384, when writing to a certain Paula, he greets a series of people including the *domesticam ecclesiam* in her home:

60. "Τίνες δὲ οἱ δύο καὶ πρεῖς ὑπάρχουσιν ἐν ὀνόματι Χριστοῦ συναγόμενοι, παρ' οἷς μέσος ἐστὶν ὁ κύριος; ἢ οὐχὶ ἄνδρα καὶ γυναῖκα καὶ τέκνον τοὺς τρεῖς λέγει." Clement of Alexandria, *Stromatum*, 3, 10, 68 (PG 8:1169). Translation from Clement of Alexandria, *Stromateis*, trans. Ferguson, 298.

61. Paul Evdokimov, "*Ecclesia domestica*," *L'Anneau d'Or: Cahiers de spiritualité conjugale et familiale* 107 (1962), 354: "On connaît l'adage des Pères: 'Là où est le Christ, là est l'Eglise'. Cette affirmation fondamentale découle de la parole du Seigneur: 'Là où deux ou trois sont réunis en mon nom, je suis au milieux d'eux' (Mt. 18,20). Une pareille 'réunion', en effet, est de nature ecclésiale, car elle est intégrée au Christ et mise en sa présence. Clément d'Alexandrie...place le mariage en relation directe avec la parole citée et dit: 'Qui sont les deux rassemblés au nom du Christ.... N'est-ce pas l'homme et la femme unis par Dieu?'"

Greet Blesilla and Eustochius, our young beginners [novices]; greet Felician, truly a fruitful virgin in [both] the flesh and spirit; greet the rest of the congregation of chaste ones and your domestic church [*domesticam tua ecclesiam*]. I fear for all of them, even those who are guarded, lest while the father of the family sleeps, the hostile man could plant in abundance darnel [tares].[62]

In another letter to Paula's mother-in-law, Laeta, Jerome reveals the composition and structure of this Christian home. Although Laeta had come from a mixed marriage, the Christian influence of her mother had a profound effect within the home (see 1 Cor 7:14). Jerome specifically quotes Paul on how the unbelieving spouse is sanctified by the Christian partner. In speaking of her pagan grandfather, Albinus, he is bold enough to say that "when a man is surrounded by a believing crowd of children and grandchildren, he is as good as a candidate for the faith."[63] This understanding has a certain affinity with the Semitic idea of corporate personality.

It is clear that this is a family that is living out its Christian faith. This is evidenced by the fact that Laeta's child, also called Paula, came as an answer to prayer. "She was consecrated from the first by Christ, before she was born, before You conceived her in the womb, before You dedicated her."[64] (This is reminiscent of the prophet Jeremiah, and of David's declarations in Ps 139.) In advising on Paula's education, Jerome places the emphasis on learning the Scriptures: "Let her treasures be... [the] manuscripts of the holy writings."[65] He then goes on to enumerate how different biblical books could be used. Finally, he urges her to send the child to Bethlehem to her grandmother, Paula, to be brought up in a convent situation. The practice of the faith is central to

62. Jerome, *Ad Paulam Epistola, Ep. 30* 14.11 (PL 22, 44): "Saluta blesillam et eustochium, tirunculas nostras; saluta felicianem vere carnis et spiritus virginitatem felicem; saluta reliquum castitatis chorum et *domesticam tua ecclesiam*, cui omnia, etiam quae tuta sunt timeo, ne dormiente patre familias inimicus homo zizania superseminet."

63. Jerome, *Letter 107: Ad Laetam,* NPNF 6 (Grand Rapids, Mich.: Eerdmans, 1989 repr.), 189–90.

64. Jerome, *Letter 107,* 190 (PL 22:870). Latin text: "quae prius Christo consecrata est, quam genita: quam ante vovisti, quam utero conceptisti."

65. Jerome, *Letter 107,* 194 (PL 22:876). Latin text: "Pro gemmis et serico divinos Codices amet."

Laeta's household and it is to this type of household that Jerome applies the Pauline term "domestic church."

Jerome here combines two aspects that we have seen before. First, as in Chrysostom, the Scriptures are seen to be the foundation of catechesis in the Christian family. Second, there is the acknowledgment that the Christian, by virtue of his baptismal identity, causes the home to become an eschatological sphere of activity in which even the non-Christian is profoundly affected. Thus, the Semitic concept of corporate personality continues to operate within the Christian consciousness concerning the family and the salvific design of God.

Other Patristic Sources

After the period of Augustine and Chrysostom, the celibate life, particularly in its monastic form, became the dominant model for religious life and was seen as the primary way of fulfilling one's vocation to holiness. However, one can still find references that at least give witness to the fact that marriage is still conceptually acknowledged as a legitimate "way of life" within the Church and, in the reference in Bede clearly shows that the phrase "domestic church" was not totally lost to the tradition. What follows are key passages from that period. They show that while the understanding of the vocational status of marriage and family—particularly its link to holiness—was not vibrant, at least there were some traces that still remained. These texts tend to replicate what had been stated early or recite Scriptural passages with little commentary.

Gregory the Great (AD 540–604)

Homiliarum In Ezechielem Lib I: Homil. VIII (PL 76:858–59)

Alia castra continentium, atque ab hoc mundo recedentium, qui contra malignorum spirituum bella quotidie in corde se praeparant. Alia castra bonorum conjugatorum, qui viventes in amore omnipoten tis Dei concorditer sic vicissim sibi carnis debitum solvent.... Quia ergo distincti fidelium ordines, ab exortu sanctae Ecclesiae usque ad finem mundi concorditer viventes contra potestates aereas dimicant.

There are other camps of [those who are] continent, as well as [those who have] retreated from the world, who prepare themselves daily in [their] heart [for] the battle against evil spirits. Another camp is of good married ones who living harmoniously in the love of the omnipotent God, thus in another way, are free from [fulfilling] the debt of the flesh.... Therefore, the distinct orders of the faithful, living harmoniously from the beginning [rising] of the holy Church to the end of the world, are fighting against the powers of the air.

Homiliarium In Ezechielem Lib. II Hom. VII (PL 76:1014A)

...quia tres sunt ordines bene viventium, bonorum scilicet conjugatorum, continentium, atque praedicatorum, et qui alii etiam in conjugiis positi amore coelestis patriae anhelant.

There are three orders of those who live well, namely, the faithfully married, the continent, and the preachers, and there are also others placed by love in the conjugal state who pant after the heavenly homeland.

Moralium Liber I: Iob 14, 20 (PL 75:535–36)

...quia post apostolorum conspectam fortitudinem, tres distinctiones fidelium in Ecclesiae conversatione secutae sunt: pastorum videlicet, et continentium, atque conjugatorum...

After having seen the bravery of the apostles, three distinctions of the faithful in the Church by way of life (now) follow: manifestly (they are) the pastors, the continent, and the married.

Fulgentius of Ruspe (AD 462–533)

De Trinitate Liber Unus (PL 65:507–8)

Unde et arca Noe, quae significavit Ecclesiam, bicamerata tricamerataque fuit; significans, ut diximus, tres gradus, aut ordines...conjugatos, continentes et virgines.... Ita etiam Ecclesia catholica in his gradibus constituta est, ut quamvis tres sint gradus, multae tamen differen tiae meritorum.

Whence, the ark of Noah, which signifies the Church, had two or three chambers, signifying, as we have said, three grades or orders...the married, the continent, and the virgins.... And so the catholic Church is established in these three orders such that whatever are the three grades, yet [they are] of many different merits.

Venerable Bede (A D 673–35)

In S. Joannis Evangelium Expositio Par. II Section I (PL 92:661)

...quia nimirum <u>tres ordines fidelium sunt,</u> quibus Ecclesia constat, <u>conjugatorum,</u> videlicet, continentium, et doctorum.

Undoubtedly <u>there are three orders of the faithful,</u> by which the Church is composed: <u>the married,</u> the continent, and teachers.

Retractatio In Actus Apostulorum (CL 1358 Cap. 19 Linea 26)

Hoc tempore commorante Paulo in Epheso dicitur primum ad Corinthios epistolam scripsisse, in qua etiam Priscillae et Aquilae meminit dicens: Salutant vos in domino multum Aquila et Priscilla <u>cum domestica sua ecclesia</u> [<u>with her domestic church</u>]; quo verbo etiam hoc ostenditur, quia non illi solummodo fideliter Christo servierint sed et fidelium in domo sua congregationem habuerint.

At that time, when Paul was staying in Ephesus he is said to have written the first letter to the Corinthians, in which he mentions both Priscilla and Aquila saying: Aquila and Priscilla greet you greatly in the Lord with their domestic church; by this greeting it is clear that not only are these faithfully serving Christ, but they also have a congregation of the faithful in their home

CHAPTER 10

VATICAN II AND THE PROBLEMS OF APPROPRIATION

MODERN REEMERGENCE OF THE TERM "DOMESTIC CHURCH"

With the end of persecutions under Constantine, a major hermeneutical shift occurred within the life of the Church. Prior to this time, to profess Christ was to endanger one's life. Consequently, only those who were earnest about their faith and willing to die embraced it. In this environment, it was clear that the vocation to holiness which informed every Christian life would be a costly path to follow. There was no need for any extraordinary measures to show one's faith, because the ordinary Christian often had to exercise heroic virtue simply to maintain the faith. After A D 313, when the edict permitting religious tolerance was promulgated, Christianity became an accepted form of life within the Roman Empire, persecutions stopped, and the "world" flood into the Church.

This expansion resulted in a "watering down" of Christian communal life and of the seriousness of the call to holiness, and it provided impetus for the development of the monastic movement for those seeking to live out a rigorous commitment to Christ. Ordinary Christian life now no longer served as the hermeneutic of committed service. The celibate life became the measure of commitment and the primary model for holiness. Predictably, the sense of the unique holiness of the Christian family and its being a "way of holiness" gradually diminished. At a cultural level (but never in terms of theology), being married and having a family grew to be seen as having second-rate status within the Church's life. In fact, the term "domestic church" disappeared from the theological landscape after the period of Augustine and Chrysostom.

Although the terminology was no longer used, the reality of the Christian family and its holiness persisted throughout the generations. In every age, there have been the many witnesses of godly Christian families who in their faith-filled lives were living out the reality of the domestic church. In essence, Christian teaching permeated Western thought and informed the structure and meaning of family life. While not accorded a formal theological place in salvation history, the family nevertheless continued to function as a primary instrument of God's salvific will. Given the stability of the cultural understanding of marriage and family in this period, there was no particular need to provide a theological articulation of its ecclesial nature. It was being implicitly lived out. However, that was to radically change in the latter decades of the twentieth century. Providentially, John XXIII called for an ecumenical council, which would, amongst many things, take up the nature and purpose of the family and resurrect an ancient understanding that would provide the modern world with a critical new paradigm for how to understand the family.

PREPARATIONS FOR VATICAN II

Vatican II was a watershed for the Catholic Church inasmuch as it allowed the perennial teaching of the Church to be applied in the modern context, using terminology and categories of thought that could be appropriated by the modern world. At the heart of the Council was the principle that first appeared in *Lumen Gentium*: the "universal call to holiness."[1] Underlying this theological concept was the belief that all

1. *Lumen Gentium*, chap. 5.

people, in all states of life, are called to attain holiness in, and through, the very states of life in which they find themselves. This doctrine prevented a bifurcation between those who were officially "religious" and those who were not. After centuries of seeing holiness and perfection through the lens of monastic spirituality, this doctrine opened up the possibility of seeing the "secular realities" of marriage and family as states of life that could help a person attain genuine holiness.

The official documents produced at Vatican II which mention marriage and family are foundational for constructing a theology of the domestic church in the modern context. But the actual debates which preceded the acceptance of these documents also contain valuable information which is helpful in constructing such a theology. An analysis of these debates enables us to understand the mindset of the Council fathers, and indeed of the Church that was operative within the Council; the conception of marriage and family and its relationship to the Church that prevailed in the pre-Vatican II era; the resistance to acknowledging the ecclesial nature or structure of the family per se; and the Scriptural, theological and Patristic foundations used to establish the family as a genuine part of the Church. Through an examination these debates we will discover the evidence necessary to confirm that the family possesses an ecclesial nature, an ecclesial structure and an ecclesial mission.

Initially, all the documents for the upcoming Council had been prepared in draft form, and it was assumed by the Holy Office (now the Congregation for the Doctrine of the Faith) that, after preliminary consultations, these draft proposals would be quickly approved by the bishops. However, the Council took a radical departure from this proposed trajectory, once it became evident that the Council fathers believed that the Church's presentation to the world had become moribund and needed to be urgently updated. It was not a question of changing the teaching of the Church. Instead, the desire of the Council was that the truth that the Church proffered might be presented in terms and categories that could be comprehended by the modern world. In the end, this became the driving force and purpose of the Council.

One of the first topics to be taken up was the question of the nature of the Church. Prophetically, it was within the debates surrounding this subject that the true nature of the family (and its teleological purpose within the salvific will of God) was to become clear. An examination of the debates clearly brings to light several aspects of the historical process:

- How the family became "inserted" into the Church and became an essential part of its structure
- The nature of the opposition to this notion and how it was overcome by appealing to the Church Fathers
- How the ecclesial nature of the family was retrieved from the tradition and crystallized in the phrase "domestic church"

At first glance, it would seem odd, as one of the Council Fathers noted, to include a section on the role of the family in a formal definition of the nature of the Church.[2] Yet that is precisely what happened in the Vatican II document *Lumen Gentium.* In studying the debates that preceded the final acceptance of *Lumen Gentium,* we will see that the Council went through four stages which finally led to the acceptance and development of the term "domestic church." Each of the stages shows engagement with the question as to what constituted the nature of the Church and how, precisely, marriage and family were related to it.

STAGE 1: INTRODUCTION OF
THE FAMILY INTO THE STRUCTURE
OF THE CHURCH

The initial drafts of conciliar document were rejected by the bishops attending Vatican II. The bishops instead sought to prepare their own initial drafts, including that on the nature of the Church. To effect this, individual bishops made submissions, and it was at this point that Bishop Pietro Fiordelli of Prato, Italy (who had worked with the Christian Family Movement) made his first contribution, on November 23,

2. *Acta Synodalia Sacrosanctii Concilii Oecumenici Vaticani II,* vol. 1, pars 4 (Vatican City, 1960–89), 309. Cf. Michael Fahey, "The Christian Family as Domestic Church at Vatican II," *Concilium* (Fall 1994/95): 87.

1962. From his speech, we learn, first, that the intimate relationship between the Church *and* Christian marriage/family had not been clearly grasped. He pointed out that in the first draft on the nature of the Church, all the constituent parts of the Church were mentioned except for marriage and family.

> But having said this, it regretfully seems, in my humble opinion, that in all of the documents nothing is to be found by way of a special chapter which concerns another state in the Church, which is of the greatest nobility and sanctity and of the greatest fecundity—to the increase of the Mystical Body of Christ-namely the state of sacramental marriage.[3]

The objections raised by the president of the assembly were most telling, for they revealed, in unambiguous terms, the prevailing (clerical) atmosphere of the day. As Fiordelli began to draw out the intrinsic relationship between the Church and the family, the president objected that these ideas were "outside the realm of this schema."[4] For the Council president, the Church primarily consisted of the ordained offices within the hierarchical Church. To include, as part of that Church, the organically structured family, which was a naturally occurring part of the order of creation, did not make sense. It was simply not a part of the subject under discussion. The family was of the natural order; the Church was supernatural by nature.

The preparatory document's lack of understanding of the value of marriage and family and its failure to include them in the structure of the Church were, in Fiordelli's eyes, deeply problematical. In some ecclesial movements prior to the Vatican II there had been a gradual awakening to the legitimacy of marriage and family as a way of life and to their unique contribution to the life of the Church. Therefore, Fiordelli was also able, in his speech on the Council floor, to develop the relationship between marriage and the Mystical Body of Christ: "For today, it seems to many that a special place in the Mystical Body of Christ

---

3. "Sed his praemissis, humiliter, mihi dolendum videtur, quod in toto schemate nullum inveniatur speciale caput quod agat de aliquo statu in Ecclesia, qui est maximae nobilitatis et sanctitatis et—ad incrementum Mystici Corporis Christi—maximae fecunditatis: scl de statu sacramentali matrimonii" (Bishop Fiordelli in *Acta Synodalia,* vol. 1, pars 4, 309).

4. "extra ordinem huius schematis" (ibid.).

must be given to those who are situated in the state of Christian mar-riage."[5]

A third point that emerges from Bishop Fiordelli's first submission is that the Christian state of marriage is intrinsic to the understanding of the Church. In order to justify including the married state in the Con-stitution of the Church, Fiordelli appealed to Augustine's emphasis on marriage as a "way of life" and also pointed to the supernatural reality operating within the Christian family (which is attested in the writings of Sts. Paul, Jerome, and Augustine). In this first stage of development, Fiordelli stated that "the Christian marital state, which most certainly proceeds from the sacrament of matrimony, is a special supernatural state, indeed, a sacramental [state]...it is not a mere formality."[6]

STAGE 2: GROUNDING THE CONCEPT
IN THE CHURCH FATHERS

In his second intervention, Fiordelli attempted to show the intrin-sic relationship between the family and the Church. He also wanted to ground the concept of the family as the domestic church in the Church Fathers, thereby giving it legitimacy in the eyes of the Council. This speech was interrupted by the illness of the Holy Father, John XXIII, but in 1963 it was submitted to the commission in written form. This full text, first, provides the conceptual basis for the term "domestic church"; it then extends the spiritual reality of Christian marriage to the whole of family life; next, it shows how procreation is fundamental to ground the sacramentality of marriage; and, finally, it provides the specific patristic witness of both Augustine and Chrysostom to the re-ality of the domestic church.

Taking each of these four in turn, we see first that Fiordelli articulat-ed clearly the conceptual basis of the domestic church:

---

5. "Plurimis enim hodie videtur quod specialis locus in Mystico Corpore Christi tribu-endus sit iis qui in statu matrimoniali christiano positi sunt" (ibid.).

6. "Status matrimonialis christianus, qui oritur ex sacramento matrimonii certissime est specialis status supernaturalis, immo sacramentalis in Ecclesia...non est mera formali-tas" (ibid., 309–10).

It seems to me that this would be the true structure of the Church of Christ.... Now, moreover, is the parish the ultimate division of the Church? No. The parish is further divided into so many holy cells, which are *Christian families,* which we can call, following the example of the Holy Fathers, small churches.[7]

For Fiordelli, the smallest articulation of the Church is not the parish but the Christian family. He strengthened his thesis even further by his contention that while the parish may change its boundaries because they are established by the legal authority of a diocese, the nature of the family cannot be altered because it proceeds "out of the will of Christ, Himself" (*ex voluntate ipsius Christi*) and is therefore "of the divine law" (*iuris divini*).[8]

Next, it was normally *only* marriage that was understood to have a spiritual dimension, but in this speech Fiordelli made a profound (and perhaps novel) contribution by extending the spiritual reality of Christian marriage to the whole of family life. For him, Christ has made the family holy and sacramental;[9] the Christian family flows from the sacrament of marriage itself. The two—Christian family and sacramental marriage—are inextricably related in Fiordelli's thought.

Fiordelli argued, thirdly, that one of the reasons marriage is sacramental is because of its relationship to the Body of Christ through the gift of procreation. The children who are born to Christian parents are inserted into the Body of Christ by baptism and thereby cause the membership of the Church to grow. Thus, the sacramentality of marriage anticipates (at least to some extent) a link with procreation. In this way, the family, which ensues from Christian marriage, provides a ground for its sacramentality. As Fiordelli argued, this sacramental dimension exists "precisely because the state of matrimony by the divine intention possesses the greatest importance for the increase both quan-

7. "Mihi videtur quod haec sit vera structuratio Ecclesiae Christi.... Nunc autem: estne paroicia ultima divisio Ecclesiae? Non. Paroecia ulterius dividitur in tot cellulas sanctas, quae sunt *familiae chritianae,* quas vocare possumus, exemplum Sanctorum Patrum, velut *minusculas Ecclesias*" (Ibid., 310–11).

8. Ibid., 311.

9. "Sanctum immo sacramentale fecit ipsum institutum familiar" ("On the contrary, he made the family itself a holy institution" (ibid., 311).

titatively and qualitatively of His Mystical Body."[10] That is, the family is divinely designed to assist in the growth of the Church and is not merely an optional social structure.

Finally, to substantiate his claim, Fiordelli invoked the patristic authority of Augustine and Chrysostom and examined how they used and understood the concept of domestic church. He chose several key citations to demonstrate that both Church Fathers saw the family as having an ecclesial nature; both used language that demonstrated that Church and family were coterminous. For both Augustine and Chrysostom, the Christian family was caught up in a salvific activity of the Church and became an instrumental part of it as we have seen above in Augustine's *De Bono Viduitatis, Letter 188* and Chrysostom's *Commentary on Genesis*.

STAGE 3: DEVELOPMENT OF SCRIPTURAL FOUNDATIONS

In a penultimate submission to these debates in 1963, Fiordelli grounded his concept of the domestic church further by appealing to Scripture and by extending the structures of the Church into the family. First, he proposed that families be seen as possessing an organic, intrinsic relationship to the Church. He asked, "What if more than just members, Christian families were considered even as organs and communities in the Church."[11] He was applying the Pauline concept of the organic body (which up till then had been used of the universal Church) to the family. Families were not merely statistical, sociological units of the Church, but actually living, vibrant members of the Body of Christ. Just like individuals, parishes, and dioceses made by the Church, so too individual Christian families were members making up the full body of Christ.

Fiordelli also made what was perhaps a novel theological contribu-

---

10. "Praecise quod status matrimonialis in mente sua divina, summum habebat momentum ad incrementum quantitativum et qualitativum mystici sui Corporis" (ibid., 310).

11. "Quod si praeter membra, in Ecclesia, etiam organa et communitates...considerentur...familiae christianae" (*Acta synodalia*, vol. 2, pars 1, 794–95).

tion here by extending +Ephesians 5:32 ("This mystery is great") to include the family and not restricting it to marriage alone. By this extension, he proffered the view that the Christian family was an actual manifestation of the love that Christ has for the Church and therefore was an extension of sacramental marriage. He asked the Council to consider the family in this new light: "It is possible to refer to the Christian family as a small church [*minusculam ecclesiam*] possessing in itself a sharing [communication] of the very mystery of the union of Christ with the Church."[12] This may have been the first time that this text was applied in this manner.

At this juncture, Fiordelli took the next logical step, which flowed from his theological analysis. If the family indeed has an ecclesial (Church-like) nature, then the structures and forms of the Church (which flow from its nature) must also be present in the family in some form appropriate to familial life. Mission derives from nature. Therefore, Fiordelli began to situate key ecclesial structures within the family; he suggested that parents be considered to have been "consecrated" (*consecrati*)[13] for their roles. While this coheres most closely with both Augustine's and Chrysostom thought (and, in fact, is central to their understanding of the domestic church), it was a rather startling admission for modern sensibilities. However, if the family is indeed to have an ecclesial nature, then it follows that "ecclesial" structures must also be present in the home. Otherwise the term is merely a poetic appellation, having no substantial reality.

STAGE 4: FAMILY AS A WAY OF LIFE

Finally, in his last intervention, Fiordelli urged the recognition of not only marriage but also the family as being a "state of life" within the Church. Again, for many within the Council, this was a new under-

---

12. "Minusculam ecclesiam familiam christianam vocare possumus, in se habentem communicationem ipsius mysterii unionis Christi cum Ecclesia" ("We can call the Christian family a small church, possessing in itself the the communon of the very mystery of the union of Christ with the Church") (ibid., 794).

13. Ibid., 795.

standing of what marriage and family represented. To substantiate his idea, Fiordelli referred to the way in which marriage had been denoted in the Fathers. This was important to him because, for Fiordelli, what could be said of marriage could equally be applied to the family.

> In verse 36 it is said that spouses "have their own gift in the Church," similar to 1 Cor 7:6. But it seems to be too little after all that has been said above; the family has not so much its own gift but a "state," according to the minds of the Fathers who called marriage a state, an order, an office, a way of life, a profession.[14]

Knowing that the citations from the early Church Fathers would be authoritative (and for many would be decisive), Fiordelli mounted a strong case for the family to be considered as a domestic church. As the debates continued, however, Fiordelli retreated from two prominent patristic ideas. The draft text had stated, "In this as it were domestic church, the parents are often the first preachers of the faith, exercising a sort of episcopal function, just as Augustine said."[15] Fiordelli, however, became uncomfortable with this close identification of the parents' role with that of the bishop; he justified his change of position by maintaining that, whereas it sounds good in Augustine, "it appears to sound bad in the conciliar text."[16] Probably, though, he was making a concession to the clerical atmosphere of the times rather than acknowledging any logical objection. It is possible that neither Fiordelli nor (most probably) the Council as a whole was ready for this type of theological conclusion to be reached.

A second issue for Fiordelli was the nomenclature that was applied to the family in this context. He himself was uncomfortable with the term

---

14. *Acta synodalia*, vol. 2, second session, part 3, 22. "Ad lin. 36 dicitur quod sponsi 'habent suum in Ecclesia donum' iuxta 1 ad Corinthios, cap 7. Sed hoc videtur nimis parum. Dicendum ex supradictis quod familia habet suum in Ecclesia non tantum donum sed 'statum', etiam iuxta mentem Patrum, qui matrimonium vocaverunt *gradum, ordinem, officium, vitae genus, professionem*."

15. "In hac velut Ecclesia domestica, parentes saepe sunt primi fidei praecones, quasi munus episcopale, ut ait Augustinus,...exercent" (*Acta synodalia*, vol. 2, second session, part 1, 259).

16. "...male sonare videtur in textu conciliari" (*Acta synodalia*, vol. 2, second session, part 3, 23).

"domestic church." He argued that although the expression is Pauline, it "has its own particular historical sense."[17] This unease may have arisen from the ambiguity in the different NT texts as to what constituted a *domestica ecclesia* ("house-church"). As the analysis in Chapter 8 shows, the use of the phrase "domestic church" does not seem philologically to clearly support the idea of a *family-as-a-church* unit. The concept of the baptized family having an ecclesial identity (*qua* the domestic church) is clearly found in the New Testament, but its theological grounding is more properly derived from the theology of baptism.[18] Perhaps because of this, Fiordelli stated that the Pauline usage was "altogether foreign to this argument on marriage about which we are speaking at this moment."[19] He concluded that the term "small church" (*parva Ecclesia*) expressed the concept better.[20] Whatever his reasons, the two phrases are similar and Fiordelli was in reality preferring the terminology of Chrysostom over that of Augustine, who explicitly uses the phrase *domestica ecclesia*.

In the final analysis, the great accomplishment of Fiordelli was to resurrect the idea of the family as the domestic church from the Church's tradition and insert it precisely where it could have the most effect, that is, into the debates concerning the dogmatic constitution of the Church.[21] He is to be credited with giving systematic justification for this ecclesial understanding of the family and encouraging the Council to include the family under the constitution of the Church and its mission, thereby making it an intrinsic part of the Church. Finally, it was Fiordelli who met the opposition to this "retrieved" tradition and

17. "Habet suum proprium sensum historicum" (ibid.).

18. One can make the case that the domestic church is properly grounded in baptism *and* the sacrament of marriage. This is true, but even here there is always the priority of baptism, because marriage becomes sacramental only when it is inserted into the reality of baptism. See *FC* 56.

19. "Qui est omnino alienus ab argumento matrimonii de quo hic est sermo" (*Acta synodalia*, vol. 2, second session, part 3, 23).

20. Ibid.

21. His frustration can be seen when he states: "Mihi videtur...quod Concilium altissimis verbis extollat *laicis* familiam christianam et praecise his loquens de constitutione dogmatica Ecclesia" ("It seems to me that the Council praises the Christian family for the laity in the most elevated language precisely with these words from the dogmatic constitution on the Church") (ibid.).

carefully provided the theological, scriptural, and patristic grounding for its eventual reception.

THE FINAL TEXT: *LUMEN GENTIUM*

After all the debates on this text (which were coextensive with the entire life of the Council), the final text of *Lumen Gentium* was approved on September 17–18, 1964. In this document, the family *as domestic church* was officially accorded recognition in magisterial teaching. Four major points germane to our discussion were ratified through this document. First, it is clear that those who had wanted marriage acknowledged as a legitimate *way of life* within the Church won the day. The way of holiness was not to be confined only to the celibate or consecrated.[22] The Council instead preferred to establish the idea of the "universal call to holiness" as its informing principle. Every human being, in whatever state of life, was call to live a life of holiness and to work out his salvation in, and through, the concrete situations in which he lived. This was particularly applied to those in the married state: "Christian married couples help one another to attain holiness in their married life and in the rearing of their children."[23]

The second major point ratified in *Lumen Gentium* is that marriage is intrinsically linked to the propagation of the human race, which, for the Christian couple, results in the perpetuation of the People of God. Human procreation can never be understood solely in terms of its societal functioning. The proper end of Christian marriage is already ordered to the advancement of the kingdom of God.

> From the marriage of Christians there comes the family in which new citizens of human society are born and, by the grace of the Holy Spirit

---

22. The Church never officially defined holiness as possible only within the context of celibacy. However, in popular imagination and culturally there was a strong link between the two, such that it was understood that those choosing to seriously pursue holiness would make the choice for celibacy, whereas those without this sense of vocation to holiness would choose marriage. Even the language revealed this: one who became a professed brother or sister was going into "religious" life. But the emphasis of Fiordelli showed that marriage was also a vocation, also a way of holiness.

23. *Lumen Gentium*, 2, 11, in Flannery, *Vatican II: Documents*, 362.

in baptism, those are made children of God so that the People of God may be perpetuated throughout the centuries.[24]

The Council affirmed this further, third point, that the role of parents not only has a sociological significance but also possesses a genuine ecclesial dimension. It accepted the Augustinian notion that parents are the first catechists of the faith for their children.[25]

Fourth, it is in this catechetical context that the term "domestic church" was confirmed as a description of the family: "In what might be regarded as the domestic church, the parents, by word and example, are the first heralds of the faith with regard to their children. They must foster the vocation which is proper to each child."[26] However, at this point in its development, identifying the family as an ecclesial reality is only haltingly made, and the family is called a domestic church only by way of analogy. It would not be until the pontificate of John Paul II that the relationship between the family and the Church would be explained fully in ontological terms.[27]

APOSTOLICAM ACTUOSITATEM

The only other document from Vatican II that deals with the "domestic church" is *Apostolicam Actuositatem* (3,11). Many of the same themes are repeated in this text, but one section is of special interest:

---

24. Ibid., 362.

25. However, the explicit extending of the *"munus episcopale"* to the parental role was dropped.

26. Ibid., 362–63. "In hac velut Ecclesia Domestica parents verbo et exemplo sint pro filiis suis primi fidei praecones, et vocationem unicuique propriam...foveant oportet": Fahey, "Christian Family as Domestic Church," 89.

27. Within the theology of the domestic church we have an observable *development of doctrine*—at least in terms of the modern appropriation of the idea of the family as having an ecclesial identity. During the debates within Vatican II, there was some hesitation as to the degree of identification that the baptized family should have with the hierarchical Church. Consequently, the relationship was set out in analogous terms. The family is *like* a church. However, within the magisterial teaching of John Paul II, the relationship shifted and was described in ontological terms. The Christian family is a realization of ecclesial communion and, therefore, should be called a domestic church (see *CCC* 2204).

The mission of being the primary vital cell of society has been given to the family by God himself. This mission will be accomplished if the family, by the mutual affection...and by family prayer, presents itself as a domestic sanctuary of the Church.[28]

Here, a slightly different terminology is used, but the parallel between "domestic sanctuary" and "domestic church" is clear.[29] It should be noted that while the family is described as a vital cell, this function extends only to society but is not applied to the Church. To forge the link between the family and the Church at this level would perhaps have been premature and certainly was too bold a step at that time. However, as this concept of family took root, it would not be long before the family was also seen as the fundamental cell of the Church. Paul VI in speaking of the family said, "Our beloved predecessor John XXIII expressed to you...[i]t is a basic, germinal cell, the smallest, to be sure, but also the most fundamental one, in the Church organism."[30] Finally, in the Catechism in 1997, there is an official, magisterial declaration that the baptized family "constitutes a specific revelation and realization of ecclesial communion, and for this reason it can and should be called a domestic church" (2204). This statement is taken from John Paul II's *Familiaris Consortio* (21) and represents the high-water mark in the development of the theology of the domestic church. Going beyond its former analogous language ("like a church"), the Church has now made a formal declaration that there is, in fact, an ontological connection between the Church and the Christian family such that they share the same nature and mission.[31] Just as a sacramental marriage is

28. *Apostolicam actuositatem*, 3, 11; Flannery, *Vatican II: Documents*, 779.

29. Here, the family is to be the sanctuary of the Church. This means that the Church lives in the family in some form. But what can that mean if not that the Church lives in the very lives and relationships of those who make up the family? In the end, there is some form of identification of the Church with the nature and structure of the family. This thesis becomes more precisely articulated in the magisterial statements *after* the Council, particularly by those of John Paul II.

30. Quoted in Maurice Eminyan, *Theology of the Family* (Malta: Jesuit Publications, 1994), 162.

31. This is not to say that each is parallel to the other, each having the same mission. Rather, the family *shares* in the mission of the Church. Looked at from the perspective of the family, one can say that the family has an ecclesial mission precisely because it is a part

reflective of and participates in the love of Christ for the Church (Eph 5:32), so too the Christian family (which emerges from this sacramental love) is *reflective of and participates in* the body of Jesus, that is, the Church.[32]

DEVELOPMENT: POST–VATICAN II

It is an arguable point but it seems fair to state that the concept of the family as a domestic church would have remained an interesting but dormant footnote in the history of the Council had it not been for the pontificate of John Paul II. Paul VI and John Paul I briefly mention the term,[33] but it is only with John Paul II that a systematic analysis is attempted and a "theology of domestic church" is sketched out. Not only did he secure a permanent place for this concept in the Church's magisterium, but he established it as the dominant hermeneutic by which the family is to be understood. Further and most important-

---

of the Church. In his *Letter to Families,* John Paul II proclaims that the Christian family is a Bride of Christ: "As the 'domestic church', it is the bride of Christ" (Boston: Pauline Books and Media, 1994).

32. The following section is a slightly revised version of my article "Family as Domestic Church: Developmental Trajectory, Legitimacy, and Problems of Appropriation," *Theological Studies* 66 (2005): 592–604.

33. Paul VI, *Marialis Cultis* 52, 53. The Second Vatican Council has pointed out how the family, the primary and vital cell of society, "shows itself to be the domestic sanctuary of the Church.... The Christian family is thus seen to be a domestic Church if its members, each according to his proper place and tasks, all together promote justice, practice works of mercy, devote themselves to helping their brethren, take part in the apostolate of the wider local community and play their part in its liturgical worship. This will be all the more true if together they offer up prayers to God. If this element of common prayer were missing, the family would lack its very character as a domestic Church. Thus there must logically follow a concrete effort to reinstate communal prayer in family life if there is to be a restoration of the theological concept of the family as the domestic Church." This appears to be more in line with Chrysostom's understanding. John Paul develops his theology of the family more along Augustinian lines.

John Paul I to a group of bishops from the United States given on September 21, 1978: "The Christian Family: A Community of Love," *L'Osservatore Romano,* September 28, 1978 (p. 11): "The Christian family is so important and its role is so basic in transforming the world and in building up the Kingdom of God that the Council called it a "domestic church" (*Lumen Gentium* 11).

ly, he did not allow this newly recovered idea to become a subjectively defined reality. Instead, he provided a definitive interpretative framework by which the domestic church was to be analyzed. He showed that theologically the family had to be understood through the prism of its ecclesiological and Christological identity. In a profound statement, he says that "families...will manifest to all people the Savior's living presence in the world, and the genuine nature of the Church" (*FC* 50). Would that statement have been possible prior to the Council?[34]

In his apostolic exhortation *Familiaris Consortio,* the "summa of the Church's teaching on family,"[35] John Paul II begins with the fundamental call of the Gospel: conversion to Christ.[36] Then in a deft move, to prevent a mere moralism from developing or an extrinsicism in regard to the life and activity of the family, the Pope unites "being" and "mission," ontology and praxis. "The family finds in the plan of God...not only its identity...but also its mission.... The role that God calls the family to perform in history derives from what the family is.... Family, become what you are" (*FC* 17). As we will see shortly, this very Pauline-sounding principle will become increasingly important in the ensuing debates over the "nature" of the domestic church. For John Paul II, it is clear that the family has a God-given nature that must be respected if it is to flourish on the societal level and if it is to fulfil its destiny within the salvific covenant.

34. As the Conciliar debates show, the understanding that the family was a part of the Church structure was initially rejected. Culturally, it would have been difficult to accept the family as having an ecclesial identity. Bishop Fiordelli overcame this opposition by showing how this idea was rooted in the patristic texts.

35. John Paul II, "La Chiesa Rinnova il Dialogo con il mondo per Favorire La Comprensione Tra I Popol," Address, December 22, 1981, in *Insegnamenti di Giovanni Paolo II,* 4/2 (1981) 1215. "...mendiante la recentissima Esortazione Apostolica "Familiaris Consortio", resa pubblica una settimana fa, che vuol essere una "summma" dell'insegnamento della Chiesa sulla vita, I compiti, le responsabilita, la missione del matrinio e della famiglia nel mondo d'oggi."

36. "The Church once again feels the pressing need to proclaim the Gospel...to all those who are called to marriage.... The Church is deeply convinced that only by the acceptance of the Gospel are the hopes that man legitimately places in marriage and in the family capable of being fulfilled" (*FC* 3). "To the injustice originating from sin...we must all set ourselves in opposition through a conversion of mind and heart, following Christ Crucified by denying our own selfishness" (*FC* 9).

John Paul II situates the identity of the family along two axes: Christ and the Church. In sections 17–49, the bulk of the document, *FC* defines the family's nature and role as being "to guard, reveal and communicate love."[37] But, once again, this is not merely an amorphous phrase but is further defined by its interior reference to Christ. "This is a living reflection and a real sharing in God's love for humanity and the love of Christ the Lord for the Church His bride" (*FC* 17). The baptized family reveals its ecclesial nature in that it is a specific revelation of the love of Christ. The family in its own unique manner shows forth and participates in the reality of Christ's love for the Church which is His Bride. Paul particularly shows this in Eph 5:32, when he reveals that the mystery of man and wife is actually related to the love of Christ for His Church.[38]

John Paul II then divides the mission of the ecclesial family into four constitutive aspects: to form a community of persons; to serve life; to participate in the development of society; and to share in the life and mission of the universal Church. These are marks of the Church, and if the family truly shares in the life and nature of the Body of Christ, then it cannot be separated from the Church but must be inserted into her very reality. Only in this way can the family become what it was destined to be. All families are called to a fundamental conversion to Christ, so that they can become the context in which the world encounters the reality of the Holy Spirit on a personal level. The family in the Old Testament functions as the carrier of the covenant, always moving towards its destined teleological fulfillment. That point is reached in

37. *FC* 17. While it is true that all baptized people have this as a personal vocation, there is a uniqueness to the family precisely because it is a community of relationships. As John Paul II says, "Its first task is to live with fidelity the reality of communion in a constant effort to develop an authentic community of persons. The inner principle of that task, its permanent power and its final goal is love: without love the family is not a community of persons and, in the same way, without love the family cannot live, grow and perfect itself as a community of persons" (18). In particular, the love of husband and wife is the icon of Christ's love for the Church (see Eph 5) and children are the fruit of that love.

38. The mission of the family proceeds from its nature. John Paul II shows how "every particular task of the family is an expressive and concrete actuation of that fundamental mission," which he sees as being ecclesial (*FC* 17).

Christ and the sending of the Holy Spirit. Now, the family functions as a privileged sphere where members of the family (and those who come in contact with these families) experience the salvific power of the Holy Spirit. As Christ begins to actually live in the members of the family, all members of the family are drawn into this sphere of holiness, because it is an organic reality. Only conscious rejection of this influence of Christ can prevent this from happening (see 1 Cor 7:12ff.).

Immediately following this presentation, John Paul II begins to develop the second axis of the family: its relationship to Christ Himself. He says that we must understand the "substance" of the family "in reference to Jesus Christ as Prophet, Priest and King" (FC 51). Here there is a close identification of the life of the family with that of Christ Himself. Each of the Lord's distinguishing roles is to be lived out concretely within the family. The *prophetic role* of Jesus is experienced whenever the family acts as a believing and evangelizing community. Like the prophets of old, the family is a sign of contradiction when it presents the values of the gospel and its claims to the secular world, inviting all to come to Christ and follow Him. The family takes on its *priestly role* when it encourages its members to enter into dialogue with God. The priest stands as a representative before God for the people. Here, the different members of the family intercede for each other and, as a family, bring before the Lord the concerns of their neighbors, the community, and all the situations in which they find themselves. In this way, they become a priestly leaven wherever they are situated and to the degree that they are open to God and to their neighbours. Finally, the family possesses a genuine *kingly role,* but always in biblical terms. To rule or have authority (which is at the root of being a king) is always, in Scripture, in terms of service. There is only servant-authority, in which the one who has authority must also lay down his life for those around him. Similarly, the Christian family as it fulfills its kingly nature in Christ becomes a community at the service of the world. As the family becomes aware of the needs of each other and of the world, they seek in concrete ways to meet those needs in the Name of Christ (FC 50). This means that the nature of the family is to be found in the nature of Christ. In this way, the threefold aspect of Christ's nature (prophet, priest, and king) are actually experienced and lived out in the home.

However, we must admit that the idea of encountering Christ in the reality of the Christian family is not self-evident; by all estimations, it is rather astonishing! We can easily draw the parallel between the family and the Church, inasmuch as both have a community-like structure and purpose. But with the injection of this Christological dimension, we are truly entering into the realm of the *mysterion*. John Paul II grounds the ecclesial mission of the family in the sacrament of matrimony and later will refine this further by saying that marriage "makes specific the sanctifying grace of Baptism" (*FC* 56). Little has been done to open these ideas further or to develop the Christological dimension of the domestic church. John Paul II has given us profound hints as to the direction this theology should go, but this has not yet been worked out. This will remain so until there is a recovery of the profound reality of baptism and how it transforms people and how it effects an ontological change (i.e., our being indwelt by Christ). Until this happens, the Christological nature of the family will remain not only a mystery (which it is in terms of the Pauline term *mysterion*), but will forever be wrapped in a Churchillian enigma. It is the inner reality of baptism which unlocks the mystery of the domestic church.

The power of John Paul II's analysis is that, like St. Paul, it cuts through the exterior layers and shows the sacramental nature of reality—in this case of the family. In Ephesians 5 Paul, drawing from the order of creation, is at pains to show how husbands and wives are to live out their marriage in terms of a Christological paradigm and are involved, not in a culturally conditioned relationship, but in a sacred order.[39] He shows how headship means that the husband must lay down his life for his wife, for he is head "as Christ also is head of the Church." That is, the Lord, out of his love for His Bride, dies for her. Towards the end of his discourse (verse 32), Paul comes alive to the deeper meanings of marriage. Verse 32 can be paraphrased thus: "In talking about the structures of ordinary human marriage, I really am speaking about

---

39. The root meaning of the word "hierarchy," which is critical to the biblical view of relationality, comes from "sacred/priestly" (*hiero*) and "order/rule" (*archē*). I want to thank Dr. Mary Shivanandan of the John Paul II Institute for pointing this out to me.

the mystery of Christ's love for the Church." Similarly, John Paul II, through the prism of the domestic church, reveals to us the profound (and, we should underline, *hidden*) mystery of the family, especially its ecclesial and Christological nature. Just as Christian marriage partakes in the dynamic and salvific relationship of Christ and the Church, so the Christian family actually participates in the nature and mission of the Church. Neither of these parallel relationships is self-evident, but they are the underlying realities of both human marriage and family. Both are caught up in the salvific design of God.

Following Vatican II and the pontificate of John Paul II, it can be asserted now that the term "domestic church" has been recovered, and this concept has become the dominant hermeneutic by which the baptized family is to be understood. But because the term has not been theologically grounded, it is vulnerable to distortion. Consequently, the great need of the moment is that its development *be* rooted in Scripture and further illuminated by patristic categories. Its nature and mission cannot be subjectively determined according to one's agenda; rather, they must be grounded in the authentic ecclesial and Christological nature of the family. Ontology is the basis for mission,[40] and it should be clear that the nature of the baptized family is ultimately revelatory of the Church herself, of which the family is an organic part.

PROBLEMS OF APPROPRIATION

Epistemological Concerns

In the present theological climate, there are serious problems regarding the authentic reception of the doctrine of the family as the domestic church. The first is the nature of modern consciousness. In *Letter to Families,* John Paul II points out that the mystery of Christ as the Bridegroom lies at the heart of marriage and family, and it is precisely this which is rejected by modern rationalism. It cannot perceive God as the Bridegroom.

---

40. This is an important area of study and is precisely where the development of doctrine lies, which must be explored further. It is clear that papal statements, such as John Paul II calling the family a bride of Christ, move in this direction.

Saint Paul uses a concise phrase in referring to family life: it is a *"great mystery"* (Eph 5:32).... Husbands and wives thus discover in Christ *the point of reference for their spousal love....* The family itself is the great mystery of God. As the "domestic church", it is the *bride of Christ....* Unfortunately, Western thought, with the development of *modern rationalism,* has been gradually moving away from this teaching.... Within a similar anthropological perspective, the human family is facing the challenge of a *new Manichaeanism,* in which body and spirit are put in radical opposition.... Modern rationalism *does not tolerate mystery.* It does not accept the mystery of man as male and female.... The deep-seated roots of the "great mystery"...have been lost in the modern way of looking at things. The "great mystery" is threatened in us and all around us. (*FC* 19; italics in original)

Unless we successfully challenge this type of thinking and show the reality of the symbolic (i.e., sacramental) value of concrete things, the world will be trapped in a materialist worldview, which is incapable of comprehending or even perceiving the spiritual.

Problems of Legitimacy

The question needs to be raised as to how legitimate this development of the family *as* the domestic church is. It is clear that the use of domestic church as a hermeneutic for the family flows directly from the Church's patrimony and an outgrowth of the reality of baptism. But little solid work has been done in grounding this concept theologically. John Paul II has sketched out a theology for us, but further extensive grounding of this is a necessity. From the initial work that has been done, it is clear that there first needs to be a recovery of the Old Testament understanding of the family, upon which the New Testament understanding is predicated. Here we will find that the family can be defined in its formal aspect in relationship to the covenant as, what I have termed, "the carrier of the covenant." Essential to its grounding is the understanding of baptism (alluded to by John Paul II) and the theology of creation (alluded to by St. Paul), as well as the recovery of the Semitic concept of corporate personality.[41] We must be careful to

41. As seen above, only by such a recovery can passages such as 1 Cor 7 be explained properly.

understand that the reality of the family as the ecclesial unit (i.e., *qua* domestic church) is found in the NT not by the mere existence of the term (which in the Vulgate is problematic); more important, this reality emerges from the NT understanding of baptism. This ecclesial identity is given particular witness by household baptisms.[42] In the New Testament, the family becomes *the sphere of eschatological activity.* That is, the baptized family becomes the place where the activity of the Holy Spirit is present to bring about the salvation of the family members and which is a foretaste of the eschaton. Finally, in our own day, we have witnessed a genuine development of doctrine. Vatican II only speaks about the relationship between the family and church analogously: "in what might be regarded as the domestic church." With the publication of the Catechism, the Church now makes an ontological connection between the two: "The Christian family constitutes a specific revelation and realization of ecclesial communion, and for this reason it can and should be called a domestic church" (2204).

Faulty Appropriation

Because the concept of the domestic church has not yet been adequately grounded theologically, it is exposed to a certain danger of faulty appropriation in the modern context. While it has potential to help rediscover the richness of the family in salvific terms, it may also become a mere theological tag which theologians might use for their own specific purposes but without due regard for its constitutive theological nature. This, in the end, can only seriously wound and deform the authentic nature of the family as the *domestica ecclesia.* Indeed, this is a danger for any theological concept. Sometimes, this faulty appropriation happens through misplaced compassion, as people seek to be inclusive. They urge people to "define family any way you are comfortable with, and behold, you are Church." But is this legitimate? Some find the ecclesial and Christological dimension of family far too restrictive and prefer to see family as principally a sociological unit that can effect its own self-definition. For some the domestic church (as christo-

---

42. Act 11:13ff., 16:15, 16:33; 1 Cor 1:16.

logically or ecclesiologically defined) might appear possibly judgmental. One modern theological writer, who brings up these themes, writes:

> Given the current state of our Church and society, it is easy to see that the guiding beliefs of domestic church might not be universally accepted. In an age where families are broken apart for a variety of reasons, and where many individuals do not experience a healthy family life, it is important to consider how this concept can be well-utilized in the Church to-day.... First there is considerable debate about the meaning of the term "family"... The official teaching of the Roman Catholic Church, for example, insists that the Christian family must spring from Christian marriage.... This raises a question as to what happens in families where kinship springs from a relationship that is not marriage, for example, the single mother who chooses to raise her child outside of marriage. According to social scientists, this would be a family, but in the eyes of the church, would this relationship constitute a domestic church? Some would say no; domestic church occurs in a family formed from Christian marriage. I prefer a definition of domestic church which respects the ideals presented in *Gaudium et spes,* but which recognizes the diversity in which contemporary families are formed....[43]

While one appreciates the legitimate concern over a legalistic approach, the danger here is that it edges close to denying that the family *in Christ,* precisely as domestic church, has any specific constitutive dimensions, or that it is uniquely defined by the created and salvific order. In fact, one can argue that it is only in this salvific identity that the family finds the truth of its being, and this cannot be manipulated but must be received as a gift. Without this safeguard, the idea of the "domestic church" can become a "concept" into which any "content" can be poured: different people or groups can then subjectively decide what meaning they prefer. But this non-objective approach leads inevitably to restructuring the very identity of the family (with implication for the salvific reality), which no longer has any objective essence. Unfortunately, domestic church, if it becomes a tool to use for whatever end one is pursuing, will become, in effect, only an empty label. This

43. Joanne Heaney-Hunter, "Domestic Church: Guiding Beliefs and Daily Practices," in *Christian Marriage and Family: Contemporary Theological and Pastoral Perspectives,* ed. Michael Lawler and William Roberts (Collegeville, Minn.: Liturgical Press, 1996), 60.

approach ends up denying there is a fundamental reality that constitutively transforms a family, giving it a new ontological reality and thereby an essential specificity which is not negotiable. If this objectivity is rejected, then we are no longer concerned with what God has designed the family for, but have rendered it simply a sociological construct, manipulable at will.

Difference can be a good thing and, indeed, is a principle of the created order.[44] But when diversity attacks the constitutive structure of an entity, it cannot be said to participate in that reality. As long as any specific diversity is not contrary to the fundamental structure of the family in Christ, there is no problem. When it is contrary, it becomes destructive of this reality. The legitimate boundaries, necessary to any definition of the domestic church, have received scant attention. But they will be properly defined only when we have fully uncovered the authentic theological foundations on which the family as the domestic church is built. At the heart of the Church is the Person of Christ. To be in Christ, to be part of His Body the Church, is to encounter the salvific power of Christ and to be converted by Him, choosing to be His disciple. To choose Him means to seek to be formed by Him, not as an ideal but in our own concrete historical reality. Surely, any reality which mitigates or is intrinsically opposed to Christ and His expressed will cannot be said to participate in Him. Can the domestic church be construed on any other terms?

CONCLUSION

The term "domestic church" serves as the hermeneutic by which we come to know the truth about marriage and family. Understood aright, the domestic church is the end for which marriage and family were created. The reality, which is attested by the Scripture and the core of Jewish and Christian tradition, is that the family as an instrument of salvation (i.e., its nature as the domestic church) is not a free-floating

---

44. Genesis 1 and 2 show that *hibdil* (i.e., the process of separating out into distinctive creations) is a fundamental principle of creation.

construct awaiting the informing principles either of theologians or of modern secular society. Rather, grounded in the Person of the Word of God, the family has been given a constitutive nature by the Creator such that it is assumed into the salvific plan of God for all humanity. In the Old Testament it functioned as the carrier of the covenant; in the New Covenant, it becomes the sphere of eschatological activity, i.e., the place where the Holy Spirit is active and bringing us into the fuller reality of salvation. In becoming part of His body, our bodies become part of Him. When, in love, we give ourselves bodily to another within a covenantal structure, our two bodies becomes one flesh in Christ, the fruit of which is the procreation of other bodily realities made in the image of God. The mystery of the baptized family is that we are called to be an organic part of the body of Jesus Christ, to participate in His nature, and to be part of His salvific mission to the world. Only here do we find our true identity as individuals, as families, and as the domestic church.

BIBLIOGRAPHY

Acta Synodalia Sacrosanctii Concilii Oecumenicii Vaticani II. Vatican City: 1960–89.

Aland, K., et al. *The Greek New Testament* 2nd ed. Stuttgart: Wurttemberg Bible Society, 1968.

Alonso-Schökel, L. "Marriage Symbols in the Bible." Edited by Joseph Atkinson (unpublished).

Ambrose. *Six Days of Creation.* Translated by John Savage. New York: Fathers of the Church, 1961.

The Analytical Greek Lexicon. London: S. Bagster and Sons, 1908.

Aquinas, Thomas. *Summa Theologiae.* Vol. X. New York: (Blackfriars) McGraw-Hill, 1965.

Arndt, W. F., and F. W. Gingrich, eds. *The Greek-English Lexicon of the New Testament and Other Early Christian Literature.* Chicago: University of Chicago Press, 1960.

Atkinson, J. "Mystery of Water, Mystery of Holiness: An Investigation of the Symbolism of Water in the Old Testament as Background to Understanding Baptism." Unpublished Dissertation. John Paul II Institute for Studies on Marriage and Family, Washington, D.C., 1998.

———. "Family as Domestic Church: Developmental Trajectory, Legitimacy, and Problems of Appropriation." *Theological Studies* 66 (2005): 592–604.

———. "The Foundation of Pauline Thought: An Investigation." In *The Incarnate Word* (forthcoming).

Augustine. *De Dono Perseverantiae.* Patrologia Latina 45.

———. *De Epistolae Nuper in Lucem Prolate.* Edited by J. Divjak. Corpus scriptorum ecclesiasticorum Latinorum, vol. 88. University of Salzburg, 1981.

———. *Enarratio in Psalm 103.* Patrologia Latina 37.

———. *Enarrationes in Psalmos 36.* Patrologia Latina 36.

———. *Epistola 188.* Patrologia Latina 33.

———. *In Joannis Evangelium.* Patrologia Latina 35.

———. *Sermones. Sermones 96, 132, 192, 196, 267,* Patrologia Latina 38; *Sermo 354,* Patrologia Latina 39.

Barclay, William. *Train Up a Child: Educational Ideals in the Ancient World.* Philadelphia: Westminster Press, 1959.

Walter Beyerlin, ed. *Near Eastern Religious Texts Relating to the Old Testament.* Translated by J. Bowden. London: SCM Press, 1978.

Block, David I. "Marriage and Family in Ancient Israel." In *Marriage and Family in the Biblical World,* edited by Ken Campbell. Downers Grove, Ill.: InterVarsity Press, 2003.

Bolle, K.W. "Priest and Priesthood, Israelite." In *New Catholic Encyclopedia,* edited by W. J. McDonald, vol. 11. New York: McGraw-Hill, 1967.

Braude, William G. *The Midrash on Psalms.* Vols. 1 and 2. New Haven, Conn.: Yale University Press, 1959.

Brueggemann, Walter. *Old Testament Theology: An Introduction.* Nashville, Tenn.: Abingdon Press, 2008.

Buber, Martin. "The Question to the Single One." In *The Writings of Martin Buber,* edited by Will Herberg and translated by R. G. Smith. New York: Meridian Books, 1956.

———. *Between Man and Man.* Translated by R. G. Smith. New York: MacMillian, 1965.

Cassuto, Umberto. *A Commentary on the Book of Genesis: From Adam to Noah.* Translated by Israel Abrahams. Jerusalem: Magnes Press, 1961.

———. *The Documentary Hypothesis and the Composition of the Pentateuch.* Translated by Israel Abrahams. Jerusalem: Shalem Press, 2006. (Published in Hebrew as *Torat HaTeudot,* 1941.)

Catechism of the Catholic Church. New York: Catholic Book Publishing Co., 1994.

Causse, A. *Du groupe ethnique à la communauté religieuse. Le problème sociologique de la religion d'Israel.* Paris, 1937.

Childs, Brevard. *Myth and Reality in the Old Testament.* 2nd ed. London: SCM Press, 1962.

Clement of Alexandria. *Stromateis.* Translated by John Ferguson. The Fathers of the Church, vol. 85. Washington, D.C.: The Catholic University of America Press, 1991.

Cohen, Abraham. *Everyman's Talmud.* New York: Schocken Books, 1995.

Cohen, Shaye J. D., ed. *The Jewish Family in Antiquity.* Brown Judaic Studies, vol. 289. Atlanta: Scholars Press, 1993.

Coogan, Michael D., ed. *Stories from Ancient Canaan.* Philadelphia: Westminster Press, 1978.

Cragg, G. R. *The Acts of the Apostles/The Epistle to the Romans.* Vol. 9 of *The Interpreter's Bible,* edited by G. A. Buttrick. New York: Abingdon Press, 1952.

Cranfield, C. B. E. *Romans. A Shorter Commentary.* Grand Rapids, Mich.: Eerdmans, 1985.

———. *A Critical and Exegetical Commentary on the Epistle to the Romans* (ICC). Vol. 2. Edinburgh: Clark, 1989.

Cross, F. L., and E. A. Livingstone. *The Oxford Dictionary of the Christian Church.* 2nd ed. New York: Oxford University Press, 1974.

Cullmann, Oscar. *Baptism in the New Testament.* London: SCM Press, 1950.

Das, A. *Paul, the Law and the Covenant.* Peabody, Mass.: Hendrickson Publishing, 2001.

Davidson, B. *The Analytical Hebrew and Chaldee Lexicon*. London: Samuel Bagster and Sons, 1959.

Davies, Richard N. *Doctrine of the Trinity*. Cincinnati: Granston and Stowe, 1981.

de Fraine, Jean. *Adam and the Family of Man*. New York: Alba House, 1965.

de la Torre, Miguel. *Genesis*. Louisville, Ky.: Westminster John Knox Press, 2011.

de Lubac, Henry. *Sources of Revelation*. Translated by Luke O'Neill. New York: Herder and Herder, 1968.

de Vaux, Roland. *Ancient Israel*. Translated by John. New York: McGraw-Hill, 1961.

————. "The Revelation of the Divine Name YHWH." In *Proclamation and Presence*, edited by John I. Durham and J. Roy Porter. London: SCM Press, 1970.

Dillmann, A. *Genesis: Critically and Exegetically Expounded*. Translated by William B. Stevenson. Vol. 1. Edinburgh: T & T Clark, 1897.

Dinur, Ben-Zion. "Jewish History—Its Uniqueness and Continuity." In *Jewish Society through the Ages,* edited by H. H. Sasson and S. Ettinger. New York: Schocken Books, 1973.

Dozeman, Thomas B. *Commentary on Exodus*. Grand Rapids, Mich.: Eerdmans, 2009.

Driver, S. R. *The Book of Genesis*. Edited by Walter Lock. 3rd ed. Westminster Commentaries. London: Methuen, 1904.

Dubarle, A. M. *Melanges Lebreton*. Recherche de science religieuse, vol. 39. 1951/52.

Dumbrell, W. J. *Creation and Covenant*. Nashville, Tenn.: Thomas Nelson, 1984.

Eberly, Don, ed. *The Faith Factor in Fatherhood: Renewing the Sacred Vocation of Fatherhood*. Lanham, Md.: Lexington Books, 1999.

Eichrodt, Walter. "In the Beginning." In *Israel's Prophetic Heritage: Essays in Honor of James Muilenburg*, edited by B. W. Anderson and W. Harrelson. New York: Harper and Brothers, 1962.

————. *Theology of the Old Testament*. Vol. 1. Translated by J. A. Baker. Philadelphia: Westminster Press, 1960.

————. *Theology of the Old Testament*. Vol. 2. Translated by J. A. Baker. 5th ed. OTL. Philadelphia: Westminster Press, 1967.

Eminyan, M. *Theology of the Family*. Malta: Jesuit Publications, 1994.

Epistle of Barnabas. In *The Apostolic Fathers*, vol. 1. Loeb Classical Library. Reprint ed. Cambridge, Mass.: Harvard University Press, 2003.

Evdokimov, Paul. "*Ecclesia domestica*." *L'Anneau d'Or: Cahiers de spiritualité conjugale et familiale* 107 (1962).

————. "Conjugal Priesthood." In *Marriage and Christian Tradition,* translated by Sr. Agnes Cunningham. Techny, Ill.: Divine Word Publications, 1966.

Fahey, M. A. "The Christian Family as Domestic Church at Vatican II." *Concilium* (Fall 1994/95): 85–92.

Fishbane, Michael. *Text and Texture: Close Readings of Selected Biblical Texts*. New York: Schocken Books, 1979.

————. *Biblical Interpretation in Ancient Israel*. Oxford: Clarendon Press, 1985.

Fitzmeyer, J. A. *Romans: A New Translation with Introduction and Commentary*. Anchor Bible Series 33. New York: Doubleday, 1993.

Flannery, Austin, ed. *Vatican Council II: The Conciliar and Post Conciliar Documents.* Northport, N.Y.: Costello Publishing Company, 1975.

Freedman, H., ed. and trans. *Midrash Rabbah.* Vol. 1: *Genesis.* New York: Soncino Press, 1983.

Gammie, John G. *Holiness in Israel.* Minneapolis: Fortress Press, 1989.

Genesis Rabbah. Translated by Jacob Neusner. Atlanta: Scholars Press, 1985.

Glatzer, Nahum. *The Passover Haggadah.* Rev. ed. New York: Schocken Books, 1969.

Harris, R. L., G. L. Archer, and B. K. Waltke, eds. *Theological Wordbook of the Old Testament.* Chicago: Moody Press, 1980.

Hammond, N. G. L., and H. H. Scullard, eds. *The Oxford Classical Dictionary.* 2nd ed. Oxford: Clarendon Press, 1984.

Heaney-Hunter, Joanne. "Domestic Church: Guiding Beliefs and Daily Practices." In *Christian Marriage and Family: Contemporary Theological and Pastoral Perspectives,* edited by Michael Lawler and William Roberts. Collegeville, Minn.: Liturgical Press, 1996.

Heidel, Alexander. *The Babylonian Genesis.* 2nd ed. Chicago: University of Chicago Press, 1963.

———. *The Gilgamesh and Old Testament Parallels.* Chicago: University of Chicago Press, 1963.

Henry, Matthew. *Commentary on the Whole Bible.* Vol. 1: *Genesis to Deuteronomy.* Old Tappan, N.J.: Fleming H. Revell Company, n.d.

Hertz, J. H., ed. *The Pentateuch and Haftorahs.* 2nd ed. London: Soncino Press, 1977.

Hertzberg, Arthur, ed. *Judaism.* New York: George Braziller, 1962.

Heschel, Abraham. *The Sabbath.* New York: Farrar, Strauss and Young, 1951.

———. *The Prophets.* Philadelphia: Jewish Publication Society of America, 1962.

Hirsch, Samuel Raphael. *The Pentateuch: Translated and Explained.* Vol. 1: *Genesis;* vol. 3: *Leviticus.* 2nd ed. Translated by I. Levy. Gateshead, England: Judaica Press, 1976.

Hodgson, Robert, Jr. "Holiness." In *The Anchor Bible Dictionary,* vol. 3, edited by D. N. Freedman. New York: Doubleday, 1992.

Houghton, Hugh. *Augustine's Text of John: Patristic Citations and Latin Gospel Manuscripts.* New York: Oxford University Press, 2008.

Irenaeus, *Against Heresies.* Edited by Alexander Roberts, James Donaldson, and A. Cleveland Coxe. Translated by Alexander Roberts and William Rambaut. Ante-Nicene Fathers, vol. 1. Buffalo, N.Y.: Christian Literature Publishing Co., 1885.

James, E. O. *The Worship of the Sky-God.* New York: Oxford University Press, 1963.

Jeremias, Joachim. *Infant Baptism in the First Four Centuries.* Translated by David Cairns. Philadelphia: Westminster Press, 1962.

Jerome. *Ad Paulam Epistol (Ep. 30).* Patroliga Latina 22.

———. *Letter 107 (Ad Laetam).* In Nicene and Post-Nicene Fathers 6. Reprint ed. Grand Rapids, Mich.: Eerdmans, 1989.

———. *Letter 107.* Patrologia Latina 22.

John Chrysostom. *Homiliae VI in Epistolam ad Titum.* Patrologia Graeca 62.

————. *Homiliae XXII In Epistolam Ad Ephesios*. Patrologia Graeca 62.

————. *Homiliae XXIV Epistolam Ad Ephesios*. Patrologia Graeca 62.

————. *Homiliae XLIV in Epistolam primam 1 ad Corinthios*. Patrologia Graeca 61.

————. *Homiliae in Epistolam primam ad Timotheum* Patrologia Greaca 62.

————. *Homiliae in Genesin*. Patrologia Graeca 53.

————. Homilies on Ephesians. Nicene and Post-Nicene Fathers, series 1, vol. 13. Edited by Philip Schaff. Peabody, Mass.: Hendrickson, 1994.

————. Homilies on First Corinthians. Nicene and Post-Nicene Fathers, series 1, vol. 12. Edited by Philip Schaff. Peabody, Mass.: Hendrickson, 1994.

    . *Homilies on Genesis*. Translated by Robert C. Hill. The Fathers of the Church, vol. 74. Washington, D.C.: The Catholic University of America Press, 1985.

————. *Homilies on Timothy*. Nicene and Post-Nicene Fathers, series 1, vol. 13. Translated by James Tweed. Edited by Philip Schaff. Peabody, Mass.: Hendrickson, 1994.

————. *Homilies on Titus*. Nicene and Post-Nicene Fathers, series 1, vol 13. Edited by Philip Schaff. Peabody, Mass.: Hendrickson, 1994.

————. *Sermones IX In Genesim*. Patrologia Graeca 54:607.

John Paul I. "The Christian Family: A Community of Love." *L'Osservatore Romano*, September 28, 1978.

John Paul II. "La Chiesa Rinnova il Dialogo con il mondo per Favorire La Comprensione Tra I Popol." Address, December 22, 1981. In *Insegnamenti di Giovanni Paolo II, 4/2*. 1981.

————. *The Original Unity of Man and Woman: Catechesis on the Book of Genesis*. Boston: Daughters of Saint Paul, 1981.

————. *Letter to Families*. Boston: Pauline Books and Media, 1994.

————. *Theology of the Body*. Translated by Michael Waldstein. Boston: Pauline Books and Media, 1997.

————. *Familiaris Consortio*. Boston: Pauline Books and Media, 1998.

Johnson, R. Aubrey. *Sacral Kingship in Israel*. Cardiff: University of Wales, 1955.

Justin Martyr. *Dialogue with Trypho*. Translated by Thomas B. Falls. Revised by Thomas P. Halton. Selections from the Fathers of the Church, vol. 3. Washington, D.C.: The Catholic University of America Press, 2003.

Kaiser, W. C. *Toward Old Testament Ethics*. Grand Rapids, Mich.: Zondervan, 1983.

Kaminsky, J. Review of *Contesting Conversion: Genealogy, Circumcision, and Identity in Ancient Judaism and Christianity* by Matthew Thiessen. *Studies in Christian-Jewish Relations* 6 (2011).

Kaplan, Aryeh. *Waters of Eden: The Mystery of the Mikvah*. New York: NCSY Union of Orthodox Jewish Congregations of America, 1976.

Kaufman, Michael. *Love, Marriage, and Family in Jewish Law and Tradition*. Northvale, N.J.: Jason Aronson Inc., 1996.

Kaufmann, Yehezkel. *The Religion of Israel: From Its Beginnings to the Babylonian Exile*. Translated by Moshe Greenberg. Chicago: University of Chicago Press, 1960.

Kelle, Brad E. *Hosea 2: Metaphor and Rhetoric in Historical Perspective.* Academia Biblica. Atlanta: Society of Biblical Literature, 2005.

Koehler, Ludwig, and Walter Baumgartner. *The Hebrew and Aramaic Lexicon of the Old Testament.* Vol. 2. Translated and edited by M. E. J. Richardson. New York: E. J. Brill, 1995.

Köstenberger, Andreas J. *God, Marriage, and Family.* Wheaton, Ill.: Crossway Books, 2004.

Kramer, Samuel Noah. *The Sumerians: Their History, Culture, and Character.* Chicago: University of Chicago Press, 1963.

Levine, Baruch. *Leviticus: The Traditional Hebrew Text with the New JPS Translation.* JPS Torah Commentary Series. Philadelphia: Jewish Publication Society, 1994.

Lewis, C. S. *Beyond Personality.* London: Geoffrey Bles, 1952.

———. *Mere Christianity.* San Francisco: Harper Collins, 2001.

Limburg, James. *Hosea-Micah in Interpretation.* Atlanta: John Knox Press, 1988.

Lohfink, Norbert. *Theology of the Pentateuch: Themes of the Priestly Narrative and Deuteronomy.* Translated by L. M. Maloney. Minneapolis: Fortress Press, 1994.

Lonergan, Bernard J. F. *Method in Theology.* New York: Herder and Herder, 1972.

Maly, Eugene H. "Genesis." In *Jerome Biblical Commentary,* edited by Raymond E. Brown, Joseph A. Fitzmyer, and Roland E. Murphy. Englewood Cliffs, N.J.: Prentice-Hall, 1968.

Marsh, John. *Saint John.* New York: Penguin Books, 1983.

Martin, F. *Sacred Scripture: The Disclosure of the Word.* Ave Maria, Fl.: Sapientia Press, 2006.

May, G. *Creatio ex Nihilo: The Doctrine of "Creation out of Nothing" in Early Christian Thought.* Translated by A. S. Worrall. Edinburgh: T & T Clark, 2004.

May, Herbert G. "Individual Responsibility and Retribution." *Hebrew Union College Annual* 32 (1961).

McKenzie, J. L. "Royal Messianism." *Catholic Biblical Quarterly* 19 (1957).

McKeown, James. *Genesis.* Grand Rapids, Mich.: Eerdmans, 2008.

Meeks, W. A. *The First Urban Christians.* New Haven, Conn.: Yale Press, 1983.

Merkley, Paul. *The Greek and Hebrew Origins of Our Idea of History.* Toronto Studies in Theology, vol. 32. Queenston, Ont.: Edwin Mellen Press, 1987.

Midrash on Psalms. Vol 1. Translated by William G. Braude. New Haven, Conn.: Yale University Press, 1959.

Milgrom, Jacob. *Leviticus 1–16.* New York: Doubleday, 1991.

Miller, John W. *Biblical Faith and Fathering: Why We Call God "Father."* Mahwah, N.J.: Paulist Press, 1990.

Miller, Yisroel. *In Search of the Jewish Woman.* New York: Feldheim Publishers, 1984.

Moffatt, J. *The Epistle of Paul to the Romans.* New York: Harper Row, 1932.

Moltman, Jurgens. *God in Creation.* Translated by M. Kohl. Minneapolis: Fortress Press, 1993.

Morgenstern, Julian . "The Sources of the Creation Story—Genesis 1:1–2:4." *American Journal of Semitic Languages and Literatures* 36 (1920).

Murtonen, A. *Hebrew in Its West Semitic Setting: A Comparative Survey of Non-Masoretic Hebrew Dialects and Traditions: A Comparative Lexicon.* E. J. Brill: Leiden, Netherlands, 1986.

Orlinksy, O. *Genesis: The NJV Translation.* New York: Harper and Row, 1966.

Ouellet, Marc Cardinal. *Divine Likeness: Toward a Trinitarian Anthropology of the Family.* Grand Rapids, Mich.: Eerdman's, 2006.

Pedersen, Johannes. *Israel, Its Life and Culture I–II.* London: Oxford University Press, 1926; reprint, 1954.

Petersen, J. M. "House-Churches in Rome." *Vigiliae Christianae* 23, no. 1 (1969): 272.

Pleins, J. David. *The Social Visions of the Hebrew Bible.* Louisville, Ky.: Westminster John Knox Press, 2001.

Porter, J. R. "The Legal Aspects of the Concept of 'Corporate Personality' in the Old Testament." *Vetus Testamentum* 15 (1965): 361–80.

Pritchard, James B. *Ancient Near Eastern Texts.* 2nd ed. Princeton, N.J.: Princeton University Press, 1955.

Rahner, Karl. *Theological Investigations.* Vol. 4. Translated by Kevin Smith. New York: Crossroad, 1982.

Ratzinger, Cardinal Joseph. *Biblical Interpretation in Crisis.* Edited by R. Neuhaus. Grand Rapids, Mich.: Eerdmans, 1989. Revised ed., edited by J. Granados. Grand Rapids, Mich.: Eerdmans, 2008.

———. *In the Beginning…A Catholic Understanding of the Story of Creation and the Fall.* Translated by B. Ramsey. Grand Rapids, Mich.: Eerdmans, 1995.

———. "On the Collaboration of Men and Women in the Church and in the World." Letter, May 31, 2004.

Ringgren, Helmut. *Israelite Religion.* Translated by D. E. Green. Philadelphia: Fortress Press, 1966.

Robinson, H. Wheeler. *The Christian Doctrine of Man.* Edinburgh: T & T Clark, 1911.

———. "The Hebrew Conception of Corporate Personality." In *Werden und Wesen des Alten Testaments.* Beihefte zur Zeitschrift für die alttestamentliche Wissenschaft 66. 1936.

———. *The Cross in the Old Testament.* London: SCM Press, 1955.

Rogerson, J. W. "The Hebrew Conception of Corporate Personality: A Re-Examination." *Journal of Theological Studies* 21 (1970): 1–16.

———. *Anthropology and the Old Testament.* Atlanta: John Knox Press, 1978.

Routledge, Robin. *Old Testament Theology: A Thematic Approach.* Downers Grove, Ill.: InterVarsity Press Academic, 2008.

Rowley, H. H. *The Faith of Israel.* Philadelphia: Westminster Press, 1956.

Sarna, Nahum M. *Understanding Genesis.* New York: McGraw-Hill Book Company, 1966.

Schaeder, Grete. *The Hebrew Humanism of Martin Buber.* Translated by N. J. Jacobs. Detroit: Wayne State University Press, 1973.

Schillebeeckx, Edward. *Marriage: Human Reality and Saving Mystery*. Translated by N. D. Smith. New York: Sheed and Ward, 1965.

Scola, A. *The Nuptial Mystery*. Grand Rapids, Mich.: Eerdmans's, 2005.

Selkin, C. "Exegesis and Identity: The Hermeneutics of Miqwa'ôt in the Greco-Roman Period." Ph.D. diss. Duke University, 1993.

Simpson, D. P., ed. *Cassell's New Latin Dictionary*. New York: Funk and Wagnalls, 1959.

Soggin, J. Alberto. *Israel in the Biblical Period: Institutions, Festivals, Ceremonies, Rituals*. Translated by J. Bowden. New York: T & T Clark, 2001.

Speiser, E. A. *Genesis*. Vol. 1 of *Anchor Bible*. Garden City, N.Y.: Doubleday, 1964.

Splett, Jörg. "Symbol." In *Sacramentum Mundi*, edited by Karl Rahner. Vol. 6. New York: Herder and Herder, 1970.

Stauffer, E. "Zur Kindertaufe in der Ur kirche." *Deutsches Pfarrerblatt* 49 (1949).

Targum Neofiti 1: Genesis. Edited by K. Cathcart, et al. Translated by M. McNamara. Vol. 1A of *The Aramaic Bible: The Targums*. Collegeville, Minn.: Liturgical Press, 1992.

Tasker, David. *Ancient Near Eastern Literature and the Hebrew Scriptures about the Fatherhood of God*. Studies in Biblical Literature, vol. 69. Washington, D.C.: Peter Lang, 2004.

Thiessen, Matthew. *Contesting Conversion: Genealogy, Circumcision, and Identity in Ancient Judaism and Christianity*. Oxford: Oxford University Press, 2011.

Tigay, Jeffrey H. *The Evolution of the Gilgamesh Epic*. Philadelphia: University of Pennsylvania Press, 1982.

Tsumura, David T. *Creation and Destruction: A Reappraisal of the Chaoskampf Theory in the Old Testament*. Winona Lake, Ind.: Eisenbrauns, 2005.

Vanhoye, Albert. *Old Testament Priests and the New Priest according to the New Testament*. Translated by J. B. Orchard. Studies in Scripture. Petersham, Mass.: St. Bede's Publications, 1986.

Vitz, Paul. "The Fatherhood of God: Support from Psychology." *Josephinum Journal of Theology* 9, no. 1 (Winter/Spring 2002).

von Balthasar, Hans Urs. "Ephesians 5:21–33 and Humanae Vitae: A Meditation." In *Christian Married Love*, edited by Raymond Dennehy. San Francisco: Ignatius Press, 1981.

von Rad, Gerhard. *Old Testament Theology*. Vol. 1: *The Theology of Israel's Historical Traditions*; vol. 2: *The Theology of Israel's Prophetic Traditions*. Translated by D. M. G. Stalker. New York: Harper and Row, 1962, 1965.

———. *Genesis*. Philadelphia: Westminster Press, 1972.

Wallace, Howard N. *The Eden Narrative*. Atlanta: Scholars Press, 1985.

Weber, Max. *Ancient Judaism*. Translated and edited by H. H. Gerth and D. Martindale. Glencoe, Ill.: Free Press, 1952.

Wellhausen, Julius. *Prolegomena to the History of Israel*. Edinburgh: A & C Black, 1885. Reprint, edited by Harry W. Gilmer. Scholars Press Reprints and Translation series. Atlanta: Scholars Press, 1994.

Wenham, Gordon J. *Genesis 1-15.* Word Biblical Commentary, vol. 1. Waco, Tex.: Word Books, 1987.

———. "Sanctuary Symbolism in the Garden of Eden Story." In *"I Studied Inscriptions from before the Flood": Ancient Near Eastern, Literary, and Linguistic Approaches to Genesis 1-11,* edited by Richard S. Hess and David Toshio Tsumura. Winona Lake, Ind.: Eisenbrauns, 1994.

Westermann, Claus. *Creation.* Translated by J. J. Scullion. Philadelphia: Fortress Press, 1981.

———. *Genesis 1-11 : A Commentary.* Translated by John J. Scullion. Minneapolis: Augsburg Publishing House, 1984.

Wilson, Peter. *Man the Promising Primate: The Conditions of Human Evolution.* 2nd ed. New Haven, Conn.: Yale University Press, 1983.

Wojtyla, K. *Love and Responsibility.* Translated by H. T. Willetts. London: William Collins and Sons, 1982.

Wright, G. E. "Theology as Recited." In *Old Testament Issues,* edited by Samuel Sandmel. New York: Harper and Row, 1968.

Wyschogrod, Michael. *The Body of Faith: God in the People of Israel.* New York: Rowman and Littlefield, 1983.

Zeitlin, Irving M. *Ancient Judaism.* Glasgow: Polity Press, 1984.

SCRIPTURAL INDEXES

OLD TESTAMENT

Genesis
1: 7n12, 35n8, 40n30,
   58n86, 60, 70, 79,
   139n28, 150, 286n47
1.1: 33, 36n11–12, 40n30,
   41, 63n93, 65, 80, 228
1.1–2.3: 65
1.1–3: 228
1.2: 39n27, 79, 228n18
1.9: 46
1.10: 144n42
1.11: 63n93
1.21: 46
1.24: 46
1.26: 7n12, 52–55, 56n79,
   171
1.26–27: 53
1.27: 47, 54–55, 120
1.28: 50, 53, 63
1–2: 40n30, 70, 148n58
1–3: 45, 58n85, 148–49,
   151–52, 159
1–11: 21n4, 33n1, 40nn29–
   30, 42n38, 59n88, 81n6
2: xi, 6n11, 7n12, 55n75,
   56n81, 58–60, 147, 152,
   155, 157, 159, 286
2.1–25: 156
2.2: 151
2.3: 135, 136n19
2.4: 46, 65
2.7: 46, 170, 173, 218n52
2.8: 59
2.11: 59
2.12: 59

2.15: 153, 155
2.18: 59, 170
2.21: 83n10, 170
2.22: 60, 170n38
2.23: 170, 203n8
2.24: 54n73, 171, 259
2.20–23: 57
2.27: 75
3: 40n31, 70, 152n69, 153,
   246
3.8: 156
3.15: 204
5.1–32: 75n135
10.1–32: 75n135
10.32: 79
11.10–32: 75n135
12: 44n43, 202, 204, 216
12–17: 79
12.1–3: 71, 204n11
12.1–5: 80
12.3: 80, 81n5, 82, 123, 124,
   205n14, 216n49, 229
12.5: 85n15
14: 172, 222
14.17: 222
14.18: 222
14.18–20: 172
14.19–20: 222–23
15: 62, 82, 83, 86n17, 118,
   205, 211, 216n50, 217
15.1–21: 80
15.2: 82
15.4: 83
15.5: 82, 83
15.5–6: 217

15.8: 235
15.8–9: 83
15.9–18: 99
15.12–14: 83
15.12–16: 73n126
17: 85n16, 86n17, 107n37,
   117, 235
17.1–27: 80
17.9: 120n63
17.10: 84, 85n14, 120n63
17.10–11: 84, 85, 122
17.12: 85n26, 249
17.13: 85
17.14: 85, 118, 235
17.23: 85n15, 249
18.19: 86, 87
22: 99n15, 202
29.14: 172
35.23–26: 75n135
36.1–43: 75n135
45.18: 249
45.19: 249
46.8–26: 75n135

Exodus
2.1–10: 109
2.24–25: 35n7
3.5: 136, 136n19
3.7–8: 35n7
4.22: 133
4.22–23: 129
7.10: 144n42
10.2: 94
10.21–29: 125
10.23: 125

Exodus (*cont.*)
11.9: 125
12.16: 136n19
12.25: 155
12.26–27: 96, 126
13: 114
13.2: 114
13.5: 155n78
13.8: 94, 98
13.14: 94, 96, 115
13.15: 114
19.1, 2a: 151
19.5: 22n7, 81n7, 205n15, 213
19.5–6: 205n15
19.6: 136
20: 140
20–23: 167
20.3: 130n4
20.8–11: 93n3
20.12: 95
23.14–17: 95n6
24.15b–18: 151
25.11: 59
25.8: 156
26.33: 136n19
28.2: 136n19
28.9: 59
28.35: 136n19
29.37: 136n19, 178
30.16: 155n78
30.25: 136n19
31.13–17: 84n12
31.16: 84n12, 136
31.17: 94, 140
31.16: 84n12, 136
33.12–21: 35n7
34.6–7: 35n7
34.14: 22
34.21: 93
34.28: 95
35.2: 93n5

Leviticus
2.10: 137n19
9–26: 141
11.44–45: 137
11.32: 178
12: 109, 236

12.1–8: 109
15: 19, 144n41, 236
15.19: 109
15.19–24: 144n41
15.25: 144n41
15.31: 109, 139
16: 139n28
16.33: 136n19
17–26: 136, 140
18.2: 140
18.3: 140
18.19: 141
18.20: 140
19.2: 137n21, 140
20: 141
20.7: 140
20.9: 141n33
20.26: 137n21
21.1–9: 169
21.8: 137n21, 140, 180n65
21.15: 180n65
23.4: 136n19
26.12: 156
27.30: 136n19

Numbers
1.1–2.34: 205
3.7–8: 155n78
4.23: 156n78
4.30: 155n78
4.47: 155n78
6.8: 136n19
8.11: 155n78
8.19ff: 155n78
11.7: 59
15.32–36: 93

Deuteronomy
1.39: 249
4.19: 22n7
4.8–9: 94
5.6: 140
5.7: 130n4
6: 96n11
6.1–5: 107n37
6.4: 54n73, 88
6.5: 88
6.7–9: 88
6.20: 97

7.6: 136n19
14.1: 129
14.2: 136
16.16: 94
17.14–20: 108n41, 275n12
18.15: 212, 212n39
23.14 (Hebr. 23.15): 156n82
23.18: 27
24.16: 178, 179
30.6: 237
32: 106
32.6: 129, 133

Joshua
4.6–7: 96
7: 166, 177, 179
7.1: 177–79
7.1–26: 178
7.11: 177, 179
7.12: 178
7.13: 178
7.15: 178
7.24–26: 177
7.25: 179
7.26: 179
22.26: 154

1 Samuel
8.7: 206n18
22.16: 248
22.19: 249

2 Samuel
6.6–7: 138
7.13–14: 206n18

2 Kings
10.11: 213n40
14.26: 122n72

1 Chronicles
23.27–28: 155n78
26.30: 155n78
28.20: 155n78

2 Chronicles
23.6: 136n19

Ezra
10.11: 20n3

Nehemiah
11.1: 136n19

Psalms
2.6: 136n19
3.4: 136n19
11.4: 136n19
30.10: 122n72
36: 278, 280
36.1–2: 278n19
46.40: 158
51: 38
51.10: 36n12
54.6: 61, 122n72
78.5–7: 90n28
87.1: 136n19
103: 55n77
103.4: 77
104: 56n77
110: 222n4, 223n6, 224
110.1: 223n6
148.5: 36n12
139: 297

Ecclesiasticus
25.1: 288

Isaiah
1.2: 130n5
9.6: 223n8
11.1: 207nn23–24
11.6: 223n8
28.16: 158n93

40.3: 227n15
43.1: 36n13
45.7: 41n35
48.6–7: 36n12
51.1–2: 175n51
52.13–53.12: 275n12
53: 207n22
54.5: 130
64.8: 130n5
65.7: 36n12

Jeremiah
2.14: 52n68
4.4: 236
4.23–26: 42n39
17.21: 93
26.1: 40
27.1: 40
28.1: 40
31: 214
31.22: 36n12
31.31: 202, 214n47, 224
31.31–32: 215
31.32: 130
49.34: 40

Ezekiel
16.8, 9: 145n48
21.30 (Hebr. 21.35): 36n13
28.13, 15: 36n13
28.13–14: 152n68
28.14: 152n68
34: 207
34.2–4: 207n20
34.11: 207
37.24: 207

44.14, 16: 155n78
47: 158
47.9: 158
47.11–12: 158

Hosea
1.2–9: 131
1.9: 214
1–3: 191
1–9: 212
2: 213–14
2.2 (Hebr. 2.4): 213n42
2.19–20: 214n45
2.21: 214n44
3.3–5: 214n46
3.5: 207n24
11: 191
11.1: 130

Joel
4.8: 158

Amos
3.2: 81n7

Zechariah
2.12: 136n20
14.8: 158

Malachi
2.14–15: 107n37
3.17: 96n9
3.23–24 MT (ET 4.5–6): 95
3.24: 95

NEW TESTAMENT

Matthew
1: 199n4, 200n7
1.1: 77, 199n3
3.2: 227
3.11: 227
5.17: 10n16, 15nn7–8, 194,
    212
5.17–18: 198
5.27: 211n35

5.28: 211n35
5.31: 211n35
5.32: 211n35
5.34: 211n35
5.38: 211n35
5.39: 211n35
5.43: 211n35
5.44: 211n35
10.34–37: 201

13.52: 206n17
18. 1–5: 89n24
18.20: 295, 296
25.24–30: 275

Luke
1.41: 254n61
3: 199n4, 200n7
3.34: 210n31

Luke (*cont.*)
8.43: 138n27
9.31: 125–26
14.26: 225n13
24.27: 15n7
24.49: 229

John
1: 53n71
1.1: 41, 55n75, 56n77
1.1–14: 246
1.21: 212n39
1.3: 41, 43n41
3.1–8: 238
3.5: 253, 258
4.14: 228n17
4.22: 79, 205n15
7.38–39: 228
10.11: 207, 288
12.24: 202, 295n57
13.34: 137n23
14.27: 289
16.7: 229
16.13: 229
19.19: 207n22
20.22–23: 230

Acts
1.5: 229
2.38–41: 82n9
2.39: 82n9, 229, 240
2.41: 232
8.36–38: 258
9.2: 193
9.4: 221
9.5: 207n26, 230
10.1–48: 269
11: 195
11.14: 186n79, 238n30, 239
11.44: 238n30
11.48: 238n30
15.7–8: 216n49
16: 9, 232, 243, 258
16.3: 110
16.11–15: 251
16.14–15: 239, 243
16.15: 186n79, 238n30, 269, 322n42

16.25–40: 243
16.30–34: 251
16.31: 186, 239, 244
16.31–34: 269
16.33: 239, 322
16.33–34: 238n30
18.2: 264
18.8: 238n30, 239, 269

Romans
3.28: 211n34
4: 210, 216
4.3: 217
4.9–16: 217
4.16: 8, 72n120, 78, 86n18, 210n30, 216, 219n55
5.8: 246n39
6: 218, 231, 232, 258
6.3: 258
6.3–4: 233
6.4: 233, 253
6. 5–6: 258
6.6: 233
6.8: 233
8.14: 134n16
8.15: 86n17
8.19: 134n16
9.4: 86n17
11: 14, 86n18, 197, 202
11.15: 216n49
11.17: 209, 212
11.17–18: 197n1
11.24: 15, 86n18, 194n2
11.25–29: 14n3
16.3–5: 262
16.5: 266, 296
16.25–26: 15n7

1 Corinthians
1.16: 186n79, 238n30, 239, 269, 322n42
5.5: 169n32
5.7: 126
6.7: 281
7: 246, 247, 257, 259, 321n41
7.10: 160n94, 169n32, 269
7.10–12: 243
7.12: 209, 318
7.12–16: 257

7.14: 186, 240n32, 244, 260, 297
7.15: 245
10.17: 219
11.3: 100n17, 286n47
12: 230n21
12.12: 230
12.12–13: 219n54
12.12–27: 166n19
12.27: 30, 220, 221n1
13.27: 261n69
16.15: 238n30, 269
16.16: 266
16.19: 264

2 Corinthians
3.14–16: 15n7
5.17: 159n94, 193, 231, 233
13.5: 232n24

Galatians
2.16: 217n51
2.20: 194n4, 231, 233, 258
3.6: 217
3.7: 218
3.16: 202, 204n11, 219n53
3.26: 134n16
3.29: xvi, 8, 15, 210n30, 216, 219n55
4.4: 77, 194n2
4.5: 86n17, 134n16
4.6: 134n16
5.6–10: 287
5.9: 169n32
6.16: 221

Ephesians
1.5: 86n17
1.10: 233n26
1.22: 100n17
1.22–23: 219n54
1.23: 231
2.11–12: 194n2
2.19: 103n26, 287
4.13: 231
4.15: 100n17
5: 133, 145n51, 233n25, 292, 317n37, 319
5.22: 108n41, 209

5.23: 100n17
5.30: 220, 221
5.32: 159n94, 309, 315,
    317, 321
6.2: 95
6.4: 257
6.5–8: 285

Philippians
2.12: 187n81, 257n64

Colossians
1.15–20: 204
1.18: 100n17
2.10: 100n17
2.11: 123n73
2.11–12: 236, 237, 250n47,
    251n50
2.12: 237
4.15: 265

1 Timothy
287
2.1: 60
3: 286n46
3.1–4: 285, 287n49
3.1–5: 103n26
3.4: 269

2 Timothy
1.5: 110
3.15: 110

Titus
2.2–5: 288

Philemon
1.1–2: 265

Hebrews
182n70, 222–24

1.1–14: 54n74
7: 172, 182n70, 218n53
7.2: 222n5
7.3: 223n7
7.5–6: 223
7.7: 224
7.5–6: 223
7.9–10: 172, 224
7.11: 224n11
11.7: 269

2 Peter
1.4: 231n22

Revelation
12.9: 204n11

HEBREW WORDS

אָדָם-'ādām (man, human being, Adam), 47, 52, 57, 60, 170, 170nn37–38, 173

אֲדָמָה-'ădāmāh (land), 80, 153n70, 205n14

אַדְמַת־קֹדֶשׁ-'admat qōdesh (holy ground), 136

אָהֵב-'āhēb (to love), 88

אוֹת-'ōt (sign), 85n14, 122

אוֹת־בְּרִית-'ōt b'rit (sign of the covenant), 85n14, 122

אֶחָד-'ehād (one), 53, 54n73, 61, 88, 171

אֵל עֶלְיוֹן-'ēl 'elyon (Most High God), 222

אֱלֹהִים-'elohim (God/gods), 33, 47, 52, 54, 60, 63, 151, 170n37, 228n18

אֶרֶץ-'āretz (earth), 33, 39n27, 40n30, 41, 228n18

אֵשֶׁת זְנוּנִים-'ēshet z'nunim (wife of fornication/prostitute), 131

אֹתָם-'ōtām (them), 47, 63

בְּ-b' (in), 38

בֵּית-bêt (house), 80, 87, 214n47, 248, 249, 250

בְּךָ-b'hā (in you), 80, 123, 205n14, 216n49

בָּנָה-bānāh / וַיִּבֶן-vayyiben (to build), 59, 60, 61, 170

בְּעָלַיִך-bōʿălayik (your husband), 130

בָּעַלְתִּי-bā 'altî (I married), 130

בָּרָא-bārā' (he created), 33, 36, 37, 38, 47

בְּרֵאשִׁית-b'rē'shît (in the beginning), 33, 36, 38, 39, 40, 42, 80

בְּרִית-b'rit (covenant), 85n14, 122, 202, 214

בָּשָׂר אֶחָד-bāsār 'ehād (one flesh), 61, 171

גּוֹי קָדוֹשׁ-goy kādōsh (holy nation), 136

גַּן-gan (garden), 153, 156

הִבְדִּיל-hibdîl (to separate), 46n49, 324n44

זָכָר-zāchār (remember/male), 47, 84, 120, 249

זְנוּת-z'nût (fornication), 131n7

חֵרֶם-hērem (ban), 178

טָמֵא-tāmē' (unclean), 109

טַפְּכֶם-tapp'hem (your children), 249, 250n44

יְבָרֶךְ-y'bāreh (he blessed), 63, 136

יָדַע-yāda' (knew), 87

יוֹנֵק-yônēq (infants), 249

כָּבוֹד-kābōd (glory), 96n9

לֹא-lō' (not), 57, 131, 213nn41–42

לֹא עַמִּי-lō' 'ammî (not my people), 131, 213n42

לֹא רֻחָמָה-lō' ruhāmāh (not pitied), 213n41

לְמַעַן-l'ma'an (for the sake of), 87

מִזְרָע-mizrā' (sow), 213n40

מְעוֹלֵל-mē'olēl (children), 249

מִשְׁפָּחָה-*misp*ʰ*hoṯ* (family), 80, 205n14
מִתְהַלֵּךְ-*mitallēk* (to walk), 156
נִבְרְכוּ-*nibr*ʰ*hû* (shall be blessed), 80, 81, 123, 205n14
נִכְרְתָה-*nikr*ʰ*tah* (cut off), 118
נְקֵבָה-*n*ʰ*qēbāh* (female), 85, 120
סְגֻלָּה-*s*ʰ*gullāh* (special possession), 22n7, 81n7, 205n15
עֲבֹדָה-*ʿăbōdā*ʰ (work), 153, 154, 155
עֵזֶר-*ʿēzer* (helper), 57, 59, 61, 122n72
עַמִּי-*ʿammî* (my people) 22n7, 131, 213n42
פְּרוּ-*p*ʰ*rû* (be fruitful), 63, 64
צֶלֶם-*ṣelem* (image), 47, 52, 53, 54
צֵלָע-*tzēlāʿ* (rib), 60, 170
קֹדֶשׁ-*qōdesh* (holy), 136, 139, 156
רְבוּ-*r*ʰ*bû* /rbw (multiply), 63, 64

רוּחַ אֱלֹהִים-*rûaḥ ʾelōhîm* (Spirit of God), 228n18
שָׁמַר-*shāmar* (to keep), 153, 154, 155
שָׁנַנ-*shānan* (to sharpen), 88
שִׁנַּנְתָּם-*shinnantām* (inculcate), 88
תַּדְשֵׁא-*tadshē*ʾ (sprouts forth), 46
תֹהוּ וָבֹהוּ-*ṯōhû vābōhû* (inchoate mass), 39n27, 41, 79n2
תְהוֹם-*t*ʰ*hôm* (primordial deep), 37n17, 228n18
תּוֹלְדֹת-*tôldôt* (generations), xii, 46, 65, 70, 71, 74, 75, 76, 79, 84n13, 198, 199, 208
תּוֹצֵא-*tôtzē*ʾ (brings forth) 46
תַּרְדֵּמָה-*tardēmah* (deep sleep), 59n89, 61, 62, 83n10

GREEK WORDS

ἁγίοις (holy ones), 256
ἀνακεφαλαιώσασθαι (to sum up), 233n26
ἀνήρηται (has taken upon himself), 286n47
ἀρχὴ (beginning), 285n44, 286, 290, 292, 294–95
δικαίωσις (justified), 210
ἑνός (one), 219n53
ζωὴν αἰώνιον (eternal life), 228
ἡγίασται (sanctified), 259n67
καινὴ κτίσις (new creation), 233

κατα (according to), 262-67, 288n50
οἶκος (house/household), 239, 241, 248-50, 261, 262, 265–66
πατρὸς (father), 224
πίστευσον (believe), 239
πληρῶσαι (fulfill), 10n16, 194
προφήτης (prophet), 212n39
σπέρματι (seed), 219n53
τέκνοῖς (children), 240
τύπος (type), 223

INDEX OF NAMES

Adam. *See General Index*

Alonso-Schokel, L., 148, 149n60, 152

Ambrose, 286, 287, 291

Anus, 28

Apsu, 44, 104

Aquinas, xv, 101, 102n23, 121

Aranzahas, 28

Aristotle, xv, 189n87

Augustine, xii, 2, 11, 13, 55n77, 197, 266, 271–83, 289, 298, 302, 306, 308–11

Ba'al, 23–24, 27–28, 132

Barclay, William, 88 , 89nn24–26, 90

Bede, 298, 300

Berger, David, 14n5

Beyerlin, Walter, 20n2

Block, Daniel I, 107-8nn39–40, 122n71

Bolle, K. W., 99n15, 102n25

Braude, William G., 223n6

Brueggemann, Walter, 34, 35n7, 42n39

Brunner, E., 47n54

Brunner, Hellmut, 19

Buber, Martin, 188–91

Cassuto, Umberto, 21nn4–5, 40nn30–31, 52n67, 59n88, 74–75, 149n60, 152n67, 153n70, 154, 158

Causse, A., 162

Childs, Brevard, 34n1, 41n35

Clement of Alexandria, **295–96**

Cohen, Shaye, 5, 21

Coogan, Michael, 27n26, 30n37

Cragg, G. R., 266

Cranfield, C. E. B., 263, 266

Chrysostom, John, xii, 2, 11, 270, 271n3, 273, **282–89**, 291, 298, 302, 306, 308–9, 311, 315n33

Cullmann, Oscar, 260n68

Das, Andrew, 11n17

de Fraine, Jean, 162–63, 165n14, 166, 167n24, 175n55, 176, 177n 62, 179, 180, 181n66, 182n69, 183, 184n74, 242n34

de Vaux, Roland, 171n40, 181n67

Dillman, A., 33n1, 40n31

Driver, S. R., 38, 40n31

Dumbrell, W. J., 81n5, 204nn12–13, 205n14, 205n16, 207n19, 229n19

Dumuzi, 26

Eberly, D., 111n44, 116n55, 121n66

Eichrodt, Walter, 23, 24n12, 33n1, 40nn29–31, 43n40, 48

Eminyan, Maurice, 314n30

Enki, 24, 25, 27–30

Evdokimov, Paul, 283n35, 296

Fiordelli, Pietro, 270n1, 273n10, **304–15**, 316n34

Fishbane, Michael, **147**, **148n57**, 149, **212n38**

Fitzmyer, J. A., 266

Fulgentius of Ruspe, 299

Gammie, John G., 137

Glatzer, Norman, 98n14

Gregory the Great, 298

Heaney-Hunter, Joanne, 323n43

Hertz, J. H., 81n7, 87

Heschel, Abraham, 92, 207n19

Hirsch, Samuel R., **64**, **75**, 91, **118–23**, 137, 145

Hodgson, Robert, 135

Houghton, Hugh, 271n5

Inanna, 26

Jacob (Israel), 90n28, 99, 146, 172, 202, 205, 249

James, E. O., 20, 28n29, 29n36, 30

Jeremias, Joachim, **248-55**

Jerome, 261-62, 271n5, **296-98**, 306

John the Baptist, 214, 227, 254n61

John Paul II, ix, xii, 3, 4n8, 14n4, 56n80, 62n92, 76, 102n24, 111n44, 112n46, 276n15, 290, 291, **313-20**, 321

Johnson, R. Aubrey, 182

Joseph, St., 291

Justin Martyr, 56n79

Kaiser, Walter C., **140-44**, 164, 165n13, 166n20

Kaminsky, J., 234n27

Kaplan, Aryeh, 143n37, 144n42, 144n44, **157-59**

Kaufman, M., 121n64, **143-46**

Kaufmann, Yehezkel, 21n4, 23n23, 30, 31n47, 34n3, 41, 42nn36-37, 45n47

Kelle, Brad E., 213n42

Kostenberger, Andreas, 89n27, 114n50, 122n71

Kramer, Samuel, 22, 23nn9-10, 25nn17-19, 26, 28n31, 30n40, 30n42, 32n48, 68, 69n114

Laban, 172

Levi, 140, 182n70, 224

Levine, Baruch, 156n83

Lewis, C. S., 51n66, 203n9, 227n16, 228n16, 232n23

Lohfink, N., 72n121

Maly, Eugene, 67n108

Marcion, 13n2, 15, 197

Marduk, 43, 104, 105

Marsh, John, 228n17

Mary, the Virgin, 148n58, 254n61, 279, 291, 292

May, Herbert G., 41n34, 165, 169n34

McComiskey, T. E., 36nn12-13, 38, 139

McKenzie, J. L., 175

McKeown, J., 35n9, 81nn5-6

McLuhan, Marshall, xi, 99, 114, **153**

Meeks, W. A., 267

Melchizedek. See General Index

Mickiewicz, Adam, 14n4

Merkley, Paul, 165n12

Miller, John, 30n38, 90n30, **103-20**, 129-30nn3-4, 146

Miller, Yisroel, 146

Moffatt, J., 266

Molech, 141

Moltman, Jurgens, 46n50

Neusner, Jacob, 200, 201

Ninmu, 27, 28

Ninkurra, 28

Oulette, Marc, 3n7

Paul, St., 11n17, 14n3, 15, 60, 86n18, 100n17, 103n26, 110, 123n73, 126, 152n69, **185-88**, 194n2, 195, 200, 202, 204, **210-21**, 225, **230-34**, **240-47**, 250n47, 253, **256-61**, 265, 266n79, 267, 269, 286n47, 288, 298, 300, 306, 308, 311, 321

Pedersen, Johannes, 100, 162, 163n3, 165n14, **173-74**, 175-76, **184-87**, 188-89, 261n69

Pelagius, 272

Petersen, J. M., 264n75

Philo of Alexandria, 155n80, 240n11

Pleins, J. David, 95n8

Porter, J. R., **167-71**

Porter, Roy, 171n40

Pritchard, James, 28nn27-34, 29n35, 30n41, 104n29, 170n36

Raba, 254

Ramban, 146

Ratzinger, Joseph, 21n4, 150, 293-94

Re, 28, 44

Rogerson, J. W., 163n3, 164n6, **167-69**

Ringgren, Helmut, 158-59n93

Robinson, H. Wheeler, 162, 163n3, **164-69**, 172n42, 179, 218n53

Routledge, Robin, 37, 50-51n65, 263n28

Rowley, H. H., 169, 170n35

Rugh, Gil, 223n10

Sarna, Nahum, 27n24, 31, 32n48, 42n38, 44, 45n46, 70n118, 72

Schaeder, Grete, 188, 190n89

Schillebeeckx, Edward, 16, 48-50, 61n90, 67n108, **132-33**, 142-43, 171n39, 192

Scola, Angelo, 3n7

Selkin, C., 59n87, 227
Smith, W. Robertson, 181
Soggin, J. Albert, 35n8
Speiser, E. A., 33n2
Stauffer, E., 248n41, 249, 250

Tasker, David, 22n8, 23, 24nn15–16, 44, 106
Tasmisus, 28n33
Thiessen, Matthew, 234n27, 235n27
Ti'amat, 37n17, 43–44, 104–5
Tsumura, David, 37n17, 59n88

Uttu, 28

Vanhoye, A., 134, 135n17
Vitz, Paul, 111n44
Von Rad, Gerhard, 27, 31n45, 33, 34nn1–2,
    41n32, 46n51, 47nn53–54, 48n55,
    48nn57–58, 49n61, 57nn82–83, 63n95,
    67–74, 142, 150

Wallace, Howard N., 155, 156n81
Weber, Max, 24, 47n52
Weigel, George, 14n4
Wellhausen, J., 36, 37n15, 39, 40n30, 102n25,
    152n67
Wenham, Gordon, 21n4, 33n1, 37n16, 37n19,
    38n20, 39nn25–26, 40n31, 59n88, 149, 158
Westermann, Claus, 21n4, 33n1, 40nn29–30,
    42n36, 42n38, 44n44, 50n64, 57, 58n84,
    63n94, 65n98, 65n100, 66, 69, 71, 74–75,
    76n138, 77n140, 79, 83n11, 149–52, 204n11
Wright, G. E., 68n113, 183
Wojtyla, Karol, 3nn5–6, 4n8, 14n4. See also
    John Paul II
Wyschogrod, Michael, 235n27

Zeitlin, Irving, 22n6, 24, 30n41, 34nn4–5,
    47n52, 67n107, 68n110, 68n113

GENERAL INDEX

Abraham (Abram) and family: Akeda, 202; beginning point of salvation, 36, **38–43**, 40, 43nn29–30, 45, **74**, **77**, **80**, 81, 152, **187**, 198, **204**, 286n47; blessing, x, xi, xii, 50–51, 62, **63–70**, 71, 72, 74, 75, 76, 80, **81**, 85, **86**, 98n12, **100**, **101**, 113–14n49, 158, 162, 174, 175, 180 n65, 187, 205nn14–15, 223, 224, 229; bodily reality of, 109, **113n46**, 141, **180**, **204**, 325; centrality of, **209**; Church and, **xvi**, 2, **6n11**, **10**, 15, **82**, **86nn17–18**, **126**, 146, 187, **193**, 194n2, 198, 200, **202**, 204, 206, **209–12**, **215–19**, 221, 240; circumcision, xi, 80, 82, 84–86, 98n12, 107n37, **117–24**, 175, 180, 181, 183, **186n79**, 197, 208, 210, 211n33, 216, 226, **234–38**, 239n31, 240, 242, 249, 250, 254, 255; corporate person, xii, xvi, xix, xx, 2n4, 9, 10, 11, **60n90**, 81n4, 83, 98, 101, 120, 124n74, 134, **161–92**, 194n2, 195, 200, 203, 208n27, 218, 220, 221, 222, 224, 225, 226, 230, 231, 232, 233, 234, 237, 238, 239, 240, 241, 242, 243n36, 244, 245, 246, 247, 248, 250, 251, 255, 256, 259, 260, 268, 269, 290, 292, 295, 297, 298, 321; covenant, xx, 2, 8, 84, 106, 120n63, 193n1, 199, 204n13, 210, 211n33, 212, 213, 215, 216, 224, 229, 236, 237, 249, 251; creation, parallel with, xi, xx, **71**, 73, 74, **80**, **174n46**, **204nn12–13**, 229; descendants, promise of, 73, 80, **82–84**, 119, 152n69, 205, 217, 219n53, 224; differentiated **80**, 93, 183, 229, 238; father of us all, **8n14**, 15, **72n120**, 78, 86n18, 100, 198, 210n30, 217, 215n55; "known" by God, 87; in NT, xvi, xx, 8, 10, 15, **72n120**, 78, **86n18**, 124, **172**, **182n70**, 194n2, 195, **197–219**, 221, 222, 223, 240; paradigmatic 8, **215–19**;

primoridal founder, 97, 118, 182n70, 216; promise to, xi, xvi, 15, 80, **82**, 83, 84, 86, 133, **194n2**, 202, 204, 210, **216**, 217, 219n53, 220, **229**, 240; sacrifice of Isaac, **202**; salvific point, 79, 80, **81**, 84, **202**, 205, 218; scandal of particularity, 81, 216; seed, xvi, 8n14, **82–83**, 84, 202, 219n53, 219n55; sleep (*tardemah*), 59n89, 62; suffering, **83**, 97; teleological conclusion, xxx, 2, 10, **82n9**, **194nn1–2**, 206; universal mission, 10, 78, 80, 81, **82n9**, 206, 219; vocation, 83, **183**, 205, **213**. *See also* Election

Adam, 57, 61, 62, 75, 81, 154n72, 157n88, 158, 159, 170, 171, 203, 205, 231; beginning of generations 199, 210n31; as prototype, 55n75, 64, 76, 174, 203, 218

'adam, 85, 122, 123, 128n 221

Akeda 202

Anamnesis (remembrance), xii, 115; related to male (*zachar*), 120–22

Anthropology. *See* Man

Autonomous, self-determining individualism, xix, 9, 60, 163, 225, 246, 247, 290

Baptism, 271; administration of, **159n94**, 232, 239, 252, 258; and autonomous individual, 9, 243, 244, 251; of a believer, xvii, 169n32, 186, 195, 221, 226, 230, **240n32**, **244**, **245–47**, 259, 260; believing spouse, 244, **245**, 259, **260**, 269, 283; birth/born again, 228, 252, 255, 258; children/infants, **186n79**, 229, 238, 239, 240, 241, **244**, **245**, 248–57, 260n68, 307; and circumcision, xi, 86n17, **123n73**, 186n79, 197, 208, 226, **234–38**, **250**; corporate dimension of, 11n17, 186n79, 187n83, **195**, **208n27**,

346

220–68, 298; and death of Christ, 231, 232, 253, 258; effects on marriage and family, 4n8, 77n140, **159n94**, 195, 226, 244–48, 257n64, 259, **269**, 296, **298**, **307**, **311**, 319; eschatological, 10, 194, **227**, **261**, **298**; exchange of natures, 231, 232, 257n64, 258; family solidarity, 249, 251, 257; freedom in, **244–47**, 290, 292, 293n55, 295; household, 9, 186n76, 186n79, 195, 208n27, 226, 234, **238–41**, 242, 243, 244, 247, 269; incorporation into Christ, 77n140, 187, 194n2, 218, 230, 233, 234, 237; individual response, 239, **242–47**; initiation, 186, 234, 235, 237, 252, 255; of John the Baptist, 214, 227; new creation, 159n94, 187n81, 194, 228, 231–33, 259; Nicodemus, 228; *oikos* formula, 250; in Paul, 86n18, 123n73, 230–34, 243–59; personal decision, 241, **242–47**, 248, 252, 259; Philippian jailer, 238n30, 239, 243, 251; proselyte (Jewish), 111, **252–56**; in Romans 6, 218, 232, 233, 253, 258; sanctifying effects, 186, 226, 259n67, 260, 319; and sins, 229, 252, 253; "sons" in the Son, 1n3, 209; unbelieving spouse, 244, 245, 260, 297
Beginning (*bereshith*), 33, 36, **38–43**, 39, 40, 41, 42, 45, 47, **50**, 55n77, 77, 80, 228n18, 232, **286n47**
beth 'ab/bēth 'ābhōth (the father's house), 108n40, 174, 182, 187, 249
Blessing. *See* Abraham and family
Body, 8, 9, 50, 112, 119, 121, 128, 144, 173, 182, 231, 233, 237, 240, 247, 256, 261n69, 267, 288, 308, 321; of Abraham, 8, 82, 83, 118, 172, 181; of Christ, ix, xv, xvi, 11, 82, 166n19, 195n5, 202, 206, 208n27, 209n28, 219, 221n1, 230, 234, 238, 257, 258, 261n79, 271, 278, 280, 281, 282, 288, 305, 307, 308, 317; inscribed with covenant, 121; in myths, 105; nuptial meaning of, 102n24; of Sarah, 118; theology of, 112; woman's, 112, 114

Catechism of the Catholic Church, 1, 4n9, 13, 55–56n77, 76n137, 145n51, 313n27, 314, 322
Celibacy, 272, 273, 276, 279, 280; charism, 276n15; and holiness, 270, **276n15**,

277, 312; and marriage, 281; objective superiority, 312n22, 281; paradigm for holiness, 298, 302; proleptic sign, 270, 276n15; proper disposition, 281; in salvific process, 280
Children. *See* Baptism
Church: fulfillment of Abraham's family, 6, **10**, 82, 126, 194n2, 198, 202, **206**, 219; body of Christ, ix, xvi, 9, 10, 11, **82**, 202, 206, **207**, 208n27, 209n28, 219, 221, 226n13, **230**, **231**, 256, 261n69, 278, 280, 288, **305**, 307, 308, 317, 324; gentiles grafted in, **86n18**, 194n2, 197, 212, 216n49; hierarchical, 209, 275, 305, 313n27; Israel of God, 221; as olive tree, 15, 86n18, 194n2, 197, 228, 212; organic nature, 15, 187, 192, 210, **219**, 233, 246. *See also* Domestic church
Circumcision: and belonging, 84, 119, 120, 175, 186n79, **235–38**, **248–51**, 254; and children, 107n37, 119, 120, 186n79, 249, 250n48, 254, 255; controversy over, 216; converts, 235, 254; as covenant, xi, 80, **84–86**, 98n9, 107n37, **117–23**, 180–83, **234–42**, 249, **250**, 255; duty of father, **107n37**, **107n40**, **117–23**, 175, 180; father-led ritual, 8, **110–26**; fulfilled in Christ, 123, 208, **250**; household rite, 240, 249; initiation, 85, 186n79, 186n81, 234, 235, 255; sign of covenant, 80, **84–86**, 119, 120, 122, 123, 180, 242, 249; spiritualization, 236, 237. *See also* Abraham and family; Baptism
Clean. *See* Spheres of reality
Collaboration of Men and Women, **293–94**
Common. *See* Spheres of reality
Conjugal chastity. *See* Marriage
Conversion to Christ, 225, 317
Corporate personality: Abraham, 83, 175, 180–81, 182n70, **183**, 186n1, 191, 218, **220–24**; Achan and family, 162, 168, 169, 177, **178–79**; in Aristotle, xv, 189n87; Church, 187, 192, 195, 221, **226**, 240; collectivism and individualism, 163n4, 166, 169, 177, 188, **189**; C. S. Lewis on, **203**, 232n23; extension into past and future, 175, 176; in household baptisms, 226; individual responsibility in, 167, 177–79, 185n77; initial ancestor, 180;

Corporate personality (*cont.*)
Levi in Abraham, 172, 182n70, 222–26; in marriage, 161, **171n39**, 185, **195**, 297; and Melchizedek, 172, 182n70, 219n53, **222–26**; Moabite example, 165n14, 176; in NT, 9, 166n19, 172, **185–88**, 192, **195**, **218**, 220, 221, 222, 224, 226, 240n32, 251, 298; one–many oscillation, 164, **165–67**, 218; ontic participation, 188; organic, 14, 97, **164**, 172, 177, 179, 182, 186, 187, 220, 246, 248, 290; Rachel weeping, 164, 172n42; as representative, 164, **165**, **166**, 173, 175, **218n53**; Semitic anthropological principle, 161–92, 243

Covenant, x–xii, xv–xvi, xx, 2, 3n7, 4n8, 5n9, 6–12, 14, 15, 17, 19, 48n55, 48n58, 49, 51, 57n81, 58–59, 62, 66, 71, 73, 74, 76, 78, **79–90**, 92–95, 97–99, 101–3, 106, 107n37, **108–10**, 111, 113n49, 114, **117–27**, 129, 130–34, 136, 140, 142, 143, 146–47, **148–60**, 161–62, 168–69, 174n46, 175n52, 176–77, 179, 180–84, 185n77, 186n79, 186n81, 187, 191–92, 193n1, 194n1, 195, 197–202, 204–16, 218–21, 224, 225, 229, 233–38, 239n31, 240–42, 244n37, 246n39, 249, 250, 251, 255, 257, 259, 260n68, 262, 268, 316–17, 321, 325; adoption into, 179, 181, 183; adultery and, 141; and birth, **85**, 145, **183**, **238**; blessing, 62, 66, 74, 76, 80, 81, **85–88**, 98n12, 101, 187, 205n14, **229**; branch theology, 207; broken, 85, 197n1, 211, 213n41, 235; conditional, 198, 213, 216; continuity, xii, xv, 86n18, 194, 195, 198, 199, 200, 206n17, 209, 215, 222, 241, 250; cut in flesh, 84, 123, 181; Davidic, 187, 200, 207; death penalty (*karet*), **141**, 143; discontinuity, 83, 86n18, 200, **206n17**, 209, 215; education in, 8, 75n137, 84n11, 87–90, 95, 98, 107, 115, 191; and election, 73, 76, 79, 80, 81, 83, 86, 180, 181, **183**, 187n82, **205n15**, 246n39; exodus motif, 72, 115, 125, 130, 212n38; as family/familial, 48n55, **83**, 123, 129, **130**, **131–34**, 186n79, 191, 205, 242, 251, 255; grace, 86, 110, 115, 118, 132, 187n81, 192n90, 195, 209, 211, 214–16, **246n39**; 251, 257n64, 260; grafted into, 15, 86n18, 194n2, 195n5, 197, 212, 216;

homosexuality and, 141, 294; and the Holy Spirit, 82n9, 192n90, 206, 209, 216n49, 229, 260, 261, 317, 325; household, 9, 80, 85, 87, 103n26, 107n39, 108n40, 114n50, **117–24**, 174, 175n52, 177, 179, 182, 186, 195, 206, 208n27, 234, 235, **238–51**, 261; incest and, 141, 142; initiation, 85, 129, 186n79, 234, 235, 237, 255, 256; language (ontological), 130, 133, 314; as marriage, 6n11, 19, 48n55, **49**, **76**, 102, 131, 132, **133**, 134, 146, **147**, **153**, 159, 161, 192n90, 195, 199, 233, 261; memorial of creation, 84; Mosaic, 102, 211, 212, 213, 216; need of family, 124, 129; new covenant, xvi, 6, 9, 11, 103n26, 169, 187n81, 197, 198, 208, 213, 214, 215, 216, 218–20, 224, 225, 241, 246n39, 251, 259, 268, 325; nuptial imagery, 102n24, 130, 133, 213, 214; old and new, 208, 212n38, **215**; remember, xi, 93, 98n12, **120–22**, 154; sign/symbol, 123–25, **128–34**, 145, **147**, 148, 149; telos of, x, 34, 50–51n65, 70, 152, 232, 261; and transgression, 141; unconditional (Abrahamic), 205, 213n43, 214. *See also* Abraham and family; Circumcision

Covenantal nomism, 11n17

Creation 66; *ad extra*, 46, 65; *barah* (create), 33, 36, 37, 38, 47; *bereshith* (in the beginning), 33, 36, 38, 39, 40, 42, 80; boundaries, 139; *Chaoskampf*, 37n17; Christocentric, 43n41, 46n51, 294; cosmic drama, 26, 34n5, 43, 45, 69, 125n76, 204; cosmos, 32, 43, 44, 45n47, 155n80; cult and cultic actualization, 67, 69, **151**, **159**; de-creation, 139; demythologization, 7, 17, 19, 47, 49, 57, 67, 68, 76, 77, 84, 131, 199; differentiation, **55n75**, **56n8**, 57, 79, 81, **120**, 152, **174**; *ex nihilo*, x, 35–43; Exodus-centered, 72; gnostic version, 36nn9–10, 47n54; *havdil* (separation), 17, 20n3, 45, **46nn48–49**, 135, 138, 149, 324n 44; history, xvi–xvii, 4n8, 13, **50n65**, **51n66**, 53, **63**, **65–72**, 73n124, 74, 75, 77; informed by Word, 34, 228n18; monotheism, 7, 17, 20n1, 29, 35n8, 46, 53, 76, 106, 131; narrative of, 6, 7n12, 37, 51n65, 61, 228, 290; non-sexualizing

of God, **48**, 56, 131; organic nature, 46, 79, 203; preexistent matter, 35, 37, 41, 45, 67; Sabbath structure of, **149–56**; salvific role 65, **72–76**, 195, 205; *shalom,* 51n65; sovereignty of God, 42, 70; *tehom,* 37n17, 228n18; *telos,* 34, 50–51n65, 152, 199; temple imagery, 58, 152n68, 154; *vestigia,* 55. *See also* Generations; Man; Mythologies; *Shabbat*
Curses: due to Ba'al worship 132n9; due to unfaithfulness, 95, 162; in Gen *1–11,* 81n6, 229; against parents, 141

Dabru emet, 14n5
David, 187, 199, 200, 204n13, 206, 207, 248, 297
De bono Viduitatis, 271, 308
De dono perserverantia, 281
Dei Verbum, 14n6, 198n2
De specialibus legibus, 155n80
Docetism, 203n10
domestica, 261–64, 271–72, 296–97, 300, 310n15, 311, 322
domestica ecclesia/domesticam ecclesiam, 261–64, 271–72, 296–97, 300, 310n15, 311, 322. *See also micra ecclesia*
Domestic church: appropriation by Fathers, 11, 269–300; appropriation by Vatican II, 12, 301–26; in Augustine, 271–82; as Bride of Christ, 315n31, 320n40, 321; cell of Church, 1, 261, 267, 314, 315n33; in Chrysostom, 282–89; in Church Fathers, 2, 6, 11, 196, 262, **269–300**; and development of doctrine, 320n40, 322, 333n 27; domestic priesthood, 101, 102; domestic sanctuary, 314; ecclesial identity, 3, 4n8, 11, 12, 192n90, 270, 272, 311, 313n27, 316, 322; ecclesial mission, 3, 187n83, 196, 303, 314n31, 319; Eph 5:32, **292–95**, 309, 319; grounded in baptism, 4, 11, **195n5**, 268, **311**, 319, 321; grounded in matrimony, 306, 311n18; icon 10, 317; in *Lumen Gentium,* 1n2, 304, 312–13, 315n33; micra- or micro-church, 11, 146, 147, **252–84**, 271; and monasticism, 2, 277n16, 298, 301, 303; ontology vs. analogy, 133, **313**, 314, 322; parallel with Temple, 160n96; parents as consecrated, 275, 309; philology

of, **261–68**; and prayer, 1, 271, 272, 273, 314, **315n33**; reading Scriptures in, 89, **283–84**, 285, 289; realism of language, 3n7, 232n24; reemergence of term, **301**; roots in OT, 191; scriptural ground, **257–61**; sphere of eschatological activity, 2, 10, 192, 209, 261, 298, 322, 355; in Vulgate, 261, 262, 265–67, 271n5, 322; and Word of God, 16, 192, **284–85**. *See also* Family

Eden/Garden of Eden, 58, 62n92, 122n72, 147, **148–60**; archetypical sanctuary, 152, 178; *'avodah* (work), 153–55; holiness of, 152n68; river, 157; sanctuary symbolism of, 148–60; *shamar,* 153–55; water as source of life, 156–58
Election, 73, 76, 79, 80, 81n7, 83, 86, 180, 181, 183, 187n81, 205n15, 246; of Abraham, **79–86**
Elephantine texts, 213
Enûma Eliš, 43, 44, 52, 60, 103–4, 170 n36
episcopatus officium, 275–76
Epistolae nuper in lucem prolatae, 272
Essenes, 227

Faith: the Way, 193. *See also* Salvation
Fall, 91, 64, 76, 152, 153, 156, 204n11, 229, 242, 294; corporate dimension, 242; Jewish roots, 152n69
familia, 266–67, 272n6, 272n9, 276n14, 296n61, 297n62, 307n7, 307n9, 308, 309n12, 310n14, 311n21
Familiaris consortio, 1, 3n6, 4n8, 102n24, 44n44, 276n15, 314, 316
Family: adopted into, 76, 86, 179, 181, 183; assumed into salvific plan, 6, 7, 17, 72, 77, 127, 191, 199, 215, 275, 325; authority (servant), 108, 275, 286, 287, 288, **290–95**, 318; baptized, 1, 2 11, 77n140, 160, 192n90, 195, 209n28, 215, 247, 261, 273, 283, 287, 311, 313n27, 314, 320, 322, 325; basic cell, 87, 267, 314, 315n33; blessing in, 50, 51, 63–**64**, **70**–72, 75–76, **81**, **85–86**, 98n12, 100–**101**, 114n49, 174–75, 187, **205n14**; blood tie, 179–82; bonding in, 94, 112; carrier of covenant, xi, xvi, 2, 7, 8, 78, 82, **91–127**, 134, 162, 191, 195, 206, 208, 209, 261, 317, 321, 325;

Family (*cont.*)
cell of Church, 194n2, 261, 267, 314, 315n33; cell of society, xix, 314, 315n33; children in, 88, **115**; Christological form, 10, 200, 202, 319, 322; and communion of love, xiii, **317n37**; communion of persons, 137; and covenant, 6, 127, 133, 159, 191, 199, 215, 325; cult/cultic, 8, **99**, 125; ecclesial nature (identity/mission), 3, 4n8, 11, 12, 192n90, 270, 272, 276, 311, 313n27, 316n34, 322; educative function, 3, 8, 75n137, 76n137, 84n11, **87–90**, **95–98**, 107, **115**, 191, 284; hallowed time, **92–94**, 150; handing over (tradition), 100, 91; head of, 9, 100–101, 108n40, 114n50, 120n63, 121, 238–40, 243, **251**, 274, **275**, **287**, 291, 294; as icon of Temple, **146–59**; image of covenant, xi, **128–60**; Jewish family in antiquity, 5; kingly role, 318; medium of covenant, 114, 123, 125n76, 146; Near Eastern context, 19–32; no family, no covenant, 8, 110n13; nuclear, xvi, 102, 108n41, 111, 263; order and differentiation, **290–95**; organic nature, 46, 219, 226, 260; original cell, 87; parents role, 111, 289, **309–13**; participates in body of Christ, 315; priestly role, 99–102, 103, **318**; prophetic role, 131, **318**; psychosomatic unity, 182, 186; relativized in Christ, 208; teachable moment, 96, 115; theology of, 315; in salvific order, 78, 215, 216, 230, 255, 294, 323; as sanctuary, 142; sexuality, x, xvi, 34n6, 144n45, 146–59, 277; state of life, 270, **276–81**, 282, 289, 298, 299, **305–10**, 312; *telos*, 77, 113n46, 150, 199, **218**; theological nature of, 104, 163. *See also* Baptism; Corporate personality; Domestic church; Father/hood; Feasts; Fecundity; Holiness; Husbands; Marriage; Messianic; Mother/hood; Shabbat; *shalom*; Woman
Fate: *Maat* (Egyptian), 30n41; *me's* (Sumerian), 25, 30; *Moira* (Greek), 30n41
Father/hood: as bishop, **273–76**, 287, 301; blessing, 100–102; crisis of, **103–8**; cultural achievement, 112, 113n47; and divine fatherhood, 107, 111, 113n47; as

foundation, 251; headship of, 100n17; instructions for, 107n39, 257; Israelite view of, **106–8**, 117; Near Eastern context, **19–26**; officiant, 100, 101; pagan view of, 104–6; *paterfamilias*, 207, 271, 274, 275; power struggle with sons, 30n38, 104–8; as priest, xi, **99–103**; psychobiology, 112–13nn46–47; reliving fatherhood of God, 111n44, 291; representative of Abrahamic community, 118, 120, 175; of Yahweh, **103**, 106–7, **117**, **129n2**; *zachar*, 120–22. *See also* Patriarchy
Father-led rituals, 110–26; Passover, 98, 124–26; redemption of first-born, 114–17. *See also* Circumcision
Feasts: Booths, 94; Passover, 124–26; Unleavened Bread, 94, 126; Weeks, 94; Yom Kippur (Day of Atonement), 139n28, 145, 252n53
Fecundity, x, 19, 25n20, 26, 50, 51, 63, 305
Flood, the, 79, 139n28, 159n93
Freedom, individual, xix, 70n117, 245–47, 295
Fulfillment, theology of, 4n8, 6, 10, 14n5, 20, 70, 82, 123, 126, 145, 192, 194, 198, 201, 202, 204n11, **206n17**, **208**, 212, 224, 225, 227n15, 229, 233, 250, 317; new Moses, 198, 211n35

Generations/genealogies (*tôldôt*), xii, 46, 65, 70, 71, 74, 75, 76; fulfilled in Christ 208, 209–10; grounded in creation, 63, 127, 203; incarnation (as safeguard), 203; theological form, 200
Genus, 277, 279–81, 310n14
Grace, 2, 86, 110, 115, 118, 132, 187n81, 192n90, 195, 209, 211, 214–17, 226, 228n16, **246n39**, 251, 253, 256, **257n64**, 260, 277, 279, 312, 319
gradus, **277–79**, 299

Haggadah, 98
Haggadic, 109
Halackic, 109
Hebraic anthropology, 8, 161–96
Heilsgeschichte. See Salvation
Hermeneutics, 21n4, 108; continuity/discontinuity, 86, 200, 206n17, 209, 215;

fulfillment in Christ (OT), 212; new hidden in old, 13, 14, 198; new principle, 209, 211; sacramental reality, 194. See also Typology

Hierarchy, 100n17, 107n39, 319

hieros gamos. See Mythology

Holiness (*qodesh*), 136, 319; family as, 134–38, 257–61; sharing in, 136, 141; Yahweh as holy, 48n58, **136–40**, 169

Holiness code, 136, 140, 141, 143, 168

Holy. *See* Spheres of reality

Holy Spirit, 82n9, 192n90, 206, 209, 216n49, 227, 228, 229, 230, 231, 260, 261, 269, 282, 312, 317, 318, 322, 325

Holy widowhood, 279, 280

hoq/hoqqoth (statutes /laws), 50

Hosea, 212–15; children's names, 131, 132; divorce, **213**–14; Jezreel, 212; not my people, 131, **213**, 214; not pitied, 212

Household baptisms. *See* Baptism

Household of God, 103n26, 287

Human person. *See* Man

Husbands, 109, 122n72, 245, 256, 259, 285, 287, 319, 321

Image forth, 53, 53n70, **129**, 132, 134, 145, 152, 191

Immersion (*mikveh*), **144–46**, 148, 227, 235; status changes, 135n17, 141, 142, 145, **227**, 253, 255

Individual(ism), 2, 81, 165 166, 168, 169, 189, 200n6, 226, 295; absolutized, **208n27**, 242; and group, 166; and personalism, 11, 166, **170–72**, 177; re-sponsibility of, 167, 177, **178–79**, 185n77, 186n81, **242–47**

In Joannis Evangelium, 274, 300

Israel: holiness of, 137, **140**; scandal of particularity, 81, 216; *segullah* (special possession), 22n7, 81n7, 205n15; separate (called out), 137, 166, 202

Jesus: priesthood of, 222–26

Jewish literature: 11Q 13, 223; *Baba Mesia,* 201; *Babylonian Shabbat,* 89; *BaMidbar Rabbah,* 159n95; *Bekorot,* 253n54; *Bikurrim,* 253n56; *Gerim,* 253n54; *Kiddushin,* 120n63; *K'ritot,* 145n47; *Midrash on Psalms,* 223n6, 223n9; *Midrash Rabbah,* 154; *Midrash Samuel,* 253n56; *Neophyti I,* 154; *Pesahim,* 98nn13–14; *Pesikta Rabosai,* 159n95; *Pirke Derabbi Eliezer,* 157n88; *Qohelet Rabba,* 253n55; *Shir HaShirim Rabbah,* 259n95; *Test Levi,* 252; *Yebamot,* 253n54, 255n62

Jewish roots of Christian faith, 4, 15, 86n18, 194n2, 197, 202

Justification, 12, 210, 217

Lex talonis, 178

Lumen Gentium, 1n2, 304, 312–313, 315 n33

Magic, 19, 31, **31nn44–45**, 34, 43, 68, 199

Man: *'adam,* 61, 62, 64, 203n8, 218n52; adamic nature, 231, 232, 258; autonomous, self-determining individual, 9, 60, 62, 163, 225, 246, 290; *basar echad* (one flesh), 54n73, 61, 171, 185, 240, 259, 325; in Christ 226, 231–34, 240n32, 258; communion (*communio*), ix, xiii, 1, 7n12, 50, 55–56, 62–63, 212n64, 134, 157, 188, 190, 208n27, 256, 313n27, 314, 317n37, 322; conjugal relationship, 277; corporate/communitarian aspect, 101, 120, **161–96**, 203, 208n27, **218n53**, 220, 225, 226, 232, 233, 240, 244n37, **245–47**, 251, 292; difference, 238, 286n47, **290–95**, 324; dignity (absolute) 52, 53, **58–62**, 238, 295; *'ezer* (helper), 59, 61, 286; female (*neqebah*), 47, 59, 61, 76, **120**, 122, 147, **171**, 236n28, 290–95, **321**; freedom (free will), x, xix, 65n99, 70n17, 114, 116, 117n57, 126, **245–47**, 290, **292–95**; gender, 7, 56, **57–62**, 102n24, **113n46**, 234; image (*imago dei*), 45, 47, **52–56**, **63–64**, 70, 92, 76, 77, 170, 181; loneliness, 56–57n81, 60, 170–71, 203n8; male (*zachar*), 47, 84, 120, 249; not chattel, 122n71; organic unity, 14, 97, **164–67**, 172, 174, 177, 179, 182, 186, 187, 246, 248, 259, 290; original unity, 46n49, 63, 229; polarity of sexes, **47**, 48; replicating "image," **64–65**, 101; responsibility (personal vs. corporate), 116, 167, 177, **178–79**, **185n77**, **186–87n81**, **242–47**; "subject, not object," 61n91; vice-re-gent, 52. *See also* Baptism; Husbands; *nephesh*; Sexuality; Woman; Work

Marriage: believing partner, 244, **245**, 259–**60**, 269, 283; conjugal chastity, 277, 279, 281, 181; covenantal, 7, 19, **132–34**, **147**, 150, 153, 159, 161, 233; cultic dimension 153, 159; great mystery, xxi, 259, 260, 321; as icon of Temple, 146–59; mixed (with pagans), 243, 245, **257–61**; procreation, 7n12, 26, 44, 48, 63, 65–70, 76n137, 282, 293n55, 306–7, 312, 325; as state of life, 270, 276, 309; as vocation, 277n17, 312n22; unbelieving partner, 244, 245, 260, 297

Melchizedek: blessing 223–24; and corporate personality, 182n70, **222–26**; eucharistic elements, 222; king of righteousness/peace, 222; messianic type, 222–23; origin 223; priesthood of, 172, 223–24; and tithe, 172, 182n70, 222–24

Menstruation/menstruant, **109**, 139, **141**–43, **144n41**

Messiah, 95, 158, 194n2, 200, 202, 203, 206n18, 207n22, 208, 210, 223; day of, 95, 158; healing/blessing, 158; return to Eden, 158

Messianic family, **200–202**; brothers and sisters, 202; claims of the father, 201; love of Jesus primary, 201

micra ecclesia, 11, 271n3, 282

mikvah/mikveh, **144–46**; and baptism, 157; bridal bath, 145; and conversion, 145, 208; gathering of waters, 144; holiness in marriage, 143–45; immersion at Sinai, 145; and primordial waters of Eden, 157n88, 158; proselyte baptism, **252–55**; reborn, 145

minisculam ecclesiam, 309

mohar (bridal gift), 214; in Hosea, **213–14**

Monasticism. *See* Domestic church

Monotheism, 17, 20n1, 29, 35, 53, 131

Mother/hood, xix, 1, 95, 107n37, **108–10**, 111, 113, 114n50, 120, 141, 201, 254, 255, 259, 291; bonding, xi, 112; interiority, 110; and Jewish identity, xvi, 110, 235–36, 238; passing on faith, 297; pregnancy, 112, 254; psychobiology, 94, 112, 236; purity 109

Mulieris Dignitatem, 291

munus episcopale, 310n15, 313n25

Mystery (*mysterion*), xxi, 14, 27, 35, 48, 57, 64, 76, 83, 132, 190, 233, 259, 260, 294, 309, 317, 319, 320, 321, 325

Mythology: Assyrian, 23, 30n41; Babylonian, 22n8, 23, 30n41, 37n17, 43, 51, 52, 103, 104; Canaanite, 22n6, 23, 27, 48; common content, **22–26**; cosmogony, 24n16, 42n38; divinization of sexuality, 48, 130n6; Egyptian, 28, 30n41, 44; *hieros gamos*, 26, 27, 45, 49; Mesopotamian, 32, 149n59, 154n76; nonteological creation, 46n51, 198; sexualized gods/creation, 24–25, 27–28, **43–47**, 103, 106; Sumerian, 23, 22n9, 24–26, 28n33, 30, 32n48, 53, 94; syncreticism 52n67; Ugaritic, 54

nephesh (soul), 9, 100, 169, 173–74, 176, 180–81, 185–87, 189, 191, 194, 195n4, 205, 218, 220; of Abraham, 100, 176, 180-81, 186n81, 187, 191, 205, 218, 220; instantation of, 172, 218n53; marked, 180, 184, 186, 187; merging with others, 185, 208n27

New principle of Christ, 209, 211

New Testament. *See* Covenant

Newness, 194, 202, 222, 253; covenant (new), xvi, 6, 9, 11, 103, 169, 187, 197–98, 208, 213, 214–16, 218–20, 224–25, 241, 246, 251, 259, 268, 325

Nicomachean Ethics, 189n87

niddah (impure), 143–44

officium, 274n11, 275–76, 278–79

Old Testament. *See* Covenant

One flesh. *See* Man

Original sin, 11n17, 186n81, 253

Passover. *See* Father-led rituals

paterfamilias, 181, 271, 274–75

Patriarchy, 107, 108n41

Peace. *See* shalom

Pelagianism, 246n39, 272

Politics, 189n87

Polytheism: cultic prostitution, 27, 45, 130n6; sexual content, 130n6, 25

Priesthood, xi, 99–103, 172, 222–25, 293

Profane. *See* Spheres of reality

professio, **277–78**

Proselytes: Abrahamic converts, 85n15; baptism, 252, **253–55**
protoevangelium, 204; cosmic battle, 43, 204, 125; seed of woman, 204
Prophet, the, **212n39**
Purification, 139n28, 145, 158, 252n53
Purity: laws of, 108–**9**, **139**, 140–44, 160n96; not moral valuation, **144**; ritual, 109, 139, 143, 144, **227**, 236–37

Questiones in Hept., 13, 198n2
quodammodo, 274

Redemption. *See* Salvation
Redemptoris Custos, 291
Responsibility. *See* Man
Rituals/rite, 22, 23, 100, **111**, 114, 116, 159n94, 236; fulfilled in Christ, 159n94; High Priest (*kohen gadol*), 59, 109, 145, 252n53; Holy of Holies, **145**, 158n93; identifying marker, 227; with water, 12n18, 158, 159n94, 227

Sacrifice, 83, 96, 99, 100, 101, **114**, 115, 117n57, 126, **154**, 202, 222, 225
Salvation: baptism and, 258; corporate nature of, xii, xvi, 2n4, 9, 10, 83, 183, 191, **195**, **200**, 221, 225, 239, 241–**42**, 251, 255, 268–69; Exodus as lens of, 72, **74**, 83, 115, 117, **205**; by faith, 216, 217, 258; through grace, 216, 228n16, **246n39**, **257n64**; individualistic interpretation, **10**, 195n5, 208n27, 242, 251; nature of, 210; removal of sin, 229, 230, 236; salvation history, xii, xvi, 2, 4n8, 6, 13, 16, 51n66, 65, 74–75, 77–78, 117n57, 133n15, 199, 205, 242, 302; trajectory of, 2, 6, 13, 65n99, 133n15, 204n13, 205n15; and works, 65, 75, 206, **210**, 216
Sarah, 109, 118, 146, 176nn51–52, 187, 202
Sermon on the Mount, 10n16, 15n8, 194, 206n17, 211n35, 212
Sexuality: demythologization, 7, 17, 19, 47–49, 57, 67–68, 76–77, 84, 131, 199; intuition about, 49, 51, 131; magical, **19**, 43, 199; role in salvific plan, **17**, 76–77, **84**, 191, 199; *telos*, x, **51**, **65**
Shabbat (Sabbath): and covenant, 84, **136**; and creation, 60, 84, **149–51**; cultic

dimensions, 93, 110, 151–52; hallowing of time, 135, 136, 151; holiness of, 92–94, 136, 152; seventh day, 93, 135, 149, 150, 152; sign of, 80, 84; structure of creation, **149–51**
shalom (peace), 51n65, 60n50, 61, 171n39, 288–89
shechinah, 146
Sign/symbol, x, 12n18, 45n46, 68, 104, 112, 116–17 123–25, 128–29, 140, 145, 147–49, 152–53, 157–59, 164, 191, 227, 253, 231
Sin. *See* Original sin
Soul. *See* nephesh
Sphere of eschatological activity. *See* Domestic church
Spheres of reality, **138–44**; borders, 144; clean, 109, 138–39, 142; common (or profane), 93, **135**, 136, **138–39**; contagion, 138, 168, 178; holy, 78, 134, 135n17, 191, 240, 245; separation, **20n3**, 45, **46nn48–49**, 137n24, **138**, 140, 143, 144, 155; and sin, 139n28, 169; unclean, 109, 138–39, 141–42, 144, 148, 169, 178, 244, 260. *See also* Temple
Spirit. *See* Holy Spirit
Stromateis, 295

tehom, **37n17**, 41, 228n18
telos (destined end), 10, 34, 50n65, 51, 65, 66n103, 70, 77, 113n46, 150, 152, 199, 218, 232, 261
Temple: *'avodah* (work), 153–55; cherubim, 159; and Garden of Eden, 58, 59, 147, **148–59**, 160; gold, 59; menorah, 59, 159; orientation, 58; *sancta*, 138n26; *shamar*, 153–55; worship, 149n59, 151, 154
Ten Words (*debarim*), 81n7, 95, 108, **111**, 140, 168, 185n77
Theogony, 30, 56
toledoth (*tôldôt*), xii, 46, 65, 70–71, 74–76
Torah, 10, 21n4, 71, 90, 108n41, 109–10, 116, 133, 137, 139, 143, 145, 154–55, 178, 183, 201, 252n53, 175n12
Typology, **212 n38**, 279; Melchizedek as messianic, 223

Unclean. *See* Spheres of reality
Universal call to holiness, 276n15, 302, 312
Urzeit wird Endzeit, 50n65

Vatican II, ix, xii, xvi, 2, 3, 12, 14, 193–96,
    267, 270–71, 272n8, 273, 276, 277n18,
    278, 302–5, 313, 315, 320, 322
Virginity, 140 n50, 279, 280, 282
vita, 227, 280, 281n30

Water, 12n18, 25, 29, 37n17, 41n35, 44,
    46, 104, 130, 135, 138–39, 144n42, 145,
    156–59, 227, 228, 235, 237–38, 252, 255,
    258, 301; as interface, 228; life–giving,
    158; living, 228; paradisal, river, 157–59;
    saving, 258. *See also* Rituals; *tehom*
Woman: menstruant, **109**, 139, **141**–43,
    144n41; wives, 63, 81n4, 87, 107n37,

108–9, 113n46, 114n50, 131, 140, 144,
    171, 174, 185, 190, 212, 213n42, 225, 244,
    245, 249, 256, 257n65, 259–60, 282–83,
    285–88, 291–92, 294, 296, 317, 319. *See
    also* Spheres of reality
Work: cultic dimension, 153–55; and
    Tabernacle, 151–52
Worship: goal of creation, 72, 149

Yahweh: as father, 106–8, **129–30**, 133,
    134, 204; holiness, **136**–37, 140, 169; as
    husband, 130–32

zachar (memory). *See* Anamnesis

Biblical and Theological Foundations of the Family: The Domestic Church was designed in Minion and composed by Kachergis Book Design of Pittsboro, North Carolina. It was printed on 60# Sebago Cream and bound by Maple Press of York, Pennsylvania.